A SHORT HISTORY
OF ROME

MONARCHY AND REPUBLIC

A SHORT HISTORY OF ROME

BY

GUGLIELMO FERRERO

AND

CORRADO BARBAGALLO

★

THE MONARCHY AND THE REPUBLIC

FROM THE FOUNDATION OF THE CITY TO
THE DEATH OF JULIUS CAESAR

754 B. C.–44 B. C.

CAPRICORN BOOKS
NEW YORK

PREFACE

THIS book has been written for the use of teachers and of the more advanced students in schools, colleges, and universities. It seemed to my collaborator and myself that there might be service to them and also to the general reader, in a work presenting a succinct view of the main outline of the great history of Rome, and giving detailed consideration to the more important periods and episodes. Our chief aim, therefore, has been to bring out clearly the connection of these larger events. No mere catalogue of facts, however complete and in however appropriate a setting, is worthy of the name of history. For history must convey the sense not only of succession but of evolution, and every part of the narrative must flow necessarily from what has already been related, and itself lead inevitably to what follows. Our general scheme, which is based on this idea, will, we hope, put our readers (whether learners or teachers) in possession of a key to Roman history which is necessary to all sound knowledge of the subject, while the more detailed accounts which have been given of particular cases will enable them to extend the scope of their studies or of their instruction.

We have included but few notes, but we need hardly say that our work is based entirely on original sources and on the authoritative treatises which deal with the successive phases of Roman history. We have deliberately avoided the methods of historical criticism which have been so much in fashion during the last ten years—methods that call themselves scientific but which are usually as sterile as they are pretentious. We have accordingly refrained from hypotheses which contradict coherent and historically attested facts, and we have not endeavoured by subtle and conjectural argument to sustain against received accounts and available evidence, inventions that can neither be proved nor disproved. We have held firmly to two cardinal principles, first, that in history we cannot hope to know everything, and secondly, that what certainty there is diminishes as we descend from great events, which can be kept in relation with each other, to the smaller incidents which escape from that correlation. The use of these principles has often enabled us to solve without difficulty, and in a manner which we hope is not repugnant to the reader's common sense, problems that have uselessly fatigued the modern school of critics.

I cannot conclude without expressing my own obligation and that of my readers to my collaborator, Corrado Barbagallo, of the Department of History in the Istituto Tecnico of Milan, whose assistance has been of the greatest value to me and to whom my public thanks are due. I am especially sensible of the deference he has shown to my opinion in cases in which we have not been in agreement, for example on the question of the part played by the senate, and of the importance of that body, under the empire, which is dealt with in the second volume. For the views expressed on that subject I am solely responsible.

G. F.

March, 1, 1917.

CONTENTS

Contents

Contents

A SHORT HISTORY OF ROME

CHAPTER I

THE MONARCHY

(754–510? B.C.)

1. Italy in the Eighth Century B.C. The uncertain earliest accounts of Rome date back to a time which for us is the beginning of history. But that time was itself the end of an extensive history, a long night in which we can barely discover here and there a gleam of light. What events, what catastrophes, what progress (to use the modern phrase) had Italy not already seen by the middle of the eighth century B.C.! She had seen the cave-dwellers who worked in stone and whetted flint arrowheads to hunt wild animals in the woods and on the hills. She had seen villages emerge from her lakes and rivers, trusting to their waters for defence. She had seen the mysterious and restless impulse of invention bring about the first great revolution in human history by fashioning bronze, by extracting and moulding iron through which men were enabled little by little to make for themselves more massive and serviceable tools. She had

seen flocks multiply and the cultivation of grain extend.
The first vines had put forth their branches, the
earliest olives had clustered on the slopes. Her hills
had been crowned with the towers of the first cities,
in which were made the first attempts at industry and
what we call the arts of peace. She had also seen
wars increase in violence and she had been invaded
from all sides by diverse peoples who fought long and
fiercely for her territories.

Towards the middle of the eighth century B.C.,
Italy was already peopled by many races. How
many and what they were, wherein precisely they
were distinguished, whence they came and where they
settled, it is impossible to say with certainty. The
scholars of the nineteenth century, who believed they
knew everything, pretended that they knew this,
but according to custom each sought to prove that
all his predecessors were wrong. It would be a
great and a vain labour to venture in their company
into this jungle of subtle and inconclusive arguments.
It is better to sum up what seem the most probable
conclusions.

In the eighth century the Greeks first set foot on
the southern coasts, and Magna Græcia already,
or soon to be, adorned by the cities of Cumæ, Posidonia, Metapontum, Reggio, Locri, Croton, and
Sybaris, rose to greatness. Meanwhile the greater
part of southern and central Italy was occupied by a
population of Indo-European origin which is usually
comprehensively described by the name Italici. This
population, which perhaps had left the East along with
the Hellenes, gathered in separate groups. The group
situated in the north and west—the inhabitants of
Latium—were destined to pass into history under the

name of Latini. Those in the east and south were subsequently named Umbri, Sabelli, Æqui, Marsi, Hernici, Volsci, Samnites, Osci, Lucani. They were all closely related in language, religion, education, and customs; all were agricultural and warlike peoples who had as yet founded few cities. None of them practised any but the most rudimentary industries. They all had little or no trade and lived in the simplest fashion. Two other peoples, probably of Indo-European origin like the Italici, were settled in the plains of the Po. The Liguri in the west occupied the stretch from the sea to the Ticino and the Alps. In the east the Veneti were settled about the Adige, and occupied the land from the mountains down to the level of the Adriatic Sea.

All the intervening free space between the Veneti and the Liguri and between these two peoples and the Italici, that is to say the best part of Italy, was held by the Etruscans. This people constituted, in the eighth century B.C., the greatest power in Italy, alike in the extent of their territories, their riches, and their culture. They occupied all the region which extends from the bases of the Central Alps to the middle of Italy and the Tiber. On one side they were bounded by the Adriatic from the mouth of the Adige to the Rubicon and on the other by the Tyrrhene Sea from the Macra (Magra) to the Tiber. They had taken possession of Elba with its rich deposits of lead and iron. They had colonized the western parts of Corsica, and in the midst of the territories populated by the Italici, they held Campania, one of the most fertile regions of Italy.

The strength of the Etruscans came not only from the extent of their possessions and the greatness of their riches but also from their cultivation of the arts. In contrast with the Liguri, the Veneti, and the Italici, who were rude and poor cultivators of the ground, the Etruscans and the Greeks were the great maritime, commercial, industrial, and (considering the times) the great cultivated and civilized powers in Italy. Their origin, their race, and the place from which they came are doubtful and disputed. Their language is all but unknown. But it is certain that, whether as pirates or as merchants, they covered the sea with their ships, that they built many cities on the mountains or in the plains, such as Mantua, Felsina (Bologna), Ravenna, Volaterræ (Volterra), Fæsulæ (Fiesole), Arretium (Arezzo), Vetulonia, Populonia, Tarquinii, Cære, Veii, Perusia (Perugia); that, like the Phœnicians and the Greeks, they did their best to foster many industries in these cities; that they professed a religion peculiar to themselves and possessed architects and painters; that they had fortified their towns and equipped them with sewers and aqueducts; that they could carve in wood and perhaps also in stone, and that they had an ordered political constitution. They did not unite to form a great empire, but set up a confederation of small states all governed by kings (*lucumoni*) and probably had an assembly which met from time to time. Like the Greeks, they were conscious of being one people and one race, but were divided into many separate cities and states.

In this Italy, dominated by the Etruscans, colonized by the Greeks, inhabited and cultivated in many parts by poor populations of Indo-European origin, Rome was founded. When? How? By whom? Under what laws?

2. The Foundation of Rome (754 B.C.). During the nineteenth century there flourished in the universities of Germany a historical school which, by the Germanization of a Greek word, termed itself "critical." The besetting sin of this school is its determination to extract at all costs from the abysses of the past historical data which are hopelessly lost. Some of its over-confident followers, as might be expected, set themselves the task of proving that the traditional stories are wrong in relating that Rome was founded about the middle of the eighth century or, more precisely, according to the date now universally accepted, in 754 B.C. And heaven knows what ingenuity these audacious critics have squandered on clever inductions and subtle arguments! An ingenious historian is never at a loss for subtle arguments in support of any thesis of which he is enamoured, but in this case, unfortunately, all these conjectures and arguments are shattered by the clear and simple fact that Rome by her chronology *ab urbe condita* always officially affirmed that the foundation of the city took place about the middle of the eighth century B.C. The ancient Romans, being nearer in time to that event, were in a better position than we to know when their city was founded. And, even if for some reason they should themselves have falsified the true date, it seems very unlikely that after so many centuries we should succeed in discovering it.

As we cannot discover, therefore, who falsified the date of the founding of Rome or how, or when, or why, we must accept the official chronology, which is, after all, a more trustworthy document than the most ingenious modern arguments. Moreover we may conclude from the fact that the years were offi-

cially reckoned *ab urbe condita* that Rome did not
arise and grow by a slow process of spontaneous development, but by a voluntary and deliberate act; that
it was, therefore, founded by a man or by a city or by
a people.   It is much more difficult to say who was,
in fact, the founder, and many are the legends on that
subject which were current in the ancient world.   The
oldest of these, recorded and transmitted to us by a
Roman grammarian, relates that Rome was founded
by a hero, the son of Jove, a certain Romus, who
naturally enough gave the city his own name.

But this and other similar stories were too simple
to explain the origin of so powerful a city.   Therefore,
in order that Rome too might have her historical
patent of nobility, research came to be made in the
archives which so many other cities of the Mediterranean world had already ransacked—that is to
say, in Greek poetry and the mythological legends of
which it treats.   Æneas was in a special manner laid
under contribution, for, having travelled much, he
might have named or founded as many places or cities
as you please.   Thus Capri boasted that its name
was derived from a cousin of the hero; Procida from a
nephew; Ænaria (Ischia) from Æneas himself; Capua
from Capio his grandfather; the Gulf of Gaeta from
his nurse.   Moreover, the Homeric legend had said
that the race of Priam would not utterly perish, and
that, through a descendant of its collateral branches,
it would arise from its ashes to greater glory than ever.
By tracing the origin of Rome back to Æneas, Homer
in person was thus made to predict the greatness of the
city.   It was imperative, therefore, that the first king
of Rome—Romus or Romulus—should be the son
of Æneas!

This fable, however, which was so flattering to the Roman *amour propre*, could not last for long owing to a chronological difficulty, which the ancients themselves, though they had never studied in the philological seminaries, could not fail to perceive. Romulus could not exactly be the son of Æneas because between the date of the fall of Troy in the Greek chronology and that of the foundation of Rome more years intervened than could be covered by the lives of a father and a son. The legend was, therefore, retouched and probably amalgamated with indigenous legends and stories. Rome descended indeed from Troy and from Æneas, but through a long genealogy of Ænædæ.

It was said that Ascanius, son of Æneas, had founded Alba Longa, capital of a mythical kingdom of Latium, and was succeeded on the throne by a long line of kings. The last of these, Numitor and Amulius, quarrelled, and the elder was dethroned by his brother, who for greater safety condemned his niece, Rhea Silvia, to perpetual virginity as a Vestal. But the God Mars avenged the usurpation, and the Vestal's twin sons, begotten by him, restored their grandfather Numitor to his throne. It was not until later that the two boys were impelled by affection for their birthplace to found a new city, and having obtained Numitor's permission and placed themselves at the head of the Alban faction, who were still partisans of Amulius against the rightful king, built a town on the Palatine Hill on the left bank of the Tiber.

3. **Was Rome Founded by the Etruscans?** Rome was thus the granddaughter of Troy and the daughter of Alba. That she descended from Troy is certainly a fable. Is it possible to maintain, however, that she

was the child of Alba? It is not in itself improbable
that Alba should have founded a colony on the left
bank of the Tiber, but here a difficulty presents itself.

In the first two centuries of her history Rome appears to have been a ,city of commerce and industry.
We shall have occasion to recur frequently to this
point, which is of capital importance in the history
of this early period. Now it is certain that at this
time the Latins were an agricultural people, who
manufactured only a few coarse things for their own
simple needs, and who bought from the Etruscans the
few articles of luxury with which they were content.
It is difficult, therefore, to understand how they
could have descended from their mountains to the
banks of the Tiber and founded a city which rapidly
became a flourishing seat of industry. Nor does it
appear how Latium could itself have provided material
for a prosperous trade. Latium had no commodities
to sell to foreigners, producing, as then it did, but
little iron, no wheat, scarcely any wine and that of
poor quality. There were no minerals in Latium
though there were magnificent ancient forests, which
might have supplied material for a great trade in
timber. We know, however, that the Latin woods
were almost intact in the second half of the fourth
century B.C., an indication that the preceding centuries had not exhausted this great source of wealth.[1]

If then, as we shall see is quite certain, Rome was
in her earliest days an industrial city, other people
besides the Latins must have had a hand in her foundation. Moreover, if she was at the same time a port
and an emporium, she must have been the port and

[1] On the subject of the forests of Latium in the second half of
the fourth century B.C., *cf.* Theophr., H. Plant. v, 8, 1, and 3.

the emporium, not of Latium, which had practically nothing to sell, but of other districts of central Italy already prosperous through industry and traffic, which required this outlet for their goods. This consideration must lead us to take quite seriously a hypothesis which has occurred more than once to modern historians and critics who have raised the question. whether Rome may not have been an Etruscan colony.[1]

This hypothesis may perhaps seem strange at first sight, but it finds some support in ancient tradition. Dionysius of Halicarnassus, who is one of our more authoritative sources for the most remote period of Roman history, says that there was a tradition, fairly widespread, that Rome was founded by the Etruscans.[2] Starting from this tradition modern scholars have set themselves to discover arguments to confirm it and they have found them in abundance. There are reasons which enable us, if not to prove, at least to maintain without temerity, that the name Rome may itself be Etruscan and derived from the family name *Ruma*. Etruscan also, according to etymology

[1] *Cf.* among others W. Schulze, *Zu den römischen Eigennahme,* in *Abhandl. d. Götting. Ges. d. Wissenschaft,* N. S., 5, 2; K. O. Müller, *Etrusker,* i., pp. 112 ff.; V. Gardthausen, *Mastarna oder Servius Tullius,* Leipzig, 1882; K. J. Neumann, *Die Hellenistischen Staaten und die römische Republik, Weltgeschichte,* ed. Ofluck-Harturg, Berlin, 1907, pp. 361 ff.; W. Soltau, *Anfänge d. römischen Geschichtsschreibung,* Häffel, 1909, p. 145; *Mythus oder literarische Erfindung in der älteren römischen Geschichte, Preussische Jahrbücher,* March, 1914, p. 453; A. Grenier, *Bologne, villanovienne et étrusque,* Paris, 1912, pp. 54, 56 and *passim;* V. A. Ruiz, *Le genti et la città, in Annuario della R. Università di Messina,* 1913–14.

[2] Dion. Halic., i., 29, 2. τήν τε 'Ρώμην αὐτὴν οἱ πολλοὶ τῶν συγγραφέων Τυρρηνίδα πόλιν εἶναι ὑπέλαβον.

and to tradition, are the names of the three tribes, *Ramnes, Tities, Luceres,* which formed the Roman people in its earliest days. The names of *all* the kings, not merely that of the Tarquins, are Etruscan. The city itself was constructed and the hovels on the Palatine reduced to an urban unity on the Etruscan model, and primitive Roman art until the third century was Etruscan in character.[1] Further, it is certain that Rome had hardly come into existence before she showed herself the enemy of the Latin peoples, and destroyed Alba and the lesser neighbouring towns. In the earlier centuries the great Roman families learned Etruscan, as later they learned Greek.[2] Finally, the fundamental forms of the old Latin religion and of the earliest commerce were Etruscan.[3]

According to this theory, therefore, at a time when the Etruscan states held so much of northern and central Italy and Campania as well, they had also, by founding Rome, secured the mouth of the Tiber, and had thus made themselves masters of the great waterway which placed all central Etruria in communication with the Tyrrhene Sea, and brought Campania, the southern part of the Etruscan Empire, into contact with their possessions in the north. This implies that Rome, when she had grown great and powerful, denied her past and her descent. But by a strange trick of destiny, the Etruscans, that great people which disappeared from the stage of history

---

[1] *Cf.* (in addition to the authorities cited in note 1 on p. 9) R. Delbrück, *Die drei Tempel am Forum holitorium in Rom.* Rome, 1903. (ed. Kaiserlich-deutschen Institut), pp. 25 ff., 28 ff., 30 ff.

[2] Liv., ix., 36.

[3] *Ibid.,* i., 8. *Cf. also* Macrobius, Sat., i., 15, 13.

and lies buried in tombs more mysterious than those of the farthest East,—that race more enigmatic than the sphinxes of the pyramids—still survives in us Italians and in our two capitals, Rome and Florence, which gave birth to the two greatest civilizations of which our history, ancient and modern, can boast.

The hypothesis is incontestably attractive, both because of the ingenious arguments with which scholars have supported it, and because it explains how it was possible for Rome to arise in the midst of rustic and simple peoples as a prosperous commercial and industrial city, the seat of a civilization which was conspicuous for those days. The Etruscans were better fitted than the Latins of the eighth century B.C., to establish a flourishing emporium on the banks of the Tiber. But, however this may be, the theory is but a conjecture which may seem probable but which cannot be proved by any conclusive argument and against which forever stands the weight of tradition.

If Rome was, in fact, founded and governed for more than two centuries by the Etruscans, how are we to explain the fact that under the Republic she Latinized herself to all appearance so completely as entirely to dissemble her origin? On the other hand, is it really necessary to invert the traditional view in this way in order to explain the history of Rome under the kings? Was it not possible for Rome, though by origin a Latin colony of Alba, to have transformed herself into a commercial and industrial city? In order to answer these questions let us examine the traditions.

4. **Rome under the Kings.** If it is impossible to discover whether Rome was founded by the Latins or the Etruscans, equally vain is our longing to know

the name of the founder who, according to ingenious calculations, on a spring day in 754 B.C. saw twelve fateful birds fly over his head, and there and then, having yoked a white bull and a white heifer, traced the furrow which was said to have marked out the ancient boundary (*pomerium*) of the city and the original site on which soon afterwards were to arise the walls of the great metropolis.

Romulus and Remus have been heroes of antique legend throughout the ages. Learned critics have thought they could prove that they were nothing but imaginary figures thrown off from the name Roma. So perhaps two thousand years hence erudite persons will be apt to teach that Amerigo was merely an imaginary eponymous hero of America, Columbus of British Columbia, and Bolivar of Bolivia. And since there is no means of proving that Romulus and Remus were historical characters, we shall not attempt to confute these modern doctrines but shall rather seek to sum up briefly the little that can with reasonable probability, if not with certainty, be inferred concerning the history of the monarchy, from the confused traditions handed down to us by the ancients.

Everyone knows that the traditional number of the Roman kings was seven, and that their names were Romulus, Numa Pompilius, Tullus Hostilius, Ancus Martius, Tarquinius I. (Priscus), Servius Tullius, and Tarquinius II. (Superbus). However much or however little we may be willing or able to believe of the many stories of these monarchs which have been handed down from antiquity, it is possible, amid the mass of fable, to distinguish two periods in their history. The first of these, which may be described as the more specially *Latin* period, covers the first

four; the second, or more specially *Etruscan* period,
the last three of these sovereigns. In the first period
the fortress founded by Alba was governed by an
elective monarchy, with a tenure of office for life,
such as existed during the first centuries of Venetian
history. It rapidly grew into a flourishing centre of
commerce and industry, at the same time increasing
its territories by force of arms. To find good reasons
for this prosperity, it appears unnecessary to suppose
that Rome was directly founded by the Etruscans.
The happy position of the city, near the mouth of a
river yet not actually on the sea, made defence easy
and trade convenient. Perhaps also the natural
impulse of a new city to grow was favoured by prudent
laws, and thus immigrants from neighbouring peoples
were naturally attracted individually and collectively
to Rome and were soon assimilated by ready admission into the thirty *curiæ* into which the Roman
territory and population were divided. Nothing
forbids us to suppose, indeed everything leads us to
believe, that among these immigrants were numerous
Sabines and still more numerous Etruscans, who
brought with them into the Latin city the spirit of
trade and industry.

In the remote period of the first kings, therefore,
we may think of Rome as a busy workshop, where
the traveller heard the shrill sound of the potter's
wheel and the constant beating of hammers in the
factories where the bronze and tin and iron workers
laboured. The first guilds of artificers were being
formed then, and Roman ships boldly sailed the
Tyrrhene Sea. On the other hand, there were also
in Rome and in Latium, within a comparatively small
radius, many cultivators, small, middling, and great,

who grew and sold grain and wine and wool, and who preferred the quiet and easy life of the country to the bustle of the port of Ostia or the mart of Rome. In a word, there then began that dissidence and antagonism between the mercantile and the agrarian elements which we shall find hereafter, sometimes more and sometimes less violent, throughout the whole course of Roman history.

In these first beginnings of the city, however, such discord as existed does not seem to have given rise to any very serious bitterness or disunion. The Etruscan or mercantile and the Latin or agrarian elements appear to have been able to develop, each after its own fashion, with the development of the city, and without any very violent conflicts, under the simple, firm, vigorous, but not arbitrary governments of the kings

The royal powers were ample but not unlimited and were of three kinds—military, judicial, and sacerdotal. The military powers, as was natural, were the most extensive. The king commanded the army in war, imposed on the people the taxation necessary for the conduct of the various operations, and had the power of life and death over his soldiers. The king's powers over the citizen in time of peace were much more restricted. He sat in judgment only on such as offended against the State or against religion, and in cases of dispute in which the parties voluntarily had recourse to his arbitrament. Justice was still left partly to private action and was partly the privilege and the duty of heads of families, who were the judges of their members. In virtue of his sacerdotal powers, the king, in the name of the people and with the assistance of the numerous colleges of priests and priestesses, performed all the sacred ceremonies. There were the augurs and the *haruspices*, who interpreted the mind of the gods, as revealed by natural phenomena, on the subject of the acts to be performed by the power of the State. There were the Vestal Virgins devoted to the cult of the Goddess Vesta, protectress of the State and of the home; the *Pontifices* who were charged with a general supervision of religion; the *feciales* and the *flamines* of whom the first were the guardians of the principles of international law, and the second were charged with the worship of various divinities.

If, however, the king's powers were ample, they were not hereditary. The king was appointed by the senate, whose choice had to be ratified by the people, assembled in their thirty curiæ. What was the senate and what were the curiæ? The senate was a body which elected the king from among its members and assisted him with their advice. In it sat the heads of the *gentes*, partly, it would seem, by hereditary right and partly by the choice of the king. The leaders of Rome were in fact a certain number of rich and powerful families, each of which gathered around it a group of poorer families—peasants, small proprietors, artisans. Each group was bound together by the religious association of common *sacra*, by their common name, and by the protection which the leading family gave to its dependents. These associations of families were known as *gentes*. How many there were at that time we do not know, but nearly all the families which gave their names and support to a *gens*, as soon as their heads were included in the senate, entered the ranks of the *patricii*. That is to say they were included in the small number of families who considered themselves, and were considered by others, superior to the rest of the population by reason of their social position and their privileges. Among the latter the most conspicuous were the religious privilege of the *auspicia* (that is of eliciting from Jove a signification of his will according to the rules of *divinatio*), and the political privilege of being chosen by the king to fill the chief offices of state. On the other hand, the rich citizens who, though they had formed a *gens*, had not succeeded in entering the senate, were apparently regarded as belonging to the common people (*plebs*) like the subordinate members of their own *gens* (*gentiles*) or like the poorer citizens who belonged to no *gens* at all.

The thirty curiæ represented a territorial and political division of all the citizens. They assembled in gatherings called *comitia curiata* in order to ratify the election of the king, to elect the magistrates, to approve the laws, and to decree peace and war, as well as to complete certain important civil acts such as wills and adoptions.

Such, in broad outline, and as far as they can now be ascertained, appear to have been the political institutions of Rome under the kings. It is probable that they did not come into existence full grown, as described, but were the product of a gradual development, though it is impossible to show how and within what period or by what vicissitudes this came about. It is certain, at any rate, that Rome was not backward in extending her borders by force of arms. The army had originally been as small as the city. Each curia had furnished one hundred infantry (*centuria*) and ten cavalry (*decuria*). In all, there-

fore, there were three thousand infantry and three
hundred cavalry. This was the one and only legion
of the Roman army of the earliest days, and in it the
soldiers were arrayed by *gentes* and served for nothing. But there is no doubt that from the first Rome
knew how to make a vigorous use of this little army
and that she was not merely eager to increase her
trade, but also to begin a warlike policy against the
neighbouring cities and peoples with a view to her
political aggrandizement. Tradition professes to be
able to follow Romulus, Tullus Hostilius, and Ancus
Martius step by step through the wars and conquests
whereby the first kings of Rome, with the exception
of the pacific Numa Pompilius, increased the territories of the State. It would be vain to attempt to
distinguish the true from the false in this tradition
and to assign to each monarch the part in these
achievements which properly belongs to him. Certain it is that Rome from its first beginnings fought
much and fortunately, and that the most important
event in these early wars was the destruction of Alba,
which achievement is attributed to the third and
most warlike of the kings. But whether it was his
work or that of another, the destruction of Alba, the
most powerful city in the Latium of the *prisci Latini*,
and the religious centre of the country, is certainly a
historical fact. It was the first great victory won
b᷍ Rome. Having destroyed Alba, Rome assumed
the hegemony of the religious and political Latin
League, began in a small way to be a real power in
the land, and succeeded in extending her territory to
the sea. According to tradition it was King Ancus
Martius who led to Ostia at the mouth of the Tiber
the first recorded colony of Roman citizens. That

under the fourth of the kings Rome had already tried
to secure a harbour on the open sea at the mouth of
the Tiber is a clear proof not only of a developed and
prosperous trade, but of conscious power, for a harbour on the sea was a point exposed to attack and,
therefore, requiring defence.

**5. The Tarquins and the Prevalence of the
Etruscan Element—Rome a Commercial Power
(Second half of the seventh century-sixth century
B.C.).** At this point the history of Rome is interrupted by a revolution which must have been profound, so many and so visible are the traces which it
has left in the fabulous accounts of the ancients.
They narrate that Ancus Martius was succeeded in
the government of Rome by an adventurer from
Tarquinii, a rich foreigner whose original name was
said to have been Lucumon. He was the son of a
great merchant of Corinth descended (it was said)
from the royal race of the Bacchiadæ, and of a noble
Etruscan lady. In his veins, therefore, flowed,
according to the story, a mixture of Greek and Etruscan blood—the blood of merchants and the blood of
nobles. Being the son of a foreigner and a refugee,
he could hope for no dignities or honours in Etruria.
He accordingly migrated to Rome, where, owing to a
favourable portent in the sky, he was hailed as a new
Romulus and was received hospitably at the Court of
King Ancus. Having distinguished himself in the
suite of that monarch by valour and sagacity, both
in war and peace, and assisting his fortunes by a dis-
play of generosity which his wealth made possible,
he succeeded on the death of Ancus in obtaining the
suffrages of the curiæ and procuring his election as
king.

So far the tradition as related by Livy agrees with the version given by Dionysius of Halicarnassus, but from this point the accounts diverge. Livy passes lightly over the reign of Tarquin, referring summarily to various wars, to some political reforms, and divers public works carried out by him. Dionysius, on the other hand, expatiates above all on his wars, and, among these, recounts long and furious conflicts with the Etruscans, which ended in the Etruscan cities acknowledging Tarquin as their sovereign. In other words, the son of the rich and noble sojourner in Etruria, having risen to the supreme office in the neighbouring State, which was new and therefore more open than the old to the ambitions of enterprising strangers, is said to have conquered Etruria and to have become king of Rome and of Etruria as well. Can we accept this tradition as true?

It seems possible. It is not in itself unlikely that Etruria may have been surprised and overcome by Rome in one of these moments of weakness and political disintegration to which all ancient states—and the Etruscan federation in a particular degree—were liable. And, if the tradition is not in itself improbable, it furthermore enables us to explain the Etruscan element in the history of the last kings of Rome without raising the ancient Etruscans from the dead in the character of founders of the eternal city. Etruria having been conquered by a king in whose veins flowed Etruscan and Greek blood, Rome became the capital of Etruria and also the metropolis of Etruscan trade and industry. Thus the Etruscan influence at Rome prevailed over the Latin tradition just as, many centuries later, the East was destined to conquer her Roman conquerors.

Though we are not yet in a position to distinguish the true from the false in the accounts which the ancient historians give of the events which occurred in the reigns of Tarquinius Priscus, Servius Tullius, and Tarquinius Superbus, these accounts enable us to understand in broad outline the course followed by the history of Rome under these kings. We see how Rome made many wars—with the Sabines, with the Æqui, with the Volscians, how she again increased her territories and took possession of all the Tyrrhene coast from the Tiber to Terracina.[1] We see also how the later monarchs surrounded themselves with a pomp and ceremony which have every appearance of being Etruscan. We see how Rome now traded with the Adriatic countries, with Carthage and Sicily, with Corsica and Sardinia, with Magna Græcia, and even with the Oriental Greeks,[2] and how within her walls the number of skilled workmen (*opifices*) and of their corporations increased, and with them the output of copper and iron work, of furriery and ceramics. We can imagine how the Greek merchants put in at the mouth of the Tiber and went up the river in order to confer with the Roman sovereigns and to obtain their favour and friendship.[3] There

[1] The power of Rome on the mainland at the end of the monarchy is proved not only by Polyb., iii., 22, but by the magnitude of the Latin League which was formed on the fall of the kings, against Rome to safeguard the recovered independence of her former subjects. *Cf.* Cato, Frag. 58, ed. Peter.

[2] *Cf.* E. Gabrici, *Il problema delle origini italiche*, in *Rivista di storia antica*, 1907, pp. 94 ff. and the first treaty between Rome and Carthage transcribed for us by Polybius (iii., 22) which was concluded in the first year of the republic and is discussed in the following chapter.

[3] Cic., *De Rep.*, ii., 19–34.

was every reason, too, for an enlargement of the city, and we find that Servius Tullius was able to enclose within a massive wall a region which comprised part of the Cælian Hill, the Esquiline, the Viminal, the Quirinal, and the Palatine, and which he divided into four districts. Neither does it surprise us to be told by ancient authors that the kings built great public monuments, such as the wall of Servius Tullius already mentioned, the Circus Maximus, the Temple of Jupiter on the Capitol, the bridges over the Tiber, and the Cloaca Maxima; or that they carried out improvements in the low-lying parts of the city, including the then untilled morass, broken up by copses and thickets and strewn with groups of neglected tombs, which was transformed into the Forum Romanum of mighty destinies. We can understand finally how, outside the sacred boundary of the pomerium, foreigners from oversea, the "metics" of ancient Rome, had installed their gods, and how, near the island in the Tiber or in the so-called Vicus Tuscus, between the Palatine and the Capitol, the new Etruscan immigrants took up their special abode. Rome had become the capital of Etruria.

6. The Constitution of Servius Tullius. But above all, this tradition enables us to explain satisfactorily the profound alteration which the ancient Roman constitution underwent in the time of these three kings—the famous constitution of Servius Tullius which imprinted on the Roman State features which remained indelible for seven centuries.

Hitherto the people had voted in the assembly, called comitia curiata, that is to say in the thirty curiæ in which rich and poor, gentle and simple, were mixed together, and the poor, being the greater num-

ber, predominated.[1] The traditional account is that
Servius Tullius divided the citizens of Rome into five
classes, to one of which, from the first to the fifth,
every man was respectively assigned according as he
possessed a fortune of not less than one hundred thousand, seventy-five thousand, twenty-five thousand,
and twelve thousand five hundred[2] asses. Each class
was subdivided into centuries, and each of these
centuries was a political, military, and fiscal unit.
Thus in electing magistrates, passing laws, or de-
liberating on peace and war the people voted by centuries, each century deciding by a majority and each
counting as one vote. In the same way, whenever
the State had need of money or soldiers, the contingent
or the impost, as the case might be, was divided among
the centuries.

Now Servius Tullius divided his first class into
ninety-eight centuries, his second, third, and fourth
classes into twenty each, his fifth class into thirty.
Besides these he created four centuries composed of
citizens who had special duties in time of war, and who
voted with one or other of the superior classes. As,
moreover, he had collected into a single century all
those who did not possess the property qualification
of the fifth class, it is quite clear what the effect of the
Servian reform was. The richer class, less numerous
but divided into a larger number of centuries, prepon-
derated in the new elective and legislative assembly,

---

[1] On the curiæ and the comitia curiata there has been much
miscellaneous discussion in modern times. It seems to us that
sufficient attention has not been given to the passage of Dionysius
of Halicarnassus (iv., 20) which we regard as entirely accurate.
Cf. also Dion., Halic., iv., 21; vii., 59; ix., 41; xi., 45.

[2] According to some authorities eleven thousand.

which was known as the comitia centuriata. On the other hand, they had to undergo military service more frequently and to pay more taxes, while the poor who were excluded from the five classes were exempt from conscription and taxation.

It was thus a timocratic constitution, or a system of privilege based on wealth, which the reform of Servius Tullius substituted for the democratic institution of the curiæ in which every man, rich or poor, counted as one. But a timocratic constitution can only be established in a state where wealth counts for more than numbers or tradition. For this reason some modern historians, German for the most part, have contended that the change dates, at the earliest, from the fourth century B.C., the Rome of the kings being too small and too poor for such a constitution. But this train of reasoning may be inverted, and, holding firmly to the tradition, we may argue that the reform shows how rich and prosperous Rome must then have been, and that, if Servius Tullius was able to introduce such a change, Rome must have been more powerful and wealthy than has been supposed. This conclusion agrees with all that we have here set forth and also with our certain knowledge of the extent and population of Roman territory in later times.[1] When

[1] From the ratio established by Servius between each class and its military contingent, it will be seen that all those fit to bear arms in each class were not counted. As a matter of fact the first class, which was the least numerous because composed of the richest men, gives ninety-eight centuries or 9800 men fit to bear arms, while each of the other classes, which obviously were progressively more numerous, gives only 2000 or 3000. In calculating the total numbers fit for military service, therefore, we may take the first class as a basis. Each of the Servian classes then contained at least 9800 men fit to bear arms, and the total

Rome became the capital of Etruria and a rich centre of trade and industry, numbering in its population many merchants and others newly enriched, the time was ripe for substituting for the levelling constitution of the curiæ a constitution based on a property qualification. The object which the kings had in view when they made the change is also clear. They wished to lean on the mercantile and industrial class, which had profited so much by the supremacy of Rome over Etruria and by the new policy, and to diminish the authority of the Latin aristocracy and of the senate which was its organ.

There are, indeed, abundant traces in the traditions which have reached us, of a struggle between the old

---

for all the first five classes of men between 17 and 60 fit for military service would be 49,000. Multiplying this number by 4, according to the usual statistical ratio, we arrive at a population of 196,000 souls for the first five classes. *But these consist only of those who possessed property.* There remain those who were without property and they, according to the usual calculation, stand to the former as 3 to 2. Their number may, therefore, be estimated at 294,000, which when added to 196,000, gives a total population of 490,000 souls or, in round figures, half a million. This, however, is still only a minimum, because we have reckoned all the first five classes as equally numerous, which cannot have been the fact. The sum total of the population may have reached six or seven hundred thousand. Now the census of the year 280 B.C. when the territory of Rome was extended over all central Italy, including part of Campania and the ancient empire of the Tarquins was reconquered, shows a population of 287,222 citizens (Liv., *Epit.*, xiii.), which gives a gross total of more than a million souls. These figures tally exactly with those we have adopted for the time of Servius. The reader will recall that by this time the greater part of Campania enjoyed the rights of Roman citizenship and that in three centuries the Italian population must naturally have increased.

Latin patriciate and the new monarchy, which tried to reinforce itself by cultivating and conciliating the new families, the rich merchants, and, generally speaking, the monied interest, while weakening the patriciate and its privileges through the introduction into the senate, and therefore into the patrician order of as many new men as possible. Livy, though he has so little to say about Tarquinius Priscus, does not omit to tell us that this king introduced a hundred new members into the senate "not for the good of the State but in order to strengthen his own position." And no doubt the last kings must have taken many liberties with the privilege of the patricians to be alone selected for the highest offices of State, and must often have had recourse to men who were not members of the privileged caste. In short, when Rome acquired supremacy over Etruria the equilibrium between the Etruscan and the Latin elements was broken. The Etruscan element predominated, and made, or tried to make, Rome a maritime and commercial power, a rich and sumptuous city, a monarchy ruled on the principle of personal power. Thus it came about that under the last three kings the struggle between the Latin and the Etruscan elements, between the king and the senate, between tradition and the cosmopolitan spirit, became gradually more acute and ended in a catastrophe.

7. **The Fall of the Monarchy (510 B.C.?).** The fables woven by the ancients about the fall of the monarchy are well known, and the best known of all is the story of the outrage committed on Lucretia. These tales have led some modern historians to throw doubt on the whole of the ancient account of what took place, and to suppose that the royal authority

was not overthrown by a revolution but was gradually eliminated through the aristocracy's taking away the king's powers one by one. This, however, is a conjecture which has no foundation in the accounts given by the ancients, which, if fabulous in part, clearly indicate that the monarchy succumbed to a *coup de main* of the patriciate. After the exposition given above we can find nothing surprising in such an event, though we may be unable to say what was the occasion of the final outbreak or how it came to be successful. Without abusing our right to criticize the text of ancient authors or the historical tradition, we may therefore go so far as to affirm that the elective monarchy with tenure of office for life, by which Rome had been governed during the first centuries of her history, fell in the early years of the sixth century before Christ, owing to a reaction of the Latin element, represented by the patriciate, against the too marked tendencies towards Etruscanism, commercialism, and absolutism displayed by the last three kings.[1]

The monarchy, according to tradition and to probability, had lasted rather less than two centuries and a half (753-510 B.C.), about the same time as the seven Plantagenet kings of England from Henry II. to Edward III., or the seven Bourbon kings of France from Henri III. to Louis XVI. Rome was deeply indebted to her seven kings. Under their sceptre the little city founded by Romulus had been enlarged, enriched, and embellished. It had conquered the Etruscans and achieved the hegemony of a great part of Central Italy. It had also become a power at sea.

[1] *Cf.* in Livy, i., 59, 9-10, the tenor of the speech which the Latin historian puts in the mouth of the conspirators of 509 or 510.

In aftertimes an obscure and sinister tradition was invented, and maintained by a persistent propaganda, in order to hide these great merits. It became a patriotic duty for subsequent generations to hate the monarchy—although or perhaps because the glorious history of the kingdom of Rome had scarcely ended when a new epoch began which for long was destined to be much less brilliant and fortunate.

CHAPTER II

THE BEGINNINGS OF THE REPUBLIC

8. The Commercial Treaty with Carthage in 509 B.C. and the Loss of Etruria. The first certain document in Roman history which we possess is a commercial treaty—the treaty which Rome concluded with Carthage in 509 B.C., the first year of the republic. Polybius (iii., 22) has preserved its text, which is as follows:

"The Romans and their allies shall not navigate beyond Cape Bel[1] unless constrained by tempests or by enemies. . . . If compelled to touch at our ports, they shall buy or take nothing except what is necessary to repair their ships and perform the sacrifices, and they shall depart again within five days. Those who come for the sake of commerce [*i. e.* to Carthage or the African coast as far as Cape Bel or to Sardinia] shall not be obliged to pay any impost save what may be due to the crier or the public notary; and for all that shall be sold in the presence of these officers the State shall be guarantee to the vendor, and this shall apply alike to sales carried out in Africa and in Sardinia. If, moreover, any Roman shall come to the part of Sicily subject to the Carthaginians, his

[1] Cape Farina, *cf.* Polybius, iii., 23.

rights shall in all respects be identical [with those of the Carthaginians]. The Carthaginians on their part undertake to do no harm to the cities of Ardea, Antium, Laurentum, Circei, and Terracina, or to any other Latin city subject to Rome. They undertake a similar obligation as regards the cities of Latium not subject to Rome. If it should happen that they occupy any such city, they shall restore it undamaged to the Romans, nor shall they build any fort in Latin territory. Should they enter the country in arms they shall not spend the night there." [1]

The text of the treaty speaks clearly. Rome renounces the right to sail or trade in the eastern Mediterranean, and the Carthaginians promise in return not to attack or damage in any way the cities of Latium whether subject to Rome or not. So true it is that the republic was founded by the Latin and

[1] The chronology of the treaty is defined by the names of the consuls of the year (L. Junius Brutus and M. Horatius), which Polybius read in the treaty itself, and there is no valid argument against its authenticity. It is a document which fits perfectly into the history of Carthage and of the early Roman republic. Polybius, moreover, quotes from actual examination of the original text, which he must have been at some pains to interpret, and in his exposition of the diplomatic negotiations between Rome and Carthage he is too precise and circumstantial to allow us to suspect any error. Contemporary German scholars, however, (most recently E. Täubler *Imperium Romanum: I Die Staatsverträge u. Vertragsverhältnisse*, Leipzig–Berlin, 1913) and, following them, some learned Italian authorities on ancient history have expressed doubts both as to the document itself and as to its date. It is another case of the mania for questioning the best established facts which characterizes so much of the German or Germanized historical criticism of contemporary Europe. Compare, on the other hand, the sensible observations of A. Pirro, *Il primo trattato fra Roma e Cartagine* (in *Annali della R. Scuola normale superiore di Pisa*, 1892).

agrarian element in revolt against the Etruscan and mercantile section of the population, that the republic was scarcely established before it began to abandon the career of commerce so ardently pursued by the last of the kings. Again it is not rash to conjecture that the republic was compelled to purchase peace from Carthage at this price because it immediately found itself at war with Etruria. We do not know whether, when the monarchy was overthrown, the Roman dominion over Etruria was as widespread as it had been in the time of Tarquinius Priscus. But it is certain, that at the very outset of its career the republic had immediately to sustain a fierce struggle with Etruria, whether because the subject peoples rebelled or because those who were independent (instigated according to tradition by the exiled Tarquins) seized the opportunity to free the tributary states. It is, moreover, beyond doubt that the republic was conquered by the Etruscans and that Rome fell under the Etruscan sway for several years. For how many it is difficult to say precisely; certainly not for many. Perhaps the period of servitude was a decade, for by the beginning of the fifth century Rome had, for good or evil, succeeded in regaining her independence.

9. **The War with the Volsci and the Æqui.** Rome was free, but only to find that she had to face new enemies who, in the years which followed the foundation of the republic, assaulted her from every side. All Latium revolted in order to secure liberty and independence. Other neighbouring barbarous populations (the tribe of the Sabines, for example), which the government of the monarchy had hitherto held in subjection or in awe, again began to ravage the Roman territories. An even more serious danger arose from

the hill tribes of the Roman Apennines—the Volsci and
the Æqui—who, impelled like all barbarous populations by the increase of their numbers, began to
swarm westward into the Latin plain as far as the
Tyrrhene coast from Antium to Circei. About the
incessant wars which the republic was forced to wage
against these peoples, and most of all against the
Volscians and the Æqui, the ancients tell many fine
stories but little that is substantial. From the text
of the treaty of alliance concluded in 493 by the
Consul Spurius Cassius, which put an end to the war
with the Latin cities,[1] we learn, however, that the
republic gave way to the Latins as it had given way
to the Carthaginians. For the Romans renounced
all ambition to hold the hegemony and officially
recognized the Latin League, with which they concluded a defensive alliance on equal terms. As regards the confused history of the wars against the
Volsci and the Æqui, all we can say with certainty is
that for more than fifty years Rome was reduced to
defending herself with much difficulty against incessant assaults, now of the Volsci, now of the Æqui,
and occasionally of both combined, and that, for
defensive purposes, the Hernici, who were not strictly
Latins and were perhaps Sabines, were admitted to
the Latin League.

10. **The First Defeats of the Republic and their
Consequences.** The little empire which the monarchy
had built up fell to pieces during the first decade of
the republic, and, when the hegemony over Etruria
and Latium was lost, commerce and industry decayed
rapidly. By 450 Rome had practically vanished from
the list of important centres of Mediterranean com-

[1] Dion. Halic., vi., 95.

merce. Rome's first attempt to become a great commercial power like Carthage or Corinth, Tarentum, Athens, and many other Greek cities had, therefore, failed.

This is a point of great importance to which the reader's attention is specially directed. Such a commercial disaster could not but impoverish the city, whose penury was increased by a series of unsuccessful wars. Booty played an essential part in the wars of Rome as in all the warfare of antiquity. The soldier went to the wars not only in order to defend his country and keep off the enemy, but also in the hope of penetrating into the enemy's territory and carrying off some of his goods. It was a settled principle of warfare, which must always be kept in view for the proper understanding of Roman military history, that the general had full power to dispose of the *manubiæ* or spoils, whether in money, cattle, or slaves, and to decide himself what share should be taken by the State and what should be distributed to the army. No doubt the largest portion of the spoils was always divided among the soldiers; and this explains why it was that during the first centuries of Roman history the armies received no pay. But the consequences of the system were twofold. A victorious war to a certain extent enriched the people, for such of them at least as were not killed brought home gold and silver, cattle, slaves, or other movable property taken from the vanquished. A disastrous war, on the other hand, impoverished the nation, for not only had the soldiers to fight for nothing, but often territory was lost, and invariably the enemy took and carried off their goods and chattels. The long and uncertain struggle with the Volsci and the

Æqui, therefore, greatly impoverished the middle and poorer classes in the first half-century of the republic. Many small and middling landed proprietors were forced to borrow, and, once entangled in debt, found it difficult to free themselves. Little by little they were stripped of their property and even of their liberty, for the terrible laws of that day provided that an insolvent debtor might be reduced to slavery by his creditor.

11. **Patricians and Plebeians. The Struggle for Civil and Political Equality.** If then we may judge by its immediate effects, the fall of the monarchy was a calamity for Rome. And yet the revolution which had overthrown the kings had modified the institutions of Rome only very slightly. The senate had retained its old powers, as had also the comitia curiata, reduced as these had been by the Servian reform. The comitia centuriata also survived. All that had happened was that the royal authority had been transferred to two magistrates first called *prætores* and later *consules*. Elected every year by the comitia centuriata, the consuls received from the comitia curiata and from the senate the *imperium* formerly exercised by the king. They were invested, that is to say, with military and judicial powers, but not with religious authority, which was conferred upon a new magistrate, styled *rex sacrorum*. Like the kings the consuls were assisted by officers known as *quæstores*.

How was it possible that a change so slight in appearance could have had such serious consequences? The answer is that the change was slight only in appearance. Under the monarchy the elective principle was combined with that of holding office for life.

It was, therefore, possible to confide the direction of the State to an energetic and active power. The republic weakened this power by making it annual and by dividing it between two colleagues neither of whom could exercise it separately. The reins of government were, in fact, transferred not from the king to the consuls but from the king to the senate, which, being permanent, predominated in the new order of things. Now, as we have already seen, the Roman senate was the organ of the patriciate, that is of a closed and privileged caste. The monarchy had tried with some success to compel the senate to open its ranks to new men. But, when the monarchy fell, the senatorial caste, left sole mistress of the State, naturally closed its ranks in a spirit of rigid exclusion, refused to admit new members, forbade all marriage with plebeians, and jealously maintained the privileges of taking the auspices, and of occupying all the offices of State. These two things were indissolubly connected, for no public act or ceremony could be performed by a magistrate without his first interrogating the heavens, or the birds or some other manifestation of the divine will. The State therefore fell into the hands of a small, proud, and exclusive oligarchy, outside which remained all the poorer families as well as the families which had grown rich in the last generation but in whose veins flowed no patrician blood.

This small and close corporation was not equal to the task of governing the State well at home and of defending it successfully abroad. This is the secret of the history of the first decades of the republic, the truth about which ancient authors have in vain tried to conceal. We do not know what were the short-

comings which caused this failure. There may have
been an exaggerated attachment to Latin tradition
or an excess of class feeling. The oligarchs may have
been too few in number, their intelligence may have
been limited or they may simply have been unlucky.
It is certain that they were unable to retain the conquests of the monarchy, that they had to resign themselves to meet with the Latins on equal terms, that
they had the greatest difficulty in defending Rome
against the attacks of the Volsci and the Ædqui, and
that they were soon attacked by an opposition which
aimed at the destruction of all their privileges. This
opposition came into being almost with the republic
itself and grew rapidly as one unsuccessful war after
another more and more discredited the narrow
oligarchical circle. The rich plebeians, excluded
from power, made common cause with the poor plebeians who were tortured by their poverty. The
former protested against the privileges of the patricians; the latter demanded the mitigation of the law
of debt and the passing of agrarian laws. All agreed
in lamenting the partiality and the uncertainty of the
laws and the arbitrary manner of their enforcement
by the oligarchy no less than the abuses of power
committed by the patrician magistrates whose pride
equalled that of the kings. The civil and political
equalization of all classes was demanded on all sides
with ever-increasing boldness.

At first the means at the disposal of the plebeians
for attaining this object were trifling. But in 495
B.C. (the date has been questioned by modern criticism
but without serious reason) all the territory of Rome
was divided, and all the citizens were distributed,
according as they owned property in each district, into

twenty-one tribes, each tribe being charged with the
duty, in case of war, of providing for the payment of
the land tax and for the levy of the armed forces
within its bounds.   The object of this reform appears
to have been purely administrative.   It is, however,
a plausible conjecture that the malcontents very
soon made it a weapon for carrying on political opposition, and that the heads of the tribe, having been
entrusted with such important duties, became in a
short time the organs of the discontent felt by the
majority of their constituents,—that is to say, by
the plebeians.   Thus is explained how it came to
pass that, some years later (the date is not stated
definitely either by the ancients or the moderns),
the patricians had to consent to the yearly election
by the old democratic comitia curiata, which by this
time appeared entirely obsolete, of two new magistrates, known as "tribunes of the peoples" (*tribuni
plebis*), who were to defend their order against any
oppression of the patricians or their magistrates.[1]

For the first time the people had a strong weapon
at their disposal and they lost no time in making it
stronger still.   By the year 471 the number of tribunes had already been increased to four or five, and
their election had been transferred from the comitia
curiata to the comitia tributa, *i. e.*, to the general
assembly of the tribes.   This change was of great
importance.   The new comitia tributa did not, perhaps, differ much in the number and nature of its
members from the comitia curiata.   On the other

[1] That the election of the tribunes of the people was originally
carried out by the comitia curiata is affirmed explicitly and without question by Cicero.   Cf. *Pro. Corn.*, fr. 24, ed. Orelli; Dion.,
Halic., vi., 89; ix., 41.

hand, as it was not yet an electoral or legislative assembly, it could meet (unlike the comitia curiata) without the permission of the senate and without any of the liturgical formalities which the patricians had so much abused for political purposes.[1]

This was not the last of the victories of the plebeians. Shortly after this the tribunes, who had obtained assistants in the plebeian ædiles, arrogated to themselves the right of using force (*ius prensionis*) against any one (even a magistrate) who dared to offend or injure a plebeian. Next they seized the truly regal privilege (*ius interdecendi*) of suspending by their veto the execution of the decrees of the government or the convocation of all the people in their assemblies, whenever they were summoned to discuss proposals which might be presumed to be contrary to the interest of the plebeians. Then again they secured the *ius agendi cum plebe*, the power of convoking the plebs in public meeting and of discussing with them their special interests and all that concerned them in the general policy of the State. Finally they obtained the right to treat directly with the senate (*ius agendi cum patribus*) on everything in the government of the State which concerned their constituents.

All these successes so much encouraged the plebeians that in 462 the tribune C. Terentilius Arsa felt himself strong enough to strike a decisive blow against the oligarchy. He proposed the appointment of a commission of five which was charged to draft a law precisely defining the powers of the consuls and putting an end to a domination which, as the

[1] *Cf.* Dion. Halic., ix., 41.

tribune said, was not less arbitrary and absolute than
that of the kings.

12. **The Decemvirate and the Twelve Tables.**
The patrician oligarchy had not sufficient authority
to resist at all points the active agitation of the plebeians.   They had been weakened by unsuccessful
wars.   They had given way on the grave issue of the
powers of the tribunes and had allowed that formidable organ of obstruction to grow up in the heart
of the State.   But they opposed the proposals of
Terentilius Arsa with much energy because, instead of merely increasing the powers of the plebs
as the appointment of the tribunes had done,
these proposals positively limited the power of the
patriciate.

A furious conflict ensued, which, interrupted by
incursions of the Volsci and the Æqui, lasted for
ten years.   It ended in a compromise.   According
to Livy, three ambassadors, Spurius Postumius Albinus, A. Manlius, and P. Sulpicius Camerinus, were
sent to Greece to study the laws of that country.
When they returned, the tribunes proposed that for
the following year all the magistracies, patrician and
plebeian, as well as the corresponding assemblies—
the consuls, the quæstors, the tribunes, the comitia
curiata, centuriata, and tributa—should be suspended.
In their place a new magistracy—the *decemvirate*—
was to be created.   That is to say there were to be
ten magistrates, invested both with deliberative and
constituent powers, who were to govern the State
and draw up a constitution, including provisions for
civil and criminal justice, which in primitive states
are incorporated in public law.   The new constitution
was to apply both to patricians and to plebeians,

therefore the magistrates charged with drafting it might have been drawn from either order.

After some discussion the law was passed. But ten patricians only were elected, who completed their onerous task in one year (451). At the end of this time, ten tables of the law testified to their achievement. Traditional history, written almost exclusively by patrician pens, eulogized in later days the moderation and the sagacity of these earliest legislators. But the judgment of the plebeians on the new constitution immediately after its publication seems to have been very different. And even from the scanty traditional accounts it is not difficult to divine the reason for their discontent. The decemvirs had sought for a compromise between the privileges of the patricians and the aspirations of the plebeians to legal and political equality. We cannot say precisely in what this compromise consisted, but we can see that the clear statement and the promulgation of the laws were in themselves two great concessions to the plebs. To balance these concessions the patricians tried, of course, to preserve in the new laws as many of their privileges as they could. Moreover, by the institution of the decemvirate, were abolished both the tribunes of the people and the comitia tributa, and with these the most precious privileges won by the plebs in recent years. It is true that, in compensation for this, plebeians could be appointed decemvirs, but as a matter of fact in the first year, as we have seen, the decemvirs were all patricians.

The plebeians were disappointed because they did not obtain from the decemvirate the great things they had hoped for, and they had also to lament the loss of several of their most valuable conquests. In the

following year, therefore, they made great endeavours
to secure the election to the decemvirate of three
plebeian candidates. They succeeded, thanks to the
help of a party among the patricians, including the
decemvir Appius Claudius, the most prominent figure
in the first decemvirate. This is a clear proof that
the need had been felt of doing something to satisfy
the people—a policy which, in fact, prejudiced the
patricians so little that in the second year of the decemvirate one of the two new tables of the law
solemnly ratified the prohibition of marriages between
patricians and plebeians. The concession, however,
such as it was, did not soothe the popular discontent.
Agitation and discord raged furiously, and this encouraged the more extreme wing of the patrician
party, which was hostile to the new constitution
owing to the favour it showed to the plebs, to declare
that the decemvirate had failed in its object and that
the ancient republican constitution ought to be restored. It seems that Appius Claudius and his colleagues tried to resist the coalition of patricians and
plebeians which attacked the decemvirate. And it
was at this point, if we may believe the version of
the republican tradition given by Livy, that the decemvirate transformed itself into an illegal despotism.
All guarantees were abolished. The caprice of the
decemvirs was the only law. Patricians and plebeians
were now companions in misfortune and victims of
the same tyranny, and at the end of the year the
decemvirs illegally prolonged their term of office.

This account does not explain how so great a change
could have been brought about in so short a time. It
is clear, on the other hand, that the decemvirs did
not succeed in overcoming the coalition of injured

interests ranged against them. They were suspected alike by patricians and plebeians. They were faced by the conservative instinct which was so strong in all classes of Roman society, and by a rooted aversion to all authority which was too wide and indefinite. Some mistakes may have hastened their collapse. (The famous episode of Virginia is, perhaps, not altogether fiction, just as the initial incidents of the Sicilian Vespers do not belong entirely to romance.) It was an unsuccessful war, however, which dealt them the mortal blow. Towards the end of the year 450 the Sabines and the Æqui invaded the Roman State. Eight of the decemvirs took command of the Roman armies. Appius Claudius, the prop and stay of the tottering government, alone remained with a plebeian colleague in the capital, which proved to be the post of greatest danger. The inexperience of the generals led to their discomfiture and the army mutinied. Under the command of its subordinate officers it marched on Rome and the ancient constitution was restored.

Thus the decemvirate, after little more than two years, disappeared like the monarchy. It left no good name behind it but, whatever may have been its crimes, it had accomplished a great work. The civil and criminal law of Rome, which for centuries were to be the foundations of its private life, and of no small part of its public life as well, was due to them, as well as the law which, notwithstanding its defects, had abolished so many of the antiquated distinctions between the various classes of society.

13. Tribuni Militares Consulari Potestate. Between the fall of the decemvirate and the end of the fifth century the external situation improved. Vic-

tories in the field improved the position of the city.
The attacks of the Volsci and the Æqui came at
longer intervals and were less violent. This was a
clear proof that the power of Rome was increasing
and that the strength of her enemies was waning,
although she still remained on the defensive. There
was, however, no corresponding improvement in the
condition of affairs inside the city. Five years after
the fall of the decemvirate the struggle for the equalization of the orders was rekindled. In 444 C. Canuleius, a tribune of the people, proposed to rescind the
law of the Twelve Tables which forbade marriage between patricians and plebeians, and his nine colleagues
proposed that the people should have the right to
elect as consul, whomsoever they chose, whether he
was a patrician or a plebeian.

The citadel of patrician privilege was thus assailed
simultaneously from the two sides of private and
constitutional law. A tenacious and vigorous resistance was, of course, offered, but less on the first than
on the second point, though the two proposals were,
in fact, connected by the question of the *auspicia*.
Now, as always happens to close corporations, the
Roman patriciate at this time must already have
begun to decline in numbers and in wealth, while
among the plebeians the number of newly enriched
families was increasing. Thus the Lex Canuleia,
though it was a blow to the pride of the patrician
caste, was capable of advancing the material interests
of that caste. Canuleius, therefore, gained his object
without much difficulty, all the more because the
patricians hoped that if they gave way to the plebs
on this point, the other demand would not be pressed.
In this they were mistaken. The other nine tribunes

were encouraged by the triumph of Canuleius and vigorously insisted on their proposal. The patricians opposed it desperately and there followed a struggle of extreme violence in the course of which the tribunes used the weapon of obstruction without mercy but also without shaking the firmness of their adversaries. As always happens when opponents are of equal strength and tenacity, the conflict ended in a compromise. A proposal was made and approved that in any year in which the senate thought fit three "military tribunes with consular power" (*tribuni militares consulari potestate*) might be elected instead of two consuls, and that they should be freely chosen from the people, patrician and plebeian alike.

The real meaning of this singular arrangement is not very clear. The *tribunus militum* was the military commander subordinate to the consul, and this suggests that the patricians, wishing formally to maintain their privilege, conceded to the plebs a sort of diminished consulship. It is at any rate certain that the new system merely added fuel to the flames of controversy. To all the other motives of discord was added almost every year a new one—the question whether consuls or military tribunes should be elected. The plebeians naturally wished for tribunes, the patricians for consuls. When it had been decided to elect tribunes, lively struggles again arose between the orders over the selection of the candidates, as each order wished to seize the majority of the posts.

The patricians manœuvred adroitly, for they had the superior political experience which comes of a long tenure of power, and for forty years succeeded in preventing the plebs from electing any of their number to the office of military tribune. The only effect, in short, of the bargain which had been struck was to diminish still further the central authority, already so much weakened by the republican constitution. This made it necessary to have recourse at every turn to the extreme expedient of the dictatorship—that is, to suspend the constitution and cause the consuls, with the approval of the senate, to appoint a dictator for a period which must not exceed six months. This magistrate, apparently of foreign (Oscan or Etruscan) origin, was invested with full powers in which for a short time was reconstituted the unity of the royal authority. The patricians also succeeded in depriving the tottering consulate of a portion of its powers. Alleging that the consuls were too much occupied with their war duties, the patricians in 443 B.C. secured the appointment of new magistrates—the censors—to whom were transferred some of the most important consular powers. These were: the power to compile a census of the citizens by which taxation and exemption were regulated; the power to settle the list of the senate; the power to administer the ordinary revenues of the State; the power to call for tenders for public contracts, and, finally, the power to supervise the morals of all the citizens, patrician as well as plebeian. The last of these, carrying with it the right of judgment without appeal, was a polit'cal weapon of the most formidable character.

The stout resistance offered by the patricians explains why in the last quarter of the century the plebeians abandoned the endeavour to take the consulate, the citadel of power, by storm, and contented themselves with a gradual approach, first securing the minor magistracies. In 421 they secured the admission of plebeians to the quæstorship, the number of these magistrates being at the same time increased to four. In 409 they secured for the first time a majority in the Quæstorial College. No doubt the quæstors had by that time ceased to be the chief criminal magistrates of the State as they had been in the early years of the republic. They were now merely financial officials, satellites, as it were, of the consuls, who were charged with the custody of the public treasury and with the supervision of revenue and of expenditure, approved by the competent authority, for the service of the State. This first step, however, was by no means useless. Indeed it was not long before the plebs succeeded in getting the number of military tribunes raised from three to six, of whom some *must* be plebeian.

CHAPTER III

THE GALLIC INVASION

14. The War against Veii and its Political and Economic Causes. At the point in the history of Rome which we have now reached, that is to say about the end of the fourth century B.C., the republic passed almost without warning from its consistently defensive attitude to the offensive. Why was this? And why was Veii the object of the first real war of conquest which the republic undertook?

A century of almost uniformly unfruitful warfare against the Volscians and the Æqui had unquestionably wearied the Roman people. It would otherwise be difficult to explain how the tribunes of this period dared to incite the plebs to oppose the policy of the senate and to refuse military service; or why they so freely accused the patricians of deliberately seeking quarrels with their neighbours in order to secure their predominance in the State by distracting the attention of the plebs from the true issue, which was between the plebeians and the patricians.

These recriminations clearly show that the citizens, who had to serve for nothing, were weary of eternal wars of defence. In these, if all went well, the best that was to be expected was the preservation of such property as the citizens possessed. If, therefore, the authority of the State and of the governing classes was to be preserved, the senate had to attempt as soon as possible one of these wars of conquest which in the opinion of the ancients, justified the burdens of military preparation even more than wars of defence. It is easy to understand the motives of the senate in undertaking such a war. Is it equally clear why they made Veii their objective?

Rome and Veii had already crossed swords more than once. Their earliest encounters, according to a probable tradition, go back as far as the days of the monarchy. Romulus himself was said to have wrested from the Veientines the salt marshes at the mouth of the Tiber and a part of the territory beyond the river, in which the Romilii, one of the most ancient of Roman families, fixed their abode. Ancus Martius had seized from them the Silva Arsia, a forest rich in timber, which was of great value for shipbuilding. It is not unlikely that Veii afterwards formed part of the Etruscan Empire of which, under Tarquinius Priscus and his successors, Rome has been the capital. After the fall of the monarchy there is no doubt that Veii successfully participated in the war of Etruria against Rome. It is certain also that for about forty years after 474 there was peace (apparently a peace imposed by Veii) between the two cities. This peace was again broken between 437 and 425 on the occasion of a war between Rome and Fidenæ in which Veii took up arms in aid of the latter. After Rome Fidenæ was the most important city on the left bank of the Tiber, and in helping her the object of Veii was to contest with Rome the dominion of the Tiber. But Rome won. Fidenæ was destroyed and again there was peace for twenty years between Rome and Veii

—this time at the expense of the latter and to her prejudice. For owing to the destruction of Fidenæ the Veientines were left entirely dependent on Rome for the navigation of the Tiber.

A people in search of glory and conquest naturally turns its attention to an adversary already vanquished, and when the truce with Veii came to an end, the ambitions and the cupidity of Rome were further encouraged by the collapse of the Etruscan Empire. Etruria, already threatened from the south by the prosperous Greek colonies of Sicily, south Italy, and Dalmatia,[1] had for some ten years been menaced from the north by an invasion of barbarians who by language and by origin were related to the Italici. These were the Celts or Gauls, who descended from the north about the end of the fifth century, seized a great part of north Italy, and greatly diminished the dominions of the Etruscans, the Veneti, and the Umbri. Veii, therefore, if she was attacked by Rome at this time, could not hope for the assistance of the other Etruscan cities.

The idea of reconquering a portion of the Etruscan territory which had already belonged to Rome and which the patrician oligarchy had lost, also counted for something in this enterprise. The monarchy had held the whole of Etruria for many years. It was natural that the republic, as soon as it felt able, should

---

[1] The Greek settlements in Dalmatia go back to Dionysius the Elder, and in particular to his colonizing activities on both sides of the Adriatic (*cf.* Diod., xv., 13–14). The chief of these settlements was Lissa on the small island of Pharos. From these secure Dalmatian bases Dionysius meditated an attack on the Etruscan empire on the opposite and (as always) much less securely held coast of Italy. (*Cf.* Diod., xv., 14.)

endeavour to reconquer at least a portion of the former possessions of the city. Another and not less powerful motive was the richness of the Veientine land. In spite of all the political struggles between rich and poor, between patricians and plebeians, the great families of senatorial rank, together with the richest families of the plebs, had retained the privilege of leasing the greater part of the public land. This probably arose from economic causes rather than from a mere abuse of power at the expense of the humbler classes. The domains of the republic embraced forests and land suitable for cultivation. They consisted of large estates, situated in many cases at a great distance from the city. They could only be turned to profit by capitalists possessed of the necessary means, who were in a position to wait, often for a long time, before reaping the fruits of their investments. Moreover, these leases were the share taken by the aristocracy in the gains of a victorious war, for, as we have already seen, all the movable booty which was not distributed among the soldiers was paid into the Treasury. From this point of view the privilege was, up to a certain point, not unjust. If, therefore, Rome could take and destroy Veii, capturing and selling into slavery the majority of its inhabitants, all the Veientine land would pass into the hands of the republic, and would be leased on very favourable conditions to the rich patrician and plebeian families, who would be able to cultivate it very profitably by slave labour.

The way was very prudently paved for the expedition by the introduction of a reform which was destined to have an immense effect on the history of Rome. It was proposed that each citizen under arms

should be paid a salary by the State. The war with
Veii might be long. It might be necessary to besiege
and destroy the city in order to get possession of all
its territories. What opportunities might this delay
not give the tribunes of exciting the discontent of the
plebeians and thus of disturbing and embarrassing the
campaign! By not merely promising the commons
a rich spoil but assuring them an immediate and
certain gain, the senate might hope to deprive the
tribunes of their most powerful argument against
wars in general and this war in particular. The
tribunes, as a matter of fact, vehemently opposed the
reform. They did not see that, had they been successful, Rome might never have been able to make great
wars of conquest at all, and would have been compelled to waste her strength in trivial defensive struggles until she disappeared from the stage of history.
This time, however, the senate had grasped the necessities of the State and at the same time had not failed
to understand the wishes of the people. The law
was passed, and the result showed that, had it been
rejected, the expedition to Veii would probably have
failed.

It would be useless to discuss whether the siege of
Veii actually lasted for ten years, as the ancient historians maintain, or whether the number was selected
in order to make the siege of Veii correspond with the
siege of Troy. There can be no doubt that in any
case the siege was long, and that the Romans had to
spend several winters in the trenches. In spite of the
arrangement for paying the soldiers, the patience of
the latter was put to the severest test. More than
once the people, weary and depressed, were on the
point of giving up the undertaking. While the army

was fighting before Veii political parties at Rome came to blows, and as the leaders of the plebeian opposition tried to make capital out of the popular discontent in order to disparage the war, the senate required all its firmness. Finally, however, the dictator, M. Furius Camillus, took and destroyed Veii. The population was sold into slavery; the Veientine territory was annexed and the movable spoils were distributed among the soldiers and the plebs. It was the greatest prize Rome had secured since the fall of the monarchy.

15. **The Invasion of the Gauls and the Burning of Rome, 390 B.C.** The victory, though costly, was very great. The republic had begun to reconquer the lost empire of the kings, and the internal effects were not less remarkable. After the siege of Veii the plebeian party passed through a crisis and began slowly to weaken. The reason for this was that the rich plebeians, or at least some of them, began to detach themselves from their former associates and, forgetting their old grievances, to gravitate towards the patricians. This movement may have been due to the new prestige which the senate derived from its victory, or to the agitation which arose among the plebeians on the subject of the Veientine land. Perhaps there was a combination of both causes. On this occasion the plebs declined to recognize the tacit assignment of the immovable and movable parts of the spoils to rich and poor respectively, which had become traditional. When they had received their share of the booty, they set up a claim that part of the population of Rome should be removed to Veii and should be given the houses and the lands of the unfortunate Veientines. This request was, of course, distasteful to the patricians and to many rich ple-

beians as well. A furious struggle ensued. The
senate could not secure the rejection of the law which
proposed to remove a portion of the Roman population to Veii without yielding a portion of the *ager
veientanus* to the plebeians and distributing it among
them at the rate of seven acres (*iugera*) per head.

Thus the conquest of Veii immediately gave rise
to new occasions of conflict. The effects of the
struggles which followed on the internal arrangements
of the republic might have been incalculable. But a
strange turn of fate intervened. Ten years after her
triumph over Veii, Rome was herself suddenly overtaken by a similar catastrophe.

The Gauls, as we have seen, had unwittingly helped
Rome to conquer Veii by weakening the power of the
Etruscans in northern and central Italy. But these
barbarians were driven on by inexorable necessity
from one conquest to another. The central mass of
their hordes was continually throwing off fresh and
furious columns, which drove ever farther afield in
search of lands and booty. In 390 according to some
authorities, in the winter of 388–387 according to
others, in that of 387–386 according to a third
account,[1] several thousand Gauls belonging to one
of their most southern tribes, the Senones, left their
homes on the Adriatic coast in the district now
known as the Marches, crossed the Apennines, and
swept towards the south-west, plundering the
Etruscans as they went. They drove on, meeting

[1] The date 390 is in accordance with the Roman tradition.
The other, 387–386, comes from Polybius, i., 6, and from Diodorus, xiv., 110 ff. There is a third date which makes the invasion take place a year earlier, viz., in 388–387., *Cf.* Dion.
Halic, i., 74.

practically no resistance, past the Trasimene Lake where then stood the splendid Etruscan city of Clusium (Chiusi). Round Clusium they stayed for some time, but their resources were not sufficient for the siege of a fortified place. After ravaging the surrounding country, therefore, they went still farther south towards Latium, their objective perhaps being the rich and fertile lands of Campania. Their course inevitably led them across Roman territory. Judging from what we know of the Gallic hordes it should not have been beyond the power of Rome and her allies to bar the way to the invaders and either to disperse or to drive them back. What happened is not clear. It would seem that Rome, either under-rating the danger or thinking it more remote than it really was, failed to take the necessary steps in time and was caught unprepared.

The fact remains that a Roman army to which Livy (v., 37) attaches the epithet disorderly (*tumultuarius*) was completely defeated at the Battle of the Allia, a small tributary of the Tiber, and that there was, in consequence, a serious panic at Rome. The whole population of Rome on receiving news of the disaster fled precipitately from the city, leaving behind in the fortress of the Capitol, only a single maniple of courageous youths under the command of the brave patrician, M. Manlius. Thus the Gauls were able to enter, sack, and destroy the city without striking a blow, while the fugitive republic was endeavouring to organize a new army to reconquer the capital.

But, just as had happened at Clusium, the efforts of the Gauls to take the rock defended by Manlius were in vain. The siege dragged on. It was not long before the barbarous but inexperienced invaders began to suffer from famine. A hot summer brought fever in its train. But the citadel still held out, and the danger of being taken in the rear by the new army which the republic was preparing grew ever greater. In the end the Gauls had to come to terms. A bushel of gold sufficed to content the barbarians and to induce them to evacuate Latium and return to their own country.

16. **The Reconstruction of Rome.** What had for a moment seemed to be an irremediable disaster to the Roman State was thus reduced to a furious but short raid by predatory barbarians. In the city, however, where the political equilibrium had been so unstable, the impression produced by what had happened was profound. Rome had been taken by the Gauls, had been burned and all but destroyed, had had to be ransomed for gold! The spirit of the people was so deeply dismayed that when the comitia centuriata met amid the smoking ruins to deliberate on the reconstruction of the city the tribunes proposed that Rome should be abandoned, that the population and the seat of government should be transferred to Veii, and that that city which had been broken up ten years before should now be rebuilt from its foundations. Already during the invasion of the Gauls and the siege, not a few Romans had fled to the territory of Veii and had taken up their abodes in the many houses there which had been left empty but intact. A small Romano-Veientine city was therefore already in existence. Would it not be better to remain where so many Romans had taken refuge, and to raise from the ashes of the great city a new Romano-Veientine State in which conquerors and conquered, patricians

and plebeians might at last achieve a real unity under new laws and institutions which would abolish all the immemorial privileges which gave Rome no peace?

The proposal was in many respects attractive and was pleasing to a number, especially among the common people whose spirits had been profoundly shocked by the great catastrophe. It was, of course, opposed by the patricians, the obstinate champions of tradition. The struggle was sharp, but tradition won. It was decided that Rome should be rebuilt and that such material as might be required should be taken from Veii, now condemned to destruction for the second time.

Thus Rome arose again from her ashes. But the new city was different indeed from the Rome of the kings. Speed was everything. The new buildings were run up without previous plan of design, without order or regularity. They were the natural offspring of the haste, poverty, and ill-will which had produced them. The broad straight streets traced by the kings were replaced by narrow and tortuous alleys which did not disappear until after the lapse of many centuries and until much more destruction had been wrought by fate or by the hands of men.

17. **The Political and Economic Effects of the Gallic Invasion.** In the city, thus hastily rebuilt, civil strife at once reappeared, embittered by poverty. The reconstruction of Rome was a more expensive undertaking than the restoration and extension of Veii would have been. Notwithstanding all the help that was given, in spite of contributions from the Treasury and the goodwill of all classes during the years immediately following 386, the condition of the

common people became more and more miserable. In addition to the extraordinary expenditure necessitated by the rebuilding of the city and to the ruin caused by the devastation of the fields, the republic had to face several short wars. For the Ædui and the Volsci, the Etruscans, and several of the allies of Rome were eager to profit by her weakness. In a short space of time, therefore, the condition of the people had again become what it had been a century earlier in the darkest days following the first defensive wars. Latium was once more covered with mortgages. Once more the bulk of the population had fallen into debt and under the iron law of the time were in danger of losing both goods and liberty. Once more the misery of the multitude issued in an agitation which sometimes humbly implored, and sometimes threateningly demanded, the reduction of debts and an agrarian law.

But the plebeians no longer had as auxiliaries in their struggles the men who had fought their battles so vigorously in the years before the war with Veii. The tribunes were now mute or feeble. The patricians had no difficulty in excluding the plebeians from the military tribunate. They turned a deaf ear to the requests of the people and busied themselves solely with the recovery of the fruits of the victory over Veii by incorporating in the territories of the State the conquered portion of southern Etruria where so much money was to be made by leasing state land. Thus in 387 were established in the new districts four new tribes,—the Stellatina, the Tromentian, the Sabatina, and the Arniensis.

18. The Agitation of M. Manlius Capitolinus (385–384 B.C.). This sudden paralysis of the plebs can

only be explained on the supposition that the schism
in their ranks which began after the siege of Veii had
persisted, and that the richer and more influential
plebeians, alarmed by the new demands of their
former friends, which threatened them with enormous
losses, had drawn closer and closer to the patricians.
The only protector of the plebeians in these years
was, in fact, the generous and glorious patrician, M.
Manlius, who for his valorous defence of the Capitol
had received the name of Capitolinus. Only a few
features of this singular personage can with difficulty
be discerned in the traditional account, which has
been coloured by patrician hatred. There is no doubt,
however, that, at the time when the rich plebeians
through fear or greed were deserting to the side of the
patricians, Manlius, induced by jealousy of Camillus,
as the ancient writers say, or possibly by sincere and
public-spirited motives, placed himself at the head of
a popular agitation for the mitigation of the universal
poverty—an agitation, that is to say, in favour of
agrarian legislation and a relaxation of the barbarous
law of debt.

The popularity with the people which the defender
of the Capitol—already the idol of the mob—soon
acquired was, of course, unbounded. Not less was
the fury with which he was persecuted by the leaders
of both parties, patrician and plebeian alike. The
tribunes of the people and the military tribunes were
equally against him. It could not be otherwise, for
Manlius, by demanding land for the people and reform
of the law of debt, threatened all the rich, patricians
and plebeians alike.

The struggle which followed was, therefore, full
of violence and cunning. It lasted, with various

vicissitudes, for about two years. In the end the rich plebeians and patricians managed to get rid of Manlius by accusing him of plotting to become king. His trial was as unjust as it was probably legal[1] and his enemies secured that he should be condemned to death. But the agitation did not cease, for it was produced by poverty, and poverty was acute. It was intensified by frequent wars, chiefly with the Latin allies, some of whom tried to profit by the critical condition into which Rome had fallen in order to recover their liberty.

The senate tried the experiment of establishing colonies (Sutrium in 383, Sesia in 382, Nepi in 381),[2] but the remedy was not adequate to cure the disease. The people were exasperated and began openly to accuse the patricians of inventing a revolt of the allies or a war as soon as anything was said at Rome about debt or agrarian laws, in order that they might have an excuse to deport from Rome all the strong partisans of the plebs.

Once again patrician obstinacy, by refusing the requests of the multitude, endangered the State, already much weakened by the war with the Gauls. Fortunately, as the situation grew worse and the evil greater, the old plebeian party gradually roused itself from its torpor and cautiously and timidly began to take up again the work of Manlius under the protection of the sacrosanct power of the tribunes. In 380 the tribunes of the people vetoed a levy for a war which had just broken out against Præneste (Palestrina),

---

[1] On M. Manlius Capitolinus, *cf.* C. Barbagallo, *Critica e storia tradizionale a proposito della sedizione e del processo di M. Manlio Capitolino*, in *Rivista di filologia classica*, 1912 (40), fasc. 2–3.

[2] On the chronology of these three colonies *cf.* Vell. Pat., i., 14.

and also forbade that any debtor should be enslaved because of his debts. In 378 the tribunes again vetoed a levy to repulse an incursion of the Volscians. This time, as the Volscian attack was a more serious matter than the revolt of Præneste two years before, the patricians gave way. A law was passed forbidding the collection of interest, or the bringing of actions for the repayment of capital, during the war. But when the war was over, the old law resumed its sway and the people recommenced their groans and curses.

There seemed to be no escape from this inextricable difficulty. The gentle remedies used by the plebeian party, which had now recovered some of its strength, to cure the ills of the debtors had proved inefficacious. It was impossible to propose a radical cure because the patrician party controlled the senate and the comitia, and because the richer and more influential plebeians would not help the poorer classes to shake the legal foundations of the existing social order by repealing the laws of debt.

19. The Licinio-Sestian Laws. There appeared to be no issue from this labyrinth, but two of the tribunes for the year 377, C. Licinius Stolo and Lucius Sestius Lateranus, found the clue. Both belonged to the aristocracy of rich plebeians which had a common interest with the patricians in opposing the laws demanded by the people, and with the plebeians in destroying the political privileges of the patriciate. They sought to reconcile these opposed interests by proposing in 377 a law dealing with debt, an agrarian law, and a law admitting plebeians to the consulship.

The law as to debt gave relief to the debtors. Perhaps it resembled the not less famous and debated *seisachtheia*, passed in Athens two centuries and a

half before by the wise Archon Solon. That measure
had enacted that from the total amount of the debt
should be deducted the sums already paid by way of
interest, and that the remainder should be paid off
in three years by instalments.

The agrarian law provided that no patrician should
possess more than five hundred *iugera* of public land
and that the land then in the possession of a patrician
in excess of that quantity should be fairly distributed
among the proletariat.

The law as to the consulship abolished military
tribunes, re-established government by consuls, and
provided that one of the consuls *must* be a plebeian.

Much has been written by modern critics on the
subject of these laws. These critics have tried to
prove that the agrarian law must have been much
later than the others, perhaps several centuries later.[1]
None of their arguments, however, seem conclusive
and the only effect of their critical speculations is to
confuse the tradition which, such as it is, explains
quite clearly the objects and the proceedings of the
two tribunes.

What they wished to do was no doubt to unite once
more the whole of the plebeians, rich and poor, who
had been divided as a result of the crisis following on
the burning of Rome. By their proposals as to debt
and the land, they aimed at relieving the distress of

---

[1] The existence of a Licinio-Sestian agrarian law is entirely
denied by B. Niese (*Die sogenannte licinischsextische Ackergesetz*
in *Hermes*, 1888, pp. 416 ff.). This view has been adopted by most
contemporary scholars. Critical revision of this theory has only
recently begun. *Cf.* W. Sinajsky *Studien zur römischen Agrar-und
Rechtsgeschichte*, Dorpat, 1908 (in Russian with an introduction
and resumé in German); also C. Barbagallo *op. cit.* pp. 233 ff.

the common people. By the law as to the consulship they hoped to gratify a long-standing aspiration
of the richer plebeians. The latter were to receive
the consulship as a compensation for the losses which
they would incur owing to the other two laws.

The manœuvre was skilful but, as may readily be
supposed, it was not easily brought to a successful
issue. Not all men are willing to pay a high price for
an increase of the prestige not of themselves individually but of their class. It is not surprising, therefore, that the struggle should have lasted for many
years—ten according to the ancient account—and
that during these years the legal weapon of obstruction should have been used without scruple on both
sides. The patricians several times found tribunes
who interposed their veto when their colleagues were
about to have the new laws put to the vote. On the
other side, the two authors of the proposed laws were
re-elected to their offices every year and retorted by
suspending the vital functions of the State.

Thus the contest lasted for a long time before the
two tenacious tribunes succeeded in carrying their
point and passing the three laws. In 367 the plebeians were delivered from their troubles by the
passage of the two enactments on the public land and
on the relief of debt. At the same time the consulship, the supreme office in the republic, ceased to be a
patrician privilege. In compensation it was decided
that, in addition to the two consuls, there should be
elected annually from among the patricians alone, a
new magistrate for the administration of justice,
styled prætor (*prætor qui ius in urbe diceret*), and
that there should be two curule ædiles (*ædiles curules*)
also chosen from the patricians.

CHAPTER IV

THE GREAT STRUGGLE WITH THE SAMNITES

20. The First Samnite War (343–341 B.C.). The passage of the Licinio-Sestian laws did not end the internal troubles of Rome. The republic was still distracted by conflicts on the subject of the consular elections. For several years the extreme faction of the patricians still tried to prevent the election of plebeians, sometimes making use of the power possessed by the Consul presiding over the elections to exclude any candidate he thought fit, and sometimes maintaining that no law could abolish or limit the freedom of the electors to elect any one they pleased. Demands for further relief for debtors were still incessant. In 357 the tribunes of the people succeeded in passing a law enacting that interest could be charged only at a fixed legal rate of one per cent. per month. In 352 a commission of five was appointed to liquidate the mass of outstanding accounts, which were in a highly confused, though not a hopeless, condition. The commission arranged for the payment of debt from public funds, substituting the State, with proper precautions, for the private creditor. They also paid off creditors with the goods of debtors, but took care that such goods should be taken at a fair valuation.

These enactments and expedients show that not

even the Licinian laws had succeeded in radically curing the evils of debt. It could not have been otherwise. No measure of conciliation between classes or parties operates at once. It was not until the second decade after the Licinian laws were passed that a certain degree of tranquillity was reached; and this was partly owing to the appearance of new grounds for public anxiety. The twenty years after the enactment of these laws were, in fact, full of conflicts great and small. The Gauls had not ceased to be troublesome. Twice, in 360 and 348, they had tried to reoccupy the country which was so closely associated with their military glories. With Etruria also there were wars and disputes. Rebellion was still smouldering among the allies. The Latin League, concluded by Spurius Cassius, was falling to pieces, either because the inconclusive blow struck by·the Gauls and the continual internal dissensions in the city had discredited Rome in the opinion of the allies, or because, with the lapse of more than a century, the alliance was worn out. We can easily understand, therefore, how the contending parties and classes may have been led by the growth of the foreign danger to accept loyally the compromise brought about by the Licinian laws. The external situation also explains two important events which happened during these years; the alliance concluded with the Samnites in 354 and the second treaty with Carthage, which was signed in 348.

The Samnites were a powerful confederation of warlike peoples. They were at first settled in the mountains between Apulia and Campania, and starting from this region, they conquered almost the whole of southern Italy from sea to sea, enslaving the indigenous peoples and subduing the Etruscans and the Greeks. Thus they became perhaps the strongest power in Italy, at a time when the Etruscans were declining and the Gauls were spending themselves in restless and tumultuous raids over the whole peninsula without taking root as yet in any one part. Rome had now secured a solid foothold in the territory of the Volsci, and her dominions marched with Samnite territory. She was, therefore, obviously bound to desire a secure friendship with that powerful confederation at a time when her old alliances were tottering.

Of no less importance is the second treaty with Carthage, concluded in 348.[1] This treaty confirmed in many respects the previous agreement of 510, but altered it in others—almost everywhere to the advantage of the Carthaginians. The new alliance now comprised the people of Utica, and the Tyrians of the far off Syrian coast. By it Latin ships were forbidden to sail beyond the Pillars of Hercules to the more westerly dominions of Carthaginian Africa. The Romans were not only not allowed to found colonies in Sardinia or Africa, but were also prohibited from trading with any part thereof but Carthage itself. In fact, if the treaty of 510 had been a hard bargain for Rome, the second edition of it was worse, for it shut the doors of Africa and Sardinia in her face.

In compensation for this Rome was assured that "if they [the Carthaginians] took any city in Latin territory not subject to the Roman dominion, they

---

[1] *Cf.* Polyb., iii., 24; liv., 7, 27; Diod. xvi., 69, 1. Diodorus mentions a treaty between Rome and Carthage in this year to which he erroneously refers as the *first*.

would negotiate as to the money and the prisoners captured, but would hand over the city itself to the Romans." The reason for the new treaty is, therefore, clear. Rome renounced Africa and Sardinia because Carthage again pledged herself formally not to pass from Sicily and Sardinia to the Italian coast. The fear that the Carthaginians might try to establish themselves on the coast was so strong at Rome in those years, in which the old alliances of the republic were falling to pieces with age, that she was willing to abandon all Sardinia in return for a renewal of the pledge that Carthage would renounce all intention of establishing herself on the continent. Once more Rome gave proof of that great prudence which always helped her in her foreign policy and which contrasted so strangely with the heedless imprudence of her internal struggles. There was indeed every reason why she should try to stand well with Carthage because, while her old allies were failing, the new ones were insecure. In 345, indeed, the Romans found themselves involved, almost without warning, in a conflict with the Samnite Confederation with which, a few years before they had concluded a treaty.

Campania was the scene and the cause of this war between two states, each of which had so far been able to extend her own dominions without crossing the other's path. This fertile region, bathed by the Tyrrhene Sea and crowned by the tablelands and scattered groups of the Neapolitan Apennines, had been inhabited from time immemorial by an intelligent and industrious population called by the Greeks and Latins the Osci (Ὄσκοι). They had tilled the ground and had introduced the cultivation of vines and cereals, the most valuable and profitable crops known to that age. By them were built the first cities of southern Italy, and they grew and multiplied on their native plains, which were so much favoured by nature, much faster than any other people in the peninsula. At a later stage in their history they had come to know the Etruscans and the Greeks, and had even submitted to the dominion and the colonization of these peoples. But they had been neither oppressed nor degraded nor destroyed. On the contrary, they had learned much by the experience.

Thus it came about that, until the middle of the fifth century, it had been possible for the three civilizations, the Greek on the coast, the Oscan and Etruscan in the inland districts, to flourish side by side. Each was, as it were, completed by the contiguity of the others—a relationship which was also apparent in their decorative and architectural art, in their monuments and even in their coinage. In this country, beside the rude wooden shrines of Oscan antiquity the traveller might admire grandiose Doric temples, among which those at Pæstum are still one of the wonders of the world. In both were to be found Greek and Oscan bronzes, coloured terra cottas, and the figures of the Gods of Homer expressed in elegant sculptures or inimitable reliefs. The courts of the Etruscan houses expanded into Greek peristyles, whose walls glowed with the many-hued marble incrustation which in the future was to face the interior of the buildings of the Hellenistic East. The modest habitations of the Oscans contained gold filigree work, articles of silver and copper, bibelots of amber, black high-glazed pottery, and vessels of glass made or imported by the Greeks and the Etruscans.

By the second half of the fifth century, however, a fourth people had come to disturb this admirable work of fusing three civilizations. The mountaineers of the Abruzzi, the Samnites, had descended upon the land occupied by the Greeks and the Etruscans. One by one they had wrested from the latter the colonies which lay nearest to them. They had pressed on towards the east and had fallen on the Greek cities far and near.[1] In these Greek states of Campania, with their vivid and sumptuous life, fierce and constant struggles for power raged, just as in their mother cities, between the aristocratic and democratic parties. In these conflicts feeling ran so high that neither party, when beaten, ever hesitated to seek support from the nearest or most powerful of their foreign neighbours. The Samnites had profited largely by these discords to extend their power in Campania. But, so far as we can discover, they were a rude and warlike people by no means suited to a strong political discipline, and they could not come in contact with Greek and Etruscan civilization without profoundly altering their character. The Samnites who had occupied Etruscan cities like Capua, or Greek cities like Cumæ, soon abandoned the customs, the ideas, and the traditions of their own race, and adopted the language, the customs, and above all the vices, of the peoples who were so much their superiors in culture and civilization. Thus, from the blending of the Greek or Etruscan civilization with the rudeness of the Samnites, had issued a new and, as it were, a bastard people, which very soon repudiated its

[1] On Campania at this period and the relations between Oscans, Etruscans, Greeks, and Samnites, *cf.* A. Sagliano, *Sanniti ed Osci* in *Rendiconti della R. Accademia dei Lincei 1912*, pp. 208 ff.

ancestral stock and claimed independence. Capua, for example, the richest and most powerful of the Campanian cities which had been taken from the Etruscans by the Samnites, and where the aristocracy was in great part composed of Samnites with a veneer of Greek and Etruscan culture, lived at constant war with the Samnite confederation.

By the middle of the fourth century, B.C., therefore, this, the most favoured land in Italy, was a chaos of discord and conflict. The Etruscans had now almost entirely evacuated it. The Greeks, distracted by internal struggles, at one moment fought against the Samnite power, at another tried to make use of that power for the satisfaction of their private feuds and ambitions. In the one case or the other they were almost always vanquished by the barbarians, but they succeeded in insinuating into these rude minds a pride, a thirst for pleasure, and a greed of riches which sooner or later made them deny their mother country and revolt against it. In short, the Greeks were constantly at war with each other, while among the Samnites there was an uninterrupted struggle with those of their own race who, having tasted the fruits of the Græco-Etruscan culture, had ceased to recognize their own kinsmen and to speak their own language.

The hour of Rome's intervention in the embroiled and always turbulent affairs of Campania was bound to strike sooner or later. It is not clear what was the first occasion and the first motive for her intervention. In 343[1], according to Livy, a new war had

---

[1] The reality of this first Samnite war as a historic fact has been called in question by some modern writers. It is attested by Dionysius of Halicarnassus (xv., 3-2), by Appian (*Samn.*, i.), and by Livy (vii., 29 et seq.).

broken out between the Samnite confederation and what may be called her rebellious colonies on the plain, the Sidicini and the Campani. The original conflict had arisen between the Samnites and the Sidicini, but the latter had eventually obtained the help of Capua. The united forces of Sidicini and Campani soon despaired of holding their own against the Samnites and went to Rome for help. They pointed out the help which Capua could give the Romans against the Volsci and the Æqui, who were always uncertain and hostile neighbours, and how important it was for Rome to prevent the Samnites from establishing themselves in Campania. Rome, allied as she was with the Samnites, hesitated for long indeed, until finally—if we may believe Livy —Capua offered to place herself in unconditional subjection to Rome. The Romans, no longer able to resist the temptation to possess themselves of the Campanian land, sent an embassy to the Samnites, warning them to respect Capua, which now belonged to Rome.

Thus originated, according to Livy, the so-called first Samnite war, which was fought in 342 and about which modern historians have disputed at great length. There can be no question that Livy's account of the struggle is to a large extent fantastic. For he states that, after the Roman army had miraculously escaped immense dangers and won extraordinary victories, the Romans and the Samnites suddenly made a very reasonable peace in the following year. But if the whole story is in fact incomprehensible, it does not seem to us possible to follow the example of modern historians and without more ado strike this war out of the history of Rome. For, on the one hand, it is not easy to explain how tradition could have invented a whole war, root and branch, and, on the other, it is equally difficult to understand how without it Rome first came into contact with Capua. It would seem probable, therefore, that Capua, if not by sacrificing her independence at least by proposing great advantages to Rome, succeeded in causing great difficulties in 342 and in starting a war between Samnium and Rome. But this war must have been short, as neither the Romans nor the Samnites wished to commit themselves too far, and both had stronger motives for arriving at a compromise than for carrying on the fight.

21. The Revolt of the Latin Allies and the New Settlement of Latium (340-338 B.C.). The peace, however (and here we leave conjecture for surer historical facts), was made at the expense of the Campanians and the Sidicini, who did not look on it from the same point of view. At Capua there was a party —the democratic party—which had only accepted the Roman alliance in order to help the Sidicini and to fight the Samnites. This party, therefore, regarded the peace between Rome and Samnium as the Sidicini regarded it—that is as a betrayal, and, in concert with the latter, they took the bold step of approaching the Latin League and offering them an alliance against Rome. Rome, in treaty with her recent enemy, had now to sustain the attack of all her allies, old and new, united against her.

The new war lasted three years. Its history, like that of the previous war, is obscure. It appears, however, that in the course of these three years there occurred one of those unexpected events which recur so frequently in history. Few wars seem in their earlier stages to have caused more anxiety at Rome. This was quite natural. No enemies could be more dangerous, to all appearance, than those who spoke the same language, bore the same arms and had for a century been making war side by side with the Romans. For such an enemy Roman strategy and tactics could have no secrets or surprises. The war promised, therefore, to be a murderous duel to the death. It was, on the contrary, short and easy. The combination, which for a moment had seemed so serious, must have been in reality very weak. A single battle at Trifanum on the frontier of Latium and Campania, in which the Romans were victorious, was enough to shatter the combined forces of Latium and Campania. It is difficult to say why the combination of the enemy should have seemed to be so much stronger than it actually was. We know only that Capua joined the Latin League at the instigation of the democratic party; that the aristocracy, on the other hand, declared for Rome and sent to the help of the legions at the battle of Trifanum a contingent of the famous Capuan cavalry, which perhaps decided the victory. The result of the battle was enough to turn the scale in favour of the Roman party in a state which was full of vacillation and strife. Perhaps in many other Latin cities the party of revolution was confronted by another party which desired to remain faithful to Rome. Be this as it may, the battle of Trifanum broke Campania and the Latin League.

This easy victory, in a war which had seemed likely to be so difficult and dangerous, had a profound effect on Rome. It is no exaggeration to say that the war against Campania and the Latin League is one of the decisive events in her earlier history. Not only did it obliterate from the public mind the last remnants of the humiliating recollection of the Gallic invasion and the burning of the city, but it infused an unwonted resolution into the policy of the republic, which had hitherto been so timid. Once the ruin of the Campano-Latin League was complete, the Romans no longer hesitated to take possession of Latium and Campania, and, after two years of war, they reduced all the cities which did not voluntarily surrender, giving them all a new form of government.

Most of the Latin cities suffered neither violence nor confiscation. They retained their land and their laws, but in every case they lost *connubia, commercia et concilia inter se.* That is to say, Rome dissolved the Latin League and forbade any one of the cities to ally itself or to trade or to intermarry with the rest, at the same time obliging each on its own account to contract a separate alliance with Rome. In this way, instead of treating with the Latins as *prima inter pares* in a powerful confederation, Rome assumed a position of hegemony over many isolated little powers, each of which was much weaker than herself. At the same time steps were taken to enlarge the Roman territory to the north, east, and south of the city. Lanuvium, Aricia, and Nomentum (La Mentana) lost their independence and were annexed to Rome with the status of *civitates cum suffragio.* In other words, their inhabitants ceased to be members of their own state and became citizens of Rome.

The same policy was followed at Antium (Anzio), whose fleet was confiscated and in which a colony was established. Other places such as Velitræ (Velletri), Tibur (Tivoli), and Præneste (Palestrina), though they were allowed to remain Latin cities and nominally independent allies, were punished by the confiscation of part of their territories. Capua lost only a small but fertile strip of land, but even in the more southerly part of the Volscian territory and in Campania the overlordship of Rome was strengthened by well-conceived regulations. Capua, Fundi, Formiæ, Cumæ, and sundry other minor states were placed under Roman rule with the status of *civitates sine suffragio*. The citizens of states in this position were Roman citizens with all a Roman citizen's rights and duties except those of electing, and being elected, to the magistracies of the State. It appears that Capua was given some special privileges. The nobility, which remained faithful to Rome during the war, were certainly treated with special favour; but in what exactly this treatment consisted is unknown.

This war was undoubtedly the most successful enterprise undertaken by the republic since the conquest of Veii. Its results at last enabled Rome to compare her existing situation favourably with what it had been in the last years of the monarchy. For the treaty concluded by Spurius Cassius with the Latin League she had substituted a solid and secure hegemony, similar to that which she had in all probability enjoyed under the last of the kings. The Roman territory, including the Latin and Campanian colonies, now extended from the Ciminian Hills nearly to Vesuvius, that is for about three thousand seven hundred and fifty square miles, to which should be added three thousand one hundred and twenty-five square miles of land belonging to the allies and to Latin colonies—in all more than six thousand two hundred and fifty square miles. Of this the Roman territory proper must have contained more than half a million inhabitants, and the less immediately subject territories almost as much again. It is thus no arbitrary supposition that Rome could now put in the field fifty thousand men—a great force for that time, especially when it is remembered that in these very years Alexander the Great set out from conquered Greece to found his immense empire with a force of scarcely thirty thousand.

In the first half of the fourth century, therefore, the republic began to reap the fruit of its long, obstinate and rather confused endeavours. There is nothing surprising in the fact that these first fruits ripened all at once as if by a kind of miracle. All great changes in history are prepared in silence and most people know nothing about them till they are accomplished. On the other hand, it may appear singular that the Samnites should have allowed the Romans to extend and strengthen themselves in this way. It was natural that the two great powers should have lived at peace until the greater ambitions of Rome turned towards the coasts of Latium and southern Etruria, while those of the Samnites were directed towards Campania. It is more difficult to explain why the Samnites allowed Rome to establish herself quietly in that very Campania which they had first conquered, then lost, and always longed to possess. Yet not only did Rome definitely take possession of Capua, Formiæ, and Fundi after the war with the Latins, but in the following years two colonies were established at Cales (Calvi) and at Fregellæ (Caprano) as outposts on the very frontier of Samnium —and the Confederation made no attempt whatever to prevent it.

22. The War between Rome and Naples. There is but one way of explaining this inertia if (as may be admitted) it is impossible to ascribe it entirely to the torpidity of the federal régime in a nation more valorous in war than experienced in the art of government. In these very years in which Rome took a decisive step towards her future greatness the Samnites were occupied with another enemy who had appeared on the coast of south Italy. This was Alexander of Molossus, king of Epirus and uncle of Alexander the Great, whom the Tarentines had hired to fight against the Lucanians and the Bruttii. Even in the extreme south of Italy the Greek colonists and merchants of the cities on the coast were constantly at war with the native populations of the interior. The Samnites, who had always combated the Greek element and championed the natives, were involved in this war, which lasted for several years with varying fortunes, and ended with the death of Alexander. It was no doubt this conflict which constrained the Samnites to leave Rome a free hand.

But when Alexander was dead, and peace had been re-established in south Italy, the Samnites would not have left so large a share of Campania to Rome had they not been convinced by events that they were unable to wrest the province from its new conqueror. Nothing but a suitable occasion was wanted to bring to grips the torpid colossus of the central Italian mountains and the agile and vigorous athlete of Latium, whose lightning movements were governed by nerves of steel. The occasion which gave rise to the great war between Rome and Samnium was supplied by the Greeks—the foreign element which from the outset had sought to found its prosperity in Italy on the discord of the native races.

It is not clear what exactly happened between Rome and Naples. But Naples was a Greek city and, as such, hostile to the Italic elements which were growing stronger in Campania; hostile, therefore, to Rome, the last comer but the most enterprising and energetic of them all. It is natural enough that there should have been at Naples a party opposed to Rome, but how the rupture between Rome and Naples came about is not known. Was it a spontaneous movement of the whole Greek population against the Roman hegemony? Did Naples conclude secret agreements with the Samnites to the prejudice of the distant republic? Was there a revolution in the politics of the city which swept into power a party opposed to that previously in office? And did that party, pursuing an illusion of liberty, drive Naples into a position from which only a miracle of political dexterity could have safely extricated it?

We are not in a position to answer these questions. All that is certain is that in 327 war broke out between Rome and Naples, and Rome ordered the Consul Q. Publilius Philo to besiege the place. By the time the consul appeared before the walls, however, Naples had been powerfully reinforced by the Samnites, and Rome found herself faced by a Græco-Samnite alliance. Stimulated by her victory over the Latins, Rome decided without hesitation to clear up the situation, even at the risk of a new war. While, therefore, the siege of Naples was begun, ambassadors were sent to demand explanations from the Samnite government and to request the withdrawal of their reinforcements from Naples. The Confederation tried to evade the demand, alleging that the Samnites who had hurried to the defence of Naples were private persons who had enrolled themselves on their own account. On this Rome cut short the proceedings by declaring war on Samnium.

23. The Beginnings of the Second Samnite War. The die was cast. The great duel between Rome and Samnium for the dominion of south Italy had begun. It was a strange and interminable war, about which the ancient historians have little to tell us, and which remains one of the many enigmas of the more ancient history of Rome. One thing alone seems clear and that is that at first each adversary in turn tried to terrify the other by diplomatic and military manœuvres without coming to a decisive issue. This curious policy, which was followed during the first years of the war, can only be explained on the supposition that the forces of the two states balanced each other, and that they were such on either side that they could not be destroyed in one or more pitched battles. Thus both parties at once understood that the war would be one of exhaustion, in which the victor would be the one who endured the longest.

Immediately on the declaration of war Rome occupied three townships in the neighbourhood of the line of the Vulturnus—Allifæ, Callifæ, and Rufrium—and made of these so many outposts thrust forward into the territories of Samnium itself, which served to protect Campania. The next move of the Romans was to seek allies in south Italy, and they succeeded in persuading the Lucanians and the Apulians to conclude an alliance with them, and to promise them arms and men for the war, thus taking the Samnites in reverse. This being assured, they did no more than continue the siege of Naples. Meanwhile the Samnites on their part seized points of vantage in Roman territory, sought allies among the Tarentines, and did their best by cunning intrigues to detach the Apulians and the Lucanians from the Roman alliance. They do not seem, however, to have undertaken any military operations, and they did not make the slightest movement to help Naples. In this year, therefore, there was no fighting except that in progress before Naples.

Naples was a splendid city, the jewel of Italy, the pride of Campania—one of the very few places in Magna Græcia not yet submerged by the tempestuous flood of native elements. She had preserved, as she was destined to preserve for centuries, all the characteristics of a Greek metropolis. Her long walls reminded the traveller of those still more glorious walls which connected Athens with her harbour. Now for a whole year she saw every outlet for her inland commerce closed. For a year her robust youth had been forced to abandon the works of peace in order to defend her walls and her gates against the threats of the enemy. The greater part of the public resources had been dissipated in paying Samnite mercenaries. The number of ships entering and leaving the famous bay grew less and less. The city festivals, the spectacles, the competitions of the theatre, the odeum, and the stadium were at an end. Strangers of all manners and all countries no longer thronged the streets of the great city, bargaining, amusing themselves, or merely idling under the sunny skies. But, in spite of these hardships, Naples, trusting to Samnite assistance, held out through the whole of the year 327, and Rome, surprised by this unexpected resistance, was obliged to take a step which was destined to be of the gravest consequence in her future history. It became necessary to extend the command of the consul directing the siege and to appoint the first Roman *proconsul*.

The procrastination and uncertainty of the policy adopted by the Samnite Confederation, however, rendered vain a resistance which might otherwise have proved fatal to Rome. Whether from want of power or want of will the Samnite Confederation did nothing to help Naples, either by attacking the communications of the besieging army or by making a diversion on enemy territory. The tenacity of the Neapolitans began to give way; the party in favour of war to the end lost ground more and more. The people, ruined and exhausted by the long siege, no longer trusted the Samnites, who had so feebly supported their ally. A day came when the leading citizens and the magistrates themselves offered to treat for surrender. The proconsul's first demand was that the mercenaries should be dismissed and a Roman garrison received. This was agreed to and peace was concluded by a treaty which left the rich city all its territories and respected its independence, subject to the conclusion of an offensive and defensive alliance.[1]

24. The Abolition of the Nexum and the Caudine Forks. Empires are founded not by force alone but by force directed by policy. By granting such generous terms Rome gave a new example of her political sagacity. In southern Italy alliances were as unstable as the soil which is constantly shaken by earthquakes. The Samnites had, in fact, succeeded

[1] On this treaty *cf.* the scattered hints which can be gathered from Strab., v., 4–7, and Polyb. vi., 14, 8.

in detaching the Lucanians from their alliance with Rome very soon after that alliance had been concluded, and had contrived to make a bargain with the Vestini. It was wiser, therefore, to make friends with the Neapolitans than to wreak vengeance on them.

After the fall of Naples the war languished. From the little that is clear in the accounts of the ancient writers it may be inferred that, in the years that followed, the Romans and the Samnites mutually annoyed each other with incursions, raids, and ravages almost always carried out on the enemy's frontiers or on the territories of the weaker allies, but never committed themselves to dangerous but decisive operations. Thus the war dragged on, and every year saw new levies raised at Rome and the army sent forth sometimes in one direction, sometimes in another.

But when military service is a national duty incumbent on rich and poor alike, the poor prefer violent but short wars to those which are waged with more caution but last longer. The plebeians soon wearied of these long delays and the upper classes were so much impressed that at this period, and more precisely in the year 326, a law was passed finally abolishing the *nexum*, making debtors responsible to their creditors with their goods only and no longer with their personal liberty. This reform, so ardently desired by the poor, was a great victory for the plebeian agitators. We may regard it as a remarkable indication of moral progress, for it showed that the savage rule of money and the interests of the possessing classes had given way to a loftier sentiment of respect for the dignity of human personality. The concession, however, was made at this time, after it had been so long resisted, by way of compensation for the sacrifices imposed on the people by the long duration of the Samnite war and with a view to persuading them to have patience. For a time it did, in fact, induce the plebeians, in spite of their sufferings, to have patience. But, as invariably happens, they began to grow weary again after a time in spite of this alleviation, and to demand a more rapid and energetic war policy, until in 322 the party in favour of war to the knife carried the day in the comitia against the party of caution.

The consuls for 321 were Sp. Postumius Albinus and T. Veturius Calvinus, two new men who had made many vehement speeches during the election in favour of a vigorous offensive and an invasion of the enemy's country. In that year four legions did, in fact, enter hostile territory from the eastern frontier of Campania through the district which in later years was traversed by the Via Appia. In those days, however, the Via Appia was not yet in existence. The march was, therefore, very rough and difficult, and rashness in the conduct of this undertaking, want of knowledge of the ground, and perhaps the incompetence of the commanders, led to a very serious military disaster.

In the gorge of Caudium, between the villages now known as Arienzo and Montesarchio,[1] a pass described in the most terrifying terms by historians, the Roman army found itself entirely encircled by the Samnites, who had occupied all the outlets of the narrow valley and had covered the crests of the surrounding heights with a strong force. The Romans tried with desperate

[1] *Cf.* E. Cocchia *I Romani alle forche Caudine; questione di topografia storica*, in *Studi filologici*. Napoli. iii., p. 378 ff.

valour to break the iron ring of their enemies, but in vain. After some days of useless efforts, their forces dwindling, their courage gone, and famine staring them in the face, they decided to treat.

The Samnites might have slain them, but they knew that the slaughter of the Roman army would have led to a war to the knife, which they were anxious to avoid. They decided, therefore, not to do this. It appears that the proposal was made to release the Romans absolutely and send them back to their own country, in the hope that by this generous act a stable peace with Rome might be re-established. In the end a middle course was adopted and the commander-in-chief, Caius Pontius Telesinus, having inflicted on the defeated army the humiliation of passing under the yoke, sent back officers and men to their homes. He required them at the same time to pledge their country to renounce all attempts against Samnium and to evacuate all the occupied territory in that country, particularly Fregellæ, the conquest of which after the Latin war had so deeply wounded Samnite susceptibilities.

But when the beaten army brought back to Rome the shame of its defeat, Rome refused to recognize it as her own. The senate, acting within its rights, refused to ratify the peace which had been accepted by their general in the field. This reply exasperated the Samnites, and in the following year (320 B.C.) they fell upon Fregellæ and carried it by storm. In their turn the Romans sent an expedition to Apulia, besieged and occupied Luceria, which was under the protection of the Samnites, placed a garrison there, and then attempted to take Samnium in the rear and cut its communications with the Adriatic. It seemed for a moment as if the two peoples intended to undertake decisive operations to fight the war to a finish, but matters again took a surprising turn, and in 319 a truce was concluded for two years. What was the reason of this? Probably each adversary realized that the struggle could only be ended by the exhaustion of one of them, and they wished to have an interval for better preparation. It is certain at any rate that the truce was used by both sides for perfecting their armaments.

So far the Romans had fought only in open plains, as in Latium and Campania, and therefore a large tactical unit such as the legion, compact, heavily armed, and similar in many respects to the Greek phalanx, had hitherto been amply sufficient for all purposes. Now they had to fight the Samnites in the mountains, where they were faced with swift mobile armies, full of dash and initiative. The legion was, therefore, divided into forty-five maniples, each of which in battle was drawn up at a certain distance from the others. They were so arranged, however, that the gaps in the first line were covered by the maniples of the second, and those of the second by the maniples of the third. The distance between one soldier and another was increased. The old and heavy spear was almost wholly abolished and for it was substituted the lighter javelin (*pilum*), which could also be used for throwing. Finally, in the place of the small but heavy shield of bronze with which only the first ninety-eight centuries had so far been armed, the whole army adopted the large square leathern shield of the second and third classes. It is probable, moreover, that the effective strength of the army for war purposes was increased.

At the same time Rome tried to renew her agreements with the Apulians and occupied Teanum, Canusium, and Ferentum. An understanding with all Apulia was successfully concluded, and by occupying Nerulum the Romans endeavoured to gain a footing by force among the Lucanians, who refused to come to terms. For their part the Samnites did their best to sow the seeds of rebellion among the Campanian cities and the neighbouring colonies whose fidelity had been shaken by the disaster of Caudium. They also prepared, by ordering a *levée en masse* of their whole population, to undertake an offensive in Latium, thus paying the Romans back in kind for their abortive invasion of Samnium.

25. The Political Effects of the War and the Censorship of Appius Claudius (315–308 B.C.). In 315, as was inevitable, the war flared up again. The Samnites, feeling that they were now ready, seized upon the pretext of an attack made by the Romans on the township of Saticula (S. Agata dei Goti) and attempted their long meditated offensive against Latium from the southern frontier. The movement was calculated to cut the communications with Campania and at the same time to prevent the Roman army operating on the Campano-Samnite border from turning round to interfere with the invasion. From there it was their intention to strike at the heart of Roman territory, raising the country in rebellion as they went.

The two armies met at Lautulæ on the Latin frontier. It is certain that the Romans, if not annihilated, were defeated and forced to retreat. The Samnites were thus able to besiege Terracina (315) and the effects of their victory were soon obvious. Southern

Latium and the Roman part of Campania, Capua included, wavered in their already uncertain loyalty. Luceria expelled its Roman garrison.

But Rome did not lose courage. The Samnites, so impetuous in their first attack, did not dare to venture into the close-set forest of Latin colonies which surrounded the city, and the siege of Terracina proved to be no slight undertaking. This gave Rome time ·to reorganize her defence. In the year after the disaster of Lautulæ two Roman armies had already taken the field against the Samnites. Of these one was in Latium facing Terracina; the other was operating in Apulia against Luceria. The battle of Terracina was the first sign of recovery. A Roman victory here was immediately followed by the reduction of the valley of the Liris, which was still in a state of unrest, and thereafter, with the help of the faithful aristocracy of Capua, the complete submission of the Campanian rebels was soon secured (314). Luceria was recaptured, and this time, that it might be held more securely, a strong colony consisting of twenty-five hundred citizens was planted there.

These successes seem once more to have paralysed the Samnites, and to have given new courage to the Romans. In 313 the latter once more took possession of Fregellæ, sacked Nola, and established a colony at Interamna (Teramo) on the Liris. In 312 they sent an expedition against the Marrucini. The Samnites appear to have been once more shut up in their mountains and to have lent but feeble aid to the cities and peoples attacked by Rome.

Thus the war of positions dragged on and spread from year to year in an interminable sequence of raids, sieges, surprises, and battles, almost all fought on the territories and at the expense of the allies or the colonies of the two belligerents. The effects on Roman society of so great an effort were necessarily many and profound. It is clear that during the Samnite war the Licinio-Sestian laws at last produced their full effect of reconciliation. The exclusive spirit of the ancient patrician families at last yielded to the spirit of the age. A considerable number of rich plebeian families filled the magistracies allowed to them by law as well as the consulship. They entered the senate and there began to mix with the patricians of ancient lineage, thus forming the patricio-plebeian aristocracy which was to govern the republic for many centuries.

The long war, however, produced other and less fortunate effects than this. It is not improbable that the struggles with the Samnites were the cause and commencement of the great crisis in Italian agriculture, which was destined to disturb the peace of the Roman commonwealth for more than two centuries. It was at this time that the decline set in of the small landed proprietors who were free men, and the subsequent growth out of their ruin of a new system of great estates worked by slaves. The Roman soldiers of this period were practically all small proprietors. At the summons of the consul they exchanged the spade for the sword and entrusted their land to the women, the old men, and the boys. Wars, therefore, such as that against Samnium, which every year required large contingents, took away from agriculture its most vigorous arms at the season when labour was required most. The loss thus caused to large families who lived on a small property may easily be imagined. The pay received by the legionary was a very slight compensation for such a loss, which was aggravated by deaths in battle; for every stroke of the enemy which did not miss its mark deprived some family of a husbandman in the height of his vigour, while the number of useless mouths did not diminish.

It is not surprising, therefore, that in these years, at Rome and in the Roman and Latin colonies, more and more ruined yeomen flocked to the cities to earn their bread, or that the rich found frequent opportunities of buying up and uniting in large slave-worked estates many little properties till then cultivated by families of free citizens. In times of constant warfare, such as these, there was necessarily an abundant supply of slaves. And what did it matter to the new landlord if the land cultivated by his slaves produced less than before of the commodities necessary to mankind? He had bought at a low price and he was satisfied with a good return on his capital outlay.

But in those days as always, though perhaps more then than now, the war, if it impoverished some, enriched others. A soldier who was lucky enough to participate in a successful expedition into a rich country under the command of a generous consul might bring home a substantial pile as his share of the spoils. Even then, moreover, war had the effect of stimulating the circulation of money, and promoted certain trades and industries, though no doubt, what it gave to one it took from another. Too often the State was obliged to give urgent orders for the provision of necessities required by the newly raised troops, which had to be sent into battle well equipped at a moment's notice. Too often the republic, in order to feed its soldiers, had to beg and send merchants to seek grain in Etruria, in Sicily, even in distant Africa. Thus, after a few years the Samnite war made a fleet necessary. Great was then the stir and bustle in the improvised shipyards on the Latin and Campanian coast, and great the fatigue of the arms and axes of the amateur woodmen employed to fell and cleave the oaks, the firs, and the magnificent pine trees of the district, which were the finest in Italy.[1]

It was at this time that silver coin was first circulated in Roman territory, bronze being no longer sufficient for the manifold needs of the State. Rome was, in fact, beginning to undertake greater tasks, to measure herself against greater difficulties, and in Campania she was beginning to gain a better understanding of what Hellenism meant. Her ideas were correspondingly enlarged. One proof of this is supplied by the appearance among the Roman aristocracy, hitherto so much bound by its traditions and so much occupied with its own immediate interests, of the strange figure of Appius Claudius Cæcus, who was censor between 312 and 308. In the midst of the preoccupations and the crises of the Samnite war, and in spite of the vast war expenditure which was being incurred, Appius Claudius commenced two public works on an immense scale and involving an enormous cost. These were a vast aqueduct and a great road from Rome to Capua—the first section of what was to be the famous Via Appia. The majority of the senators were shocked at his proposals. For many a year the Romans had drunk water from the Tiber or from the cisterns and wells excavated within the city, and no one had complained. The old roads had sufficed for the legions which had first conquered

[1] *Cf.* Theophr., *Hist. Plants*, v., 8, 1.

and then defended Campania. Was this the moment, when the State was exhausted by the expenditure on the war against Samnium, to engage in works so grandiose and so costly?

But, like all the Claudii, Appius was a proud, resolute, and obstinate man. He knew that times were changing and that Rome was no longer the little city it had been. He saw that there were many hands no longer occupied in tilling the ground, and that those who required to be fed should by no means be left idle. Therefore, notwithstanding the opposition of the senate and the difficulties of finance, he resumed the splendid architectural traditions of the monarchy, which had been in abeyance for two centuries.

This was not enough. He wished also to rejuvenate the constitution. Among the families which had been enriched by the war there were some who were capable of rendering useful service to the State by reinforcing the new patricio-plebeian aristocracy. Were not these *nouveaux riches* of the same flesh and blood as the plebeians who, for the last half-century, since the passing of the Licinio-Sestian laws, had so lightly leapt to the summits of political power and taken their seats in the senate? Appius Claudius did not content himself, however, with this process of renovating the governing class, which for the last two generations had been proceeding rapidly enough. When he came to compile the list of the senate, he inserted the names of many rich and active plebeians even though they were not provided with famous ancestors, and he did not hesitate to add to the list some of the freedmen, who now began to be the backbone of the commercial class of Rome.

Further, while he provided for the rich plebeians,

Appius Claudius did not forget the multitude of the artisans of Rome who lived by the work of their hands. These were excluded from the centuries because they did not possess the required property qualifications, and they were all enrolled as members of the fourth urban tribe. Thus, they could take no part in the comitia centuriata and they counted for little in the comitia tributa. They had no rights, therefore, but they had duties. The Servian constitution was still in force, and under its provisions the theory was that only those included in the centuries were required to perform military service. In practice, however, when the need for soldiers arose, recourse was often had to these plebeians. Appius Claudius decided that any man might choose the tribe in which he was to be registered without regard to his place of residence. The workmen accordingly distributed themselves among all the country tribes and thus their political influence was increased.[1]

As may be imagined, all these reforms were not effected easily. The Roman aristocracy cried out against the audacious innovator who was turning the social order upside down and undermining the most sacred foundations of civil life. The consuls of the following year refused to convoke the new senate, so the historians of the patricio-plebeian aristocracy inexorably condemn Appius Claudius and invoke in their support the expressed opinion of the gods themselves, who, according to their account, did not hesitate to punish the great censor by depriving him of the greatest of all blessings, which is sight.

Nevertheless, the appearance of this aristocratic and revolutionary censor, in the very midst of the

[1] Diod., xx., 36, 3; Liv., ix., 46.

first great war which Rome had to wage for the conquest of her empire, is, as it were, a ray of light which
permits us to discern the tremendous work that had
been wrought on Roman society as the result of
foreign wars. The force of tradition was declining.
New families, new energies, new ideas, new needs were
arising. The political constitution and the social
order had become more popular and equalitarian.
The classes, in spite of their mutual hatred and contempt, and of the insults which they had exchanged,
had been brought together in the brotherhood of
arms, which had been imposed upon them and in
which all had to labour, suffer, and die together in
order to conquer.

Another proof of this is to be found in two laws
which were proposed by three tribunes of the people
and passed in 311. The first of these provided that
sixteen military tribunes should be elected every
year, not by the consuls or by the dictator, but by
the people. The second provided that the people
should elect the *duoviri navales classis ornandæ
reficiendæque*. The need for an armada had begun
to make itself felt and it was laid down that the
magistrates who were to be charged with meeting it,
and who were to have the duty of distributing the
labour and the contracts, should be elected by the
people. The authority of the comitia, even in military matters, was on the increase.

26. The End of the War (311-304 B.C.). In
times so full of arms and war, however, the reforms
of Appius could be no more than an episode. In
311, the very year in which Appius Claudius was rejuvenating the constitution, a new peril developed
in the north. The Etruscan Confederation had long

resigned itself to the loss of the southern territories which, after the war with Veii the Roman state had annexed to its dominions. At first the outbreak of the war between Rome and Samnium had apparently failed to rouse this slothful people. Perhaps this was attributable to the fact that, if the Romans had taken southern Etruria, the Samnites had despoiled them of Campania, a loss to them even more painful. However that may be, as the war dragged on and became more complicated, even the Etruscan Confederation was at last moved to action and decided to attempt the reconquest of some of its lost territory —not of distant Campania, which had been lost for so long, and where the Roman armies seemed so solidly established, but of southern Etruria. In 311, therefore, they allied themselves with the Samnites and laid siege to Sutrium between the Ciminian and the Sabatine lakes, which are now known respectively as the Lago di Vico and the Lago di Bracciano. This town had been conquered by Rome at the time of the war with Veii and was now the seat of one of her most loyal Latin colonies.

Notwithstanding all her losses Etruria was still one of the greatest powers in Italy, and, if the alliance with Samnium had been concluded sooner, she might have seriously endangered the nascent power of Rome. She took arms somewhat too late, when Rome had begun to temper herself to resist even this new combination. But, late as it was, the intervention of Etruria could in no circumstances be regarded as a slight danger. The Romans were, in fact, compelled to thin their armies operating against Samnium, and to arm new forces to rush to the defence of the imperilled town. It was soon clear that it would be a difficult task to dislodge the enemy from his positions, and the Roman armies spent themselves upon it in vain.

In the following year, therefore, the consul, Q. Fabius Rullianus, who had remained in Etruria, decided to leave Sutrium and its besiegers on one side. His colleague was to go to Apulia to detain the Samnites by threats in that direction, while he himself was to strike at the heart of Etruria itself, and try to compel the Etruscan army before Sutrium to rush to the defence of their threatened country. The manœuvre was obviously one of very great difficulty. Its success might end the war in a short time; but its failure meant the destruction of the army. As a matter of fact, it succeeded. The Etruscans, collected in furious haste from all sides, were beaten at a place variously indicated by the ancients. The cities of central Etruria, Arretium (Arezzo), Cortona, and Perusia (Perugia) hastened to conclude peace with the victors, and shortly afterwards, the siege of Sutrium having meanwhile been raised, their example was followed by all the cities of southern Etruria (310).

On the other hand, things did not go so well in Samnium where the other consul, Caius Marcius Rutilius, appears to have been defeated in this year. There was undoubtedly a panic at Rome, and Papirius Cursor was made dictator. He was the most experienced of the generals who had fought against Samnium, and in 309 he seems to have returned against the Samnites the blow which they had struck at the Romans in the previous year. Meanwhile Rullianus, in a second battle near Perusia, had finally overcome the Etruscans who had again made peace.

But no sooner was Etruria pacified than, in 308, several of the peoples of central Italy, who were allied to Rome more by force than from inclination, to wit, the Umbri, the Marsi, the Peligni, and some of the Hernici, seized the opportunity offered by the difficulties with which the great city was struggling and attempted to recover their independence. Rome was thus confronted with a set of new enemies, among whom the leading influence was the Umbrian Confederation. Their want of discipline soon counterbalanced their few initial successes, and about the same time Nocera, the other Campanian town which was still in possession of the Samnites, fell.

By this time Samnium was exhausted, and Rome nearly so. The moment for the final push was near, when the belligerent who had still in his possession a last reserve of energy might impose his will upon the other. Rome understood that the time for a supreme effort was come. The consuls of 306 at the head of four legions tried again the enterprise which had failed in 321. That is to say, they undertook the invasion of Samnium notwithstanding the fact that fifteen years before a similar attempt had ended in the disaster of the Caudine Forks. Samnium was quite finished, and was invaded, traversed, and devastated from one end to the other by the Roman army without offering serious resistance. But the Samnites did not give in. They collected their forces once again, and, in the following year (305), they attempted an incursion into Campania. Their army was beaten, their territories again invaded. Bovianum, one of their principal centres, and (what was much worse) their commander-in-chief, Statius Gellius, fell into the hands of the Romans.

The war was over, and in the following year the peace, which had been so long delayed and was so much desired by both sides, was concluded. We do not know what exactly the terms were, but, from the little that is known, they do not appear to have been adequate—at least from the point of view of the victor—considering the length of the war. In substance the old alliance between the Romans and the Samnites was to be re-established. Possibly some of the provisions were made more favourable to the Romans and some less favourable to the Samnites. But the alterations were inconsiderable. On the other hand, not an inch of Samnite territory, properly so called, was ceded to Rome. The Samnites lost only the best of their conquests and, among them, all Campania, which even at the beginning of the war was, as a matter of fact, no longer in their hands.

Notwithstanding these (from the point of view of Rome) rather hard terms of peace, the power of the Samnites was virtually destroyed by the war. Not only were they reduced to the limits of their ancient territory, but, having been cut off from the Tyrrhene Sea by the loss of Campania, it was inevitable that they should soon be cut off from the Adriatic also. On this side they still communicated with the sea through the territory of the Ferentani, who were their subjects. But the weakness produced by the war and the skilful diplomacy of Rome were destined soon to close for ever this outlet as well.

On the other hand, the political and military power of Rome had correspondingly increased, not so much perhaps by her victories in pitched battles as by the energy and tenacity of which she had given proof, and by reason of the new territory she had acquired.

Rome at the end of the first Samnite war was not only the most formidable but the most extensive of the Italian states, for her own dominions were now nearly five thousand, and, if we include the territories of her allies, seventeen thousand five hundred square miles.

CHAPTER V

27. The Coalition of the Umbrians, the Gauls, the Etruscans, and the Samnites (299–290 B.C.). The peace of 304 could not possibly last. The Samnites had been defeated but not destroyed. Rome had been victorious but not so completely as to be reputed invincible. The Samnites devoted themselves, therefore, to preparing their revenge, and Rome did her best between 304 and 299 to reinforce her position by alliances and colonies. Two of the latter, Alba and Carseoli, were established in the territory of the Æqui; another, Sora, among the Volsci; a third, Narni, among the Umbri. But these measures merely increased the suspicion and fear with which Rome was regarded and hastened the renewal of the war. In 299 the Samnites attacked the Lucani in order to compel them to accept an alliance with Samnium. The Lucani appealed to the Romans, who, not wishing that the enemy should receive such an accession of strength, granted the desired assistance and declared war on the Samnites.

From the outset of this new conflict there had been rumours that the Samnites meant to ally themselves with the Etruscans, who had been restless for some time. However this may be, the Romans for the

first two years had only to face the Samnites, who succeeded without much effort in defending their country.
This fighting seems, however, to have been merely a
feint intended to conceal from the Romans the preparation of the great league which was in course of
formation. For in 296 an army under Gellius Ignatius
suddenly issued from Samnium and entered Etruria
without interference. There they effected a junction
with the Etruscan army and opened negotiations with
the Gauls. The Umbri also adhered to the combination, and the Lucanians, on whose behalf the Romans
had taken arms, deserted the alliance and went over
to the Samnites. The coalition, long and skilfully
prepared in secret, became suddenly manifest and it
was formidable indeed; for, while a large army of Samnites, Gauls, and Umbrians concentrated in the
north, another Samnite army fell upon and ravaged
Campania and Latium.

Rome was undoubtedly surprised but was not dis-
heartened by the coalition. Before the end of 296
a vigorous counter attack threw back the Samnite
forces, probably of no great strength, which had invaded Campania and Latium. For the year 295 were
elected the same consuls as for 297, that is to say
Q. Fabius Rullianus and P. Decius Mus. According
to law they were not apparently eligible for re-election,
but they had the confidence of the people. Great
preparations were made for the war, and, as Gellius
Ignatius also required time to organize the forces at
his disposal, Rome had a breathing space in which to
make her arrangements.

When sufficient forces were available, the consuls
of 295 decided not to rely on the leisurely methods of a
war of exhaustion, which had been employed in the

first struggle with the Samnites. They foresaw that a coalition, such as that with which they had to deal, would not survive a vigorous blow, and they made up their minds to seek out the main body of the enemy and to try to destroy it in a pitched battle. An advance guard, amounting to a legion, was surprised, encircled and destroyed by the Gauls and the Samnites at Camerinum. But this did not discourage the Romans. From Camerinum they attempted to enter the territory of the Senones and, near Sentinum in Umbria, they came in contact with the army which the Samnite leader Gellius Ignatius had succeeded in getting together and with which he sought to bar their progress. Ignatius, like the Roman consuls, was anxious to give battle, because a great victory was the only means of keeping together an army composed of such heterogeneous elements.

The clash came at Sentinum. In after years tradition spoke of a combination of at least 350,000 Gauls, Samnites, Umbrians, and Etruscans of whom more than 100,000 were said to have been killed. There is no doubt that the fighting was of the most desperate character. The Romans fought heroically, and one of the consuls, P. Decius Mus, was killed. The defeat of the coalition was complete, and Fabius was not slow to turn the victory to good account. With conquering legions he invaded the country of the Gauls and compelled them to abandon the coalition. In the following year the war in Etruria was also brought to a close, and the Etruscan cities surrendered, for the most part on easy terms.

The Romans were not in a position to be too exacting. For, if the great coalition had been discomfited, thanks to the fortunate audacity of the

consuls, the Samnites were by no means conquered,
and with them it would be necessary to recommence
the eternal war of exhaustion. Rome's contest
with Samnium was, in fact, to continue for another
five years with many vicissitudes of defeat and victory,
all of them costly in life and none decisive. It was
not until the year 290 that it was possible to conclude
peace, after having successfully founded in 291 a
Latin colony at Venusia in Apulia. This colony consisted of 20,000 settlers, the greatest number which
had ever been sent to an Italian colony up to that
date. With the establishment of so strong an out-
post of Rome in Apulia, the fate of the Samnites might
be considered as sealed. The terms of the new peace,
however, were very mild. In substance it was merely
the renewal of the old alliance. The Samnites had
to submit to some very slight diminutions of territory.
The independence of the Samnite Confederation was
confirmed, but it was now surrounded on all sides
and cut off from the sea.[1]

28. The Lex Hortensia (287 B.C.). Rome had
defeated a formidable coalition of Gauls, Etruscans,
Umbrians, and Samnites. She had fought another
long and bloody campaign in Samnium. She had
succeeded in weakening her powerful rival and in
winning the reputation of being the strongest power
in Italy. But, as indeed had been the case at the
end of the previous Samnite war, she had not gained
any territorial advantage of the slightest importance.
Reputation could not be regarded as a sufficiently
solid gain. In the same year, therefore, in which
the republic made peace with the Samnites the consul,

[1] On the third Samnite war *cf.* Bianca Bruno, *La terza guerra
Sannitica*, Roma, 1906.

Manius Curius Dentatus, profiting by the weariness and the terror of the vanquished (and probably on the pretext that the Sabines had helped the Samnites) conquered all the Sabine territory south of Umbria, one of the richest and most populous districts of Italy. Thence he invaded and conquered southern Picenum —the so-called country of the Prætuttii—and there founded Hadria (Atri), thus definitely reaching the Adriatic.   The territories of the republic were thus greatly increased.   The census of 288–287 had shown a population greater by more than 100,000 citizens of the superior class than that returned by the census taken immediately before the war.   There were now 272,000 citizens, a total number of more than 900,000 free persons, and, if we include foreigners and slaves, there were about a million inhabitants distributed over an area of 12,500 square miles.   In this way the Sabines and the Prætuttii paid the expenses, as it were, of the victory won by Rome over Samnium and the coalition.

The benefit of these increases of territory could, however, only be realized in time, and it was not immediately possible to alleviate the sufferings caused by such a protracted war.   At Rome the peace with the Samnites was succeeded by a lively agitation on the part of the plebeians on the eternal question of debt.   It is not apparent what measure of relief was demanded by the debtors.   We only know that the agitation generated "*graves et longas seditiones*" and that it was necessary to appoint a dictator in the person of Quintus Hortensius.   To this dictator is attributed a law providing that plebiscites, that is decisions of the comitia tributa, should henceforth have the force of laws binding on patricians and plebeians alike. The effect of this was to place the comitia tributa on an equal footing with the comitia centuriata, and from this single fact, isolated from the narrative vouchsafed by the governing classes of the day, we may infer that the measures demanded by the people were resolutely opposed by the upper and richer classes, who were predominant in the comitia centuriata. The tribunes of the people gave up hope that that body would ever pass their proposals and thenceforth decided to lay them before the comitia tributa. Thus the question, which had probably been already touched upon more than once, was now definitely raised, whether the decisions of the comitia tributa were or were not to be regarded as the law of the land.

The patricians, the rich plebeians, and all who were opposed to the movement on behalf of the poor, said no. The comitia tributa could be convened at will without the consent of the senate or any religious formality. It was nothing more, they held, than a private gathering of the plebs and could only decide upon purely plebeian questions. The leader of the plebeian party naturally supported the opposite contention. The issue was of great importance. The victory of the plebeians would mean that the Roman constitution would in part lose the timocratic character which Servius Tullius had impressed upon it, and that the comitia centuriata would be compelled to surrender part of its privileges in favour of an assembly in which, as in the old comitia curiata, numbers and not wealth predominated. It is not surprising that on this occasion, as before, the question became the focus of violent conflicts and gave rise to threats of secession. But the plebeians won their victory and it is not difficult to understand why. Was it possible to deny this satisfaction to the victors of Sentinum and Samnium, to the conquerors of Picenum and the Sabine territory, at a time when Rome, victorious though she was, saw herself surrounded with enemies who had not yet resigned themselves to acknowledging her victory as final? The Lex Hortensia[1] proved again, what had been demonstrated by the censorship of Appius, that these long and sanguinary wars had altered the constitution of Rome. Old traditions had been weakened, classes and interests had been mingled, new ideas and new energies had been awakened, with the result that the ancient institutions of the republic had become more democratic.

29. **The Recovery of the Gauls and the Etruscans (285–280 B.C.).** It was indeed well for Rome that satisfaction had been given to the multitude on this point. Hardly had Hortensius quieted the serious tumult which had arisen, when the republic was faced with a renewal of the war in practically all Italy. Difficulties first arose in the south, where the Lucani, presuming perhaps on their alliance with Rome, had given offence to the Greek cities on the coast. One of these, Thurii (Turio), having been attacked by the Lucani, complained to Rome. The Romans, from what motive we do not know, perhaps from a desire to preserve a balance of power in south Italy as elsewhere, ordered the Lucani to respect Thurii. The Lucani turned a deaf ear to this injunction and the Romans were about to draw the sword in defence of the Greeks in the south when a much graver danger suddenly appeared in the north.

[1] Plin., *Hist. Nat.*, xvi., 10, 37; Gell., *Noct. Att.*, 15, 27, 4; Dig., i., 2, 8.

In 285 some of the Etruscan cities which had been conquered in the previous war, assisted by a contingent of the Senones, attempted a renewal of hostilities and besieged Arretium (Arezzo), an Etruscan city which remained faithful to Rome. Arretium appealed to Rome for help. It was impossible to refuse, for, if Arretium were taken, the way to Latium would lie open to the enemy. The danger was all the greater as rebellion was being openly fomented all along the Via Cassia as far as Volsinium. Rome, therefore, sent assistance, but, near Arretium, quite 13,000 Romans, including the consul Cæcilius Metellus, were killed, while great numbers fell into the hands of the enemy. Sentinum seemed to be avenged and the disasters of Caudium and Lautulæ repeated. The inevitable consequences immediately followed. Insurrections against the Roman domination broke out anew all over the peninsula—in Etruria, in Samnium, and in south Italy where the Lucani seized the opportunity to avenge themselves for the protection given by Rome to Thurii and dragged the Bruttii with them into revolt. An embassy sent by the Romans to the Senones to demand explanations of the assistance which they, as allies of Rome, had given to the Etruscans, was murdered by the Senones. The situation was again critical, but Rome did not lose courage. Two strong armies were formed. One of these was sent to hold the enemy in check before Arretium, the other was despatched into the territory of the Senones to avenge the murder of the ambassadors. There they slew the able-bodied men, took the women and children prisoners, and wasted and sacked the country far and wide.

The punishment was exemplary, but the extermination of this Gallic tribe disquieted another, the Boii, who joined the Etruscans and raised an army with which, in 283, they attempted a move against Rome. Against this new assault, however, provision had also been made. The Gallic horde was completely destroyed near the Lacus Vadimonis (Lago di Bassano) on its way along the Tiber (283). This battle decided the fate of the coalition, though fighting went on until the year 280. The Samnites, shut in on every side, could do little. First the Boii and then, one by one, the Etruscan cities, made peace, each on its own account. The Lucani and the Bruttii, now isolated, could not resist for long. The new war brought Rome enhanced prestige and a new strip of territory, the land belonging to the Senones between the Æsis (Esino) and the Rubicon. She also gained some hundreds of miles of coast line on which was founded the colony of Sena Gallica (Sinigaglia). Following their usual policy, the Romans took advantage of the confusion into which Italy had been thrown by their new victories, to compel the Lucani, who were still besieging Thurii, to obey the injunctions which had been given them before the war. In 282, therefore, they sent a strong force to the help of Thurii. Thereupon a new war broke out and one which was much more serious, being nothing less than a regular struggle with the Greeks.

30. The Causes and the Occasion of the War with Tarentum (282–281 B.C.). Early in the third century B.C. the Greek cities of Magna Græcia had ceased to be the uncontested masters of that region as they had been two or three centuries earlier. Magna Græcia had now become a small and weak power, hard put to it to defend its own civilization and independence against strong and threatening neighbours. The indigenous population was rebellious and the iron-shod boots of the Lucanian, Messapian, and Bruttian peasants were treading closer and closer on the heels of the shining buskins of the citizens of such towns as Croton, Tarentum, Rhegium, Velia, and Posidonia. Like all powers conscious of growing weakness, the Greek cities had for a hundred years been trying to fortify themselves against the dangers surrounding them by seeking alliances in Rome, in Sicily, in Greece and, in fact, wherever such alliances could be found. But states incapable of defending themselves without assistance, and dependent on alliances, can only secure safety by choosing their allies with skill and dealing with them consistently and firmly. Now the foreign policy of these cities was as unstable as the sea on which most of them were situated. The factions alternated, attacked, and overthrew each other in civil strife, which boiled and foamed like breaking waves. Even in their foreign politics they exploited to the uttermost whatever happened to be the popular craze of the moment. Their whole proceedings were, in fact, a rash trifling with the danger which threatened the cause of Hellenism in the peninsula where, for all its brilliant civilization, it was a foreign and so far an adventitious element.

This frivolity, as well as the instability of their party system and of their foreign policy, explains how it was that the Greeks not only failed to make use of the power of Rome but, on the contrary, were so heedless as to make the Romans their enemies. In the nature of things Rome was bound to be averse from Hellenism. Her citizens, like the people of Lucania and Bruttii, were of Italic stock. But the

Gallic invasions, the Etruscan and Latin wars, and, above all, the Samnite wars, which had sprung one from another like the heads of the Lernæan Hydra, had hitherto prevented Rome from taking up any very definite attitude in the great struggle between the Italians and the Greeks of which south Italy was the scene. For the Greeks, moreover, who were masters of all the arts and sciences, the Romans had the feeling of respect which was natural in a people growing in power and wealth and beginning to feel the desire for a more sumptuous civilization; and the fact was that, if they had chosen, the Greeks of south Italy might have sheltered themselves for some time behind the shield of Rome. Thurii had understood this and so had Locri and Rhegium, cities which, when Rome threatened them, had followed the example of Thurii. But the pride and self-interest of Tarentum prevented Hellenism from turning the discord among the native elements to account.

Tarentum was the richest and most powerful Greek city in south Italy. For some time she had been in the habit of speaking by herself in the name of all the rest. She aspired, in fact, to a sort of political hegemony which was intended to reinforce her trade interests and to make them prosper at the expense of the other Greek cities. For this reason Thurii and the other Greek states had preferred to seek help against the danger threatened by the Lucanians and the Bruttians at the hands of an Italian power like Rome rather than to be under obligations to a Greek power like Tarentum. For this very reason Tarentum regarded the overtures of these states to Rome as an attempt to upset the balance of political forces in this remote part of the peninsula. Tarentum was ruled by a democracy which, like all democracies, aimed at flattering the most powerful passions of the masses, and, above all, the pride which in a Greek city could not fail to be intensified by the contrast of their civilized refinement, with the poverty, the rudeness, and the ignorance of the native Italians. In the eyes of the Tarentines the Romans themselves were merely insolent and presumptuous barbarians, who had the impertinence to interfere in the concerns of people whom they should have revered as their masters. Roman intervention at Thurii had exacerbated this sentiment, and a single incident was enough to precipitate war.

The incident in question was a military operation carried out in the course of the campaign at Thurii. An ancient treaty between Rome and Tarentum forbade Roman ships to pass the promontory now known as Cape Noto but then as Lacinium[1] where the Italian peninsula projects farthest into the Ionian Sea. The object of the clause containing this provision, which resembled others of a similar character contained in the treaties between Rome and Carthage, must have been more commercial than military. But in order to succour Thurii it was so convenient to make use of the sea that Rome did not hesitate to infringe the stipulations of a treaty of such ancient date. Moreover, if these provisions had been made for the protection of Hellenic interests, what harm could there be in Rome's breaking them in order to defend a Greek city?

It would appear, therefore, that convoys of troops and munitions were sent from Rome to Thurii by sea. The Lucanians were repulsed. Thurii was relieved

[1] App. *Samn,* 7.

and protected by a Roman garrison. But the Roman
victory exasperated the Tarentines, who had awaited
the issue of the campaign, perhaps hoping for a Roman
reverse, and who now made the old treaty a pretext
for revenging themselves. One day a Roman squadron
appeared off the wide entrance to the Gulf of Tarentum. It was challenged by the fleet of the great Greek
city, which was cruising suspiciously in these waters.
The Roman admirals were summoned to observe the
treaty, but in vain. On this the enemy attacked,
sank some ships, and captured others of the Roman
fleet. Immediately afterwards a Tarentine army
marched on Thurii, occupied the place, compelled the
Roman garrison to withdraw, and restored the reins of
government to the Philhellenic party, in other words
to the democrats.

The provocation was serious, but Rome refused
to be distracted from the Etruscan and Gallic danger
which menaced her in the north. It was not difficult
to divine that Tarentum had made an alliance with
the Samnites and the other Italic peoples, and Rome
did not wish to be caught between a coalition of Gauls
and Etruscans in the north and a coalition of Greeks
and Italians in the south. She accordingly sought by
means of an embassy to obtain an amicable and
diplomatic settlement of the affair. The haughty
democrats of Tarentum refused, however, to hear
reason and it became necessary to support the vain
attempt of diplomacy with a show of force. The
consul Q. Æmilius Barbula, who was encamped in
Samnium, was ordered to march immediately in the
direction of Tarentum, and to make an appropriate and
imposing military demonstration under the walls of
the city. He was not to commence a war, but (if it

could be done) to force a solution which would not be dishonourable. Even this energetic move failed to secure a settlement; indeed it produced the opposite effect. Tarentum retorted by summoning to her assistance a Greek prince named Pyrrhus, who was then king of Epirus.

31. Pyrrhus in Italy. The Battles of Heraclea (280 B.C.) and Asculum (271 B.C.). South-eastern Europe and part of the west of Asia had not yet recovered their balance since the cataclysm produced by the death of Alexander the Great. Kingdoms and empires continued to rise and fall, only to re-emerge in new forms and with new proportions. Pyrrhus was one of the petty monarchs who appeared, disappeared, and reappeared so frequently in this disorderly time. On the throne of Epirus he had been preceded by his father, Æacides, but he had been compelled to go into exile, had returned, and had been restored to his throne, only to be forced to fly a second time. In the end Fortune had again smiled on him and he had not failed to take advantage of her favours without being too scrupulous about the means he had to use. He returned to Epirus as king in 295, and had extended his dominions to the north, south, and east. These conquests failed to satisfy him. He aspired to increase his States still further to make his name illustrious and to augment his treasures.

He therefore accepted the invitation from the Tarentines, who called upon him to become the champion of Hellenism in Italy, and, early in 280, he hastened to disembark with rather more than 20,000 infantry, 3000 cavalry, and a certain number of war elephants. Tarentum promised to contribute a somewhat larger army, in addition to which there were to be the contingents placed in the field by her Italian allies and by the Greek cities which had espoused her cause and with which in the meantime agreements had been concluded.

Tarentum, a Greek city, had placed herself at the head of a coalition of Greeks and Italians against the Romans, who had appeared in south Italy as the allies of Greeks against Italians. The confusion of interests and ambitions was thus strange enough, and it was increased by a kind of misunderstanding between Pyrrhus and Tarentum, which was the hidden cause of many of the curious vicissitudes of this singular war. Tarentum summoned Pyrrhus as a mercenary to defend her against Rome. Pyrrhus came, not as a mercenary making war for pay, but as an old officer of Alexander, ambitious of founding an empire, large or small, as so many generals had done since the death of the great condottiere of Macedon.

In any case a new coalition threatened Rome, and she had to take up a new challenge. It appears that at first she hoped, vainly as it proved, to dispose of this coalition by a bold and resolute stroke, such as that by which in 295 Fabius and Decius Mus had broken the coalition of Greeks, Samnites, Etruscans, and Umbrians. While Pyrrhus in the spring of 280 was awaiting the concentration of his various forces and those of his allies, a Roman army attacked him without warning in a valley between Heraclea and Pandosia (the modern Acri and Sinni) near the Tarentine coast. But Pyrrhus had learned war in the school of Alexander the Great; he had served as an officer at the Battle of Issus and he was a very different adversary from the Etruscan, Gallic, or

Samnite generals. Moreover, the force which attacked him, unready as he was, was only a single consular army of two legions, which, with its complement of auxiliary troops, consisted of barely 20,000 men.

The Romans fought with great valour, but were in the end defeated, and in a few days such was the impression produced by this reverse, that the Roman hegemony seemed to totter throughout south Italy. The Roman garrisons either had to be removed or were taken prisoners and sent to Pyrrhus, who, reinforced by the Samnites and the Lucanians, moved resolutely upon Latium. Was his object to raise the surrounding country in rebellion, or to attempt a direct surprise attack on Rome? Or again was he trying to effect a junction with the Etruscan cities in the north against which Rome was again at war? It would be difficult to say. Perhaps Pyrrhus had no very definite plan but wished to put the firmness of his adversary to the proof by taking a determined offensive, while keeping himself free to take any course which might be suggested by events in the course of the campaign. Be this as it may, Rome proved to have pertinacity and courage enough to confront even the genius of a great soldier, and opposed his vigorous offensive with a tremendous effort. Such an agreement as was possible was made with the Etruscans. All citizens down to the poorest were recruited and two armies were sent against the invader. Pyrrhus, who had experienced Roman valour at Heraclea, did not venture to attack, and having encamped for some time at a respectful distance, he fell back, retiring to Tarentum in the autumn. The campaign of 280 was over.

The war recommenced in the spring of 279. Pyrrhus invaded Apulia and took several cities. The Romans hastened against him with two consular armies and attacked him at Asculum (Ascoli di Puglia). The battle lasted two days. At the end of the second day the Romans were defeated but not routed. They left on the field 6000 of their comrades; but they had inflicted serious losses on the enemy and were able to retire in good order to their own encampment. Thus, although these two battles brought defeat to the Roman arms, they nevertheless decided the war in favour of Rome. Pyrrhus was too good a general not to recognize from these two difficult and by no means decisive victories that he had not force enough to crush Rome.

He had to put aside his idea, therefore, of founding an empire, the hope of which had led him to cross the sea to south Italy. There a military power had appeared which was too strong for him. Just at this moment, however, persistent invitations began to reach him from Sicily, which was near at hand. Syracuse, the citadel of Sicilian Hellenism, was then beset by land and sea by a Carthaginian army and fleet. This invitation suggested a new plan to Pyrrhus. He would make peace with Rome, hold the Greek cities of south Italy which had invited his assistance, and, using them as a base of operations, he would conquer Sicily. Thus he would unite under his sceptre and in a single empire all the Greek cities of Sicily and the larger Greek cities of south Italy. He accordingly began the negotiations for peace with Rome round which have gathered so many famous legends. All he asked was that Rome should evacuate that part of Italy the occupation of which constituted a permanent danger to the Greek cities under the hegemony of Tarentum, and that the Roman agreement with Tarentum should be re-established as it was before 282. The senate was weary of the long war and was, moreover, anxious about the sullen resistance which was being offered by the agricultural class to the demands for recruits. In 280 this resistance had made it necessary to arm the poorest class, in spite of the increase of the population (287,222 against 272,-000 at the previous census). The senators were inclined, therefore, to accept the proposals made by Pyrrhus, when quite unexpectedly there arose a new speaker to combat any suggestion of an accommodation. This was Appius Claudius, who had been censor in 312 and consul in 307 and 296. He was now old and blind, and broken by the infirmities of his years, but his spirit was as high as ever. His boldness had already done violence to many class prejudices and many traditions of prudence, and now he burst forth once again to denounce the timorous longing for peace which threatened to make Rome renounce south Italy at the very moment when it might be hers for ever.

The eloquence of Appius Claudius found a potent auxiliary in the Carthaginians. The government of Carthage, having learned that the Sicilian cities had appealed to Pyrrhus, hastened not only to renew the former treaties with Rome but by the insertion of new articles to transform them into a regular alliance offensive and defensive against Pyrrhus.[1] By abandoning Sicily to the Carthaginians Rome might, therefore, hope for the definite conquest of south Italy. The opportunity was too good to be lost. The war party prevailed, the projected peace

[1] *Cf.* Polyb., iii., 25, 3-4.

with Pyrrhus broke down, and hostilities were officially reopened.

32. Pyrrhus in Sicily: his Return to Italy and his Final Departure (278-275 B.C.). Rome's refusal to treat did not induce Pyrrhus to alter his plans. He believed that he had sufficient force at his disposal to conquer Sicily and to defend the Greek cities and the points in south Italy which best secured them against Roman attacks. No doubt his change of objective looked to the Tarentines like a betrayal. They had summoned Pyrrhus to crush Rome and not to conquer Sicily. But owing to the army which he commanded and the prestige with which he was surrounded, Pyrrhus was then the stronger. Towards the end of the summer of 278, after two years and a half of sojourn in the peninsula, he left for Sicily with about half his forces, leaving the rest to guard the Greek cities which had invited his assistance.

Pyrrhus was not mistaken in believing that he could conquer Sicily while maintaining the defensive on the main land. During the three years of his absence the Romans were again able with varying fortune to invade Samnium, which was as unconquerable as Antæus. By force of arms or by successful intrigue they might succeed in taking here and there a Greek city, such as Locri, Croton, or Heraclea. But they could do nothing against Tarentum or seriously threaten Pyrrhus's position on the continent.

Meanwhile in a series of brilliant and rapid campaigns Pyrrhus succeeded in driving the Carthaginians out of all Sicily except Lilybæum (the modern Marsala). His design of founding an empire which should include the Greek cities of Sicily and south Italy seemed in a fair way to succeed, and, in order to hasten its realization, Pyrrhus began to build a great fleet, intended as a powerful instrument of this dominion, which was everywhere bounded by the sea. The opposition of the Siceliots, however, brought the great plan to nothing. Sicily was not a unified and homogeneous State capable of a stable and continuous policy or of protracted and sufficient sacrifices. Pyrrhus, on the other hand, though a great soldier, was not a skilful politician, and he seems to have damaged many interests and wounded many susceptibilities even among the Greeks, by the summary methods of his rapacious military government.

Disaffection soon began to grow. Some of the Greeks, having summoned Pyrrhus to help them against the Carthaginians, began to conspire with the Carthaginians against Pyrrhus. At the same time on the mainland Tarentum and the other Greek cities grew more and more discontented. They were perpetually threatened by Rome and never ceased recalling their ally in order that he might help them to put an end to the war. The time came when he could not prolong his absence without risking his hold on south Italy, and he had to return. But he had not yet so securely mastered Sicily that he could safely leave the island to itself. He was scarcely gone before the Carthaginians, who were still at Lilybæum, took courage again and attacked and defeated his fleet. On the news of this reverse the whole island rose in rebellion, and Sicily was lost before Pyrrhus could come to the rescue.

He was now pledged to a new struggle with the Romans. In the spring of 275 he attempted to surprise one of the two Roman armies operating in

Samnium and Lucania. The consul M. Curius Dentatus was then encamped not far from Benevetum,
on the part of the Via Appia which runs from
Caudium to the heart of Samnium. He had made
up his mind not to yield to any provocation which
the Epirot king might offer him to fight before the
arrival of his colleague from Lucania. In the result
Pyrrhus decided to attack the mobile fortress which
the Roman Castra always presented. As might
have been anticipated, the attack was a failure,
and as the king was not in a position to face
both the Roman armies which were on the point of
effecting a junction, he had to decide on a retreat.
Moreover, he saw that his double plan against south
Italy and Sicily had now failed, and immediately
afterwards he made up his mind to leave Italy and to
seek his fortune in another field, that is to say in
Greece, where, in his vain dreams of Italian successes,
he had too much neglected his old ambition to wear
the crown of Macedon. For the time being, however,
in order to disguise his flight in an apparent intention
of soon returning, he left behind him a detachment
of the Epirot army under the command of his son,
Helenus, whom he appointed his lieutenant. Soon
afterwards both this force and its commander were
recalled from Italy.

33. The Conquest of South Italy (275–270 B.C.).
While the king's triremes were fleeing towards Illyria,
Rome, with less haste and less genius, but with a
greater tenacity and firmness, prepared for the complete and final conquest of south Italy. Once the
Romans felt themselves to be the strongest, nothing
could prevent the struggle in which they had begun
by defending themselves from being transformed

into an offensive war of conquest. There were still to be, however, five years of expeditions, battles, and sieges, of partial and disjointed operations against such members of the coalition as still held out with their several forces and with their own objects. But, as soon as Pyrrhus was gone, the victory of Rome could only be a question of time, and accordingly, about the year 270, she became mistress of south Italy. There was no longer any reason why she should be indulgent. Most of Samnium was annexed, therefore, to the Roman State and covered with Roman colonies. Only the central part, known as the country of the Pentri, was allowed to remain in a certain degree independent, as if to indicate where the State of Samnium once had been. The great duel was finished for ever.

Bruttii and Lucania had no better fate. They too were forced to cede part of their territory. On the coast of Lucania at Posidonia (Pæstum, Pesto) was founded a colony of Roman citizens, and that great city, whose marvellous ruins between the sea and the sky even now attract the admiration of the traveller, made another step on her tragic downward path towards barbarism. Only the ancient Hellenic cities, including probably Tarentum, the cause of all the mischief, were allowed to become allies of Rome, retaining at least a nominal autonomy.

Shortly before this catastrophe, in 273 or 272, Pyrrhus, who was on the point of securing the Macedonian crown he so much desired, perished obscurely in a trifling skirmish on the outskirts of Argos.

CHAPTER VI

34. Rome a Great Mediterranean Power. The end of the war with Tarentum was a great event. Rome had now conquered all Italy, or at least all that the ancients meant by the name, which was the whole peninsula from the Arno and the Rubicon to the Ionian Sea. Beyond these boundaries lay Cisalpine Gaul and the islands, countries inhabited by people not of Italic stock—another world. Rome had become, therefore, what would now be called a great power. In less than two centuries and a half the republic had progressed indeed, though it had been by toilsome and stumbling steps, and at the cost of more than one dangerous fall. But in these two hundred and fifty years great changes had taken place in the whole of the Mediterranean world and new great powers had arisen on the ruins of older empires.

Etruria was now hardly more than a name. The Persian Empire had ceased to exist a hundred and fifty years previously, and with it what survived of the Phœnician power in the East had fallen to pieces. Henceforth all the East was Greek and the Greek genius reigned supreme in art, in politics, in literature, in culture, in industry, and in commerce. Three great powers had formed themselves from the ruins of the empire of Alexander—the three so-called Hellenistic monarchies—reigned over by the dynasties founded by Alexander's generals.

First of all there were the Seleucids, rulers of Syria, whose dominions included not only that country but all the various and uncertain territory which extends from the Ægean coast of Asia Minor, across Syria proper, Mesopotamia, and Iran as far as the basin of the Indus and the Oxus. Secondly, there were the Ptolemies, who reigned over Egypt, the Cyrenaica, and southern Syria, some of the larger Mediterranean islands, for instance Cyprus and Crete, and certain territories on the confines of Thrace, the Hellespont, and Asia Minor. Finally, there were the Antigonids of Macedon, the most restless and rapacious of all, and the most desirous of enlarging to the north and the south, in Dalmatia and Greece, the difficult heritage bequeathed to them by Philip II. of Macedon, in the middle of the preceding century.

Besides these, another Hellenistic power, Syracuse, had more than once attempted, through her tyrants, and condottieri, such as Dionysius, Timoleon, and Agathocles, to create an empire, forming relations with the Hellenistic monarchies of the East, insinuating herself into the affairs of Italy and Greece, and lording it over the Siculo-Greek, or, as they are often termed, Siceliot cities. But after the expedition of Pyrrhus, Syracuse had been completely overthrown by Carthage, which was then the greatest and the most ancient power in the western Mediterranean. The Carthaginian empire embraced the whole of northern Africa, from the borders of the Cyrenaica to beyond the Pillars of Hercules, and in Europe the coast cities of southern Spain, Corsica, and Sardinia, northern Sicily and all the rest of the island west of the river Halycus (Platani).

35. Carthage and her Empire. Carthage, Syracuse, and the three Hellenistic monarchies of the East, were, therefore, the great powers of the Mediterranean world in the first half of the third century when Rome, the youngest of them all, emerged. It will be convenient at this point to compare, as far as possible, the most ancient with the most recent of these great powers, which were on the point of engaging in a mortal struggle. In accumulated treasure, in commerce and industry, Carthage far surpassed Rome. She had, moreover, an army which has, perhaps, been too much depreciated by historians on the ground that it was composed of foreigners and mercenaries. But, if we may hesitate in our valuation of the land forces possessed by Carthage, there can be no doubt that she had the advantage over Rome at sea.

Carthage, like Rome, was governed by an aristocracy. If at Carthage the old nobility, which possessed the more martial spirit, were at variance with those more recently promoted from the ranks of the merchants and the traders, we must remember that Rome was no less agitated by constant class conflicts, and that the Carthaginian government, shortly before this period, had been pronounced by Aristotle to be perfect. In many respects, therefore, Carthage was Rome's superior.

The two states seem to have been formed and guided on different principles and by different methods. Apart altogether from the transmarine possessions of Carthage, such as Spain and the islands, which were useful appendages but not vital organs of her empire, northern Africa was inhabited by two different races. The Phœnicians, when they occupied the country, had everywhere established agricultural colonies, intended to teach the aborigines a settled habit of life to found villages and practice husbandry. The population of these colonies being intermixed with the natives, a composite race known as the Libophœnicians had arisen. Thus all the Carthaginian territories were covered with innumerable towns and villages, some inhabited by Libophœnicians, others by pure Libyans, who all lived by cultivating the ground, or by carrying on a few industries and exploiting the natural riches of the soil. Part of the army of Carthage was recruited among the Libophœnicians and the Libyans. The rest was made up of Spanish, Ligurian, and Gallic mercenaries.

Carthage, however, and this is the important point—was above all not a military but a great commercial power, buying and selling everything which by exportation, either from barbarous to civilized nations or *vice versa*, could be made to fetch a higher price. She drew her soldiers from her Libophœnician and Libyan colonies; but her motive in founding these colonies was not the increase of her military power but the development of trade. This fact explains the organization of the Carthaginian empire. In the ancient world commerce prospered only by monopolies, and a monopoly can only be imposed by peace. As a matter of fact we know that the subject populations were not allowed to buy or sell without observing the rules laid down by Carthage in her own interests, and it is not surprising to find that autonomy in any shape or form was denied them.

The Libophœnician cities were, in fact, governed directly and despotically by Carthage, through officials appointed by the central government. The Libyans were divided into tribes under the rule of kings who in their turn were in strict dependence on Carthage. The nomad populations who dwelt beyond the cultivated zone—the Numidians, as the Romans called them—alone enjoyed some measure of self-government. Even they, however, had to recognize the authority of Carthage, by furnishing contingents of cavalry and by refraining from attacking their richer and more settled fellow subjects. This being so, it is not difficult to see why so many of the Carthaginian towns remained unfortified. Carthage had no reason to impose on her subject cities fortifications whose chief use would have been to give support to some rebellion against the metropolis and its privileges.

36. The Roman State and its Composition. Carthage, in short, had covered a great part of her rich territory with agricultural and commercial but not with military colonies. In the Roman dominions we find a very different arrangement. At this time the little empire which Rome had got together with so much labour, was not a civilized State governed by a bureaucratic organization, but a bundle of various elements, held together by the colonies, by the authority of Rome as well as by the interests of her subjects. It was made up of two very diverse parts—the territory composing the Roman State and the territory of the allies. The area of the first was about twenty thousand square miles and was administered by many cities, each of which controlled its own land and belonged to one of three categories: (*a*) Roman colonies, (*b*) Latin colonies, (*c*) *Municipia*.

The Roman colony differed from the Greek colony in that it was founded by State initiative, and from the Carthaginian colony in that it had not an economic but a political and a military purpose. Its inhabitants, the Roman colonists and the ancient occupants of the place, coalesced to found a new administrative unit. They were Roman citizens who enjoyed civil and political rights in Rome though distance might prevent them from using them. In the colony they were autonomous, as we should say, in the administrative sense. That is, the colony, while politically incorporated with the Roman State, had its own magistrates (*duoviri* or *prætores*), a council (*decurionum ordo*), priests (*flamines*), popular assemblies (*comitia*), and independent finances. Finally every Roman colony was a fortified city.

Before the middle of the third century there were but few Roman colonies. These were almost all on the sea and all were small because as a rule three hundred colonists and no more were sent out. The sinews of Roman power in Italy were, in fact, the so-called Latin colonies, which Rome founded in great numbers. These, so far as the metropolis was concerned, were sovereign states. They had their own laws and institutions, the right to coin money, entire administrative independence, immunity from tribute, and the right of banishing their citizens. Their territory was not included in the organization of the Roman tribes. On these sovereign rights Rome imposed only two limitations, the obligation to furnish contingents to the Roman army and to leave to Rome the question of making war and peace, and of making all alliances and treaties with other states. To the inhabitants of Latin colonies, moreover, Rome granted the *ius connubii* and the *ius commercii*, the right to contract marriage and the right to hold property under Roman law. Roman citizenship was, of course, not granted to them, for that would have been incompatible with their own citizenship.

The government of the Latin colonies was thus based on principles entirely opposite to those followed by Carthage in the ordering of her empire. While Carthage took care to keep her colonies in a state of total subjection, Rome did not fear to multiply the number of these small and quasi-independent states in every part of Italy and to allow them to fortify themselves and so to cover Italy with fortresses, any one of which might be made a rallying point for a revolt against the metropolis. The policy of Rome may at first sight seem singular. But in this fact—of great consequence, as we shall see, in the destinies of Rome—we can trace a remote but profound result, visible after the lapse of two hundred and fifty years, of the revolution which had upset the monarchy and interrupted the action of the forces which were making Rome a commercial power like Tarentum and Carthage. As she was not a commercial power, Rome had no monopolies to impose, and, this being so, it was open to her in planting her colonies to be guided chiefly by military considerations. Her aim was to have, not colonies which she could exploit, but colonies each of which was capable of providing many soldiers and of defending itself without assistance.

The *Municipia* formed the last class of communities dependent on Rome. These comprised all the Italic cities which had lost their former independence and had fallen under the Roman dominion. The least favourably treated of this class, to which had been given the *civitas sine suffragio*, might be compared with the subject cities of Carthage. Their inhabitants had no right to vote and were not eligible for the Roman magistracies. On the other hand, they had to render military service, to pay tribute and to obey Roman laws, in the making of which they had no share. Their local organs of administration, if not entirely abolished, were reduced to a nullity, and they were governed by a *præfectus iuri dicundo* sent from Rome. Others were a little better treated, and retained, in a more or less modified form, their ancient communal autonomy. Others, again, whose numbers increased as time went on, enjoyed full Roman citizenship, and were known as *civitates optimo iure.* The inhabitants of all three classes of *Municipia* were on the same footing as those of the Latin colonies in that rights of citizenship were completed by the possession of the *ius commercii* and the *ius connubii* with Rome.

Beyond the territories which formed part of the Roman State extended the greater expanse of the possessions of the allied cities, which by this time amounted to about 62,500 square miles. To these cities was applied as far as possible the system imposed on the Latin League after the great war of 340–338. In a word, the Romans aimed at breaking up all the old confederations and at uniting the members singly to themselves. Cities which were powerful enough to be dangerous, were humbled. Weak but loyal communities were reinforced, In the midst of every city Rome made a point of creating and imposing a Roman party at the expense of the nationalists.

The allied cities remained autonomous saving, of course, for such interference as the stronger party always practises on the weaker when it seems advantageous, and saving also the cases of dispute in which the only tribunal of arbitration was Roman. They lost all semblance of liberty in foreign policy and were bound to Rome by the obligation, which grew heavier every year, to enrol, equip, and pay a prescribed proportion of naval and military forces for any war, offensive or defensive, which Rome might choose to undertake.

37. Messina—the Apple of Discord. It is not surprising then, that two states like Rome and Carthage, whose aims and ambitions were so different, and which for so long had been separated by the sea, should for centuries have lived at peace with each other; or that Rome, poorer, ruder, and weaker than her rival, as we have seen, should for so long have been content to do as Carthage willed. But now two centuries and a half had passed since the foundation of the republic. Rome in her turn had grown great, and the two empires were separated only by the Strait of Messina, that is to say they almost touched. Thus it was that the peace which had lasted so long was broken in the course of a few months of the year 265 by an incident which to all appearance was trifling.

Twenty-four years previously a corps of mercenaries, most of whom were Italians, and who had been hired by Agathocles of Syracuse to make war on Carthage, had been disbanded. But, instead of returning to their own country, they had attacked and taken Messina, had established themselves there, had assumed the high-sounding title of "Sons of

Mars" (*Mamertini*), and had even extended their sway over the neighbouring cities on both sides of Cape Pelorum (Faro). Pyrrhus had waged war on them, and, after Pyrrhus had departed, the Romans took up the contest when they set themselves to subdue the Italian cities in the extreme south of the peninsula.

The Mamertini, however, succeeded in holding Messina until the year 270, when they were first beaten in the field and then besieged in the city by Hieron, a young Syracusan general, who made this victory the pretext for assuming a royal crown. The Mamertines, finding themselves in great danger, sought for help. Some looked to Carthage and handed over the citadel of Messina to a Punic general, while others turned to Rome.

38. Peace or War? The Two Parties at Rome and their Ideas. Messina thus invited the great Italian power, which had been led victoriously but by slow degrees to the shores of the Sicilian Sea, to cross the strait. It is a narrow arm of the sea, and from one bank the eye clearly discerns the cities, the villages, and even the separate houses on the other. But the step which Rome took in crossing it was great indeed, for it was her first towards the conquest of a world empire. The Romans were aware of this. We know that the request of the Mamertines caused an agitation at Rome more serious than any incident or accident of her foreign policy had ever yet aroused. The dangers which would have to be faced if the Mamertines were to be relieved, were patent. To intervene in Sicily was the same thing as to declare war on Carthage. True, Sicily was one of the gems of the Mediterranean; but could Rome, even to get a footing in so opulent an island, run the terrible risks of war with a power like Carthage, so formidable both in arms and in resources? We need not be surprised when the ancient authors tell us that the senate evaded the request of the Mamertines.

Public opinion showed no such hesitation. Polybius[1] has recorded for us the arguments which the partisans of intervention opposed to the sagacious calculations of the party of prudence. They said that Carthage was now mistress of a great part of Spain, of Corsica, of Sardinia, and of all the other smaller islands scattered about these seas. Moreover, she already possessed most of Sicily. If Messina and therefore the whole island, fell into her power, Italy, to use the actual words of the Greek historian, would be "encircled and suffocated" by Carthage. What else could Messina be but a bridge-head for the invasion of Italy? Polybius adds that those in favour of war also insisted on the benefit which the war would confer upon the citizens individually.

Rome found herself, in fact, at the crucial point in her history. We have seen how for a century wars and conquests had been rapidly altering at Rome the ancient aspect of fortunes, classes, ideas, and traditions, overturning, destroying, revolutionizing, and renewing now this and now that part of the old order. But there were several reasons why the war with Tarentum and the conquest of south Italy should have given a new and potent impulse to this movement. First and foremost to have conquered Pyrrhus, a general educated in the school of Alexander the Great, had not only added to the prestige of the Romans; it had also increased their pride, their con-

[1] Polyb., i., 10.

fidence in their own strength, and their ambition. At the same time the conquest of the central region of the Apennines and the reduction to *ager publicus* of so much of the vast conquered territories had accelerated the great economic transformation which probably commenced, as we saw, in the middle of the Samnite war, and which was characterized by the formation of great landed estates, either freehold or leasehold, and by the growth of an urban proletariat as well as an expansion of industry and commerce.

In these years the Licinio-Sestian laws were for the first time violated by the Roman nobility, who having, willingly or unwillingly, made war on Pyrrhus, threw themselves in haste upon the new booty which the victory provided. At Rome began to appear, chiefly among the nobility, great fortunes in real estate, which had been easily made out of the lands of the conquered peoples, and the passion for this lucrative kind of speculation spread among the upper classes. Moreover, it is certain that, after the victory over Tarentum the old aspirations to make Rome a commercial city, as the kings had tried to do, revived. These aspirations could not but be encouraged by Rome's growing knowledge of the Greek world, her confidence in her own strength, the greater abundance of her available capital, and the opportunities offered by her more extended dominions. To the growth of riches and the rise of new families and of greater fortunes was added a renovation of customs and ideas. Hellenism made rapid progress at Rome after Magna Græcia had been incorporated in the empire, and, with Magna Græcia, the most direct route to Greece and the Hellenic East. At this epoch Livius

Andronicus, a Greek of Tarentum, brought to Rome the Greek epic, the Greek drama, and a passion for all branches of Greek culture. The Greeks began to flock into the ancient city from south Italy in greater swarms than the Etruscans in the days of Tarquinius I. and Tarquinius II., bringing with them the culture, the customs, the vices, and the luxury of Hellenistic Asia. As early as 275 a consul had been expelled from the senate because of the excessive splendour of the plate on his table, and two years after the conquest of south Italy Rome found it necessary to strike silver coins and to open mints for the purpose in Latium and Campania.

39. The Comitia Decide on War with Carthage. All these aspirations, inclinations, and ambitions combined to form a current of opinion which urged the republic to cross the strait even at the risk of war with Carthage. Great landed proprietors who had grown rich on the conquered lands of Samnium and south Italy, young lords who had acquired a taste for Greek literature and philosophy, contractors for the army and for public works, workmen and artisans who lived by war and by public expenditure, senators, knights, rich freedmen who were beginning to try their hand at commerce in imitation of Tarentum, obscure plebeians, and small proprietors—all alike forgot how many had been killed or ruined in the previous wars. They saw only those who had returned with a pile of money and had made their fortunes. With one accord they spurned the timid prudence of their advisers. Carthage, the friend of centuries, had become the danger of the hour. Carthage, which had occupied Africa and Sardinia, and was in the course of occupying Spain, would some day,

if Rome did not make haste, be found to have invaded
Italy as she had already invaded Sicily.

This current of popular opinion was so strong that
the senate did not dare to oppose it directly. But
they were equally unwilling to take action; the responsibility was too tremendous. They, therefore,
took a step to which recourse was rarely had in the
whole course of the long history of Rome and referred
the request of the Mamertini to the comitia centuriata.
At this supreme moment the people were called upon
to be judge and arbiter of the fate of Rome! In the
comitia centuriata the counsels of the bolder party
prevailed; and thus began a war which, with longer
or shorter intervals of truce, was to last 122 years
and was destined to change the course of the history
of the Mediterranean.

CHAPTER VII

THE SECOND EFFORT OF ROME TO BECOME A COMMERCIAL POWER

40. The First Punic [1] War (264–241 B.C.). The first war between Rome and Carthage began with the expedition to Messina. In 264, Rome sent an army under the command of the consul Appius Claudius to the assistance of the Mamertines who, immediately on hearing that their request for Roman protection had been granted, had expelled the Carthaginian garrison in possession of the citadel. Carthage, however, had lost no time in sending a fleet and an army against Messina and had, moreover, concluded an alliance with the Syracusans. Thus, by the time that Appius Claudius arrived at Rhegium with his legions in the summer of 264, Messina was already invested by sea and land by the forces of Carthage and Syracuse. What was to be done? To cross the strait without having first conquered the Carthaginian fleet was too perilous an enterprise, and Rome had no navy which could confront the Carthaginian ships. This, the first difficulty which presented itself, was

[1] Punic means Phœnician and is the name which the Roman historians gave to the three wars between Rome and Carthage, calling them, as they invariably did, after the name of the adversary.

133

serious. It was not without reason that the senate had hesitated before this narrow strip of sea. For, when all was said and done, it was a singularly rash proceeding to risk a war, with no fleet, or next to none, against a great naval power, for the conquest of an island.

But the comitia had not stopped to consider this difficulty. War had been declared, and Appius Claudius could not remain at Rhegium an inactive spectator of the siege of Messina. Having no alternative he faced the extreme dangers of eluding the Carthaginian blockade by night and of throwing himself into the city after having forced the lines of the besiegers. Both these enterprises were extremely rash. Had either failed the army was lost. But Appius succeeded in both. Once inside the city, he lost no time. In two battles he succeeded in defeating the Carthaginians and the Syracusans and in liberating the city. When they had mastered Messina, the Romans had a sufficiently secure line of communication with the main land, though it was still to some extent threatened by Syracuse. They did not delay to profit by this, and, in the following year, a new army was sent to Sicily which was to operate against Syracuse and deprive Carthage of all her *points d'appui* on the eastern coast. The action of this army was successful. So long as the Romans had no base of operations in Sicily, Syracuse might hope to exclude them from the island by making use of her old enemy Carthage. But, now that Rome was mistress of Messina, Syracuse felt too much oppressed by the Roman power to be able to continue the alliance. The party opposed to the Carthaginians prevailed at Syracuse, and Hieron, abandoning the Carthaginian connection, allied him-

self with Rome. By the end of 263, Rome had established a solid foothold in Sicily.

But these successes were not enough to daunt a
power like Carthage. Without losing a moment
she assembled a great force of Ligurian, Gallic, and
Spanish mercenaries. Soldiers and arms were hurried
off to Sicily. Agrigentum was made the new Carthaginian base of operations against Rome and Syracuse, and a fleet was dispatched to harry the coast of
Italy. On their side the Romans and the Syracusans
laid siege in 262 to Agrigentum. With this opened
the second phase of the war, which was to last as long
as the siege, that is to say for the last eight months
of the third year of hostilities.

It was not until the late autumn, and after having
been more than once on the point of raising the siege,
that the Romans managed to defeat in pitched battle
a Carthaginian army which came to the assistance of
the garrison. This success gave them possession of
the city but they did not succeed in capturing the
Carthaginian garrison, which managed to escape
through the Roman lines and to effect a junction
with the defeated Carthaginian army outside. But
this new victory, the recovery of the other cities which
followed on that of Agrigentum, and above all the
hitherto unheard of magnitude of the spoils, produced
an outburst of public exultation at Rome. Great and
small were now at one in thinking of nothing but
building a fleet and expelling the Carthaginians from
Sicily.

Tradition has depicted this effort in somewhat
too brilliant colours. It is narrated that Rome,
being ignorant of shipping, used as a model a quin-
quereme which had been wrecked in a storm on the

southern coast of Italy. As a matter of fact Rome was familiar with ships, possessed both men of war and merchantmen, and, moreover had at her disposal the fleets of her Italian and Syracusan allies. The legend may, however, be nearer to the truth than modern critics think, if it is interpreted in the sense that before this time neither the Romans nor the Italians understood the handling of vessels with five banks of oars such as formed the greater part of the 120 warships of which their first large fleet was composed. The Romans, moreover, distrusting their skill in sea fighting, provided their navy with a new contrivance, the so-called *corvi*, boarding gangways with which each ship could run alongside an enemy vessel and so give passage for the legionaries to enter her.

The whole of the year 261, in which no great feats of arms are recorded, seems to have been spent in preparing this armada. And the interval will not seem too long when it is remembered that not only had the ships to be built, but the crews had to be got together and trained. At the beginning of 260 the Roman fleet was at sea, and in the spring began the third phase of the war (260–255). Under the command of the consul C. Duilius the fine new squadron sailed for Sicily, eagerly seeking the veteran fleet of Carthage, which was familiar with every sea and laden with trophies, and which had for centuries been used to fighting in Sicilian waters. After a first unsuccessful attempt the Romans found their adversaries at Mylæ (Milazzo) near Messina and gave battle (260). The *corvi* were tried with great success. The Romans fought with great tenacity, wishing to show that they were a force to be reckoned with at sea as on land. The Carthaginian fleet of 130 sail lost more than half of its effectives; the Carthaginian admiral himself barely escaped with his life, and unprecedented honours were conferred on C. Duilius when he returned to Rome.

It is not difficult to understand the reason for these honours. The victory of Mylæ had made on Rome, on Carthage, and on the neutrals an impression such as few other battles have made. Rome had scarcely launched her first great fleet when at once she had won a great victory over the greatest naval power of the day. The military effect of the victory, however, was less than its moral effect. Carthage did not lose heart. She proceeded with great vigour to reinforce her fleet. She defended herself insistently against all the Roman attacks, and sought to protract the war, hoping thereby to wear out the Romans, who had to call their own citizens to the colours every year while the Carthaginians used mercenaries.

As a matter of fact, in the three years which followed, we find the Romans fighting in Sicily, attacking Corsica and Sardinia, coming back again to fight in Sicily, seeking to reap the fruit of the battle of Mylæ, but without forcing Carthage to make peace. At last, being anxious at any cost to terminate a war which had now lasted nine years and was imposing such terrible sacrifices on the population of Italy, Rome resolved in 256 to repeat the enterprise of Agathocles in 310 and attempt a landing in Africa. The undertaking was arduous and dangerous, for the passage was strongly guarded by the Carthaginian fleet. The preparations made were great and adequate to the affair. Near the mouth of the Himera (the modern Salso), not far from Cape Ecnomus,

(Monte S. Angelo) on the southern coast of Sicily, was prepared a great fleet of three hundred ships of war and transports and in these were embarked about 140,000 men, including soldiers and galley slaves. The expedition was under the orders of L. Manlius Vulso and M. Atilius Regulus. The Carthaginian fleet tried to bar the way in the neighbourhood of Ecnomus itself. A fierce naval action ensued, in the course of which the Romans succeeded in getting through. Having defeated the Carthaginian fleet, they succeeded in reaching the coast of Africa and occupying the city of Clypea to the west of Cape Bon.

It seems probable that the Carthaginians thought themselves safe from an attack of this kind and were surprised with insufficient forces. We know, moreover, that the Roman army had scarcely disembarked in Africa when a serious revolt broke out among the Numidians, who raided the Carthaginian territory. Nothing but want of preparation and the Numidian revolt can explain why the Roman army was allowed to range over a huge space undisturbed and to ravage towns and villages which, being for the most part unfortified, could not defend themselves, or why the invaders were permitted to collect an immense booty, chiefly cattle and slaves, and to send all this back to Italy undisturbed together with one of the consuls and a considerable part of the army of invasion.

Regulus remained behind with part of the army— a most singular piece of imprudence, due, we must suppose, either to the difficulty of keeping a large force for long in Africa or to a mistaken belief that Carthage was already conquered. This was far from being the case. Carthage had been taken unprepared, and again she temporized, sent a small army to amuse rather than to fight the Romans, and, when this army was beaten, opened negotiations for peace. But all the time reinforcements were being urgently prepared. Soldiers were being enrolled in Numidia, in Spain, and in Greece. A Spartan general, a certain Xanthippus, was hired, who understood the art of war better than the Carthaginian leaders. Regulus, who aspired to the honour of finishing the war, willingly agreed to negotiate for peace; but, believing that the resistance of Carthage was broken, he sought to impose very hard conditions. By this time the new Carthaginian army was at hand and, when all was ready, the Carthaginians rejected the conditions and Xanthippus took the field. That clever general overthrew the Roman army and Regulus himself was taken prisoner (255).

The audacious move of the Romans, which had at first been favoured by fortune, thus ended in a catastrophe. Rome was undismayed, however, and immediately got ready another fleet, which was sent to Clypea to embark the remains of the Roman army, which had fled thither and fortified itself against the assaults of the Carthaginians. But fortune had now turned against the Romans. After having defeated a Carthaginian squadron and embarked the survivors at Clypea, the Roman fleet was, on its return voyage, almost entirely destroyed by a storm near Cape Passaro. Out of 364 ships only 80 were saved. The Carthaginians were much encouraged by this new disaster to Rome, and immediately prepared an expedition, the object of which was to take the offensive and drive the Romans out of Sicily. Rome met this move by sending a fleet and an army in 254 to take Panormus (Palermo) and by preparing a new expedition to Africa in 253. The war therefore had burst forth again more violently than ever, both on land and on sea, but this was the last flicker of audacity. The new expedition of 253 failed before Africa was reached; partly owing to errors committed by the leaders, and partly to another tempest, which again seriously damaged the fleet. The new misadventure finally discouraged Rome from the ambitious design of striking at Carthage in Africa. She now despaired of competing with Carthage at sea, and restricted her efforts to securing the conquest of Sicily.

Now began the fourth and last period of the war, which was entirely Sicilian (253–241). This period covered fully thirteen years, and its very length, as well as the incessant vicissitudes of defeat and victory, shows that the combatants were weary. In 251 the consul Lucius Cæcilius Metellus inflicted a serious defeat before Panormus on the Carthaginians, who were endeavouring to raise the siege. The Carthaginians thereupon evacuated all the fortresses of Sicily and contented themselves with defending Lilybæum and Drepanum (Trapani) on the west coast. Sicily was now almost entirely in the hands of the Romans, who took new courage and determined to finish the war by a supreme effort. They again built a fleet and with it laid siege to Lilybæum. But in 250 the consul Publius Clodius lost a squadron in an attack on the Carthaginian admiral Adherbal near Drepanum, and another was lost in the following year by the consul Lucius Junius Pullus on the south coast of Sicily.

Owing to these defeats the Romans were compelled to raise the siege of Lilybæum and to renounce once more the idea of supremacy on the sea. It was, indeed, well for them that Hieron remained faithful and in 248 renewed his alliance with Rome. For, had it been otherwise, they might have found themselves in an awkward position in 247, when Carthage at last sent to Sicily a great general in the person of Hamilcar Barca, the father of Hannibal. Hamilcar reorganized his army, took up a formidable position near Panormus (perhaps Monte Pellegrino), and captured Eryx. Then he commenced a series of rapid raids over the whole of Sicily and by sea against the coasts of Italy, trying to conquer Rome by a war of attrition, to exhaust her finances, and wear out her people, who year by year were called to the colours. The Romans had the worst of this struggle from 247 until 242, and seemed on the point of confessing defeat, so deeply were they discouraged. At last, in a final spasm of energy, they grasped the fact that they could not subdue Hamilcar and force him to abandon the formidable positions from which he was threatening both Sicily and Italy, unless they finally reconquered the command of the sea and cut his communication with Carthage. For this, however, it was necessary that a new fleet should be launched, for most of the ships they possessed had been destroyed by fire or water. And how was that to be managed amid the discouragement which was so universal? The richer citizens, on whom the greater share of responsibility for the undertaking devolved, came forward at this point to save the State and their own popularity, which was now hopelessly compromised, by equipping a new fleet at their own expense.

In the spring of 242 the last two hundred ships of war which Rome could produce were sent to sea with

orders to attempt a decisive action. With this fleet
the consul Q. Lutatius Catulus ventured on a strong
blockade of Drepanum and Lilybæum. A Carthaginian fleet tried to break the blockade and to reinforce
and revictual Hamilcar. Lutatius Catulus attacked,
conquered, and in part destroyed this fleet off Lilybæum, near the Island of Ægusa (the modern Fa-
vignano), one of the Ægates group.

The supreme effort had had its effect. Rome was
once more mistress of the sea. Communication between Carthage and Sicily was interrupted. Hamilcar
could no longer maintain himself unless Carthage recovered her naval supremacy without delay. This she
was unable to do, either because she could not rebuild
her fleet in the time available, or because her finances
also were exhausted. War carried on by means of
mercenaries cost Carthage much more than Rome had
to pay her conscript levies, and the struggle with
Rome had lasted so long and required such large
forces that even the riches of Carthage were inadequate to the necessary expenditure. The State was
no longer in a position to pay the hire of its soldiers,
who were becoming turbulent and rebellious. It
became necessary, therefore, to treat for peace—a
course which even Hamilcar advised. Rome on her
side was not too exigent, for she also was exhausted,
and there can be no doubt that she was content with
much less than Regulus had demanded. Carthage
had to cede the whole of her possessions in Sicily,
including the neighbouring islands between Italy and
Sicily, and had to promise to pay Rome within ten
years the sum of 2200 talents.

41. The Reform of the Comitia Centuriata (241
B.C.). Rome had won, but at what a price! A cen-

sus taken in the very year peace was concluded showed
that the Roman population possessing full rights of
citizenship had diminished by nearly 40,000, from
297,797 to 260,000. Five years previously the diminu-
tion had been greater by 20,000, for the figure then
was 241,212. No doubt there was a proportion-
ate or even a greater decline among the population of
the Latins and the allies.

We have no particulars of the finances, but we
may readily conjecture that, after so long a war,
and before the indemnity from Carthage began to
restore the deficit, there were grave embarrass-
ments. On the other hand, the State required
more ample means if it was to keep a firm grasp
on the part of Sicily which had been conquered,
and to face the liabilities involved in the prosecution of a policy which was now framed on a much
grander scale.

The difficulties created by the war were met by
Rome in the usual manner. Political concessions
were made to the classes which were most numerous
and most distressed. The war had had the effect of
making the constitution more democratic. In the
last year of hostilities the censors had been so generous
in conferring citizenship on the Italians that there
were enough to constitute two new tribes—the
Velina in Picenum and the Quirina in Samnium—
which were intended, at any rate partly, to conceal
the decline of the population. Very soon, however,
matters went further than this. The constitution
of the comitia centuriata was reformed in such a way
as to increase considerably the powers of the middle
and lower classes at the expense of the rich. At the
same time the property qualification of the lowest

class was reduced in order to increase the number of citizens liable to military service.

As citizens had been called upon with growing frequency to serve when required, even though they were constitutionally entitled to exemption, the reform did no more than legalize an already established practice. But, on the other hand, the rights corresponding to the duties had to be recognized, and this was done by admitting these citizens not merely to the files of the army but also to the ranks of the legislators. Such an innovation would not by itself have altered the balance of the parties and social classes in the comitia centuriata. But a change was also effected in the number of centuries in each class by assigning to each the same number of voting units. This was carried out by a complicated revision of the existing scheme, the details of which have not all been recorded with sufficient clearness. It would appear that the number of centuries to be assigned to each class was suggested by the recently increased number of the tribes. In other words, the five classes were, so to speak, merged in the thirty-five existing tribes, which had hitherto been entirely separate. While, previously in the formation of the centuries the citizens had been indiscriminately collected from all the tribes, now and henceforth the components of each tribe were to be distributed according to their fortune among the five classes, each class being represented in each tribe by two centuries. Thus in each tribe there were to be ten centuries (2×5) in all 350 (10×35) centuries. Each class was to have seventy centuries (35×2), and since to these must be added the eighteen centuries of knights of the first class, and the five centuries which had for long been formed outside the classes, the new body of Roman citizens was divided in all into 373 centuries equally distributed among all the classes. The result of this was that the majority now lay with the third and fourth classes, and that the centuriate assembly now represented the wishes and intentions, no longer of the aristocracy but of the middle classes.[1]

42. The Conquest of Sardinia and Corsica (238–235 B.C.). Peace with Rome was hardly concluded when Carthage found herself involved in two new wars. One of these was with her African subjects, the other with her dissatisfied mercenaries, who refused to be disbanded. Nor was this all, for, immediately after this mutiny was suppressed, the Sardinian mercenaries also rose in rebellion and invoked the aid of Rome, or rather offered their co-operation in conquering the island. Rome hesitated for an instant, but soon yielded to the temptation, and once more

---

[1] The original authorities do not indicate precisely either the time or the manner of this reform. They show, however, that, in all probability, it coincided with the reduction of the census (property qualification) of the lowest class, of which we only learn indirectly from Polybius, vi., 19, 2. Scholars have therefore hazarded various possible views, none of which can be justly regarded as certain. We have preferred the date 241, not only for the reasons of internal policy adumbrated in the text but because this was the year in which the tribes reached the number of 35, and in which the conquest of the first transmarine province confronted the Roman State with a new military necessity.

As regards the actual substance of the reform, regarding which the hints given by our authorities are really insufficient, we have adopted the hypothesis which was first advanced by an Italian humanist, Ottavio Pacato (il Pantagato) some centuries ago and which is still the most sensible and the most widely accepted. *Cf.* G. Bloch, *La République romaine.* Paris, 1913, pp. 132 ff.

declared war on Carthage. The pretexts were specious. They were: that the Carthaginian armaments intended for the reconquest of the island were really aimed at Italy; that certain Roman merchants had been maltreated in Africa during the war with the mercenaries; and, finally, that Sardinia, being territory between Sicily and Italy, came within the scope of the previous treaty (238). Carthage had no forces with which to resist these claims and for the moment bowed her head. She ceded Sardinia and in addition consented to pay an indemnity of 1200 talents.[1] The conquest of Sardinia was followed by that of Corsica, which Carthage had perhaps already abandoned, and indeed had never very securely held.

Rome had in a few years become possessed of the greater part of Sicily and of all Corsica and Sardinia. But these islands were outposts beyond the bounds of Italy proper, and inhabited by peoples no longer related to the Italians either in language or in customs. Was it possible or necessary to govern them as the conquered regions of Italy were governed? Rome did not think so. After the conquest of Sicily, Sardinia, and Corsica she began to elaborate a new political and administrative system, which was destined in later times to be applied to all the provinces which one by one came to form part of her empire. Sicily, Sardinia, and Corsica, in fact, became the first provinces of the Roman Empire. The two principles on which the management of the provinces was based were that the soil and the government belonged entirely to Rome. The soil was, in the strict sense, the property (*prædium*) of the Roman people. It was open to them to confiscate it for their own benefit

[1] Polyb., i., 88, 8–12; iii., 10, 3.

as *ager publicus*, or to leave it to its subject owners. The latter had merely a shadow of ownership and were, of course, obliged to pay in kind one tenth of the revenue (*decuma*) as tribute. The whole province was under the absolute control of a governor, in this instance of a prætor (Rome had in 227 at least four prætors), who was invested with full power—military, civil, and judicial, and who acted as ruler and administrator. Many were the peoples and many the countries to which those two principles were one day to be applied, and infinite were the abuses of which they were the source!

43. **The Conquest of Both Sides of the Adriatic** (229–215 B.C.). For the moment, however, no one at Rome imagined that in Sicily, Corsica, or Sardinia there was being tried for the first time an experiment in administration and institutions which were for centuries to be the framework, as it were, of a vast empire. Rome had hardly settled the affairs of the Mediterranean after the long struggle which has just been described when she was obliged to turn her attention to the Adriatic, for reasons and in circumstances which deserve special consideration.

While the Romans were engaged in fighting Carthage, an Illyrian principality had been formed on the Dalmatian coast. Having secured the friendship of Demetrius, the new king of Macedon, this State threatened Epirus and the cities on the western coast of the Balkan peninsula. This State, according to the invariable habit in antiquity, did its best to monopolize the trade in its own part of the world, and to exclude all rivals, partly by competition and partly also (and to a much greater extent) by violence and piracy. Now that the war with Carthage was over and the difficulties which had followed were settled, the senate was beset with lamentations from every part of Italy over this state of matters. And the lamentations were accompanied with the most urgent prayers for armed intervention by Rome to secure free trade in the Adriatic for Roman merchants.[1]

These lamentations and prayers in the end proved sufficiently powerful to compel the senate in 230 to send an embassy to Teuta, Queen of the Illyrians. This fact is in itself enough to show how much the mercantile spirit, the progress of which since the war with Tarentum was so notable, had grown and strengthened in Italy during the First Punic War. It shows also that Italian merchants were now trying to secure the Adriatic trade, and how greatly the number of senators had increased who desired that Rome, having conquered Carthage in war, should rival her in commerce also, and create a mercantile empire not less vast and rich than hers. After three centuries, in fact, the republic was returning to the mercantile schemes and ambitions of the monarchy, but in circumstances which were different indeed!

The embassy sent to Teuta obtained no satisfaction, and war was declared. A fleet of 200 ships and an army of 22,000 men were sent to Illyria. The enemy were easily overcome and Teuta had to accept the peace imposed upon her. The southern boundary of the Illyrian principality was fixed at Lissus (Alessio). The Illyrians pledged themselves not to sail south of Lissus with more than two ships and to pay tribute.

Almost all the confiscated territories were given to Demetrius of Pharus, Teuta's general, who had

[1] Polyb., ii., 8.

treacherously surrendered Corcyra to Rome. The power of Illyria was shattered, and the commercial interests of Italy were in every respect secured. An article in the treaty of peace opened up a new field of political action for Rome. Several Greek cities— Corcyra, Apollonia, Epidamnus—and their dominions, in fact all southern Dalmatia from Lissus to the frontiers of Epirus, including the neighbouring islands, were added to the Italian confederation. With great political wisdom the treaty of peace was announced to several of the Greek States,—to the Ætolians, the Achæans, the Corinthians, and the Athenians,—who received the message and the messengers with enthusiatic demonstrations of joy. The Greeks, like the rest of the world, were turning to Rome, hoping for the protection against their enemies, and more specially against Macedon.

44. The New Reaction of the Small Rural Land Owners: Caius Flaminius. The Illyrian war had been one new sign of the growing influence of commercial interests. Another, which manifested itself a few years later, was even clearer. In spite of the most vehement opposition of the senate, there was passed in 218 in the comitia tributa a Lex Claudia which forbade senators to own vessels of a capacity exceeding 300 amphoræ (about 8000 litres)[1] and capable of transporting anything beyond the products of their private estates. What could indicate more clearly that the thirst for wealth and the passion for speculation and gain had invaded the highest classes, and even that citadel of social tradition in ancient Rome, the senatorial order? Trade, which was theoretically incompatible with the supreme political dignity of the

[1] Livy, xxi., 63.

senate, was beginning to be tolerated in practice. And this had gone so far towards fusing the interests of finance and politics that it was necessary to provide against the evil by imposing a legal check.

But the mercantile class received a larger reinforcement than the members of the senate who gave themselves up to trade, in the increasing number of public contractors. The fact is that Rome was no longer a little city but a great State. Her needs were many and various, and, unlike modern States, she had no numerous bureaucracy at her disposal to undertake the task of supplying them. There were only a few magistrates, most of whom were elected annually, whose duties were laid down on a scale suited to the requirements of a town. Although the number of these magistrates had been increased, the government found itself continually obliged to have recourse to the assistance of private enterprise in order to discharge the necessary public services.

The list of contracts which the senate found itself forced to allocate every year had suddenly become much longer and more lucrative. They had to arrange for public works, transport, military supplies, the collection of the *decumæ* and other imposts and duties in the provinces, the letting of public land, the management of mines, salt works, forests, etc. The established practice of the Roman administration was to divide up these contracts among a large number of middling and small capitalists. It came about, therefore, that, as the Roman Empire increased, there grew up at Rome a class which we should describe as a comfortable *bourgeoisie*, who undertook this or that public service. This class came between the senators and the knights, with whom they were always in contact (as it was from them that they received their contracts and sometimes capital to invest) and the *menu peuple* of artisans and proletarians, who lived by the labour they gave out.

This class was the very prop and stay of the policy of expansion under a social system in which industry on a great scale, depending on machinery, was unknown. Nothing but the continued aggrandizement of Rome could give these avaricious and enterprising people new sources of wealth and new opportunities for making fortunes. Thus was formed a long chain of interests which went down from the senate through this middle class to the urban proletariat.[1] All these had but one object, to rekindle Roman ambition to become a second Carthage by her commerce, to urge on the State to schemes of vaster conquest, and to cast off and weaken in every possible way ancient forms and traditions and with them the influence of the agricultural classes.

And, as a matter of fact, while the increased and enriched mercantile class was getting the State into its power, the ancient yeoman class, which in the days of her poverty had been the very sinew of Rome, were rapidly declining and dying out. The reasons for this were many. The blood tax grew heavier every year. Nearly four legions were now annually called to the colours, and the number of effectives was often even more. Moreover military service tended to be prolonged from one year to another. Many soldiers had lost all count of the service they had performed. Others had not seen Italy for years and were already beginning to grow old in the ranks. Many of them

[1] As appears from Polyb., vi., 17, this process was to be completed by the middle of the second century B.C.

never came back at all, and the necessity should have been apparent of continuing the policy of sending out colonies to the conquered territories, thereby multiplying these veritable nurseries of small landowners and soldiers who had been so useful during the first centuries of the republic. The plantation of colonies had, on the contrary, now for some time been discontinued. The land which Rome conquered was no longer allotted in small parcels to the poor but was almost always hired out to the great capitalists who were for the most part senators.

This does not prove that the great ones of Rome were actuated merely by selfishness and greed. It was easy for them to take the land from the people because the people had ceased to desire, as in times past, to have the land. And this was because the business of landholding on a small scale was falling more and more into ruin, owing to a social and economic tendency which, as wealth increased, grew up gradually beside the other tendencies which we have already examined. Ancient Italy was at that time for the most part under grain. But much of the country was mountainous and badly watered by rivers, which were few and small. The climate was in many cases unfavourable to vegetation and crops were not great. Small proprietors had been able to keep going so long as their families were content to work hard and live very simply, consuming the products of their own land, clothing themselves in the wool of their own flocks, making for themselves everything they required, and buying as little as possible.

Now, however, more frequent intercourse with the Greeks, and military expeditions into rich countries such as Sicily, had disgusted the yeomen with the hard work of their forebears, and had awakened a desire for better living, at a time when the growing abundance of the precious metals had raised prices. Yeomen like other people, therefore, felt a greater need of money than before, but grain, which was their chief product (and of that merely a small quantity), could be sold only at low prices in the neighbouring markets, for there was no means of transporting it to a distance. Nor could they hope to profit by the scarcity which frequently recurred, more especially at Rome. The State, urged by the clamorous complaints of the plebs, amassed in the magazines of Ostia and of Rome huge cargoes of corn, coming for the most part from Sicily and Sardinia, and sent in payment of the *decuma*. These stores were thrown upon the market whenever prices threatened to go up.

Thus the life of a small proprietor became every year more precarious. All who could, abandoned it. Those who had enterprise and good luck became contractors or merchants. The duller and less fortunate fell back among the working classes and the proletariat. One result was that it became easy to extend the term of military service, for many were not unwilling to remain for a long time with the colours, as they liked the pay and the prospect of booty. The professional army was beginning to grow up on the ruins of the yeoman class, which was ceasing to be a force in politics. It is true that some censor would at times try to annul the reform of Appius Claudius, who had distributed the poor among all the tribes, and would again place them in the four city tribes. But this was in vain. The change never lasted for long, and, after a few years, a new censor always returned to the practice of Appius Claudius.

Rome, however, had been a peasant republic for too many centuries, and the distrust of merchants, inculcated by the aristocracy at the foundation of the republic, had been too intense, to enable the commercial element to take possession of the State without meeting an obstinate resistance. Between the First and the Second Punic War, indeed, the yeomen agitated and sought to defend their interests and their principles against the invasion of mercantilism. They formed themselves into a democratic country party, and found a leader in Caius Flaminius, a great man destined to win undying fame in history. Flaminius was tribune of the people in 233, the very year in which the merchants, when their plans in the Adriatic were threatened by the Illyrians, were besieging the senate with their complaints. He proposed a law providing that the land taken from the Senones since 283, which had hitherto lain idle as *ager publicus*, should be distributed in small holdings among the poor plebeians of Italy. The reform intended by this law is plain, and the idea behind it, as we shall see, was to become a fixed point in the Roman party controversies of the next two centuries. This idea was as follows: Small ownership, the nursery of soldiers, was declining. It was important, therefore, to prevent the rich from appropriating all the land. Colonies, on a larger scale than ever, must be planted in order to reconstitute that rural middle class which the wars and the new tendency of the times were gradually destroying. The senate violently opposed the bill, but Flaminius used without scruple the privilege conferred on the plebs by the Lex Hortensia in 287 in order to secure at any cost that his plebiscites should become law. He succeeded, but, while his supporters

were looking forward to a renascence of small ownership, a new war broke out which was destined to be as
important as the Punic wars in the history of Rome.

**45. The Conquest of the Valley of the Po (225–
222 B.C.).** The colonization of what had been in
ancient times the country of the Senones awoke once
more the energy and the hatred of the Gauls. This
people had never reconciled themselves to the loss of
the *ager Gallicus*. In 237, indeed, the Galli Cisalpini
after concentrating a numerous force of mercenaries
about the Rhone, had made an attempt—which proved
vain—to recover it. Now, however, fearing no doubt
that the new measure of colonization was only the
first step towards further conquests by Rome, they tried
a forlorn hope. The Gauls of Italy and those beyond
the Alps combined to set on foot a strong army.
They burst into central Italy across Etruria, and
reached a point three days' march from the capital
of Latium.

Rome had to prepare an energetic defence. She
mobilized the whole of the Italian League. She
enlisted the support of some of the peoples of the
Italian country beyond the Po, the Cenomani and the
Veneti. She waited till the barbarians, in their con-
cern for booty, had forgotten the real object of the
war, and she succeeded in encircling and overthrowing
the great Gallic host near Cape Telamon on the coast of
Etruria. The destruction of the main strength of the
Gallic armies placed Cisalpine Gaul for some years,
at least, entirely at the mercy of the Roman army.
And Rome was no longer the timid power that she had
once been, stopping her advance as soon as she
had gained a success. The democratic party, which
had insisted on the allotment of the *ager Gallicus,*

saw that the best way to secure this domain in future from the assaults of the Gauls was to seize the opportunity which now offered itself to conquer the valley of the Po and annihilate the Gallic danger for ever. The people understood this, and, though there was a strong party in the senate opposed to the new war, Gallia Cisalpina was invaded in 224.

The war lasted three years (224–222). In 224, after having conquered the country of the Boii, which covered the eastern portion of the Cispadane territories, the consuls crossed the line of the Po, and occupied the country of the Insubres in Gallia Transpadana. In the following year one of the two consuls was C. Flaminius, who had been tribune in 233, and who was principally responsible for inspiring the Gallic War. To him and to his colleagues of the succeeding year was due the complete conquest of Transpadane Gaul, which was crowned by the storming of its ancient capital, Mediolanum, the modern Milan. In the country of the Boii was planted the Roman colony of Mutina (Modena) while the line of the Po was secured by the colonies of Placentia (Piacenza) and Cremona (218).

Thus, while the mercantile class had pressed the senate to conquer the eastern shore of the Adriatic and to fight Carthage, the rural middle class, starved for land, had urged Rome into the valley of the Po, that great plain covered with woods and silent marshes, but strewn also with splendid lakes, furrowed with numerous watercourses, and traversed by the greatest river the Romans yet knew or that Italy possessed. The people, ruined by war, had as it were trusted to the remedy of the spear of Achilles, and by war itself had sought to cure the wounds which war had inflicted.

Their hopes were vain. Not even the conquest of the valley of the Po could save the small landowning class of Rome as it then was. But, in the pursuit of this illusory expectation, the old rustic yeomanry, which was on the point of disappearing for ever, had secured for Rome what in centuries to come was to be the fairest jewel of Italy. Thanks to Flaminius, the country which he conquered could be described in less than 150 years thereafter as the garden of Italy and the bulwark of the Roman Empire.[1]

[1] *Cf.* Cic., *Phil.*, iii., 5–13; Strab., v., 1, 12.

CHAPTER VIII

THE SECOND PUNIC WAR

46. Carthage in Spain. We know little of what happened at Carthage after 241. Two facts, however, are certain. One is that political power passed into the hands of a ring of rich families of which Hamilcar Barca, the great warrior and statesman who had distinguished himself in the last years of the war with Rome, was the mainstay. The second fact is that Carthage gave up the attempt to recover the lost islands and preferred to seek compensation in Spain. Shortly after 238, indeed, we find Hamilcar Barca in Spain at the head of a powerful army and armed with full powers. His object was the conquest of the Iberian peninsula, and not, as might be supposed from what followed, to make Spain a bridge by means of which to attack Italy. Having lost Sardinia and Sicily, Carthage was reduced to the defensive. For an attack on Italy she was at a disadvantage. None but a madman could at that time have played with the idea of attacking Rome from Spain, for the conditions which a few years later made that enterprise possible did not as yet exist. Carthage went to Spain, therefore, because she had resigned herself to leaving Sicily and Sardinia to Rome, and was seeking compensation elsewhere.

For their part the Romans had no obvious reason for regretting that Carthage should involve her forces in the attempt to conquer Spain rather than in an endeavour to repossess herself of the islands, and we need not be surprised that for nine years Hamilcar was left undisturbed to enlarge the Spanish dominions of Carthage. Hamilcar having fallen in the ninth year of these operations, was succeeded as commander-in-chief by his son-in-law, Hasdrubal, who continued the work of his predecessor rather by treaties than by battles, but with such invariable good fortune that Rome began to be disquieted.

Spain was rich in minerals. Her population was warlike. If Carthage became mistress there, would she not at one stroke obtain a numerous supply of soldiers and the means of paying them? It became, therefore, the aim of Roman policy to cultivate friendly relations with the more important cities not yet subject to Carthage. With one of these, Saguntum, the Romans concluded an actual alliance, and in 226 (whether shortly before or shortly after this event is not clear) they induced Hasdrubal to enter into a treaty whereby he promised that his army should not cross the Ebro.[1] It cannot have been agreeable to Carthage that Rome should take upon

---

[1] Polybius (ii., 13, 7; iii., 27, 9) gives the text of the fundamental clause of the treaty: μὴ διαβαίνειν Καρχηδονίους ἐμ πολέμῳ τὸν Ἴβηρα ποταμόν. This, as historians have not observed, was an agreement whereby Carthage accepted a limitation of her military activity and undertook not to send troops across the Ebro on any pretext whatever, not a reciprocal delimitation of spheres of influence. As Polybius himself observes, the Romans by the document above cited, did not actually acknowledge that all Spain on the farther side of the Ebro was Carthaginian territory (ii., 13, 7).

herself to limit in this way her Spanish ambitions. But Carthage had still so much to do on her own side of the Ebro that, for the time being, the treaty did not embarrass her in the least. Hasdrubal could sign the agreement, therefore, without disturbing the relations of the two great Powers.

In a few years, however, there was an abrupt change in this situation. In 221 Hasdrubal died, and Hannibal, the son of Hamilcar, then twenty-six years of age, by the acclamation of the armies of Spain, was elected commander in his place. The senate at Carthage ratified the choice of the soldiers, and Hannibal immediately attacked Saguntum, the city which the Romans had received into their alliance. After a siege Saguntum was taken in 219, and no attention was paid to the request from Rome that it should be respected. An embassy was, therefore, sent to Carthage threatening war if Hannibal was not delivered up to Rome, and within a few months war had again broken out between the two great Mediterranean Powers.

47. The Underlying Cause of the War: Hannibal's Plan of Campaign. How was it that the course of events was so precipitate? Was it the ambition of Hannibal, and his hatred of Rome—as was repeatedly asserted—that hastened the catastrophe? Hannibal was a great man and it is incredible that he would have risked a tremendous conflict merely because it seemed to him a fine thing to do so. Moreover, in beginning and carrying on the war he was supported and countenanced, not only by a great party among his countrymen but also by the constituted government of Carthage, which must have had solid reasons for challenging Rome a second time after having tried for years to live at peace with the rival Power. These reasons—or at least the most important of them—are no doubt to be found in the Roman conquest of Cisalpine Gaul. If it displeased Rome that Carthage should grow too strong in Spain, it could not suit Carthage that Rome should establish herself in the valley of the Po. This district was near to Spain. By possessing themselves of it the Romans gained a vast region, rich, fertile, and (what was more important) populated by the very Gauls and Ligurians from among whom Carthage recruited part of her armies. Further, it was a humiliation for Carthage that Rome should be allowed to extend her sway freely over the valley of the Po while Rome forbade her to cross the Ebro.

These were the sentiments and considerations which made the incident of Saguntum the occasion of the Second Punic War, the real cause of which was the conquest of Cisalpine Gaul by Rome. In that conquest we shall find also the explanation of the plan conceived by Hannibal when he set out on his great adventure. As we have seen, Carthage was in a position of strategic disadvantage as against Rome, because, having lost Sicily and Sardinia, it had become very difficult for her to take the offensive against Italy. Hannibal's remarkable manœuvres in this war will be inexplicable to us unless we suppose that he wished to do away with this initial disadvantage.

His intention was not to make a direct assault on Rome but to reach south Italy, with his army, to seize a port, raise a revolt among the Roman subjects and allies, and shut up a part of the Roman armies in Italy. He would next proceed to a combined attack on Sicily from Italy and Africa. Having

reconquered Sicily and Sardinia, he would clinch his
success by a final attack in Italy, after forming as
strong a coalition against Rome as he possibly could.
For this coalition he had already cast his eye on
Macedonia, whose new king, Philip, was already
anxious about the continual progress made by the
Romans on the eastern coast of the Adriatic, which
had recently been increased by the results of a short
but successful war, waged in 220, against Demetrius
of Pharus.   But to attack Italy in this way from
Spain would have been madness while the valley of
the Po remained independent of Rome.   Immediately
after the conquest of this region the enterprise became
possible (though still dangerous), provided the Gallic
populations came to his assistance.   As we shall see
Hannibal meant the first step of his undertaking to
be the conclusion of an alliance between Carthage
and the Gauls, and to make Cisalpine Gaul his first
base of operations against Rome and Italy.   In short
the Roman conquest of the valley of the Po was at
the same time the cause of the Second Punic War
and the basis of the strategical plan which Hannibal
adopted.

48. **The Passage of the Pyrenees and the Alps
(Summer and Autumn 218 B.C.).**   Hannibal's plan
was bold and certainly very complicated, but his
courage was equal to the attempt.   He took measures
to provide Spain and Africa with adequate defences
against any attack which might eventually be made
by the Romans, and, in the early summer of 218, he
left the Spanish territories of Carthage with a force
of fifty thousand infantry and nine thousand cavalry.
This was certainly not an army sufficient to conquer
a country shown by its latest census to be capable

of mobilizing 800,000 men.[1] But, if it be admitted that it was intended, not to conquer Italy but merely to prepare the strategic situation and the coalition which was to strike the heart of the power of Rome, one can readily see why Hannibal thought it sufficient.

The journey of the little force was not easy. In addition to the cold and the natural obstacles met with in the Pyrenees, they soon had to reckon with the hostility of some of the Celtic populations in the Rhone valley. After crossing the Rhone, the number of the army had fallen to thirty-eight thousand men, and eight thousand horse. When the Carthaginian forces had marched up the left bank of the river and began the ascent of the northern slopes of the Alps, things went even harder with them. They managed, however, to baffle the ambuscades of the Alpine tribes and in nine days reached the summit of the ascent. It has been a matter of dispute for centuries whether the pass they took was the little St. Bernard, the Monginevra, or the Mont Cenis. There is no means of settling this question definitely, but it is certain that at the beginning of the autumn Hannibal began his descent. His losses had been tremendous, but, five months after leaving Carthagena (the Spanish Carthage) he was able to pitch his camp at the foot of the Alps in the friendly country of the Insubres with the remnant of the army—twenty thousand infantry and six thousand horsemen.[2]

[1] *Cf.* Polyb. (ii., 24); one of the most important chapters in the whole work of that great historian.

[2] These figures, like those given before and after, come from an inscription at Lacinium, dictated by Hannibal himself in memory of his achievements in Italy, which was known to Polybius and was followed by him in his great work (iii., 56). We

Meanwhile what was Rome doing? She had commenced the war with the ambitious plan of a double offensive against Carthage, carried out simultaneously in Spain and Africa. The consul, P. Cornelius Scipio, had been sent to Spain with a fleet of sixty sail and two legions. His colleague, Tiberius Sempronius Longus, with two other legions and 160 quinqueremes, had gone to Sicily with orders to enrol as many troops as should appear necessary and to attack Africa. But immediately the news of Hannibal's movements was known in Cisalpine Gaul, the Boii and the Insubres fell upon the new Roman colonies of Placentia and Cremona, and forced the colonists to fly to Mutina where they were besieged. In order to succour the three colonies the senate ordered Scipio to send one of his legions to the valley of the Po and to raise a new one. Obedience to this order meant loss of time, and so, when Scipio disembarked at Massilia (Marseilles) with his army, he learned to his great surprise that Hannibal was already proceeding by forced marches towards Italy. What was to be done? After a feeble attempt at pursuit he sent the greater part of his army into Spain under the command of his brother Cneius, with the object of cutting Hannibal's communication with his Spanish base. He himself returned with the remainder of his force

---

have not accepted the doubts expressed by modern German critics on the presumed exaggeration of these losses, both because in our opinion Hannibal was in a better position to know how many men he had lost than modern scholars, and because military history teaches us that in many great campaigns, both ancient and modern, losses incurred by armies, owing to the inclemency of the weather, have been much more serious than those caused by actual pitched battles.

to Pisa, where he took command of the legions which were operating in Cisalpine Gaul, and with them he moved to meet Hannibal in the Valley of the Po.

He hoped to find the enemy exhausted by the crossing of the Alps and to annihilate him more easily than if he had continued the pursuit from Massilia. What Scipio had done on his own initiative the other consul did by order of the senate. No sooner did they grasp the fact that Hannibal had decided to carry the war into Cisalpine Gaul than they recalled Sempronius in furious haste from Sicily and ordered him to concentrate his army at Ariminum on the borders of that province. The revolt of the Boii and the Insubres and Hannibal's great advance had frustrated the plan of attacking Carthage in Africa and Spain, and instead, Rome was concentrating for a defensive campaign in the valley of the Po, which had been the first cause of the war.

49. The Battle of the Trebia (December, 218 B.C.). Meanwhile Scipio had crossed the Po and also the Ticinus, and was advancing rapidly westward against Hannibal's army, which was stationed in the neighbourhood of Victimula in the Vercellese, with the fixed intention of attacking it as soon as possible before it had time to recuperate. For all Scipio's attempts at haste, however, Hannibal had had time to reorganize his army and to open negotiations with the Gauls for the necessary assistance. The negotiations had not had much result, as the approach of the Romans held the Gauls in suspense. But he had completely succeeded in restoring the efficiency of his army, and he soon showed his adversaries that they had to do with a soldier who had all his wits about him. On the right bank of the Ticinus, at about two days' march from the river,[1] the advance guard of the Roman army was surprised by a strong body of Carthaginian cavalry and was utterly routed. The Roman squadrons were broken, enveloped, and overthrown. The consul himself was severely wounded and extricated himself with great difficulty. He owed his life to the valour of his son, a youth of seventeen, who sixteen years later at Zama was destined to prove to his father's conqueror how much he had profited by the lessons of this trifling cavalry skirmish.

Although only his cavalry and light infantry had been put to the test in this affair, Scipio decided not to renew his attempt to surprise the Carthaginian. He rapidly recrossed the Po, therefore, and retreated on Placentia, where he decided to wait for his colleague, who was then collecting his army at Ariminum. The retreat was skilfully conducted and Hannibal, though he harassed, was not able to impede it. As was to be expected, however, a certain number of Gauls declared for Hannibal immediately the Roman armies recrossed the Po, and a certain number also of the Gallic auxiliaries serving under the Roman flag revolted.

Hannibal was now master of the whole course of the river as far as Placentia, and it was in his power to cross to the right bank above that city. Scipio was, therefore, in danger of being taken in reverse at Placentia. To avert this danger he fell back rapidly on the Trebia, in order to make a stand behind this defensive line, his right resting on the fortress and his left on the Apennines, and so cover the road to the Adriatic, to Rome, and, therefore, to all Italy. At

[1] The traditional name of this encounter is the battle of the Ticinus, but the precise place in which it was fought is uncertain.

the Trebia he was joined by his colleague Tiberius Sempronius Longus. The two consular armies consisted of four legions and an equal number of Italian auxiliaries, the whole force amounting to about 35,000 men. To these Hannibal could oppose 20,000 infantry and thanks to the new contingents of Gauls which had joined him—about 10,000 horse. The opposing forces were, therefore, about equal. Notwithstanding this Scipio thought it would be best to await Hannibal's attempt to force the line of the Trebia. Sempronius, on the other hand, wished to attack, and no doubt the Romans, no less than Hannibal, had reason to desire a battle, and a victory, in order to gain the assistance of the Gauls, who were merely awaiting events in order to declare themselves on the side of the stronger party.

This explains the impatience of Sempronius, but, as the armies were separated from each other by a river, and as their strength was about equal, it was clear that to attack would be most dangerous, and this justified the view taken by Scipio. Hannibal profited by the dissensions between the consuls, the uncertainty of the position, and the impatience of Sempronius to provoke his enemies to attack. In the month of December a body of Numidian cavalry crossed the Trebia and assaulted the Roman camp. Sempronius (Scipio being still incapacitated by his wound) launched upon the enemy the whole of his cavalry and six thousand light infantry. Immediately, as if conquered, the enemy cavalry retreated in disorder to the left bank of the river. Thereupon Sempronius, thinking the enemy was in flight and that his opportunity had come, hastily called out the whole army, without giving them time to have a meal, and hurried them through the icy water to the attack. But, when they had crossed the river, the Romans were confronted by the whole of the Carthaginian army drawn up in a single line, with the cavalry on the flanks and the elephants in front, the men fresh and primed for combat and not benumbed by a cold plunge like their adversaries. The conditions were too unequal. At the first shock the Carthaginian cavalry overthrew the Roman cavalry and uncovered their infantry on both flanks. It was in vain that the two front lines of the Roman centre struggled nobly and courageously. The Carthaginians swooped down on their flanks. Hannibal had hidden two thousand men in ambush in a wood near by, and these fell upon the rear of the third Roman line of reserve. The third line having been thrown into confusion, the ambushed troops turned upon the second and the first lines. Thanks to the desperate valour of the soldiers, the Roman army escaped complete destruction, but it was so severely shattered that what remained of it had to retire to Placentia.

50. **The Trasimene Lake** (217 B.C.). It was a great disaster. Except for the Roman fortresses all Cisalpine Gaul was lost and in revolt. If Hannibal meant to proceed with his attack on Italy, the way to the centre of the country was now open. It appears that at Rome the government, uncertain as they were regarding Hannibal's intentions, feared a resolute and simultaneous attack on Italy from the north and from the sea. Thus, though Cneius Scipio had fought with some success beyond the Pyrenees, and had succeeded in cutting the communications between Hannibal and Spain, the senate took defensive measures on a large scale. The consuls of the

following year (217), C. Flaminius, the conqueror of Cisalpine Gaul, and C. Servilius Geminus, were directed to take large forces and bar the two roads of access to central Italy,—the eastern, which passed through Ariminum, and the western, which passed through Arretium. All the fortresses were reinforced. Troops were sent to the coast towns and to Sicily and Sardinia, a Carthaginian fleet having already been driven out of the Tyrrhene Sea. Finally they requested assistance from friendly states, among which was Syracuse under King Hieron. What the senate had in mind is clear. They meant to return to the defensive strategy which Scipio had advised in vain. Their idea was to force Hannibal to break his head against Ariminum and Arretium as Scipio had tried to induce him to do against the line of the Trebia.

The senate was at least partly right. If Carthage was not yet thinking of an attack on Italy, Hannibal could not subsist in the valley of the Po. He must, therefore, advance with his little army as rapidly and as cautiously as he could, in order to reach southern Italy as soon as possible, inciting the Italians to revolt as he went. Immediately after the Battle of the Trebia he had, in fact, released his Italian prisoners, begging them to say to their compatriots that he had come to free Italy from vassalage to Rome, and to restore to every city what Rome had taken away. During the winter he had reinforced his army by enrolling many Gauls, and, in the spring of 217, he set his forces in motion by the western road.

He met no impediments in crossing the Apennines and reached Fæsulæ (Fiesole). Here he learned that Flaminius was waiting for him with a large army at

Arretium, and, wishing to avoid a frontal attack on this fortress as he had wished to avoid attacking the line of the Trebia, he imagined a new stratagem more audacious than any of his previous inventions. From Fæsulæ he marched towards Arretium by the high road, burning and plundering the surrounding country. Then he suddenly left the road and, with all his army, threw himself into the vast marshes formed in early spring by the Arno in its upper course, with the object of making a detour to the north of Arretium. For four days and three nights the Carthaginian army had to make its way through mud and water and suffered unspeakable privations. But in the end they debouched in the rear of Flaminius.[1] The manœuvre was daring, for, when all was said and done, Hannibal was risking a dash towards south Italy while leaving two strong armies intact on his

---

[1] There has been much discussion among the learned about the location of these celebrated marshes. The argument has been all the more lively because Polybius and Livy not only contradict each other, but are both obscure and vague on this point. The only way to resolve the doubts which have arisen is to look at the military necessities of the position. Hannibal could never have imposed on his army the fatigue of marching for many days, up to their knees in water, through the marshes, except to avoid an obstacle which barred their way. Now between the battle of the Trebia and the battle of the Trasimene Lake the only serious obstacle that he can have encountered was Arretium, where Flaminius was waiting for him. On the other hand, we know that Hannibal eluded Flaminius and suddenly appeared in his rear, compelling him to change his front and pursue the Carthaginians towards Trasimene. It is clear, therefore, that Hannibal threw his army into the marshes in order to circumvent the position of Arretium and compel Flaminius to come into the open instead of having to assail him in the fortified position.

rear. If Flaminius had only waited till his colleague joined him at Ariminum, things might have been different! But no doubt he was furious at Hannibal's having slipped through his fingers in this way and, moreover, he was the leader of the country party. No sooner had Hannibal emerged in the rear of the consul than he recommenced ravaging and burning the countryside. Could Flaminius, after allowing Hannibal to get the better of him, permit the ruin of the country and all his farmers? Would his want of skill not be blamed for all the losses they sustained? Flaminius could not restrain himself, and pursued the invader, who was marching southwards. Hannibal at first acted as if he desired to evade the pursuit. Then, at a certain point near the Trasimene Lake, he slackened his pace. In his impatience to attack his adversary, Flaminius allowed himself to be drawn into a narrow valley situated between two mountain chains and closed at one end by a high hill difficult of access, and at the other by the lake. In this valley the Romans were surprised and attacked in front, flank, and rear by the Carthaginians, who had waited for them in ambush. Some were thrown into the lake. Others were killed before they had time to get into order of battle or to strike a blow. Flaminius himself, the conqueror of the valley of the Po and one of the greatest of the makers of Italy, lost his life. A few days later the cavalry of the other army, four thousand men in all, which had rushed to the aid of Flaminius, was also destroyed.

51. Cannæ (August 2, 216 B.C.). This second victory won by the enemy in the heart of Italy was greater than the first, for a whole Roman army had been destroyed. There was panic unspeakable at

Rome, for the city itself seemed to be in danger. Heroic remedies were prepared. Four new legions were raised. A dictator was appointed in the person of Q. Fabius Maximus, a great figure who had already been twice consul, censor, and dictator. It was he who in 232 had successfully fought the Ligurians, and he had won the reputation of a brave but most prudent soldier.[1]

Hannibal, however, did not attack Rome. For this, indeed, he had not sufficient forces; and, following his plan of reaching south Italy, he turned eastward. He entered Umbria, and, after an unsuccessful attempt to take Spoletium (Spoleto), he made a very wide detour round Rome as he had done round Arretium shortly before. Passing into Picenum he crossed the territories of the Marrucini and the Frentani in the direction of Apulia, undermining the loyalty of Rome's allies as he went. Possibly he had already chosen the great port of Tarentum as his objective. In Apulia he found Q. Fabius Maximus, who had now taken over the command of the force under Servilius, which had retreated thither from Ariminum. Fabius hung upon Hannibal's rear, harassed him without ceasing, did his best to interfere with his supplies, but always obstinately refused battle. Hannibal, on his side, recommenced the game which had been so successful with Flaminius. He burned and sacked the countryside under the eyes of the Roman general, and, as Fabius seemed indifferent to the devastation of Apulia, he turned off to the west, passed into Samnium and thence straight into Campania, ruining the

[1] The most trustworthy account of the public life of Fabius Maximus is contained in an inscription set up to honour his memory. C. I. L. I., p. 288, No. xxix.

richest and fairest part of Italy in full view of the
Roman army. These tactics were vain; the sagacious
dictator let him do as he would and refused to change
his plan.

But this temporizing policy, if it avoided defeat,
put a severe strain on the patience of the Roman
people, who had not equipped all these legions in order
to leave central Italy in the possession of the enemy.
The lamentations and complaints of the Italian allies
were not less insistent. Was it thus that Rome proposed to defend them and their possessions? Political discord envenomed the strategic discussion. Caius
Flaminius had been the leader of the rural democratic
party, which of late years had come in conflict with
the aristocracy. The latter had not spared their
reproaches against the rash general who had lost the
battle of the Trasimene Lake, and ostentatiously proclaimed their approval of the caution of Fabius as a
necessary corrective of the imprudence of Flaminius.
Flaminius's followers resented this, stimulated popular discontent, and openly accused the senate of purposely prolonging the war, thus repeating the old
charge which had always been a prominent feature of
civil controversies at Rome.

When Fabius resigned the dictatorship in the
spring of 216, the aristocratic party could only secure
the election of one of their candidates, L. Æmilius
Paulus. The other consul was C. Terentius Varro,
an ardent supporter of the party of Flaminius. The
elections had given a clear indication of the popular
discontent, and this discontent grew so great that
the senate resolved to try a great stroke in order to
secure a decision against Hannibal. It was resolved
to send one legion to begin an attempt to reconquer

Cisalpine Gaul. Eight others, each of them consisting of five thousand men, were detailed for the campaign against Hannibal. Reckoning the contingents
of allies, the consuls of the year had, therefore, at
their disposal a force of nearly ninety thousand men,
against an enemy whose forces in Apulia might perhaps amount to half that number. This time the
offensive was to be attempted with adequate force.

Hannibal had returned meanwhile to Apulia, still
perhaps with an eye on Tarentum, and in Apulia
near the River Aufidus (Ofanto), he was met by the
two consuls. It is related that dissensions had very
soon arisen between the aristocratic consul and his
democratic colleague, for the perennial reason that
the aristocrat counselled prudence while the democrat
would have none of it. However this may be, the
two armies came face to face on the 2d of August
near the southern bank of the Aufidus, the Romans
facing southwards, the Carthaginians towards the
north.

The Roman army was drawn up in the usual way,
but Varro, profiting by bitter experience in the
past, had given the maniples of his three lines a greater
depth than was customary. Hannibal, on the other
hand, had drawn up his infantry in a continuous line,
thinner than usual, and certainly much thinner than
the Roman. He placed his best troops, the Africans,
on the wings, and distributed his cavalry on the wings
of his phalanx in such a way that on the left his horse
should have a decisive superiority. He then advanced
the centre of his infantry so as to form a convex
curve the extremities of which rested on the lateral
bodies of Africans, which remained drawn up in a
straight line. When the battle began, even before

the light troops, who usually opened the combat, had finished their action, the Roman cavalry of the right wing had been defeated and cut to pieces by the superior numbers of cavalry concentrated on the Carthaginian left, which, thereupon, immediately proceeded to attack the Roman left wing. The result could not be doubtful; in a short time the flanks of the Roman infantry would be uncovered. Meanwhile the heavy Roman infantry had attacked the centre of the thin Carthaginian line, had flattened the curve, and forced it back. The first two lines of the Romans in their apparent success dragged the reserve (the *triarii*) with them, for the Roman generals had not grasped the fact that the wings of the Carthaginian infantry had not yet come into action. Thus, when the Roman line, bent in two at an obtuse angle, had sufficiently penetrated the gap which it opened before itself by its own weight, it was possible for the two lateral bodies of Africans by a slight change of front to attack the Romans in flank. The threatening Roman wedge was caught as in a pair of tongs. But Varro's army had a sufficient numerical preponderance to sustain front and flank attacks at the same time, and might have prevailed had not the heavy Carthaginian cavalry, which had overthrown the two cavalry corps of their adversaries, at this moment, made an assault on the Romans from the rear.

No effort and no heroism could now extricate the Romans from envelopment. There followed a scene of carnage in which fell seventy thousand men, including one consul, Æmilius Paulus, two proconsuls, two quæstors, twenty-one military tribunes, and eighty senators. Ten thousand men who had been left to guard the Roman camp were attacked and made prisoners after the battle. On their side the Carthaginians had lost only eight thousand men.[1]

52. The Struggle for Sicily (213–210 B.C.). The impression made by this disaster was immense, not only in Italy but in all the Mediterranean world. This time it was south Italy that was shaken. Bruttii, Lucania, part of Apulia, all the Samnites except the Pentri, went over to the invader. Part of Magna Græcia and Campania revolted. Capua opened her gates to Hannibal. Philip of Macedon, who had hitherto held his hand, decided to make common cause with Carthage.[2] The blow was so severe that Rome abandoned all idea of an offensive, imposed a truce on her internal struggles, collected as many soldiers as she could, and entrusted them to a vigorous general, the prætor Marcus Claudius Marcellus. Marcellus was directed to content himself with preventing Hannibal from getting possession of all Campania and in particular of any seaport. Hannibal, on the other hand, once solidly established in south Italy, resolutely began to develop the second part of his plan, which he intended to be decisive, namely to reconquer Sicily and through Sicily to re-establish communication with Carthage. Thus the scope of the war was enlarged at the very time when it split up into a number of small operations.

The last months of 216 were spent in combats of small importance between Hannibal and Marcellus in Campania. Hannibal took Nuceria (Nocera), Acerræ (Acerra), and Casilinum. The Romans managed to retain Cumæ, Nola, and Neapolis. In 215,

[1] The description we have given of the battle of Cannæ is founded chiefly on the account of Polybius (iii., 110 ff.).

[2] The text of the treaty is given in Polybius (vii., 9).

however, the war blazed up again, and not merely in Italy. Indeed greater things happened outside Italy than within its boundaries. In Spain the Romans made notable progress south of the Ebro, because Hasdrubal, who commanded in Spain, was compelled to return to Africa to quell a revolt led by Syphax, King of Numidia, and instigated by the Romans. The Carthaginians, for their part, were preparing large reinforcements to send to Italy and attempted an attack on Sardinia, which was unsuccessful. In Italy, Carthaginians and Romans continued the struggle in Campania and Apulia; but Hannibal did not succeed in getting possession of a harbour and the Romans did not manage to retake Capua. To all appearance, therefore, the war languished in Italy. But Hannibal relaxed none of his activity, and, if he fought no great battle, he at any rate succeeded this year in concluding an alliance with Philip of Macedon, and began to carry into effect his designs on Sicily. King Hiero, the aged and faithful ally of Rome, was dead, and, at Hannibal's instigation, his nephew, Hieronymus, who had succeeded to his throne, denounced the ancient alliance with Rome and joined the Carthaginians. The long prepared attack on Sicily had begun.

On the whole things had gone badly for Rome in 215. What had happened in Sicily was particularly serious. It was clearly understood at Rome that this was the decisive point of the whole war; for, if Sicily were lost, Rome would be in the gravest danger, being practically surrounded on all sides. In the following year (214) no less than four legions were raised to be sent to Sicily, and were placed under the command of Marcus Claudius Marcellus, the best

available general. Carthage on her part made great
preparations for a Sicilian expedition. In Italy, on
the contrary, the minor warfare went on, while the
Romans continued to progress in Spain, extending
their dominion in the southern portion of the country
and beginning to rebuild Saguntum. In this year,
too, a new war was added to the rest. Philip of
Macedon had undertaken to reinforce the Carthaginian fleet with two hundred ships and to attempt a
landing on the coast of Italy. But, either because
he had no secure communications with Hannibal and
with Carthage, or because he was not a man of much
resolution, the king of Macedonia acted with little
energy and did not give much trouble to M. Valerius
Lævinus, who had been sent from Rome to attack
him.

The year would, generally speaking, have turned out
well for the Romans had not matters come to a crisis
at Syracuse. Shortly after joining Carthage, Hieronymus had been killed as the result of a conspiracy,
and the monarchy had been abolished. For a moment
it seemed that the supreme power would pass into
the hands of an aristocratic party which was friendly
to the Romans. But a democratic revolution upset
the government almost at once and restored the
Carthaginian alliance. Marcellus, who had begun
by attempting to negotiate, hesitated no longer. He
marched against Syracuse and invested the city.

In 213 the war continued to go well for the Romans
in Spain, and in Illyria, and not too badly in Italy,
where they took Arpi, and again succeeded in preventing Hannibal from occupying a port. But it was in
Sicily that the great events of the year developed.
The Carthaginians occupied Agrigentum and sent a

fleet to the aid of Syracuse. Most of the island rose in rebellion against Rome. Syracuse obstinately held out, one of her defenders being Archimedes. Marcellus continued the siege operations and at the same time defended himself against the attacks of the Carthaginians with extraordinary vigour. Everything depended on his army. If Marcellus could take Syracuse, Rome might hope to save Sicily. If he were to be destroyed in the attempt, the war was as good as lost.

The fighting in Sicily continued the whole year without a decisive result. At the beginning of 212 Hannibal at last succeeded in getting possession of Tarentum. He now had a harbour which might have served the Macedonian fleet as a base of operations capable of being used in concert with the Carthaginian fleet to dispute finally the mastery of the seas with Rome and complete the conquest of Sicily. It was a heavy blow to Rome, for the issue of the struggle around Syracuse was still doubtful. In compensation for this the senate succeeded in concluding an alliance with the Ætolian League whereby the latter pledged themselves to make war on Philip. The Romans also profited by the absence of Hannibal with the bulk of his forces at Tarentum to draw the lines of investment about Capua tighter. Soon, however, Rome found a greater compensation for the loss of Tarentum in the conquest of Syracuse. In spite of the vigorous efforts which were made by the Carthaginians, Marcellus took the city. The immense booty which was seized somewhat restored the strained finances of the republic, and the victory re-established the prestige of the Roman arms in Sicily. The island, however, was not yet won back, for the Carthaginians still maintained themselves at Agrigentum and were determined to hold out to the last.

In 211, the war continued more fiercely than ever. Rome won a new and great victory in Italy by taking Capua. Hannibal had in vain made a dash from Tarentum to save the city and had made a final effort to divert a part of the besieging army, by pretending to march on Rome. His forces were, however, too few to assault the entrenchments behind which the besiegers retreated on his approach, and the feint at the capital did not deceive the Romans. The fall of Capua was a shrewd blow to the prestige of Hannibal in all south Italy, which from this moment began to have doubts of his power and his fortunes. His weakest points were now manifest. These were the feebleness of Philip of Macedon whom the Romans were now involving more and more completely in a net of diplomatic intrigues, the excessive difficulty of communicating with Carthage, owing to the fact that Rome was still so strong in Sicily and on the sea, and finally the lack of siege train. Carthage has been reproached for not having sent proper support to Hannibal. We have too little information as to what Carthage actually did, and was in a position to do, to enable us to pronounce judgment on this point, but we may observe that Carthage did equip a large force to succour Spain, and made a notable effort to reconquer Sicily. It is reasonable to suppose, therefore, that she did no more because she could do no more, Sicily being a constant obstacle between her and Italy, the sea being watched by the Roman forces and all the harbours having been for many years in the hands of her enemies.

However this may be, the fall of Capua, if it was

a mishap for Hannibal, was by no means a mortal blow. He still had great forces and numerous *points d'appui* in Sicily. The Carthaginians still held Agrigentum and in this very year fortune suddenly turned against the Romans in Spain. Hasdrubal, having composed matters in Africa, returned, and, after a series of successful operations, succeeded in driving the Romans back across the Ebro. The two Scipios, who were in command of the army, were killed, and their legions were nearly annihilated.

53. The Battle of the Metaurus (207 B.C.). During 210 the encounters between Hannibal and the Roman armies in Italy continued to be of slight importance, but in Sicily the Carthaginians finally lost Agrigentum and evacuated the island, which again fell under the sway of Rome. This was a great success for the Romans and a serious misfortune for Hannibal, for it meant the failure of one of the principal aims of his vast plan of campaign, the success of which depended on the reconquest of Sicily and the re-establishment of secure communication with Africa through that island.

Hannibal did not, however, give up hope. The Romans had won their successes at a very high price. For some years now they had maintained more than twenty legions under arms, that is to say, more than two hundred thousand men, without counting the fleet or the allied contingents. The finances of the State were in a critical condition. Italy was half ruined by the ravages of the enemy, the death of so many men, the ruinous taxation, and the neglect of agriculture caused by the long absence of the farmers with the army. In this year, too, the country was desolated by a terrible famine for which there would have been no remedy but for the friendly conduct of the King of Egypt, who furnished grain in large quantities. Hannibal believed that the moment had come for a supreme effort. He had failed in his plan to conquer Sicily and could not expect, therefore, any longer to be reinforced by sea. His idea was that reinforcements should reach him by land, and that they should take the same route as he himself had done. The thing was possible now that Spain, since the victories of 211, had been restored to Carthage. He accordingly arranged with the Carthaginian government that his brother Hasdrubal should prepare a strong army in Spain with which he was to follow in Hannibal's own footsteps and swoop down on Italy exhausted by so many years of war. He was then to effect a junction with his brother and the decisive blow would be struck.

At Rome there must have been some suspicion of this new plan, for it was decided to send a capable leader to Spain. The man chosen was Publius Cornelius Scipio, son of the consul who had commanded at the Trebia and who had been killed shortly before in Spain. The young Scipio in 211 was twenty-four years of age. He was extremely popular owing to his noble birth, the proofs he had already given of valour and ability, and his courteous manners. It was to him that the senate turned, in their great need of generals for their vast armies, to command the expedition to Spain. Scipio was too young to hold either the prætorship or the consulship, and, to obviate this difficulty, a special law had to be passed giving him proconsular authority.

The event showed that this notable exception had not been made without good reason. Scipio's arrival in Spain in 209 was distinguished by a master stroke. He attacked Nova Carthago (Carthagena), the capital of the Spanish empire of Carthage, which was universally believed to be impregnable. The city was taken, or rather surprised, by a single assault, together with the provisions in the fortress, the reserves of metal which were kept there, amounting to about six hundred talents, and much booty besides. The effect of this was immediate. The Iberian peninsula was at once aflame with an anti-Carthaginian insurrection, which immobilized the three Punic generals whose forces were dispersed through the various districts.

In the same year the Romans succeeded in recovering Tarentum, which, like Syracuse, was mercilessly sacked. For the Romans, therefore, 209 was a distinctly successful year, but 208 was less fortunate. For though in the east they succeeded in inducing Attalus, King of Pergamus, to move against Philip, they lost Marcellus, their greatest general, who was killed in Lucania. What was worse Scipio failed to confine Hasdrubal, who had continued in the meantime to prepare the new army of invasion, to Spain. He brought him to battle at Bæcula on the Bætis and claimed a victory. But Hasdrubal got away and crossed, first the Pyrenees and then the Alps with much greater ease than his brother, because, after ten years of war, the Alpine tribes had become accustomed to the passage of armies. In the early months of 207, Hasdrubal unexpectedly appeared in the valley of the Po at the head of a formidable army, again (and not unsuccessfully) rousing the Gauls, the Etruscans, and the Umbrians to revolt.

It was a moment full of terror for the Romans

and for the Italians who had remained faithful. It seemed clear that, if Hasdrubal and Hannibal succeeded in effecting their junction, Rome was lost. In furious haste one of the consuls, Marcus Livius Salinator, was sent northward to meet Hasdrubal, while the other, Caius Claudius Nero, was dispatched to the south to hold Hannibal in Apulia. The former, having reached Sena Gallica (Senigaglia), decided to wait for Hasdrubal whose intention was to follow the Via Flaminia from Fanum Fortunæ (Fano), and perhaps to join Hannibal on the road to Rome. Nero meanwhile fought with varying fortune against Hannibal and seems to have succeeded in holding him in Apulia. Probably Hannibal did not yet intend to set out to meet his brother as he had had no news of him and did not suppose he could have arrived so soon.

One day, however, Nero intercepted a letter which Hasdrubal had sent to Hannibal, and which revealed Hasdrubal's intention to march in the direction of Fanum Fortunæ and the Via Flaminia. Rightly conjecturing that his colleague would in a few days be at close quarters with Hasdrubal, and seeing that if Salinator were defeated, it would be an irreparable misfortune, Nero did not hesitate to assume a tremendous responsibility. He chose seven thousand men, the best he had, and, leaving the rest to contain Hannibal, he left secretly at their head and hastened by forced marches night and day to his colleague's assistance. By this bold move Nero rendered an immense service to Rome, for he arrived at the very moment when Livius was faced with the alternative of allowing Hasdrubal to pass or of attacking him.

The battle was fought near the Metaurus River, at a spot not far from the modern Cagli in the Marches.

Nero's seven thousand men decided the victory. Hasdrubal was conquered and slain, and his army annihilated. Thus Hannibal's new plan also failed owing to Nero's energy and to the singular accident that Hasdrubal, having met with less serious difficulties in the Alps than his brother, had reached Italy sooner than was expected.

54. The Roman Counteroffensive (207–201 B.C.). The Battle of the Metaurus greatly improved the position of the Romans. Hannibal evacuated Apulia and Lucania and stood on the defensive in the country of the Bruttii, and the war languished in Italy where the Romans reduced their forces. Things went even better for them abroad. In the following year (206) the Carthaginians were again defeated by Scipio at Bœcula, and almost all Spain fell into the hands of the Romans. Carthage tried to recover herself, and sent Mago with the remains of the army to attempt an attack on Italy. In 205, Mago took Genoa, raised a force of Ligurians and Gauls, and attempted to rouse Etruria against Rome. But, after the failure of Hasdrubal, he was unable with the scanty forces at his disposal to achieve any important success. In the same year, too, Philip of Macedon, wearied by ten years of war with the Greeks, the Romans, and their allies, and after having a few months previously concluded peace with the former, made up his mind to settle finally his long-standing differences with Rome in Illyria and retired from the war.

The moment was at hand when Rome, after having remained so long on the defensive, might at last take the offensive against Carthage. Publius Cornelius Scipio, who had returned from Spain, was elected consul in this same year and immediately suggested to the senate that they should revive the plan of Attilius Regulus, which had failed in the First Punic War and had for a moment found favour at the beginning of the Second, of carrying the war into Africa. Scipio was equal to the task and the situation was more favourable to such an enterprise than it had ever been. Difficulties, however, arose at home, and in Rome itself. As the danger diminished, the party truce tended to relax. The youth who was ready to take so much upon him, and in whose favour the fundamental principles of the Roman constitution had been set aside, excited both envy and distrust. Many were still terrified by the recollection of the catastrophe into which Attilius Regulus had rushed the country, and asked whether such an enterprise was really possible. The senate, in fact, was against the plan. It was necessary to threaten that body with an appeal to the assembly of the tribes before it could be induced to give Scipio the province of Sicily with permission to invade Carthaginian territory if opportunity offered. In the event he was able to set out for Africa at the beginning of the year 204 with 35,000 men, 40 ships of war, and 40 transports.

Following the example set by Hannibal on his arrival in Italy, Scipio meant to detach the allies of Carthage from their allegiance. In securing this object he counted much on the assistance of Syphax, King of Numidia, with whom until very recently the Carthaginians had been at war. But just at that time Syphax had made up his quarrel with Carthage, and had sent to her assistance 50,000 infantry and 10,000 horse. Scipio's only course, therefore, was to come to terms with another Numidian chief, Massinissa, the rival of Syphax, who had fought in

Spain with Hasdrubal, but whom the Carthaginians had finally abandoned in favour of his more successful rival, and who for the moment was consequently without a kingdom.

In these circumstances Scipio had only his 35,000 men with which to begin the campaign. His first move was to besiege Utica, but he was compelled to desist when the Carthaginians and Syphax approached with superior forces, and to retire to an entrenched camp on a promontory between Utica and Carthage, where he spent the winter putting forward proposals of peace, which were intended more as a means of deceiving the enemy than as serious negotiations. In the early spring by a surprise attack he succeeded in defeating separately first the Numidians and then the Carthaginians. He defeated them a second time in a pitched battle, as a result of which Massinissa, at the head of a Roman army, invaded the kingdom of Syphax, defeated the king and took him prisoner.

After these disasters Carthage opened negotiations for peace. Scipio demanded the cession of Spain in addition to an indemnity. An armistice was arranged on condition that Hannibal and Mago were recalled from Italy. This sad message reached the great Carthaginian in Calabria. He was at the time in the ancient city of Croton not far from the Lacinian promontory, where, in the last years of his sojourn in Italy, he had caused to be engraved on an altar dedicated to Juno, a narrative of his achievements in the Greek and Punic tongues, which was destined to be the foundation of the masterly account composed by Polybius. He was for the second time meditating and plotting an alliance with Macedonia. Nevertheless, he obeyed the summons, and, undefeated, he voluntarily evacuated the soil he had occupied for more than fifteen years.

The news of the departure of Hannibal was for Italy the removal of a horrible obsession. The news of his return to Africa was fatal to Carthage. There the war party recovered its ascendancy. Soon afterwards a Roman fleet sent to revictual Scipio's army was captured. Hostilities were immediately reopened, and Hannibal, who had come home merely to confirm a peace, had to take the lead in conducting a new war.

55. Zama (202 B.C.). The decisive battle was fought in Numidian territory near Zama. The order of battle adopted by Hannibal on this occasion recalls that which distinguished the greatest feats of arms in his Italian campaigns. He placed the mercenaries newly enrolled by Carthage in the first line, flanked by his excellent cavalry and supported by eighty war elephants. These were to attack the Roman legions immediately they had been thrown into confusion by the onset of the elephants. Should the elephants be repulsed or checked, they were, with the assistance of the second line, composed of the new national Carthaginian militia, to inflict the first shock on the enemy and wear him out as much as possible, even if they were finally beaten and forced to retreat. The third line, composed of veterans brought back from Italy, would then intervene and strike the final and decisive blow.

Scipio's great anxiety, on the other hand, was the formidable line of the eighty elephants. He arranged his army in the usual three lines, but not in the usual chess-board pattern. He left the same interval between all the maniples of the three files so that between the maniples there ran, through the whole depth of his army, a series, as it were, of lanes or corridors. In the intervals between the maniples of the advance guard he placed the skirmishers (*velites*), who, when the elephants arrived, were to fly and disperse, thus enticing the elephants into the open corridors between the maniples where they could be pierced with arrows from both sides. As a matter of fact, his anxiety was to a great extent groundless. Terrified by the trumpets and galled by the darts of the skirmishers, most of the elephants rushed back on the Carthaginian cavalry of the left wing. This made it easy for the opposing body of Roman cavalry to charge and rout them. The mainspring of Hannibal's successful tactics—the stereotyped initial cavalry success—had this time been put to profit by the Romans and turned against him. The failure on the Carthaginian left was all the more serious as on the other wing their cavalry had also been thrown into confusion.

It was, therefore, urgently necessary for Hannibal that the battle should be decided before the return of the victorious enemy cavalry. But, though his first line fought with honour, it proved almost impossible to move his second, composed, as it was, of recently enrolled Carthaginians, who were unaccustomed to war and were seized with panic. The mercenaries of the first line at once concluded that they were betrayed, and fell furiously on the second line. Thereupon the mass of the Roman army swooped down on the two parts of the Carthaginian host which were struggling together, and the shameful scuffle became a rout.

Hannibal did not even yet give in. He collected on the wings what remained of his first and second lines, while Scipio, embarrassed by the heaps of corpses, which lay before him in the middle of the field, extended his front, placing his second and third lines on the flanks, and in the centre what remained of the first. Thus the two armies came together in the final and most terrible shock of the battle. The issue of the combat still seemed doubtful; but the Roman cavalry returned from pressing the enemy and appeared in the rear of Hannibal's forces. The Carthaginian army was encircled, and the surprise manœuvre of Cannæ was completely reproduced by the Romans with all its terrible consequences. Of the 60,000 Carthaginians a good 20,000 remained on the field. As many more were taken prisoners. Hannibal himself with a handful of horsemen escaped with difficulty to Hadrumetum.[1] From Hadrumetum the fugitive general soon regained Carthage and, like his father after the battle of the Ægates Islands, forty years previously, he advised peace. Peace was accordingly made. Carthage recognized the independence of the new Kingdom of Numidia, within frontiers to be indicated by Rome, and Massinissa as its ruler. She promised to pay Rome for fifty years an annual contribution of two hundred talents, to disperse her war elephants and all her ships of war but *ten*, to abandon, then and for ever, all external conquests, to limit her armaments, to give up her levies of foreign mercenaries and, even in Africa, to make war only by licence of Rome (201). Thus, after more than sixty years of war, the greatest State of

[1] The chief source of the description of the battle of Zama is, as usual, Polybius (xv., 9–14).

the European and African West disappeared from the ranks of the Great Powers.

Rome had conquered chiefly for three reasons: In the first place, the possession of Sicily gave her a strategic advantage, for Carthage could only attack her by making the long circuit followed by Hannibal. Secondly, she remained on the defensive for the greater part of the war and did not pass to the offensive until nearly the end. Thirdly, her Latin colonies remained loyal, and surrounded her with a cuirass of impregnable fortresses, while of her subjects, whether Gauls, Italians, Greeks, or Etruscans, only a part rebelled against her.

CHAPTER IX

56. The War with Macedonia (200–196 B.C.).
In the war with Hannibal, Rome had shed her blood in
torrents. But she had conquered all Sicily, including
the Syracusan territory, which was the best part of
it, and Spain, which was so rich in men and minerals.
Mistress of Sicily, Sardinia, Corsica, and Spain,
Rome now dominated the western Mediterranean.
Circumstances, the errors of her enemies, the wisdom
of the senate, the valour of her soldiers, the tenacity
of her public spirit, good fortune, which is sovereign
in such matters,—all had conspired to make Rome
in less than a hundred years one of the greatest
Powers in the Mediterranean basin, and perhaps the
greatest of all. It might have been expected that
she would now go forward with ever-growing vigour
and dilated ambition to new conquests in order to
increase her empire. Is not this the natural tendency
of all empires in the period when their fortunes are
in the ascendant? Why should not Rome have sought
to exploit to the uttermost the fortune that seemed
so favourable, and have done, perhaps more slowly,
what Alexander had accomplished less than a century
before?

After the Second Punic War, however, a sudden

change came over Roman policy, which affected its scope, its methods, and its objects. This change is one of the most important phenomena in Roman history, and we must thoroughly grasp it if we are to understand how it was that Rome managed to create the most durable empire of the ancient world. The first impulse towards the new departure was given by certain grave complications in Eastern affairs which arose during the last years of the war with Hannibal. While Rome was at grips with Carthage, the Kingdom of Egypt for various reasons, chiefly internal, had entered on a period of decline. Syria, on the contrary, under the powerful régime of Antiochus the Great, and Macedonia under the intelligent, if vacillating, rule of Philip, had become notably stronger.

The death of Ptolemy IV. in the year 204 and the accession of Ptolemy V. Epiphanes, who was a minor, sufficed to produce an alliance between the sovereigns of Macedonia and Syria, the object of which was the partition of the possessions of the Lagidæ situated outside Egypt. In 202, moreover, Antiochus invaded Palestine while Philip fell upon the Cyclades, the Thracian Chersonese, and the coasts of Bithynia, and Egypt under its rapacious and incompetent regency could not raise a finger to prevent this. Even though Egypt had abandoned them, however, the cities, which preferred the nominal protectorate of the Lagidæ to the severe rule of Macedonia, had offered resistance. The free cities of Rhodes, Chios, Cyzicus, and Byzantium, terrified by the ambition of Philip, had formed an alliance, had hired mercenaries—Ætolians, for the most part—and had equipped a fleet. Attalus, King of Pergamus, had joined this alliance. Philip, however, resumed the war in 201 with such vigour that Rhodes and Attalus came to Rome for help. Besides these there shortly arrived on the same errand, an embassy from the Athenians. Owing to a chance incident, they had become involved in war with Philip, one of whose generals had been ordered to invade Attica. Egypt being impotent, Rome alone could save the East from the hegemony of Macedonia and Syria.

But Philip and Antiochus had chosen their moment well. If Egypt was impotent, Italy was overwhelmed with difficulties. Sparks from the great conflagration which had so lately been extinguished flew in clouds and everywhere kindled minor fires, which lasted for years. There was war in Spain, which was conquered but not pacified. There was war on the plain of the Po, where the Gauls had fought desperately to the last for the cause of Carthage, and even yet, though peace had been made, refused to lay down their arms. There was fighting in Liguria, whose natives infested the maritime communications between Italy and Spain as well as the Gallic and Iberian coasts. Was it possible or right for Rome, immediately after the great effort demanded by the war which had just been concluded, to intervene seriously in Oriental affairs, which after all concerned her but little, merely in order to prevent Philip and Antiochus from unduly enlarging their states at the expense of the Lagidæ?

We know that at Rome public opinion demanded peace. The senate, however, did not hesitate to grant the assistance which was requested. An embassy was sent to Philip calling upon him to cease making war on the allies, and, when the ambassadors returned without an answer, the senate proposed at the consular elections for the following year (200), in the teeth of popular opposition, that war should be made on Macedonia. How are we to explain the obstinacy of the senate on this point? Livy puts in the mouth of the tribune of the people who most strenuously opposed the war, a speech in which he accuses the senate and the nobility of purposely creating one war out of another so that war might never cease. To the consul who supported the senatorial policy he attributes another speech, which may be summed up as follows: "We must make war on Philip in Macedonia, otherwise Philip will very shortly come and make war on us in Italy."[1] In these speeches, though we may admit that they are fictions composed by Livy, are set forth the actual views of the two parties, the party of peace and the party of war.

The people did not wish for this new war because they were tired of fighting. But the senate was an assembly full of experienced politicians. To all who could see beyond the events of the day the war with Hannibal had demonstrated that, though Rome had extended her empire beyond the seas, Italy was by no means secure. Hannibal had managed to enter Italy and to maintain himself there for sixteen years, and what was more, had contrived to obtain soldiers and support of every kind. This time Italy had escaped from a great danger, but the adventure had been too perilous, and a wise people would do well to take care that it did not occur again. From this moment the inviolability of Italy became a cardinal principle of Roman policy. The reason why the senate wished to go to war against Macedonia in 200 was

[1] Livy, xxxi., 6 and 7.

that they felt bound to block the path of a new Hannibal before he could march against them. Macedonia was strong in arms and rich in money. She had been Hannibal's ally. She had already shown that she feared the Romans and their influence on the eastern shore of the Adriatic. Macedonia, finally, was no farther from Italy than Carthage, and she enjoyed an advantage which Carthage never had— she was a Greek state. It must not be forgotten that at this time southern Italy was still half Greek. A Greek state, therefore, might well regard that region as its own predestined sphere of influence. What would have happened if one day, while the Carthaginians continued secretly to foment and sustain rebellion among the Gauls in northern Italy, Macedonia had attempted an attack on Rome from the south, raising against her the Greeks of Magna Græcia and reproducing the designs of Pyrrhus? The senate must have been all the more inclined to obstruct the excessive growth of an Adriatic Carthage by means of what we should now call a preventive war, because, now that the rich mines of Spain belonged to Rome, the means at their disposal were ample.

The people, however, would not be convinced and the comitia voted against war. The senate, on their side, insisted. They did their utmost to overpersuade the citizens, and caused them to be addressed by many orators on the subject. Finally they managed to get the matter referred again to the comitia and this time the war was approved.

This fact is important because it shows how much the authority of the senate and of the aristocracy of which the senate was the organ had grown during the war with Hannibal. The rural democratic party, which before the Second Punic War had been gaining ground, had disappeared altogether before the war was over, and it is easy to see why. In these terrible years Rome had no time for political disputes. She had to defend herself. Thus the senate, which alone had the knowledge and the power requisite for the conduct of so long and so great an undertaking, became for more than ten years the central institution of the State. It was filled with men who were the heroes of these innumerable battles and with their sons. It was in a state of unity and concord such as had never been seen before; for the old party rivalries, the old jealousies and family feuds had died down, and the ancient difference between the patrician and the plebeian senators was almost completely done away with. Between 312 and 216 we have the names of 148 senators in virtue of the so-called curule offices—that is to say the offices of dictator, censor, consul, and curule ædile. Of these 73 were patricians and 75 plebeians; and while the 73 patrician senators came from only fifteen families, the 75 plebeian senators came from thirty-six.[1]

The war with Macedonia, then, was imposed by the senate on the people as the first war against Carthage had been imposed by the people on the senate. The senate, however, was under no illusions as to its power of making a war of conquest in Macedonia at a time when they had to send an army every year to Cisalpine Gaul to fight their Gallic subjects, who, under the guidance of Carthaginian irregulars, were waging an atrocious guerilla warfare of surprises and ambuscades, with alternations of simulated peace

[1] *Cf.* G. Bloch, *La république romaine; conflits politiques et sociaux*, Paris, 1913, p. 138.

and sudden revolt. Rome merely wished to compel Philip to keep his vaulting ambition within more modest limits. They proposed to effect this, not by arms alone but also, and even more, by diplomatic arts whereby they hoped to turn to account the envenomed discords of the Greek world.

Rome was already allied with the King of Pergamus, with Rhodes, and with Athens. It was desirable to gain over the Ætolians who were old enemies of Macedonia, and possibly the Achæans, who, on the contrary, somewhat inclined to the Macedonian party, and several other peoples and states if it could be managed—the object, in fact, being to encircle Philip and force him to give in by restricting his supplies of men and money. This explains the strange and uncertain progress of the war. In the first year of hostilities the two principal adversaries seemed rather to avoid than to seek an encounter. The consul Publius Sulpicius Galba disembarked with an army at Apollonia in Illyria, and there he stayed to organize Illyria as a base of operations against Macedonia and to conduct intrigues with the Ætolians, the Achæans, and the petty Illyrian principalities. Philip, on the other hand, struck hard against Attica, where forces had been disembarked by Rome, Rhodes, and Pergamus for the defence of Athens. They succeeded in taking Chalcis by a surprise attack, but did not dare to face Philip, who ravaged Attica by way of reprisal, and carried on an intrigue the object of which was to induce the Achæans to join him.

The year 200 came to an end without any decisive event. Sulpicius had succeeded in winning over the Atamani and some unimportant Illyrian princes, but not the Ætolians, nor had he come in contact with

the Macedonian army. Philip on his part had made
no progress with the Achæans. Both Ætolians and
Achæans meant to see how events were shaping before coming to any decision. Sulpicius grasped the
fact that the mere presence of a Roman army in Illyria
was not enough to bring them into the war, and in the
following year, that is to say in the summer of 199,
he made an incursion across Illyria into upper Macedonia, while the Roman fleet, conjoined with those
of Attalus and Rhodes, attacked the Macedonian
coast, Eubœa and the lesser islands. In spite of this,
however, the war was not waged with any greater
resolution in the course of this year. Philip went
so far as to face the Roman army but did not commit himself very deeply. On the other hand, the
Roman consul did not attempt to compel the enemy
to fight a decisive battle, either because he would not
or because he could not. There were several encounters favourable to the Roman arms, after which
the Ætolians declared for Rome, but Sulpicius, instead of advancing into the heart of Macedonia,
retired again into Illyria as if he had accomplished
his object.

In the second half of 199 the situation seemed to
change. Sulpicius handed over the command to the
consul Publius Villius who, having arrived from Italy
after the Ætolians had joined the Romans, changed
the plan of campaign and conceived the idea of threatening Macedonia not, as before, from the north but
from Ætolia and Thessaly. At the beginning of 198
he carried out this plan and attempted an invasion of
Thessaly. Philip, however, was too quick for him,
and barred the way by occupying a very strong position in the gorge of the Aous. Villius could not out-

flank the enemy and did not feel equal to a frontal attack. He stopped, therefore, and for some time the two armies were immobilized in opposing camps. It is impossible to say how long this state of inaction might have lasted had it not been for the arrival in the following spring of Villius's successor, Titus Quintius Flamininus, a young man of great skill and resolution. After observing the enemy for forty days without moving a step, and after a vain attempt to come to terms with Philip, Flamininus, with the assistance of an Epirot prince, contrived to circumvent the king's position by using certain little known mountain paths. Philip retired slowly, first into Thessaly, which he laid waste as he went, and then into Macedonia. He was not immediately followed by Flamininus, who returned to Epirus to receive the submission of the tribes hitherto loyal to Philip. Then, in concert with the Ætolians, he entered Thessaly and commenced the siege of all the cities which adhered to the Macedonians or were occupied by Macedonian garrisons. With the approach of winter he went back to the Gulf of Corinth to arrange for winter quarters. By a supreme effort and the promise that they should have Corinth, he succeeded in winning over the Achæans to the side of Rome, and with an Achæan army, assisted by a Roman fleet, he advanced against that city. Flamininus, in fact, like his predecessors, made no attempt to cut the main stem of Macedonia but only lopped off the longest of its branches, which too much overshadowed Rome.

The third year of the war, however, was now drawing to its close, and there was no sign of an end. This gave rise to much discontent at Rome by which Flamininus's friends profited to secure the prolonga-

tion of his command. They convinced the senate and
the people that the reason why the war was protracted
was that the general was changed every year. Flamininus then tried in the winter of 198–197 to finish
the war by negotiation. Rome, however, insisted
that Philip should abandon all Greece, including the
fortresses of Demetrias (Volo), Chalcis, and Corinth,
and thus demanded what only a victory could give
her. No settlement on this basis was possible. In
197, therefore, Flamininus concentrated his army
and made a resolute attack on Macedonia. Philip
was compelled this time to make a serious reply.
The two armies at last met at Cynoscephalæ, and
the Macedonians were defeated.

After the battle came an armistice and then a truce,
during which terms of peace were arranged. The
allies demanded the destruction of Macedonia, but
Rome would not permit this. The existence of Macedonia was necessary. Moreover, Macedonia must be
strong enough to be a bulwark for Greece against the
barbarians of the north but not so strong as to
be dangerous to Rome. Macedonia was, therefore,
allowed to make peace on condition that she abandoned all her possessions in Illyria, Greece, Thrace,
Asia Minor, and the Ægean islands, and on payment
of a thousand talents, one half immediately and the
other half in ten years. She was to reduce her army
to five thousand men and her navy to five decked
ships, and she was forbidden to make war or any
alliance outside Macedonia without the consent of
the Roman senate. She was, in fact, reduced to less
than the condition of a protected State. But the
proof that all the Romans wanted was to remove the
Macedonian danger from their flanks lies in the fact

that they did not keep for themselves one square foot of the enormous territories which they had conquered. The Ætolians recovered all they had lost in the first Macedonian war. The Achæans received Heræa and Triphylia. The Illyrian territory was given to the Illyrian princes. For the rest, all the Greek cities which had been subject to Philip in Greece and Asia were declared free by Flamininus, a decree which amid a scene of wild enthusiasm was read by the proconsul at the Isthmian Games of the year 196.

For the Greek cities to be declared free meant that each should be autonomous, as in the days the memory of which was still so glorious in comparison with the decadence into which Greece had now fallen. To the Romans this arrangement was welcome, for it relieved them of the burden and embarrassment of looking after all these cities, a responsibility which they did not at that time wish to assume. They did not wish to hand them over to any Power which would make use of them to the detriment of their empire, and they were glad to pay homage to the ideal of republican liberty, which they delighted to contrast with the servile character of monarchical institutions.

57. The New Policy of the Military and Diplomatic Hegemony. To those who consider this peace in the light of the insatiable lust of territory which for two hundred years has possessed the states of Europe and America, this peace may seem a strange one. It may seem incomprehensible that Rome could have all Greece and all Macedonia in her power and yet resist the temptation to make them her own. But since the end of the struggle with Hannibal there had gradually grown up at Rome, as the years passed,

ochus a pressing invitation to cross over into Euro
Last, but by no means least, Hannibal, who for so
own reason had been compelled to leave Cartha
ived at the Court of Syria in 195.

kept a watchful eye on all these transactio
anxious to avoid a war in the east. She h
troops to Cisalpine Gaul every year to car
dy war of ambuscades and stratagems. Spa
restless and turbulent. These were anxiet
She made several attempts, therefore,
Antiochus in a friendly way to aband
nia, to return to Asia, and to free the Gre
t was in vain. Antiochus flaunted his hi
ms to the cities of Thrace; he advised tl
if they had the freedom of the Greek citi
at heart, to free Tarentum and Syracus
a word inclined more and more to the ant
party by which he was surrounded. Finall
autumn of 192, trusting in the promise of th
ans that as soon as he appeared in Greece th
peninsula would rise in his favour, he set sa
orty ships and landed in Thessaly with abou
infantry, and 500 horse. Rome could no
the challenge, and acted with much energy
year, by good fortune, Cisalpine Gaul wa
nd in 191 the senate was able to send a stron
ainst Antiochus.
other side the Achæans, Athens, many of the
ties, and Philip of Macedonia himself, took
of Rome. The army of Antiochus was too
hold Thessaly against so many adversaries
diately after the disembarkation of the
rmy in Greece, he returned towards the
Greece. At the Pass of Thermopylæ he

an aversion to territorial aggrandizement. All agreed that, if it was necessary to keep watch on the whole of the Mediterranean and crush in the bud the coalitions to which envy and fear of the growing power of Rome were likely to give rise, it was best not to extend the frontiers of the empire. The military forces of Rome were barely sufficient to keep what she already possessed.

It is easy to understand and to appreciate the wisdom of this idea. We have seen that the Roman army consisted of two parts, the legions composed of Roman citizens and the Italian contingents. It was necessary to preserve a certain proportion between these elements, so that the citizens should not be too much submerged by the allies. Now, between the year 294–293 and the year 199–198, after twenty full years had had their way in healing the wounds made by the Hannibalian war, the Roman population had declined from 263,321 to 258,318 adult males. The number of Roman citizens was therefore small, and was diminishing. Moreover, at Rome, as we have said more than once, military service was a civic duty and not a profession. Owing to this Rome could keep under arms a more numerous army at less expense than Carthage or the kings of the east, who used mercenaries. But the Roman army could not be used with the same freedom for distant expeditions, nor could it be kept in being year after year. At all times conscript armies have been much better for defending their own country than for the conquest of distant territories by a long war. The legions sent to the Macedonian campaign had, in fact, threatened to mutiny more than once.[1]

[1] Livy, xxxii., 3.

If it was not easy to increase the number of the soldiers, still more difficult was it to multiply the number of superior officers, and the whole administrative staff, as would have been necessitated by any further extension of the empire. Such a staff could have been controlled only by the senatorial aristocracy. This was so both because all the political and military administration of the republic was in the hands of the aristocracy, and because, by its long domination and constant success, the nobility had acquired such an ascendancy that the middle and lower classes, alike in Rome and Italy, could no longer conceive the possibility of military command being entrusted to a man of any other class. But the Roman nobility was a narrow oligarchy, consisting of about a hundred families, and it was beyond its power to provide a very large number of generals, ambassadors, lawyers, and civil servants.

58. The War with Syria (191–189 B.C.). It is not surprising, therefore, that at this point in the history of Rome we should find all parties in agreement on the policy of not further extending the borders of the empire. The most illustrious and the most resolute champion of this doctrine was the victor of Zama himself. The reorganization of the finances, the final reconquest of the valley of the Po, which had been the cause of the Second Punic War, the consolidation of Spain, where resistance was still smouldering, an attitude of wakefulness as regards the rest of the Mediterranean, and a fixed determination to prevent in every possible way the growth of too powerful rivals—these were the cardinal points in the new policy.

Rome was prepared to make war but not to conquer.

Such was the curious motto of this negative policy whereby, feeling, rightly or wrongly, that she could expand no further, she hoped to prevent other stat from beating her in the race for power. It policy which was difficult to carry out and means inexpensive, for it brought with it wars, which arose one out of another in a fatal concatenation. Before the war with M was finished dangerous complications wit had already arisen. In 198, while Rome was Macedonia, Antiochus had conquered seve on the southern coast of Asia Minor. In occupied Ephesus; in 196 he set foot in F Lysimachia. The cities of the Troad turne and implored assistance, some of them a the decree whereby Flamininus had li Greek cities of Europe and Asia. Ror manner pledged to support them, and in missioners sent by the senate to rearran saw Antiochus at Lysimachia and in c requested that the freedom of these respected. These *démarches*, howe rupted by a false report of the deat Egypt, which compelled the King to his dominions. Rome, not wis a new war too lightly, decided to another time.

Meanwhile, however, a new d the direction of Ætolia. The not received the spoil they h ruins of Macedonia but the conceded to Greece had They began, therefore, to i by stirring up the Greek

hoped to repeat with greater success the exploit of Leonidas. But the Romans were not Persians. Antiochus was conquered and compelled to recross to Asia, while all Greece, except the Ætolians, submitted to Rome again. Shortly afterwards the Roman fleet, reinforced by those of Rhodes and Pergamus, and supported by help of all kinds from the great cities of the Ægean islands—Samos, Chios, and Lesbos—defeated the fleet of Antiochus in Chian waters and secured the command of the sea. Rome immediately profited by this to prepare an expedition against Asia, which in the following year was to strike at the heart of Syria. The enterprise was great and difficult, and the obvious commander was the victor of Zama. But Publius Scipio could not be re-elected consul because the legal interval had not elapsed since his previous election. It was decided, therefore, to elect as consul his brother, L. Cornelius Scipio, and to associate Publius with him with the title and authority of proconsul.

At the beginning of 190 Scipio crossed to Greece with the new army, concluded a truce with the Ætolians, who would not yet admit defeat, collected a contingent from the Achæans, and crossed Macedonia and Thrace on his way to Asia, where Eumenes of Pergamus and the Rhodians had made great preparations to assist him. Antiochus on his side assembled reinforcements from all his allies in Asia Minor—from Galatia, Paphlagonia, the Lycian League, and the King of Cappadocia. He reinforced the fleet which had been defeated in the previous year, and placed Hannibal in command of part of it. Hannibal, however, was beaten by the Rhodians. Antiochus failed to prevent the passage of his adversaries into

Asia and tried in vain, first to conquer the King of
Pe~~r~~ ~~~us~~ before he could effect his junction with the
R *un* and then to make terms.

had kn e end of 190 he had to accept battle near
ar nd his forces were entirely scattered,
Rome g to the assistance of Eumenes. Han-
but was hope was gone and he fled to Bithynia.
to send ished monarch surrendered all Asia up to
on a bloo s to Rome, promised to pay in twelve years
was still nity of fifteen thousand talents, to reduce
enough. , and to keep no more war elephants. The
persuade of the war were copious, but Rome kept only
Lysimac demnity for herself, and distributed among her
cities. I s all the territories ceded by Antiochus. The
toric clai eek cities were liberated. Rhodes was granted
Romans, ost of Caria and Lycia. The King of Pergamus
much obtained the larger and the better part of what had
in a for long been the garden of the kingdom of the Seleu-
n - cidæ, in addition to the Thracian Chersonese, Lydia,
Phrygia, and part of Caria (189)[1]. There was no
discussion or disagreement at Rome about the peace.
Everyone agreed upon the formula of the new policy,
"we are prepared to fight but we want no conquests."

In the course of a few years Rome had conquered
Carthage, Macedonia, and Syria, the three greatest
Powers of the day, and had compelled them to pay
her enormous indemnities. She was now the leading
Mediterranean Power, and, in the eyes of the Romans,
this hegemony, maintained by the money of the
vanquished, was of more value than any territorial
aggrandizement.

[1] Polyb., xxi., 14, 3 ff.; xxii., 7, 7 ff.; xxii., 26, 1 ff.

CHAPTER X

THE TWILIGHT OF ANCIENT ROME

59. Economic and Social Changes in the First Half of the Second Century B.C. If the wars described in the last chapter did not increase the Roman Empire, they produced an effect which was even more profound. They precipitated the end of the old Rome which had founded the republic, which had conquered and Latinized so much of Italy, but which for more than a century had been slowly changing under the influence of Hellenism. What alterations had she not seen in the last fifty years! In the first place, after two centuries of uninterrupted embarrassment, the Roman State for the first time knew the joy of having plenty of money to spend. The treasury was choked with money, which poured in from the rich silver mines of Spain, the huge indemnities imposed on Carthage, on Macedonia and Syria, the spoils of the wars in Cisalpine Gaul, in Spain, and in the East—spoils which took the form of precious metals, profits from mines, lands, forests, and slaves.

Rome could, therefore, spend lavishly, not merely on her war requirements but also on her civil services. The first twenty years of the second century are deservedly celebrated for the great public works which were then undertaken. In 187 was begun the con-

struction of the Via Æmilia, which continued the
Via Flaminia across the Cispadane territories from
Ariminum to Placentia.   In 181 the sewers of Rome
and the drainage of the Pomptine marshes were
completed.   In 177 the new Via Cassia across Etruria
was opened.   The censorship of 174 was destined to
be famous for the great number of public improvements which were ordered, both in Rome and in the
colonies.   Never had the State contracts been so
many, so lucrative, or so varied as in these thirty
years, whether for military supplies or the collection of
taxes or excise, or for the exploitation of mines,
forests, or lands belonging to the State.   Many
young men who had brought back a little capital from
the war in the East or the West, applied for and easily
obtained these contracts, using either their own funds
or combining with others to find the necessary money,
or again borrowing what was necessary from some
rich man who was to participate in the common
gain.   The theory and practice of this sort of business
became so widely known, and the number of these
middle-class capitalists who made a good thing out
of supplying the public increased so rapidly, both
in Rome and Italy, in the course of these thirty years,
that a few decades later, Polybius was able to say
"that all citizens of Rome without distinction,"
participated in these enterprises.[1]

Agriculture and grazing also seemed to enter on a
new phase of development.   Since the end of the
war with Hannibal there had been a great deal of
speculation at Rome in south Italian land, which had
depreciated owing to the ruin wrought by the war and

[1] *Cf.* Polyb., vi., 17, 2 ff., one of the most important passages
in Polybius's works.

the death of so many of its former owners. As money and slaves became gradually more plentiful, it followed that all Italy gave itself up to speculation in the new *ager publicus*. Many proprietors among the Latins and the allies obtained allotments without difficulty which they added to their original patrimony and cultivated by means of slaves bought out of what they had saved from their share of the spoils of war. The greater capitalists, on the other hand, leased vast tracts of the public domains in Italy or abroad in order to pasture great herds of cattle, swine, goats, or sheep. Pasturage on a large scale must have been very profitable in these years for the armies consumed large supplies of goatskin for the machines of war, and many carcases of salt pork for victualling the soldiers. In the ranks of the Roman senate and aristocracy there was, therefore, a large increase in the number of great fortunes drawn from landed properties. The old agrarian policy was resumed on a greater scale than ever. In the new colonies of Cisalpine Gaul, which were founded between 189 and 177—Bononia (Bologna), Parma, Mutina (Modena), Aquileia, Luca (Lucca), Luna (Luni)—the new owners received much larger grants of land than had been customary in the colonies of an earlier day.

The mercantile spirit, that trading propensity which twice already had nearly made Rome a second Carthage, now acquired an even greater force and an even wider diffusion. Already during the Second Macedonian War the Roman soldier had taken to practising usury among the native races. In the years that followed many Romans and Italians, citizens or small landowners, who either as soldiers or army contractors had come to know the riches and the commerce of Greece and Asia, put all the money they could scrape together from the sale of their paternal acres, or their share of the prize money divided after the war, into the purchase of a ship. Some established themselves at Delos, which after 192 became a flourishing centre of Roman trade. There they opened depots of Asiatic goods for the merchants who came from Italy to load their ships with varied cargoes, and who found Delos a more convenient port of call than Rhodes, or Corinth. Others again traded between Delos and Rome or in the western Mediterranean. On the coasts of Italy there grew up numerous small shipbuilding yards. The woods of Sila, which produced pitch, brought in a very high rent to the State, for pitch was required in very large quantities for tarring the new vessels. Members of the senatorial nobility, in spite of all prohibitions,[1] participated in the profits of this transmarine traffic by lending to the traders, whether citizens or freedmen, the capital necessary to set them up in business.

With these changes of fortune old customs and old ideas also changed. The soldiers and the merchants who returned from the East brought with them the seeds of new forms of luxury and new needs, which rapidly gained a hold on the new generation. Rome was still regarded in Greece—and not without reason —as a rude city, lacking monuments and palaces. But she was ready to enjoy and to flaunt her new riches, and all Italy followed her example. Shortly after the Second Punic War, the first public baths

[1] The prohibition was enacted by the Lex Claudia of 220 (Liv., xxi., 63).

were opened at Rome. Hitherto the Romans had
bathed in the Tiber. At the same time, too, clever
cooks began to command very high wages. The
wines of Greece and the costly delicacies of far countries were imported at great expense, and the Greek
art of fattening poultry came into vogue. Citizens
in a state of intoxication—a new scandal—were seen
even in the assemblies, and half-tipsy magistrates
were found wandering in the forum. So much was
this the case that in 181 a law was passed to restrain
a widespread tendency to debauchery. Beautiful
slave girls and boys fetched large prices. Among the
ancient, simple, and too rare Latin holidays new and
costly spectacles were intercalated, such as the hunt-
ing of wild beasts and the gladiatorial shows customary at funerals. The Lex Oppia against luxury
was repealed in 195. Oriental perfumes, Babylonian
carpets, furniture inlaid with gold and ivory, began
to be seen all over Italy, but principally at Rome.

Among the upper classes Greek culture made great
progress. All the youths of good family now studied
Greek. Greek philosophy opened their minds to
general ideas. Political theories elaborated by Greek
thinkers began to be known and dicussed by the
aristocracy, which hitherto had governed by rule of
thumb and according to tradition. Latin literature,
which had first been essayed fifty years earlier, now
for the first time began, amid the new spiritual and
social ferment, to put forth works showing originality
and artistic skill. It was the age of Plautus, of
Ennius, of Pacuvius, of whom the first wrote the
finest Latin comedies, the second introduced Greek
metres to Rome and composed the first Roman Epic,
while the third was the first to write tragedy in Italy.

60. Marcus Porcius Cato and the Traditionalist Movement. The first thirty years of the second century before Christ were for Italy one of these fortunate epochs in which even he who starts with little can make a fortune, because the whole edifice of civilization, the standard of living, the wants of the people, industry, commercial enterprise, are growing simultaneously. At such a time there is abundance of labour and gains come easily. Each new fortune that is made gives rise to new occasions of profit. Riches beget riches, and capital rapidly accumulates. We can now say that in those thirty years Rome and Italy made great progress. But contemporary observers lament, on the contrary, the growing corruption of the age. What we call progress and civilization, the ancients regarded as decadence. These thirty years, which to us seem so prosperous and fortunate, had not passed before the upper class—especially the better spirits—became distressed by a dull anxiety about the state of the nation, and it was in that very period that a new personage, Marcus Porcius Cato, made his appearance in Roman politics in the character of the harsh puritan raging against the evils of the times.

Cato was born at Tusculum in 234. He was, therefore, a contemporary of Scipio Africanus, and belonged to the generation which had fought Hannibal. He came of a modest family of landowners of the middle class, and had spent his youth in fighting the Carthaginians and cultivating his paternal acres. It was not easy in an aristocratic city like Rome for a man of moderate fortune to reach the highest positions in the State. But Cato was intelligent, eloquent, energetic, courageous, and honest, and the times were too difficult to dispense with so powerful a personality. The influence of a patrician, Lucius Valerius Flaccus, who was the patron of his family, enabled Cato to be elected quæstor at the age of twenty-nine, ædile at thirty-five, prætor at thirty-six, consul at thirty-nine, and censor at fifty. At the point which we have now reached in the history of Rome, that is to say at the close of the war with Syria, Cato was one of the greatest figures in the republic. He was the most redoubtable, energetic, and authoritative champion of the traditionalist and conservative movement, which narrowly watched, and sought by all means to restrain, what we should now call the "progress" of Roman society.

He wished the rural middle class to be, as they had anciently been, the prop and stay of the republic. At the same time he revered the authority of the senate, and only opposed such senators, or groups of senators, as departed from old traditions and favoured too much the innovating tendencies of the day. For him the chief cause of all evil was Hellenism. "Cato," says one of his ancient biographers,[1] "genuinely despised all the characteristic studies of the Greeks. He said that Socrates was a loquacious and violent person who did his best to encourage tyrants, to overthrow the established usages of his country, and to convert his fellow citizens to opinions which were contrary to the laws." And he prophesied to his son that "when this evil genius [Greece] had succeeded in diffusing her literary culture at Rome, all things would come to ruin." He opposed, therefore, with all his strength the new movement towards education, whether public or private, the love of Greek things,

[1] Plut., *Cato Major*, xxii., 1–2.

and all that that love implied—above all the new-fangled luxury and the mania for pleasure which pervaded all classes.

He combated this tendency with sumptuary laws, which limited the number of guests and the cost of banquets, and the magnificence of feminine apparel. And when this weapon was struck from his hands by the opposition of unbridled appetites and vested interests, he revenged himself in his second censorship by imposing prohibitive taxation on all costly and luxurious articles. He narrowly watched, denounced, and, so far as he could, ruthlessly put down the rapacity of money lenders, the frauds of the tax farmers (*publicani*), and the abuses of provincial governors. He waged energetic war on the insolence of the resident aliens and the freedmen, who, in spite of innumerable rebuffs, continually renewed their endeavours to secure admittance to the tribes and to the citizenship of Rome. Finally he wrestled with the great aristocratic ring formed by the Scipios, who, emboldened by the glory of Africanus, were tending to acquire an almost excessive power and authority in the State.

61. Corruption and Progress. Cato would not have succeeded in making himself one of the first personages of his age by defending these principles, had he not been supported by a great consensus of public opinion and sentiment. That such a body of opinion should have existed will surprise only those who judge of antiquity by the standards of modern times, of which the ancients knew nothing, and which would have appeared to them the very antithesis of wisdom and truth. We shall not be able to understand either the ancients or the moderns if we do not grasp how much the ideas of mankind on this subject

have been turned upside down. Since the steam
engine was invented, and a means was thereby discovered of rapidly creating wealth on an immense
scale, the idea has gained ground that it is a sign of
perfection—and therefore a duty—to increase one's
personal needs and to spend lavishly. But it is not
more than a hundred and fifty years since men learned
to use fire in this way, and for this purpose. Before
that they had only such tools as their own hands or
the muscles of animals could actuate, and, though
they could make excellent and very beautiful things,
they could only make them in small numbers. It is
obvious, therefore, why, in those ancient days, simplicity and parsimony were prized as precious virtues,
and why luxury was feared as a danger. It was luxury
that brought disorder into the fortunes of families
and individuals of high or low degree, who allowed
themselves to be tempted to spend too much. In all
ancient states, therefore, moralists and legislators,
systems of government and of religion, impressed on
the citizen the necessity of moderate desires and
simple habits.

In this Rome was necessarily no exception. On the
contrary, there were special reasons why she should
not live too well, for there was a real danger that, if
she did, the foundations of her military power might
be undermined. In all this there was an insoluble
and tragic contradiction, which we must clearly understand if we are to follow the tremendous crisis
which arose at this time. We have seen how small
was the number of Roman citizens (between two and
three hundred thousand) among whom were recruited
the legions on which the might of Rome depended.
If the majority of these citizens laid aside the spade

and the plough and gave themselves up to the pursuit of commerce and public contracts, if they became rich and accustomed to the conveniences, the pleasures, and the luxuries of life, would they be able to support the fatigues and the privations of a long war? In the course of the wars with Macedonia and Syria signs of decadence had already multiplied in the armies. Some legions had demanded leave of absence; the subterfuges for evading recruiting had become more ingenious. Soldiers were seen who went to war accompanied by a slave, who carried their burdens and prepared their food. The antique severity of discipline was relaxed, because the army found means of revenging itself on a too strict general by its vote at the next election.

But this was not the only danger. Riches, Greek culture, and scepticism had weakened the spirit of civic abnegation among the nobility no less than respect for the law, the sentiment of concord, and the sense of honour and right. In these thirty years, in fact, there were signs and symptoms which could not but cause uneasiness to any one who knew how many enemies surrounded Rome. There arose a new generation of statesmen, ambitious, impatient, greedy of innovations, who respected law but little and tradition still less. Many presented themselves as candidates for public office before they had reached the age required by law. Electoral corruption became bolder and more shameless, and the suspicion grew that magistrates abused their powers to make illegitimate gains, more especially by appropriating for themselves an undue share of the spoils of war. It would be difficult to decide whether this suspicion was justified; all the more so because, as often hap-

pens, the facility with which such charges were bandied about may itself be considered as a symptom of
an evil which was actually growing, though more
slowly and less seriously than the credulous public
was willing to believe. On the other hand, these
exaggerations of a real evil were, in their turn, the
sign of another kind of mischief—the exacerbation
of rivalry and discord among the great Roman
families.

With the growth of the riches, power, and culture
of Rome grew also the pride, the ambition, and the
cupidity of the nobility who were her governors.
This is shown by one of the most flagrant scandals
in Roman history, which came to light shortly after
the Syrian war, and was one of its direct consequences.
The two conquerors of Antiochus, Lucius and Publius
Scipio, were accused, the former of misappropriation
of part of the spoils of Syria, the latter of actual
treason, it being alleged that he had received money
and promises of advantage from Antiochus in the
course of the peace negotiations. Ancient authors
give very confused accounts of this episode, and it is
impossible to say whether the charges which were
made were or were not well founded.[1] It is certain,

[1] On this famous case of the Scipios there has been much
discussion, especially in Italy. I may mention the most important researches. Th. Mommsen, *Die Scipion-prozesse*, in
Römische Forschungen, ii., p. 417 ff.; C. Pascal, *Il processo degli
Scipioni*, and *L'esilio di Scipione africano* in *Fatti e leggende di
storia antica*, Florence, 1903, pp. 53–84. Pascal's work is very
interesting in that, by arguments difficult to contest, he cuts
short the tendency of contemporary German and Italian scholars
to discover in the original accounts of these trials endless falsi-
fications made at subsequent periods. Two later studies, G.
Bloch, *Observations sur le procès des Scipion* in *Revue des études*

however, that in the senate accusers and defenders
contended with the utmost ferocity, that among the
accusers Cato took a leading part, and that Africanus,
wearied and disgusted with the struggle, departed
into voluntary exile from Rome. Whether they
were true or false, the fact that such accusations were
made was an ugly sign of the times. If they were
false, it was shocking that the victor of Zama should
have been treated so unjustly. If they were true,
it was appalling that such a man should have been
guilty of betraying his country.[1]

62. **The War with Perseus and the New Settlement
in the East (171–168 B.C.).**   All this serves to explain
the movement of which Cato was the visible champion
and which was genuine enough. It might almost be
said of Rome that, in this supreme moment, she was
afraid that she might become too rich and powerful,
and that she foresaw with terror the glory and the
greatness of the mighty empire which was to be hers.
Strange are the complications of human fortune!
Rome was now to be driven on till she secured the
hegemony of the Mediterranean world by circumstances so numerous and powerful that she was compelled to found a great dominion in spite of all her
fears.   The generation of men who lived in the first

---

anciennes, 1906, and A. Barbato, *Il processo degli Scipioni in
Livio*, Aversa, 1913, are on the same lines. Another volumi-
nous essay on the subject, Fraccaro, *I processi degli Scipioni* (in *Studi storici per l'antichità classica*, 1911, pp. 217–414),
on the other hand, inclined to the excessive and so-called
"radical" school of criticism characteristic of German philological seminaries.

[1] On the argument of this paragraph, *cf.* G. Ferrero, *The
Greatness and Decline of Rome*, London and New York, 1907,
vol. i., chap. ii.

thirty years of the second century had imagined that, by means of their ingenious policy of limited interventions, they could preserve the balance of power in such a way that the Oriental states would not be able to aggrandize themselves at the expense of Rome, while Rome would not be compelled to aggrandize herself at theirs. But these Oriental states differed acutely among themselves, and for centuries had been used to struggle, each to get the advantage of the · other. Many could boast of a longer and a greater history than Rome, and possessed great resources of culture, riches, territory, and men. It was, therefore, impossible to petrify the Orient in the artificial equilibrium which happened to be most convenient to the Romans. The living facts of the situation asserted themselves at every turn, and the hard-won equilibrium threatened to collapse at any moment.

It would be impossible to enumerate all the troubles which Roman policy encountered in the East after the victory over Antiochus. One day it was the Achæan League which was making war on Messene. The next it was the Ætolians, lacerated by internal discord, or Philip of Macedon, who, presuming on the services he had rendered to Rome in the war against Antiochus, was trying to recover his old dominions in Greece and Thrace, and was striking terror into the Ætolian League and the kingdom of Pergamus. The King of Pergamus, on another occasion, came to blows with the King of Bithynia, or, in league with the King of Cappadocia, waged war on the King of Cappadocia Pontica; whilst the new King of Syria, Seleucus IV., who had succeeded Antiochus III., wished to assist the latter and began to intrigue and fight against Egypt, the eternal antagonist. Rome was constantly forced to intervene. Her task became a very labour of Sisyphus, which at every turn interfered with vested interests, wounded susceptibilities and multiplied her enemies. It is not difficult to imagine the effect of these continual interventions. In the twenty years which followed her great victory over Syria, hatred of Rome grew all over the East, and men's minds turned towards Macedonia, by force of opposition rather than from any impulse of natural sympathy.

Although Rome had not allowed the new encroachments which Philip was attempting to make at the expense of Eumenes and the Ætolian League, Philip was not discouraged, and had turned his attention to possible enlargements of his dominions in Thrace, to the reorganization of his finances, and to cultivating the friendship of the warlike but barbarous peoples beyond the Danube. He was thus able, when he died in 179, to leave to his son Perseus a powerful and flourishing State. Perseus continued his father's skilful game. He made friendships in Greece and Illyria, both secret and avowed. He married a daughter of the King of Syria. He succeeded in establishing good relations with the Rhodians, the ancient allies of Rome, who had begun to weary of their powerful protector. He tried to secure a *rapprochement* with the Achæans, and in a word he became the hope of all Rome's enemies in Greece and in the East.

Little by little the policy which had aimed at the balance of power began to produce the very opposite of what had been intended, and political storms and confusion grew worse and worse. Perseus had become the champion and the hope of the enemies of Rome rather by force of circumstances than of set purpose. He was a man not devoid of intelligence but he was timid and parsimonious. He feared to commit himself to the issue towards which he was being driven by pressure from all sides, yet had not the intelligence or the firmness which would have been necessary to resist that pressure and to deliver Macedonia from the compromising aspirations of the anti-Roman party. Thus he gradually allowed Macedonia to drift into a posture of opposition to Rome without making any resolute preparation for war.

There could be only one result of these proceedings, and that was to ensure that war would break out at the moment which suited Rome best. And so it happened. Rome had one sure friend in the East, the King of Pergamus, who had been anxiously watching the manœuvres of the party opposed to Rome, which was growing more powerful every day. His activity (both in word and deed, for he paid a personal visit to Rome) was such that he succeeded in persuading the senate of the necessity of removing the danger from their path,—by fighting and destroying Macedonia. Any other course, he pointed out, would mean the downfall of Roman prestige in the East. Following this decision the senate availed themselves of the first pretext which offered itself, and, in 171, declared against Macedonia what would now be called a preventive war. Once more Rome attacked for fear that, if she did not do so, she would be attacked herself thereafter.

The first two years of the war which followed held for Rome and her friends a series of disagreeable surprises. It was suddenly revealed to everyone how much her military prowess was weakened. In the legions there were too many soldiers who went to war attended by their slaves, who refused to obey orders when it happened to be inconvenient, and whose object in pursuing the campaign was much more to secure booty than victory. The comitia were too prone to elect as consuls and prætors frivolous and incapable men whose only skill lay in flattering the vices and weaknesses of the multitude. Owing to the want of discipline among the troops and the ineptitude of the generals the war began with several serious reverses to the Roman arms, and then dragged on for two years, 170 and 169, uncertain, slow, and dubious. The prestige of Rome in the East was shaken. All her friends and allies except Eumenes began to waver. The Romans had to dispense with the aid of the Greek and Ætolian contingents, so uncertain did their loyalty appear. The Macedonian party prevailed in many Greek cities, and in many states of Epirus and Illyria. Finally the Rhodians, the ancient and faithful allies of Rome, hesitated in their allegiance, and sent an embassy to propose that they should enter the conflict, no longer as allies but as mediators between Rome and Macedonia. The new King of Syria meanwhile prepared once more to attack Egypt.

Things would have gone ill for Rome if Perseus had been more active and intelligent, and had known how to profit by his early successes. But Perseus was slow, timid, and mean. At Rome, on the other hand, defeat and danger awakened the public conscience. The people were thoroughly alarmed, and in their need turned to Lucius Æmilius Paulus, son of the consul who fell at Cannæ, an illustrious relic of the generation which had fought Hannibal, and a prominent member of the traditionalist party of which Cato was the head. Æmilius Paulus had lived in retirement for many years, for he had small affection for the new men by whom the republic had been invaded. He was now elected consul, and in 168 was sent to Macedonia with powerful reinforcements.

Æmilius Paulus restored the discipline of the army, and, in a short but vigorous campaign, succeeded in ending the war in the same year by a single decisive victory over Perseus at Pydna.[1] The King of Macedonia was taken prisoner, and, a few days later, Macedonia submitted. No sooner, in fact, had Rome decided to develop sufficient force, than the danger which had been so much feared was dissipated. Macedonia had been brought low and it was necessary to decide what should be her fate. Some proposed annexation. But Cato, Æmilius Paulus, and their party, who were then all powerful, would not hear of this. What was to be done? The old policy was applied, but this time in a more drastic form. Like all Powers which have to repress vital movements of peoples or of classes, Rome was gradually driven to the use of terrorism. The ancient kingdom of Alexander the Great was this time dismembered and divided into four principalities, nominally independent but really vassals of Rome, and, what was worse for them, completely isolated the one from the others. Trading and intermarriage between the states was forbidden. The country was disarmed. Many of its noble families were deported to Italy. Half of the taxes paid into the Macedonian treasury were

[1] On the battle of Pydna, *cf.* T. Kromayer, *Antike Schlacht-felder in Griechenland*, Berlin, 1907, vol. ii., pp. 310 ff.

made over to Rome. The gold mines which belonged
to the Macedonian kings were closed. This singular
measure must be attributed to the influence of Æmilius Paulus and the traditionalist party, who did not
wish Rome to grow too rich.

Epirus was barbarously sacked. Seventy cities
were destroyed and 150,000 Epirots were sold into
slavery. Rome did not deprive Greece of liberty
but inflicted on her more than one punishment for
her faithlessness, and took cruel but effective precautions against a repetition of her doubtful and uncertain conduct. The Ætolian notables who had taken
part against Rome were put to death, and the territory of the confederacy was restricted. A thousand
citizens of the Achæan confederation were deported
to Italy, among them the great historian Polybius.
In every city the Macedonian party were persecuted,
decimated, and ruined, and many were at this time
made victims, on political pretexts, of family feuds
and private vendettas.

Rhodes, also, was punished for her momentary
hesitation. The mercantile party at Rome wished
for her extinction, so that they might be rid of a
rival; but Cato and his political friends saved her
from utter ruin. The commercial interest did succeed, however, in having her deprived of practically
all her continental possessions, and in having Delos
declared a free port and ceded to Athens. Delos was
henceforth thronged with Italian merchants and grew
in prosperity as rapidly as Rhodes declined. Eumenes,
finally, was also made to feel the wrathful distrust
of Rome, and Antiochus of Syria, who was still at
war with Egypt and had already practically conquered
Cyprus, was ordered by Caius Popilius Lænas to re-

turn to his own dominions and to leave Egypt in peace—a summons which he hastened to obey.

Greece and the East had been reorganized with sudden and brutal completeness. Roman policy had become more suspicious, violent, and cruel as the difficulties for which she was herself responsible produced their inevitable consequences. She was driven by her own policy to terrify, divide, and destroy, in order to impose her will. But how far could she have secured by force the artificial arrangement and the impossible equilibrium of which she dreamed?

CHAPTER XI

63. The Great Rebellion in Spain (154 B.C.).
After the battle of Pydna there followed several years
of quiet. The whole of the Mediterranean was terrified into silence. Only in Syria, Egypt, and the
Adriatic were there some difficulties, and these were
of little account and quickly settled. On the other
hand, the Macedonian War was followed by a new
and remarkable burst of prosperity. The treasury
was so full of the spoils of war, of the tribute paid by
Macedonia, and the revenue which flowed in from
the other provinces, that in 157 it contained 16,810
libræ of gold, 22,070 libræ of bar silver, and more
than 61,000,000 sesterces in silver coin.[1] Rome had
never been so rich and powerful.

Now, however, that all cause for alarm was over,
and that money was so plentiful, the good resolutions
which had led to the election of Æmilius Paulus began to lose their fervour. The new current of pluto-
cratic, mercantile, and Hellenizing influences regained
its ascendancy over the traditionalist party. Nearly
everyone was carried away by the new tendencies,
Cato himself among the rest. We know that this
bitter enemy of Hellenism himself took up the study
of Greek literature in his old age; that, though he was

[1] Plin., *Hist. Nat.*, xxxiii., 3, 55.

the champion of small holdings, he became in time a great landowner; that, though he was a persecutor of usurers, he engaged, *salvis legibus*, under cover of one of his freedmen, in speculations, in money lending, and commerce, which were forbidden to senators.

The ancients, as we have seen, regarded as corruption and dissipation many things which we look upon as signs of progress. But, then as now, human nature failed to resist the temptations presented by riches and novelties, as soon as the danger which had grown out of their excessive enjoyment seemed less imminent. Rome again closed her eyes, surrendered herself to the enjoyment of the moment, and gave rein to the obscure forces which were undermining not only the State but the army. The consuls, when making their levies, exempted Roman citizens—particularly the rich—in large numbers in order not to make enemies. The officers closed one eye, and sometimes both, to the presence of slaves and prostitutes at the camps. They allowed the soldiers to get drunk, to take hot baths, to commit crimes of rapine and violence, to shirk fatigue and dangers. Every means was studied of lightening the burden of military service to the indolent masters of the empire. The term of service was reduced to six years. Soldiers who had served six campaigns were exempted for ever. The Latin and Italian contingents were increased.

And yet in these years, behind this specious appearance of prosperity and tranquillity, a great and terrible crisis was preparing. The first signs of this came from Spain. In 154 several tribes of Celtiberia—the Belli, the Titti, and the Arevacæ—revolted. The Romans were accustomed to these periodical rebellions, and at first no one thought of being anxious.

But one of the consuls of 153, Quintus Fulvius Nobilior, who had been sent to quell the revolt, was beaten first at some distance from Numantia and then, a second time, under the walls of that town. He lost —if the figures handed down to us are exact—six thousand men in the first encounter, four thousand in the second, and was perforce reduced to the defensive. The rebellion spread, and his successor, Claudius Marcellus, who arrived with reinforcements amounting to eight thousand men, thought the most prudent course was to negotiate, and, in fact, succeeded in concluding peace. In 152, however, while Marcellus was treating with the Celtiberians, the Lusitanians rose in revolt, and in 151 Lucius Lucullus replaced Marcellus in Spain with every intention of recruiting the modest fortunes of his family by the proceeds of a fortunate campaign. He found Celtiberia pacified for the moment, but, having attacked the Vaccæi without any reason, he started a new war.

64. **The Third Punic War (149-146 B.C.).** Rome very soon realized that the war in Spain was a more serious affair than an ordinary rebellion—all the more so in view of the shortage both of soldiers and officers[1] —and once again she became cruel in the presence of danger. In Spain her generals began a war of extermination, outrage, and dishonourable stratagems. No one at Rome protested against this except the aged Cato, and his protests were academic. But

---

[1] Polyb., xxxv., 4, 4 ff. The fragments of the new epitome of Livy discovered among the Oxyrhyncus papyri have thrown a new light on the bitterness of the disputes provoked at Rome by the Spanish insurrection. Cf. *Oxy. Pap.*, iv., pp. 90 ff.; ii., pp. 177; 182-184; 207-209; E. Kornemann, *Die neue Livius-Epitome aus Oxyrhyncus*, Leipzig, 1904, pp. 107 ff.

cruelty and perfidy exasperated, while they failed to terrify, the proud races of Spain, and the war became so violent that dark rumours of it reached—and by no means displeased—Carthage, a city for whom Spain held the memory of a lost empire.

After Zama, Carthage had loyally accepted the situation created by the peace, and, in 196, had brought herself to sacrifice even Hannibal. Many Italians had settled in Carthaginian territory. Carthaginians and Romans lived peacefully together in Sardinia. Friendly relations had been established between Carthage and Massinissa's new kingdom, and, in spite of her acceptance of the adverse result of the war, Carthage had not declined, at any rate in the commercial sphere. The Carthaginians were so much more dexterous and skilful than the Romans in trade that, in spite of their defeat and the loss of their empire, they had contrived, with the resources they had retained, their knowledge of merchandise, and their old established business relations, to retain the commercial hegemony of the Mediterranean; and they continued to keep in their hands all the trade which came towards the Mediterranean from central Africa.

After a time this began to excite the fear and envy of Rome. The merchants and the publicans, who were now so influential and so numerous at Rome, and through them the senators and the plebeians who followed the trend of the times, had formed the ambition to make Rome a great centre of commerce. For them the successful competition of Carthage was a source of insupportable humiliation and loss. Others, who thought that Rome was being weakened by corruption were terrified by the riches of Carthage.

What if Carthage should one day produce a second Hannibal? Thus from year to year there grew up at Rome a sort of general animosity against Carthage which, for want of a better means of expression, issued in a policy of pin pricks. Massinissa was encouraged to usurp here and there portions of Carthaginian territory. When the dispute was referred to Roman arbitration, as the treaty of peace required, the decision was always in favour of Massinissa. This treatment was requited by Carthage with a hatred as deep as it was tenacious, but between 151 and 150 the situation took a graver turn.

A swing of the political pendulum had brought the popular party into power at Carthage and some forty of the most eminent citizens had been banished. They took refuge with Massinissa, who demanded that they should be reinstated. Carthage refused, and, making this his pretext, Massinissa again invaded Carthaginian territory. This time the party in power at Carthage refused to submit to the arbitration of Rome, declared war on Massinissa, collected an army, placed it under the command of Hasdrubal, and assumed a posture of defence. Unluckily for Carthage, Massinissa inflicted a severe defeat on her army, and on this the storm of envy and hatred, which for some time had been brewing at Rome, broke at last. From all sides came the cry that Carthage had violated the treaty, that war must be declared, and that she must be taught a sharp lesson.

The mercantile interest, which longed to weaken Carthage, in order to get rid of her competition and to take possession of her trade, fanned the flames, and when the senate, driven on by the popular clamour, summoned a new army to the colours, volunteers flocked in from all sides. No one wished to serve in Spain, where there were plenty of hard knocks but little booty to be earned, but all were importunate to go to Africa, where it was hoped that spoils would be copious and easy to come by.

The Carthaginians were terrified. They upset the popular government, condemned Hasdrubal to death—a sentence which he managed to elude—and sent an embassy to Rome to effect an agreement. It was too late. Things had gone so far that war was now inevitable. The embassy returned, having received only an obscure and ambiguous reply. The senate, on the other hand, did not wish to commit themselves to war in Spain and Africa at the same time. What was to be done? The senate met in secret session, and, after a long debate, decided to put an end to the Carthaginian danger by destroying Carthage like any Spanish village, and interning the population. In order to avoid a new war, Carthage was to be surprised and betrayed to her ruin, so that she might be destroyed without striking a blow. Never, perhaps, in the whole course of history has a civilized state decided, in cold blood, in a time of profound peace, and without serious provocation, to commit so monstrous an outrage. But in this case pride was exacerbated by fear, and pride and fear combined were envenomed by greed.

The plan was carried out with diabolical perfidy. The Carthaginians in vain sent a second embassy with instructions to reach an understanding at any cost. When the ambassadors arrived at Rome at the beginning of 149, the senate had already declared war, and the two consuls, Manius Manilius and Lucius Marcius Censorinus, had crossed to Sicily with the army and the fleet. The ambassadors, fearing that all was lost, fell into the trap set for them by the senate, and declared that Carthage committed her fate into the hands of Rome. The senate pretended to be appeased, and, having expressed satisfaction that Carthage was coming to her senses, replied, rather ambiguously, that if within thirty days they handed over three hundred hostages from their best families and obeyed the orders which would be given to them by the consuls, Rome would not touch either their liberty, their laws, or their territories. Not a word was said about the city. This silence disquieted first the ambassadors and then the Carthaginians themselves, who were quite aware that at Rome many powerful interests were clamouring for the destruction of the city. But, if the silence on this point concealed some trap, how was it to be avoided? The Carthaginians allowed themselves to be deceived. They sent the hostages to Sicily and referred to the consuls, who had meanwhile disembarked at Utica, in order that they might fulfil the orders of Rome. The consuls first directed that the people should be disarmed. Again the Carthaginians hesitated, fearing the consequences. But again the order was obeyed.

Then, and then only, was promulgated the ferocious decree of the senate which ordered the destruction of Carthage and the compulsory settlement of its inhabitants at a distance of eighty stades (9½ miles) from the sea. Her laws, her liberties, and her territories were respected. The city was to be destroyed because (according to one of the consuls) Rome wished well to her ally, and his injunction, if carried out, would remove her citizens from the treacherous pursuits of commerce to the more healthy occupation of agriculture! But the great city, which had not known how to live, wished at any rate to die worthily. All that the fury of despair could suggest was done with lightning rapidity. Carthage still disposed of large resources, and thus, when the Roman army arrived beneath the walls, they found that a long siege would be necessary.

65. The Rebellion of Macedonia and its Annexation (149-148 B.C.). The fine plan of taking Carthage by stratagem without drawing the sword had, therefore, failed. Already involved in Spain, Rome had to face a new war in Africa. But worse was in store. In the same year new difficulties arose in Macedonia. There too the negative policy of Rome had brought forth its inevitable fruit. The splitting up of the kingdom had injured too many interests and destroyed too many vital traditions. Once the royal power had fallen, local rivalries, feuds, and overbearing ambitions no longer curbed by any superior authority, destroyed the peace of the country. Moreover, the Macedonian party, which was faithful to the old régime, hated the existing government, as being friendly to Rome, and therefore, in their opinion, traitorous, and never ceased to stir up discontent. Thus there arose a general and growing unrest, which was bound to break out into open warfare at the first opportunity. Finally, it is not improbable that the news from Africa and Spain tipped the balance of the Macedonian situation, which had for some time been precarious. However this may be, the mere appearance in 149 of an adventurer named Andriscus, who gave out that he was the son of Perseus, was sufficient to raise all Macedonia in his favour. It was necessary to get ready a new army which crossed the Adriatic in 148, under the command of the prætor Quintus Cæcilius Metellus. Meanwhile from Africa there came bad news. The subject populations remained faithful to Carthage and the Roman troops had the worst of it in the preliminary operations against the city.

The spring of 148 saw great movements of troops in Spain, Macedonia, and Africa. In Spain the situation remained much the same, for the war dragged on its slow and murderous course. In Africa the consul Lucius Calpurnius Piso not only failed to take Carthage but did not even succeed in winning over, either by force or by negotiation, the Libophœnician cities. Battles were fought and men lost with no other result than to encourage the Carthaginians in their resolve to resist to the last. Hasdrubal, the general who had been condemned to death in the previous year, was summoned to Carthage and invested with the supreme command. In Macedonia, on the other hand, things went better. Metellus in a short time was able to quell the insurrection led by the impostor and to reconquer the country. But no sooner was Macedonia pacified than new tumults arose, this time in Greece. There, too, the news from Africa, Spain, and Macedonia had produced the customary effect. Rome was tottering, now was the time to rebel! The Achæan League, weary of the Roman suzerainty, which prevented them from settling their long standing differences with Sparta, gave the first signal for the revolt. As at Carthage the oligarchical party, which was favourable to Rome, had been displaced by the democrats, who were nationalist and anti-Roman. In 148 this party threw

caution to the winds, defied the orders of Rome, and
declared war on Sparta.

At this point the Roman public lost patience, and
it is easy to understand why. What, they demanded,
were all their consuls and prætors doing at the head
of all these legions? Was it no longer possible to
find among the great houses of Rome a leader capable
of conquering Lusitanians and Carthaginians? Was
there not already reason to apprehend a coalition of
Carthage, Spain, and Greece? Cato once more gave
expression to the public anger when he described the
generals of the republic as shadows, not men.[1] But
out of this uneasy situation came a new and unexpected development.

At the time of the elections a certain young man
had come from Africa, where he had been serving as
military tribune, to present himself as a candidate
for the office of ædile. This was Publius Cornelius
Scipio Æmilianus, a son of Æmilius Paulus, who had
entered the family of the Scipios by adoption. His
descent was as illustrious as any in Rome, but he
was distinguished not only by the name he bore but
by his own virtues and achievements, for he had done
good service first in Spain and then in Africa. It
was to his advice that any success that had been won
in Africa was due. Attracted by the great name and
the high reputation of the youth, the public became
persuaded that he was the man required to finish the
war with Carthage, and he would have been at once
nominated for office, not as ædile but as consul, had
not the difficulty arisen that he was not legally
qualified for the latter office either by age or by
having previously held the other magistracies

[1] Liv., *Epit.*, xlix.

prescribed. The people swept away this obstacle by passing a law suspending the ordinary rules in his favour, and Æmilianus was elected consul for the year 147. This time the people had made no mistake. In Cato's words the new consul was really a man among the shadows. He reached Africa early in 147, with reinforcements of men and ships, and, immediately on his arrival, he restored the discipline of the army and finally completed the investment of Carthage, which he succeeded in blockading at the cost of enormous and painful efforts.

Things in Africa, therefore, took a turn for the better, and a decisive result was achieved in Macedonia, which in 147 was once more entirely in the power of Rome. This time the senate declared the country a Roman province like Sicily, Sardinia, and Spain. This was a grave decision, for, at a moment when Rome had so many enemies and so much trouble on her hands, she was adding to her empire a vast province which was bounded by barbarian peoples and therefore required to be strongly defended. But Rome could not help herself. Having abolished the native dynasty, and having tried in vain the expedient of breaking up the country, her only alternatives were to annex or to abandon Macedonia.

In contrast to the improvement in Africa and Macedonia the situation in Lusitania and Greece grew worse. It was at this time, when the Romans thought they might begin to hope that the Lusitanian war was dying down, that a certain Viriathus, a gallant soldier, put himself at the head of the rebels. Viriathus was a common shepherd whom the war transformed into a hero. He commenced a guerilla warfare which was destined to be memorable for defeats inflicted on the Romans. Moreover, the danger of grave disturbances had increased in Greece, where the senate had decided to punish the Achæan League by depriving them of certain important cities acquired after the second Macedonian war. This led to tumult and disorder and to a new fermentation of discontent.

66. The Destruction of Carthage and of Corinth (146 B.C.). In 146, however, Rome reaped the first fruits of the election of Scipio Æmilianus. First he succeeded in defeating the army which the Carthaginians had collected to come to the aid of the besieged city, and afterwards he took the city itself. It was necessary first to scale the great walls and effect an entrance. The invaders had then to hack their way step by step through the narrow, tortuous, barricaded streets, fighting for six days and six nights without ceasing until they reached the citadel where fifty thousand citizens had taken refuge. When at last these also had been overpowered, Rome was mistress of Carthage. She did not hesitate as to the next step. Feeling her security was menaced, she was determined to remove all dangerous rivals from her path. The senatorial commission sent to settle the affairs of Carthage proceeded at once to destroy the city. Buildings, monuments, whole quarters which had escaped the ravages of war, were demolished. The surviving population was dispersed, and the site of Carthage was consecrated to the Infernal Gods—a rite which signified that no man would thenceforth be allowed to live there.

After the destruction of Carthage the question arose as to what should be done with her territory. The same choice presented itself as in the case of

Macedonia. It must either be abandoned or, at any rate in part, annexed. Necessity once more triumphed over reason. All the Carthaginian dominions were reduced to the status of a Roman province under the name of Africa, except the eastern part, towards the borders of Cyrenaica, which, with Emporiæ and the cities of Sabrata, Œa, and Leptis Magna, were left to Numidia; while Utica, Hippo, and a few other places, in recompense for their defection from Carthage, were granted independence and a share of the old Carthaginian possessions. The survivors of Carthage, in order to make a livelihood, had to scatter over the country and give themselves up to cultivating the ground. An agricultural State was founded on the ruins of the most prosperous of the ancient commercial empires. Part of the Carthaginian territory was confiscated by the Roman State and formed the greatest tract of *ager publicus* hitherto possessed by Rome outside Italy. The rest was left to the population of the new province who had to pay a fixed tribute (*stipendium*).[1]

Carthage, the terror which had weighed on Rome so long, was no more. But while Carthage was burning, Greece rose in rebellion. The Achæan League had succeeded in winning over the Bœotians, the Phocians, the Locrians, and the Eubœans, and in 146 again declared war on Sparta. Rome intervened, this time resolutely. After conquering Macedonia and Carthage she had no fear of Greece, even though in Lusitania Viriathus had been winning successes which increased both his resources and his prestige. Metellus came down from Macedonia and inflicted a first defeat on the League. King Attalus II.

[1] Cic., *Verr.*, iii., 6, 12.

sent his fleet to help the Romans. The consul Lucius Mummius, who arrived shortly afterwards, defeated the enemy at Leucopetra. The League collapsed and in a few days Mummius was able to occupy Corinth and quell the revolt.

For the third time in three years the senate was confronted with the problem what was to be done with the vanquished. Always averse to annexations they were glad to preserve the independence of the cities which had taken no part in the war. But could this be done in the case of those which had rebelled? And, if not, what could be done but reduce them to the state of subjects? Their territories were accordingly incorporated with Macedonia and declared part of that province. All the leagues were abolished, and all the cities isolated. In each, as in Italy, the democracy was abolished and replaced by an oligarchical government, which was made responsible for administering the city in accordance with the will of Rome. All who had favoured the war and the anti-Roman policy were pursued and severely punished. The country was ravaged and part of it appropriated as *ager publicus*. Finally, the splendid old city of Corinth, famous in history for its beauty, its monuments and its riches, was burned and destroyed.[1]

---

[1] For the conditions imposed on Greece, in 146, *cf.* G. Colin, *Rome et la Grèce de 200 à 146, A.J.C.*, Paris, 1903, pp. 640 ff.

CHAPTER XII

THE GRACCHI

67. The Economic Crisis in the Second Half of the Second Century B.C. The mere fact that Rome had dared to destroy, in the course of two years, two cities so ancient, rich, and famous as Carthage and Corinth shows that with her power there must have developed in her some terribly abnormal and morbid growth. History records few outrages which, from any standpoint of reason and justice, are more execrable than these. Something might be said for the destruction of Carthage. Carthage, after all, had really tried to annihilate Rome, and Rome, in her turn, might claim the right to apply to her rival the *lex talionis*. But Corinth had never dreamed of engaging in mortal combat with Rome. She was destroyed simply because the mercantile interest, which was so powerful among the Romans and was then exalted by the destruction of Carthage, seized the opportunity of getting rid of another dangerous competitor. Public opinion, irritated by the prolonged struggle, and carried away by a long deferred success, refused to interfere.

Rome, however, had now reached a critical period of her history. The sagacious policy of the Scipios had sought in vain to preserve her from the danger of a too vast ambition. This time, as so often happens, the force of circumstances had been stronger than human wisdom. The recent annexations had sprung from the exhaustion of the policy of hegemony. Rome had been forced to bow to that logic of events, which in real life corresponds so little to the logic of reason; and now possessed a scattered dominion, individual portions of which might be profitable, but which, as a whole, was a burden, and committed her to new schemes of conquest. It was a burden because, by multiplying her points of contact with other powers, it multiplied also the possibilities of conflict and the responsibilities of defence. It committed her to new ventures because, in the first place, the necessity of holding what she had, and, secondly, that of establishing secure lines of communication between the separate parts of her new possessions, could not fail to compel the conquest and annexation of more territory.

But the strength of Rome had not grown as fast as her possessions and she was therefore becoming weaker as her empire increased. An economic crisis had already begun which was soon to become menacing and terrible in the extreme. Not that the new impulses of cupidity and ambition which had driven Italy to seek new wealth in the provinces and on the sea showed any signs of slackening. Many Italians grew rich at Delos, in Asia, and in Egypt. Publicans and usurers from Rome and Italy plundered Sicily, Macedonia, and Spain in ever-increasing numbers. The slave trade continued to flourish in secret alliance with the pirates all over the Mediterranean. Throughout the Italian peninsula agricultural methods were being perfected. The traditional empiricism was no longer thought sufficient, and the scientific treatises on agriculture produced by Greece and Carthage were carefully studied. Vines and olives began to be cultivated. Education was more widely diffused. Latin became the national language, displacing the Oscan, Sabellian, and Etruscan tongues. Rhetoricians and grammarians, both Greek and Latin, now opened schools everywhere with unprecedented success. Among the small and middle-class landholders many began to send their sons to these establishments, in the hope that education might be the key to a more ample fortune. Among all classes, also, luxury and the desire to spend became more widely spread. In the year 143 the Lex Didia Cibaria was passed, which extended to the whole of Italy the provisions of the Lex Fannia against the excessive prodigality of banquets.

All classes, in a word, wished to enrich and educate themselves and to rise in the social scale. But these ambitions were less easy to realize than in the first thirty years after the war with Hannibal. The prosperity of that period, as we have seen, had several causes. The quantities of precious metal then imported into Italy, as war booty or in the form of indemnities, had enabled the senate to meet a large public expenditure without burdening Italy. The enormous confiscations of land, especially in the valley of the Po, had given opportunities for many successful agricultural speculations. There was, moreover, an abundance of slave labour, also produced by the war. But in the thirty years which followed the war with Perseus, these three sources of gain tended to dry up. It is certain that the great struggles after 154, with the exception of the war against Carthage, cannot have been so profitable to Rome.

Macedonia and Greece had already been much exhausted by previous wars, and the interval had been too short to enable them to accumulate new treasures sufficient to satiate their greedy invader's hunger for gold. The Spanish war was already in all probability costing the Roman treasury more than it was bringing in, and was likely in a short time to upset the finances of the State, which had been so prosperous thirty years before. Finally, although in the ancient world nations were not connected by such a strict community of interests as in our time, we must suppose that the destruction of Carthage and Corinth was a new cause of impoverishment for the whole Mediterranean world. When these two flourishing centres of commerce fell, many industries, in the products of which their merchants traded, must have languished or entirely perished for want of middlemen. Rome and Italy did not succeed in replacing the merchants of Corinth and of Carthage in every branch of their trade. Their vanity and cupidity were not equalled by their command of capital, their knowledge of their business, or their commercial ability. This was yet another cause of poverty for all countries including Italy.

The greatest gain from these wars was, in fact, the growth of the public contracts for collecting the taxes and leasing the public property in the new provinces. But these contracts, and the small amount of commerce which the Italians could scrape together out of the smoking ruins of Carthage and Corinth, enriched only a small number of fortunate persons. The ease which the whole of Italy had enjoyed during the first thirty years of the second century sprang from the great income and the great expenditure of the State. When these declined, the ease that depended on them also departed. The evil of debt began, therefore, to increase again, this time in a new and more dangerous form. Now the nobility themselves, being unable to live up to the new standard of life with their old fortunes, which in many cases they were unable to increase, began to run into debt and become entangled in corruption, and to try to exploit their political power for their own profit. The evil must by this time have made much progress, for it was in 149 that the first permanent tribunal whose business it was to try cases of extortion on the part of magistrates and senators to the prejudice of allies and provincials, the first *quæstio perpetua de pecuniis repetundis*, was established. The equestrian order, on the other hand, was more and more filled up with publicans and enriched merchants whose pride and power increased as the old aristocracy grew more corrupt and impoverished. Discord began to gather in secret between the two highest orders in the State while the condition of the lower orders was not less serious. Everywhere, even in the more remote country districts, the cost of living increased, either because of an increase in the needs and the luxury of the population, or because the currency became depreciated with the increase of the available quantity of the precious metals. There was, however, no corresponding rise in the price of the commodities which the landowner had to sell in order to pay for the new luxuries. In districts which were far from the great roads or from any rich city, and which were, therefore, not in a position to export their products, the price of provisions dropped the moment production was even slightly increased. Thus

Polybius tells us that in his time in the valley of the Po provisions cost very little indeed.[1] The slightest extravagance, therefore, on the part of the landowner plunged him into debt from which it was difficult to extricate himself, especially at a time when there were fewer opportunities of making money out of war.

The crisis among the small holders became acute, and, all over Italy, the rural middle class, from which the legions were recruited and which was the very nerve of the military power of Rome, began to decline. Italy was invaded by *latifundia*, and with them came large areas of pasturage and a servile population freely imported from oversea. The great landowners were flourishing on the military decadence of Rome. Tiberius Gracchus said about this time that, though the wild beasts had their dens, those who fought and died for Italy had nothing to bless themselves with but the air they breathed. The question of the military levies became, in fact, graver every day. Now, whenever there was any chance of a really serious war, all sorts of expedients were necessary in order to secure soldiers.

This strange situation, owing to which Rome found herself obliged to preserve and extend her empire with diminished forces, explains the unrest of public opinion, the panics to which it so often gave way, and its frequent outbursts of irritation. Rome was afraid of her own power, though the many victories she had gained over her numerous foes might have sufficed to tranquillize her. True, she had conquered this time once again, but with what an effort! And then if Macedonia, Carthage, and Greece had,

[1] Polyb., ii., 15.

for good or ill, been overcome, Viriathus gave them no peace in Spain, and the war went on implacably. From 145 it had again to be entrusted to the command of one of the consuls. It seemed that Rome would soon perish like Carthage if the aristocracy had not the wisdom to return to the ancient simplicity of life, if the Romans did not remember that the first duty of the citizen is to produce a large family; above all if something were not done to prevent the ruin of the lower and middle-class landowners, the reservoir of the soldiers who had conquered both Italy and the empire. These were the ideas which after the fall of Carthage stirred the enthusiasm of the better part of the Roman nobility which gathered round Scipio Æmilianus, now the leading figure in Rome.

These ideas very soon emerged from the restricted circle of private conversations. In 145 the tribune C. Licinius Crassus proposed an agrarian law with the object of reconstituting the system of small holdings[1] and, shortly before or shortly after this, the prætor Caius Lælius, an intimate friend of Scipio and his *legatus* in the Carthaginian war, brought forward a similar measure. We do not know what its leading provisions were; we are only told that it excited so much opposition in the senate that Lælius, in spite of Scipio's support, dropped the bill, a proceeding which earned him the title of *Sapiens*—the sage.[2] This compliment reveals the insoluble self-contradiction of the times. The evil was thoroughly diagnosed, the remedies fully discussed. Up to this point everyone agreed. But, when it came to taking action, the vested interests took alarm and there were always so

[1] Varro, *Re Rust.*, i., 2, 9.
[2] *Cf.* Plut., *Tib. Gracch.*, 8.

many plausible reasons for putting aside any remedies that might be suggested, that the wisest doctor seemed to be he who renounced the use of them.

Thus things went from bad to worse. All wise men agreed that it was necessary to curb the spirit of greed which now pervaded the mass of the people. But it was found that no plans or undertakings succeeded except those the effect of which was to intensify it. Most of what is now Piedmont was still independent of Rome, nor had any of the tribes composing it ever given any pretext for Roman aggression. But one of these tribes, the Salassi, possessed auriferous land, and, in 143, the consul Appius Claudius during the unsuccessful campaign against Numantia made an entirely unprovoked attack on them, took away part of their gold mine, and handed it over to be worked by a company of publicans. Victumulæ near Vercellæ became henceforth a flourishing centre of the gold industry.[1]

68. Disasters and Scandals of the Spanish War: Numantia. This was a weary and depressing period in which Rome had the feeling that things were going wrong and that there was no means of putting them right. A disconsolate pessimism invaded the upper classes and stimulated the germs of discord which were already plentiful. Feuds and vendettas among the great families became envenomed, and were exasperated still more by the truly scandalous incidents of the Spanish war. Sometimes victorious and sometimes vanquished, but always in the field, Viriathus gave the Romans no peace, but, on the

[1] On the Salassi and the auriferous mines of Piedmont in antiquity, *cf.* Polyb., xxxiv., 10–18; Strab., v., 1, 12; Plin., *Hist. Nat.*, xxxiii., 4, 78.

contrary, enlarged the area of rebellion. Between 143 and 142 he again succeeded in stirring up against Rome the Arevacæ, the Titti, and the Belli, the three tribes among whom the Spanish revolt had first begun years before. The city of Numantia was the central point of the new war. It seemed as if all had to be begun over again, and that all the blood and treasure expended by Rome on the conquest of Spain had been thrown away!

The discouragement at Rome was so great that, during the year 141, the proconsul Q. Fabius Maximus Servilianus, who was in command in Spain and was reputed a wise man, entered into negotiations with Viriathus and concluded with him an honourable peace, which he succeeded in inducing the comitia to ratify. The Lusitanians being pacified, all that remained was to reduce Numantia. In 140, however, Q. Servilius Cæpio, the brother of Fabius, became consul and intrigued so energetically that he persuaded the senate to allow him to recommence the war with Viriathus—at the very moment when the consul Q. Pompeius Rufus had been beaten by the Numantines. The war was on the point of breaking out again with all its former violence when Servilius Cæpio managed to get the better of Viriathus by having him murdered by hired assassins.

Viriathus having been removed by treachery, the resistance of the Lusitanians soon declined. Their army melted away, and what was left of it was satisfied by the grant of lands in the neighbourhood of Valentia. But the means by which this victory had been procured were not such as to encourage the Romans to carry on the war against the other Spanish peoples. At the end of 140, therefore, Q. Pompeius opened negotiations with Numantia. The Spaniards knew that they could not conquer Rome and were willing to discuss terms. Peace was accordingly concluded, on what terms we do not know, but there must have been special provisions for the Numantines if they consented to give hostages and pay an indemnity.

M. Popilius Lænas, the successor of Pompeius, arrived at the beginning of 139, after this peace had been made. But thereupon Pompeius, either because he had negotiated only to prevent any further attack on him until his successor arrived, or because at the last moment he feared that his treaty might not be ratified at Rome, denied that he had ever treated with the Numantines. The resulting scandal may easily be imagined! The Numantines cited as witnesses to their contention the senators, prætors, and military tribunes who had taken part in the negotiations. A violent controversy followed, which was cut short by Popilius Lænas, who referred both parties—Numantines, on the one side, and Pompeius, on the other—to the judgment of the senate. The discussion was recommenced at Rome and, as may be imagined, it was bitter. In the result it was decided that Pompeius had negotiated and concluded peace, but that the senate could not ratify the promises he had made. A law providing that Pompeius should be handed over to the Numantines was not passed.

It is not difficult to understand the disgust with which so disgraceful an affair was viewed by the better part of the population, who were distressed to think that Rome could have sunk so low. But the mischief was done. The war flared up again furiously in Spain. Popilius Lænas had done practically nothing, as the greater part of the year 139 had passed while the discussion about the treaty was proceeding at Rome. But hostilities were recommenced as soon as the senate had declared that there was to be no peace with the Numantines, and in 137 Rome experienced a new and tremendous disaster. The consul C. Hostilius Mancinus was defeated and his army of twenty thousand men surrounded. In order to save them from destruction, it was necessary to ratify the treaty of peace which the Numantines offered. This time, however, the Numantines, who had learned by experience, refused to agree to the treaty unless a certain quæstor in the Roman army, Tiberius Sempronius Gracchus, would guarantee its ratification at Rome. Gracchus was the son of the consul of the same name who had held office in 177 and in 163, and who had administered Spain with humanity and justice, leaving golden memories behind him among the Spanish population, who regarded him with veneration. The younger Gracchus was related to Scipio Æmilianus, who in a certain sense was responsible for his upbringing; he was the son-in-law of Appius Claudius, the consul of 143, and thus he represented all the better elements that survived among the Roman aristocracy. The Numantines, therefore, trusted him. They were mistaken. When the conditions of peace were known at Rome, public opinion was unanimous in declaring them unacceptable. The authority of the Gracchi went for nothing, and even their influential relations like Scipio could not entertain the view that a family pledge should bind the republic. The two consuls of 136 proposed to the people that the treaty should be rejected and this was approved.

The war accordingly went on, but spasmodically. In 136 and 135, the Roman armies, if they escaped conspicuous defeat, failed to accomplish anything of importance. But that the government should refuse peace without knowing how to make war was too much for the patience of the Roman public, whose eyes again turned to Scipio Æmilianus. Scipio, however, was absent on a mission to the East, which had been entrusted to him by the senate. Moreover, the interval required by the law between his first election to the office of consul and re-election to that office had not elapsed. Public opinion, on this occasion, as before, swept aside these obstacles. A special law was passed and Scipio was elected consul for 134. He left at once for Spain where he found the army in a parlous condition. The camps were full of prostitutes, traders, and slaves. The soldiers had accustomed themselves to the use of hot baths. It was necessary, as it had been before Carthage, to re-establish discipline and to teach his troops the elements of their business. Fortunately the army had still a few good officers, among others a certain Caius Marius, a tax farmer, who, after having failed at his business, had taken to soldiering, and who was certainly born to handle steel rather than gold.

69. **The Tribunate and the Agrarian Law of Tiberius Gracchus (133 B.C.).** While Scipio was preparing to bring the war with Spain to a decisive conclusion, a series of grave events had occurred at Rome. The year 133 was to be memorable in history. Tiberius Sempronius Gracchus, the youth who as quæstor had vainly guaranteed to the Numantines the treaty of peace concluded with the consul Mancinus, had been elected tribune for this year. Like

many of the nobility he had been alarmed by the crisis which threatened alike the small landholders and the army. But while others were content with unfruitful lamentations, he decided to take action. Either the increasing gravity of the evil gave the final impulse to a nature more ardent and more prompt in decision than those of his contemporaries, or his youth prevented him from realizing the difficulties of the enterprise; or again he may have been embittered by the affront put upon himself and his family by the senate and the people when they refused to sanction the peace made by Mancinus. However this may be, it is certain that as tribune of the people in 133 he took up again the idea which had been so lightly abandoned by Caius Lælius.

His agrarian law of that year, the first which had been worthy of the name since the Licinio-Sestian measure of 367, was chiefly inspired by the anxieties of the traditionalist party. True the peninsula contained no public lands of which disposal could still be made. But the vast domains in Italy which the rich had hired or usurped might, as *ager publicus*, be legally resumed by the State. If, after they had been resumed, the State could redistribute them in small allotments to the poor of Italy, would not the gravest of all Italian problems—nay the only problem which Gracchus recognized—be solved, and would not Italy again become a country of small cultivators and gallant soldiers?

His concrete proposals were: (I) That no Roman citizen should be allowed to hold more than 500 jugera of public land, or more than 750 if he had only one son, or more than 1000 as a maximum if he had two or more sons. Within these limits the public land was to become the absolute property of the citizens and was to be exempt from tribute. (II) That the State should reclaim from every Roman citizen all public land occupied by him in excess of the prescribed quantity, but should indemnify the occupier for all expenses incurred by him in breaking up the land or introducing improvements. (III) That the Latins and the allies should similarly be deprived of public land illicitly or irregularly acquired, without prejudice to their right to participate on equal terms with the Roman proletariat in the new distributions. (IV) That all public lands made available for distribution by the operation of the law should be distributed in small allotments, probably of 30 jugera each, which should be inalienable and charged with a yearly payment to the State. (V) That the application of the law should be entrusted to a special commission, consisting of three members to be elected annually by the comitia tributa—*tres viri agris iudicandis adsignandis*. This body was to proceed to measure out and thereafter to distribute the domanial lands, and was given power, in the event of a dispute, to hear the case and to pronounce sentence without appeal.[1]

The principle of the law was not entirely new, but its provisions were much more thoroughgoing than those of the Licinio-Sestian law, which it explicitly repealed. It met with the fiercest opposition. The reception it got from the senate is comprehensible, if we assume that the majority of the members of that body were in occupation of great tracts of public land in excess of the quantity allowed under the pro-

---

[1] For an illustration of Tiberius's agrarian law, *cf.* E. de Ruggiero, *Agrariæ leges* in *Enciclopedia giuridica italiana*, i., 2, pp. 798–808.

posed law. This is all the more probable as we have already seen that the *ager publicus* was traditionally the share of the spoils of war with which the senatorial aristocracy compensated themselves for the risks and fatigues of a campaign. But, if the senators and the rich knights were the first to suffer, the law was no less threatening to many of the Latins and the allies. They were to be compelled to prove their title to landed property in their occupation which had been handed down from one generation to another, sold, regularly acquired, pledged for debts, given as dowries, divided, subdivided, and consolidated again with other lands assigned and received at other times. Lands, moreover, which had been regularly assigned were often confused with others occupied without regular allotment, and in both kinds vast capital sums had been invested, and frequently much labour had been expended on them.

Tiberius's law, therefore, could not be put in force without causing an infinite number of lawsuits, confiscations, and bankruptcies. It meant the complete overthrow of many private fortunes, and, what was more serious, the practical annulment of federal compacts with the allies, which no Roman law had ever before had power to vary. The fact, therefore, that one of Gracchus's colleagues, M. Octavius Cæcina, vetoed the law is in itself no proof that Octavius was himself in occupation of great tracts of public land or that he was in the pay of those who were. Gracchus had, however, kindled a great conflagration which it was no longer in his power to quench. His adversaries were many and determined, but his law had been received with great enthusiasm by the remains of the old Roman peasantry, by the urban lower classes and, generally speaking, by all the poor who, then as always, were ready to blame the rapacity of the rich for the misery they had to endure. He had also on his side a certain number of senators who either had no great amount of public land or who placed the good of the State above their private loss. All these formed a great party and, what was more than a party, a great current of public opinion, which drove Tiberius before it.

To the obstruction of Octavius, Gracchus, when he saw that all his entreaties and arguments were vain, retorted by calling on the people to remove his colleague from office. Was this an unprecedented and revolutionary proceeding? It was not unprecedented for it had been done more than once in times both recent and remote, and that on the initiative of the senatorial assembly. But Gracchus found a new justification for his action which gave it a revolutionary character. The duty of a tribune of the people, he said, is to defend the people. If he fails in this duty, the people who appoint him can deprive him of office. In other words, the tribunes' right of veto must no longer be used, as had often happened in recent times, in the service of the aristocracy and the party of the rich. This theory could not but meet with general acceptance at a time of popular commotion, and Octavius was deposed by a unanimous vote of the tribes. After his deposition the law was passed, and its execution entrusted to the best of all possible commissions, which consisted of Tiberius himself, his brother Caius, and his father-in-law Appius Claudius, one of the few senators who were favourable to the tribune's proposals. To simplify the great difficulties in the reckoning, Tiberius had ended by omit-ting the clause providing for an indemnity, by which he had vainly tried to placate the opposition of the interested parties.

70. The Testament of Attalus and the New Province of Asia (133 B.C.). In the midst of these agitations and struggles, there arrived at Rome a curious piece of news. Attalus III., King of Pergamus, had died and, having no sons, he left Rome his kingdom, or rather, he handed over to the republic all the numerous and varied rights which he exercised over the Greek cities and the native races. How and why, and as the result of what intrigues the last king of a dynasty which had prospered as a client of Rome, conceived this singular idea we do not know. But Fortune seemed determined to put Roman wisdom to a severe test. At the very moment when it was proposed by means of Gracchus's drastic law to reconstitute the ancient rustic and warlike Italy in the heart of her own peninsula, fortune was offering, as a free gift, one of the richest domains in the ancient world, in which flourished all the arts and sciences, and traffic in all the things which were blamed for corrupting the healthy tissues of primitive times!

The kingdom of Attalus was not large, but how rich it was! Through it passed all the most frequented trade routes between the East and the West. Chaldea, Phœnicia, Syria, Persia, India sent incense, cassia, resin, myrrh, aloes, cinnamon, sugar, tortoise-shell, diamonds, sapphires, emeralds, amethysts, topazes, pearls, textiles, yarn of cotton and of wool, dyed stuffs, silk, indigo, ebony, teak, nard, purple, glass, crystal, all the treasures of India and all the rarities of China which fed the luxuries of the Mediterranean countries. The soil was fertile beyond compare. Here were contracts to farm, tribute and taxes on the land, customs and excise duties to collect, more valuable than in any other province of the empire. Here for a century and a half had reigned in splendour, the richest, the most cultured, and perhaps the most generous of the Hellenistic courts. To its liberality we owe to-day the latest masterpieces of Greek sculpture and architecture, such as the famous frieze of the Giants in the Berlin Museum, which formed the decoration of a colossal altar sacred to Zeus and Athena, the Dying Gaul in the Capitoline Museum at Rome, or the group wrongly named Arria and Pætus in the Villa Ludovisi.

It required no prophet to see that the gift of Attalus would be a fatal one, at any rate if its consequences were to be judged according to the ideas which moved Tiberius Gracchus and his friends to propose the agrarian law. By accepting it the republic was setting foot in the East, the region which, in the eyes of the Roman traditionalists of the school of Cato and Scipio Æmilianus, was the perilous home of the corruption which they feared so much. Furthermore, an opportunity was offered for the extension of Roman commerce, that other vehicle for dangerous riches and evil examples. To increase commerce and the number of points of contact with the Orient, and to restore the ancient rustic simplicity of Italy, were two contradictory propositions. Tiberius Gracchus and his party, to be strictly logical, should, therefore, have advised Rome to refuse the gift, as after Cynoscephalæ she had refused Macedonia and Greece. But the generation which lamented the disappearance of the warlike rusticity of the antique days no longer had the strength to put aside the temptations of power and riches. Neither the man nor the party existed that could have persuaded Rome to make such a renunciation. Tiberius was less qualified than any one for such a task, for he was menaced by all the powerful interests he had injured and against which his only defence was to create new interests. Driven by this necessity he did not scruple to make use even of the testament of Attalus, and proposed that the treasures bequeathed to the Romans by the late King of Pergamus should be used to furnish the poorer of the new colonists with agricultural implements, and that the organization of the new province, which was to be known by the name of Asia, should be handed over to the people. The first proposal, to provide implements, was opportune; but the second, which deprived the senate of the control of the new province, was highly revolutionary, for it threatened one of the most ancient and important prerogatives of that assembly. New struggles and disputes arose, therefore, on this point, adding fuel to the flames of hatred and a new venom to the accusations which were bandied about.

Meanwhile most of the official year had passed away and it was necessary to arrange for holding new tribunician elections. According to law no term of office could be renewed; but if Tiberius ceased to be tribune, the application of the agrarian law could make no progress. Moreover, it was necessary that he should be elected in order to escape the prosecution for subverting the constitution which his adversaries, in view of the deposition of Octavius, would in all probability launch against him. Tiberius, who was certainly of a somewhat rash disposition, and who had been driven much farther than he originally intended by the exigencies of the situation, decided to stand again. This audacity frightened his friends. The Romans were slaves of convention, especially political convention. The election of the same tribune twice in succession was a thing unheard of for many a day. Tiberius's enemies had a splendid opening. Many of his friends abandoned him and others vacillated.

The election took place in the month of July, the month devoted to the harvest. Many small holders who would certainly have voted for Gracchus could not come to Rome. His adversaries made a tremendous effort. Nevertheless, the voting of the tribes at first went in his favour, so much so that his opponents feared he would succeed and set up the claim that the votes cast for him were null and void. A tribune could not be re-elected; therefore his election was bad. This caused a riot. The comitia were thrown into confusion, and immediately a group of senators, with Scipio Nasica at their head, pressingly invited the consul to do his duty and repress the revolution which was being attempted by Tiberius and his partisans.

Scipio Nasica was a great landed proprietor, but he had also been a determined opponent of the destruction of Carthage. This friend of peace had, perhaps, been less truly responsible for the Italian crisis than the Catonian generation that supported Tiberius and had insisted on Carthage being razed to the ground. Yet he now demanded what the Roman State had only allowed very rarely in cases of extreme danger at the time of the great struggle between the patricians and the plebeians,—that is to say, the proclamation of martial law, the *senatus consultum ultimum* as it was soon to be called. This meant that a state of siege was to be proclaimed because of a trifling disturbance caused by an election of doubtful legality.[1] The consul did not dare to comply with the requisition, and accordingly Nasica himself with a band of senators and knights, supported by their clients and their slaves, issued from the Temple of Fides where the senate was sitting and threw themselves on the crowd, which was divided into two parties and still tumultuous. After a feeble and brief resistance, Tiberius and three hundred of his supporters were killed (133).

71. **The Destruction of Numantia and the End of the Spanish War (134–133 B.C.).** Thus ended the first serious attempt to arrest the development of that "corruption of manners" which threatened to bring Rome to ruin before the eyes of her wisest citizens. To the timid and wavering attempts of Tiberius at revolution, the vested interests, entrenched in the citadel of the senate, had replied by an act of resolute and open violence. How powerful these interests were and how infuriated by the proposals of Gracchus was proved by the success of their unprecedented act of violence. Nasica was a man of authority; the senate was the highest power in the State. Once Tiberius was crushed, everyone came to the conclusion that he had attempted to subvert public order by force and had, therefore, deserved his fate. Even Scipio Æmilianus, who was then engaged in besieging Numantia, took this view. The party of Tiberius was dispersed by terrorism.

But the work of the unfortunate tribune was not

[1] On the *senatus consultum ultimum*, *cf.* Barbagallo, in *Rivista di filologia classica* (1912), p. 49.

entirely destroyed. After his death the commission entrusted with the application of the agrarian law proceeded to northern, central, and southern Italy, and endeavoured to reconstitute the ancient *ager publicus* which had been usurped. They did not allow themselves to be discouraged by the difficulties of all sorts which the lapse of time, vested interests, and the duplicity of mankind had thrown in their way. The *cippi*, or terminal stones, precisely defining the limits of the *ager publicus* and the *ager privatis*, which were set up between one estate and another and were marked with the names of the triumviri,[1] still testify to their labours. Another fact which the partiality of ancient historians cannot distort bears a still more eloquent testimony to their achievement. Whereas since the year 164–163 the number of Roman citizens had been declining, that number in the single generation between 131–130 and 115–114 grew by more than 75,000, amounting to 394,336 as against 317,823. This was certainly due, at least in part, to Tiberius's law.[2] "The land," as was in later days observed by one of the most implacable opponents of the Gracchan party, "had been rescued from the shepherd in order to be restored to the plough."[3]

In 133, the year in which Tiberius Gracchus tried to restore by law the antique rural and warlike efficiency of Italy, Scipio Æmilianus succeeded in taking and destroying Numantia, thus finally ending the terrible Spanish war. A commission of senators, acting with Scipio, reorganized the country and reestablished the government as in 197. Under this settlement Spain was divided into two provinces,

---

[1] C. I. L., i., 552–556, 583; 1504; ix., 1024–26.
[2] *Cf.* Liv., *Epit.* lix., lxiii.   [3] C. I. L., i., 551.

Hispania Citerior and Hispania Ulterior, separated by the Sierra Morena (*Saltus Castulonensis*) and each under the rule of a prætor.

Meanwhile a new war had arisen in the ancient kingdom of Pergamus. Time had been lost owing to the dispute between Tiberius and the senate about the control of the new province. A certain Aristonicus, who appears to have been an illegitimate son of Eumenes, seized the opportunity to claim the kingdom. He collected men and money, freed the slaves, and won over all the friends and artisans of the extinct dynasty. He played his cards so well that the kings of Bithynia, Paphlagonia, and the two Cappadocias, who were allies of Rome and had, as such, been requested to deliver the province from the usurper, failed in their attempts to do so. It was necessary to send troops from Italy, and these had the worst of the first encounters, in which one of the consuls lost his life. It was not, in fact, till 129 that Manius Aquilius, the consul of that year, succeeded in recovering the new province.

In spite of all, however, so rich a spoil was never secured at so low a price. The republic had all at once become an Asiatic power and occupied a position in Asia beside the two great monarchies formed from the fragments of the empire of Alexander. This was a decisive step, and all the more serious because it had not been preceded by a long preparation. At the moment, however, no one at Rome seems to have realized its significance. Internal questions monopolized public attention. The application of the agrarian law gave rise to, or rather exacerbated, a very serious question. We have seen how Tiberius's law provided for Roman citizens—justly perhaps, but at the expense of the Latins and the Italians. They were all deprived of the public land which they had unjustifiably occupied; but only some of them could participate in the new distributions, for Roman citizens were to have a preference and Latins and Italians were only to have what the Romans left. Too many Italians had received a sterile tract of marshy ground in exchange for a fine farm planted with vines and olives.

The evil was all the more serious because for some time political discontent had been smouldering and growing among the Latins and the Italians. Since the end of the first Punic War no new Roman tribes had been formed. The new municipia or colonies to which Roman citizenship had been granted had been incorporated in a limited number of the existing tribes. At the same time grants of the rights of citizenship had become rarer. The Latins, who had immigrated into Rome, and had for many lustres enjoyed these rights in practice, had little by little been removed from the lists of the citizens. The Latins who had enrolled themselves in the colonies of Roman citizens and who thought that they had acquired the same rights by long prescription were similarly disappointed. Rome had not only become more jealous of the privilege of her citizenship but harsher in the exercise of her metropolitan jurisdiction. Since she had risen to be a world power she had become too much accustomed to treat Italy as a province, and this at the very time when she was compelled to levy a larger tribute of blood than in the past. The agrarian law was the crowning stroke and its effect may easily be imagined.

The opposition of the Latins and the Italians to

the agrarian law was too serious a development not to produce an immediate effect at Rome. The adversaries of the measure profited by it to renew the struggle, and, thanks to the Italians, they were able to secure the support of Scipio Æmilianus, the greatest personage of the day. Scipio was favourably disposed to the Italians, of whose work in Spain and Africa he had seen much, and he well knew that they were now the mainstay of the military power of Rome. In 129, therefore, he intervened in their favour, using his influence to secure the passage of a law depriving the commission of the powers which had given rise to so much contention, and transferring these powers to the consuls. From this it may be presumed that the consuls would almost always be against agrarian laws, and would be glad to leave in suspense the interminable questions of the legality of this or that occupier's title, thus, in fact, paralysing the work of the commission. This indirect concession, however, did not satisfy the Latins and the Italians, who wished for the abolition of the law, and who flocked to Rome in hordes to protest against it and to defend their interests. The supporters of the law, on the other hand, who had been dispersed but not destroyed by the death of Tiberius, closed their ranks again and rushed to the aid of the threatened statute. The struggle became furious. Scipio himself was threatened by the partisans of the law, and, as he died suddenly in the middle of the controversy, the friends of Tiberius were accused of having murdered him to gratify party spite.

For a moment, indeed, the partisans of the law hesitated whether it would not be best to cut short the opposition of the Latins and the Italians by an act of force. In 126 the tribune Marcus Junius Pennus proposed to expel them all from Rome. Fortunately wiser and more conciliatory counsels prevailed. The consul-designate for 125 was Fulvius Flaccus, a senator who had been a friend of Tiberius and who was warmly in favour of the agrarian law. Flaccus proposed a law granting Roman citizenship to all the Italians who claimed it, and to those who did not want it he proposed to give the privilege of *provocatio*, hitherto reserved for Roman citizens alone, which would enable those upon whom it had been conferred to appeal to the comitia centuriata against any sentence of corporal punishment passed by a Roman magistrate.[1]

The object of the law is clear. It was intended to compensate the Italians for the losses inflicted on them by the agrarian law by making a political concession of great value to the Italians and at the same time useful to Rome. Italians and Romans would have been made one single people with equal rights. But the proposal came too soon. We know that neither the senate nor the comitia accepted it and that it was, therefore, abandoned by the consul. The Roman oligarchy was too egotistical and proud to extend its precious privilege so widely. An insurrection at Fregellæ, in protest against the abandonment of the proposal, was not enough to shake the obstinacy of that oligarchy. But the problem was stated, and it was soon to be taken up again by Caius Gracchus, the greatest statesman of his time.

72. **Caius Gracchus (123–121 B.C.).** Three years after the failure of Fulvius Flaccus's proposal, Caius Gracchus, the brother of Tiberius, was elected tribune

[1] App. *B. C.*, i., 34.

of the people at a meeting of the assembly of the tribes attended by an unprecedented number of electors from town and country. Caius had been present at the fatal scene in 133. He had been a member of the commission charged with bringing his brother's law into operation. He, too, had been persecuted by his political opponents, who controlled the senate, and who had first tried to keep him away from Rome by shutting him up in a perpetual proquæstorship in Sardinia, and then to ruin him by accusing him of complicity in the insurrection of Fregellæ. But, though sorrow and rancour may have been secretly consuming his heart, Caius was not a man to waste his term of office as tribune in a policy of reprisals. He wished to continue his brother's work, but to continue it in the only way in which a man of intelligence can carry on the activities of a predecessor, namely by enlarging its scope and bringing it to completion. What had been the lesson of the struggles and the agitations of the previous ten years? That the agrarian law of Tiberius had yielded but few of the advantages hoped for, because, on the one hand, the senatorial aristocracy and, on the other the Italians and the Latins, had done their best to impede its operation. It was clear, therefore, that the policy of the agrarian law required to be recast in such a way as to restrict the power of the aristocracy and of the senate and at the same time appease the just complaints of the Italians.

Each of these objects implied the other. But how was it possible to restrict the power of the aristocracy and the senate, which since the second Punic War had become the supreme arbiter of the republic? Caius Gracchus was too intelligent to attempt to imitate the policy of Caius Flaminius and to rely on the common people, the small holders, and, generally speaking, the poorer classes. Times were changed. The senate was now too powerful in riches, culture, and prestige. A stronger weapon was needed. Caius Gracchus cast his eye, therefore, on the knights, that second order of nobility, which included the citizens who were not senators but who possessed fortunes of at least four hundred thousand sesterces, and whose membership comprised so many rich publicans and well-to-do merchants and landowners. Two aristocracies cannot live side by side and treat each other as equals, and as the purse-proud knights had for some time back been unwilling to submit as they had formerly done to being regarded as the inferiors of the senate, it may have seemed to Caius that it would be easy to weaken the senate by arming against it the equestrian order.

The method he adopted to secure his object was skilfully chosen. One of the most important prerogatives of the senate was its jurisdiction in criminal matters. For the various *quæstiones perpetuæ* the *iudices*—juries as we should call them—selected annually by lot to decide each class of charge, consisted of senators alone. It was at this point that Caius Gracchus launched his first attack. He proposed a *lex iudiciara*, which provided that the *quæstiones* should be composed no longer of senators but of knights. The political motives of the proposal were cleverly cloaked by an appeal to the principles of justice. The most important of the *quæstiones* was the *quæstio de pecuniis repetundis*, which was instituted, as we have seen, in 149 to try cases of malversation. Such cases involved sums of money alleged to have been improperly received by magistrates in connection with some branch of the public service, and included cases of provincial governors accused of corrupt practices. Cases of this kind had of late become so frequent that public opinion called for severe measures. In this very year another tribune, Manius Acilius Glabrio, had brought forward the elaborate *Lex Acilia de repetundis*. Now the governors of provinces were all senators, and was it to be expected that senators would apply the law strictly to their own colleagues? If the law was not to be a dead letter, senators should be tried by men belonging to a different order, such as the knights.

Caius, however, was not content with this first proposal. The Roman Government had not yet settled the taxation of the new province of Asia. It had to choose between the fixed impost adopted in the case of Africa and the proportional system which had already been tried in Sicily. Each of the two systems had its advantages and its disadvantages for the State; but the hundred and more years of the provincial régime in Sicily had proved that the proportional impost secured enormous profits to the publicani who farmed it. By a second law Caius proposed that the Sicilian system should be adopted for Asia, and that the contracts for collecting excise duties of the province—in a word all the taxes of the country—should be assigned to the Roman knights.

By these two laws Caius might hope to attract to his party the whole equestrian order. He next proceeded to devise a series of provisions which would in one way or another be of advantage to the lower classes and thus unite the whole people in one compact party. Before all he intended to rescue his brother's agrarian law from the lethargy into which it had fallen, by restoring to the triumvirs the judicial powers which Scipio had transferred to the consuls. But the agrarian law benefited only the peasantry and the poorest class of landholder. It meant nothing to the urban proletariat, which had much increased at Rome and which, being resident in the city, was very powerful in the comitia. For this class Caius provided by a *lex frumentaria*. This law provided that every month in Rome the State should sell corn at less than the current price, and that only persons officially recognized as poor should be able to buy it. Perhaps he also intended that the State should make large purchases of grain in Italy and so assist Italian agriculture, and, by ordering the construction of vast granaries at Rome, should give work to the small contractors and the artisans. The interests of these latter classes as well as those of agriculture, were studied in a further law, the *lex viaria*, a grandiose project of new roads to be built in various parts of Italy, with a view to helping farmers to sell to greater advantage products which could thereby be transported to more distant markets.

To these he added a *lex militaris*, which forbade the enrolment of any Roman citizen before he was seventeen years of age, and obliged the treasury to pay for the soldiers' kit. This law was bound to be extremely popular with the lower orders both in the town and in the country.

Rome had never yet seen a body of laws so well thought out, and so skilfully interrelated, and all intended to help the multitude in despite of the great. Caius became in a moment the idol of the plebs, the favourite of the knights, and the head of such a formidable coalition of interests that all opposition melted away. The tribune was able to pass all his laws through the comitia tributa without first asking for the approval of the senate. He was able, also, to put them into immediate operation, hiring out the contracts for building granaries and roads, which he caused to be constructed on a scale of hitherto unheard of magnificence. All day long he gave his attention tirelessly to a thousand things, making his house the rendezvous of the publicani, of the men of letters, and the savants of Rome, and the hope and rallying place of the multitude.

The landowning oligarchy of the senate raged in silent fury. The influence and the popularity of Caius were so great that he was able to try again with success where his brother had failed, and to secure his re-election as tribune for the year 122. Tiberius had set an example which Caius followed for a better reason than mere personal ambition. One reason for the impotence of the democratic party had been the brevity of the term of office for the various magistrates. If the republic was to renew its youth, new principles and new methods were necessary. The people understood this and Caius was re-elected.

Triumphantly re-elected tribune for the second time, he found himself at the height of his power and popularity, and in the full flood of public work, at that unique moment in the career of a great public man at which his power, under whatever name it may pass, has something of an absolute character. He seemed, indeed (and it must have occurred to many to make the comparison), to be the Pericles of the Roman republic in which, and perhaps not unconsciously, he had accomplished many things that recalled the Athens of the second half of the fifth century— the democratization of the courts, the subventions in kind to the urban proletariat, the impulse which had been given to public works. But the laws he passed during his first tribunate were for Caius merely a preparation for the two capital reforms which he regarded as a radical cure for the evils of the time.

Rome was growing too large. Too many artisans, merchants, artists, savants, adventurers, and beggars were crowded together from all parts of the world into the new metropolis. This led to evils of all kinds, the greatest of which were the high price of bread and excessive rents. The *lex frumentaria* was a remedy not without its dangers, in view of the great expense to a treasury already swamped by the Spanish war. It was necessary to lighten Rome by inducing some of the Roman merchants to transfer themselves from the capital to other cities convenient for navigation and commerce; for then many of the poorer class would follow them to their new abode. Caius chose for this purpose three points on the Mediterranean coast. Of these Scylaceum (Squillace) already had a custom house for imports from Asia. Tarentum had long been famous for its trade and its riches. For the merchants who traded with Greece, Macedonia, and the Orient would not Tarentum and Scylaceum, renamed Neptunia, and Minervia, be more convenient places of residence than Rome? The African trade (or at any rate the little that had survived the ruin of Carthage) had passed into the hands of Roman merchants, who could have established themselves more conveniently in Africa than at Rome. Many had, in fact, settled at Cirta. Was it not possible to rebuild from the ruins of the Punic city a new Roman Carthage, which should be known as Junonia? At Scylaceum, Tarentum, and Carthage, therefore, he proposed to found three colonies, not of poor people as had been the practice of old, but of persons of good position[1] to whom vast estates should be granted in order to make them willing to leave Rome.

These proposals were also passed, though it would seem with some reluctance, for the emptying of Rome was likely to injure many people. Finally, however, Caius was bold enough to express his supreme idea, long meditated in silence. He wished to grant Roman citizenship to all the Italians, as had already been proposed by his friend Fulvius Flaccus, and thus to give new strength to the little oligarchy of Rome, which resembled a slender column worn by time and storms, on which improvident architects had piled an ever-increasing fabric. The design conceived by Caius was, in a word, to base the empire, not on the cupidity and pride of the narrow Roman oligarchy, but on the solid and simple virtue of the rural population of all Italy, to restore the ancient seats of ruined and decadent commerce, and to relieve Rome of the congestion of riches and population from which she was suffering.

Rome had not yet seen, and was never again to see, a reformer possessing ideas more profoundly organic and creative. If one man had been able to perform a task which only several generations could accomplish, Caius Gracchus would have regenerated Rome and solved the perennial problem with which she

[1] Plut., *C. Gracchus*, 9. *Cf.* also E. Callegari, *La legislazione sociale di C. Gracco*, Padua, 1896, p. 99.

was wrestling. But he was merely a great man, not
a god. When he proposed to grant the citizenship
to the Italians, Gracchus had passed the bounds which
must be respected even by men as great and powerful as he. Although the proposer of the law was on
this occasion a man to whom so many owed admiration and gratitude, the opposition which had constrained Fulvius Flaccus to abandon his proposals
revived. The senate, the knights, the farmers, the
urban proletariat, all found themselves this time
united in opposition to Caius Gracchus. Hatred of
innovation, pride of privilege, the selfishness of threatened interests, prevailed over every other consideration. The Roman oligarchy had no intention of
sacrificing their privileges. When the tribune Livius
Drusus vetoed the proposal, the people who had deposed Octavius broke into clamorous applause; the
popularity of Caius Gracchus began to totter. To
make matters worse, Caius had agreed to join the
commission appointed to conduct the new colony to
Carthage, and had, therefore, to leave Rome at this
critical moment, although a tribune of the people
was by law forbidden to leave the city. He tried to
force the pace and decided to return within seventy
days. But his absence gave his enemies the opportunity of ruining completely what remained of his
popularity.

Their instrument was the tribune Livius Drusus,
who with perfidious cleverness proposed three roga-
tions much more generous in their scope than those
of Caius. One of these promised the people, not
three colonies, composed of a mixture of poor and
well-to-do persons, but twelve, entirely recruited
from the proletariat. Another made the new allot-

ments of public land exempt from the tribute to the State required by the Lex Sempronia. The third abolished corporal punishment for all Italians, even when under arms. The fickle and foolish populace fell into the trap and was easily persuaded that the senate and the oligarchical party to which Drusus belonged had turned over a new leaf, and had become more truly their friend than Caius Gracchus, who wished to compel them to share their privilege of citizenship with the Latins and the Italians, whom he liked better than Roman citizens.

When Caius returned from Africa, popular favour had so completely deserted him that his enemies began to aim at no less than the repeal of the law founding the colony of New Carthage. They commenced, indeed, to prepare the public mind for this by whispering of threatening prodigies seen by the first band of colonists—a sure sign of the impiety of those who had dared to affront the anger of the gods by founding a colony on the accursed soil of Carthage.

It is not surprising, therefore, that the elections of the year 121 were unfavourable to Caius. He may not have presented himself as a candidate; in any case he was not re-elected. Worse still, the consul who was elected was Lucius Opimius, one of the most implacable and violent of his enemies. Encouraged by the result, his adversaries decided to strike their first blow at his work. The tribune Minucius Rufus proposed the abrogation of the law relating to the Carthaginian colony. Caius could not refuse the challenge, and, on the day on which the vote was to be taken, he went to the comitia to defend, at least by a speech, what had been one of the noblest and most fertile measures in his political career. But men's minds were in a ferment. Once more a tumult arose. And once more his opponents in the senate exhorted the consul, as Scipio Nasica had vainly done ten years before, to declare the country in danger, to proclaim a state of siege, and to treat a trifling riot as an attempt at revolution.

This time however, the consul was Lucius Opimius, who did not wait to be pressed. The *senatus consultum ultimum* was passed, a provision was renewed which for about 263 years had, in the case of imminent revolution, taken the place of the old dictatorship. In virtue of this decree Caius and his followers were attacked and many slain. He himself, seeing all escape cut off, ordered a faithful slave to kill him.

CHAPTER XIII

TOWARDS REVOLUTION

73. The Scandal of Jugurtha (117 B.C.). Truth and Fiction. After the carnage in the streets followed prosecutions, confiscations, and condemnations. The party of Caius was dispersed as the party of Tiberius had been, and the aristocracy remained masters of the State. They immediately decided to secure for themselves that part of the spoils of victory to which they attached most importance, namely the Italian lands. It was not possible to destroy the whole of the work of Caius Gracchus. The " lex judiciaria," the laws on the subject of Asia, the " lex militaris," the "lex frumentaria" were not touched. The agrarian law, however, bore the brunt of their attacks and was soon destroyed. In the very year of Caius's death the senate repealed the provision forbidding alienation, which the Lex Sempronia imposed on the new small holders. In this way the poor were led to squander their substance by first mortgaging and then selling their holdings, while the rich formed latifundia. Two years later, in 119, the comitia passed a measure repealing the agrarian legislation of the Gracchi and providing that the proceeds of letting the land should be distributed to the people. Thereby the people, in consideration of this pittance, renounced the rights and privileges as owners of the public land of their county which the Gracchi had won for them. The *ager publicus* could now be leased by any citizen without any special regulations, limitations, or conditions.[1]

The party of Caius Gracchus had been merely dispersed, however, and not destroyed, and soon began to collect its forces again, though at first, partly owing to fear and partly to weariness, it had little influence on events. The times were quiet and the empire at peace. Many Romans, by contracting for the collection of the taxes and by engaging in trade, were beginning to make their fortunes in the new province of Asia. The only warlike enterprise of any importance was the expedition undertaken between 125 and 121 B.C. to put an end to the raids of the Gauls into the allied territory of Massilia, and to secure the roads which led to Spain. To attain these objects Rome made war on the Arverni and reduced to the status of a province Gallia Narbonensis, a country which included those parts of southern France which lie between the Alps and the Rhone. To prevent the Arverni from becoming dangerous again they deported to Rome their king, Bituitus, and his son whom they had made prisoners. In 121, Metellus, son of the victor of Macedonia, conquered the Baleari; but thereafter the war was confined to the barbarous tribes of the frontier or of the countries conquered, and consisted merely of minor operations of which no notice was taken at Rome. Within and without the frontiers of the empire there reigned, in fact, an ap-

[1] *App., B. C., i.,* 27. The date of the law is indicated by the words πεντεκαιδέκα μάλιστα ἔτεσιν ἀπὸ τῆς [sc. Tiberii] Γράκχου νομοθεσίας.

parent calm, but beneath this, there was still a violent
ferment of discord, hatred, rancour, and jealousy.
Any accident was sufficient to cause a new explosion,
and Africa supplied the occasion.

Micipsa had succeeded Massinissa as King of
Numidia in 149, and had died in his turn in 118, leaving the kingdom to his two sons, Hiempsal and Adherbal, who were still very young, and to a man who
was much more powerful than the two put together.
This man was Jugurtha, whose father was an illegitimate son of Massinissa. Jugurtha had been in
command of the Numidian contingents sent by Micipsa
to the assistance of the Romans at Numantia. He
had distinguished himself greatly in this service by
his valour and sagacity. He had made friends with
many Roman senators, and even with Scipio Æmilianus himself, who esteemed him highly for the services
he had rendered to the army during the siege.

There is nothing improbable in the supposition
that a Numidian prince who was intelligent, energetic,
and courageous, and who, moreover, had known how
to acquire many friends at Rome, should have conceived the design of getting rid of Micipsa's two sons
and making himself sole monarch, or that he actually
did make away with his cousin Hiempsal by treachery
and then attacked Adherbal in his own kingdom.
When, however, Adherbal fled in terror to the neighbouring province of Africa, imploring the assistance
of Rome in the name of his father and grandfather,
are we to believe Sallust when he tells us that Jugurtha's ambassadors had no great difficulty in convinc-
ing the most influential senators—by means of very
solid arguments—that Hiempsal had perished justly?
And is it necessary to accept his story that Jugurtha

himself scattered handfuls of gold among the senators, in order to explain their decision in 117 to send a commission to Africa with instructions to divide Numidia between Jugurtha and Adherbal?[1] Numidia had to be governed by one or other of the two princes or by both. It would assuredly have been unjust to exclude Adherbal. But might not the senators believe in good faith that they were doing a just and politic thing in giving part of the kingdom to Jugurtha? Jugurtha was a man of parts. He had rendered signal services to Rome before Numantia and had earned the praises of Scipio Æmilianus. He had many friends in the senate, though these were doubtless not all disinterested. It might well appear useful to many senators to have so friendly and clever a prince as Jugurtha in Africa, even though he was not a model of virtue.

It appears probable, therefore, that the decision to divide Numidia between Jugurtha and Adherbal was taken by the senate in good faith. But Jugurtha's admirers and supporters in that assembly belonged chiefly to the party of the enemies of the Gracchi. This did not tend to win him much sympathy from the other side. His far from agreeable relations with a certain number of senators (no doubt the least influential) might also have given rise to suspicions. But at the time no one suspected—or at least expressed any suspicion—and the commission proceeded to divide the kingdom between the two princes, whether fairly or not it would be difficult to say. It

[1] On the so-called Jugurthine War the Roman historian C. Sallustius Crispus (86–31 B.C.), a contemporary of Cæsar, who belonged to the democratic party, wrote a monograph entitled *De Bello Jugurthino,* which is a good but highly partial book.

is at any rate certain that the peace was soon broken, and we may accept Sallust's view that Jugurtha was entirely to blame, for he attacked Adherbal without any justification, defeated him, and shut him up in Cirta.

The senate sent two successive embassies, and it is difficult to see what more could have been done. The second was headed by no less a person than the *princeps senatus*, Marcus Æmilius Scaurus, and, like the first, it endeavoured to persuade Jugurtha to suspend hostilities and refer the issue to the judgment of the senate. It is not necessary to suppose that Jugurtha corrupted the ambassadors in order to explain the failure of their mission. Jugurtha wished to remove Adherbal and to confront the senate with a *fait accompli*, hoping that, when there was no surviving prince but himself, the Romans would recognize him as king, the more so because about this time anxieties were beginning to arise about the northern frontier of Italy. The Cimbri, a barbarous nation from the north of Europe, had invaded northern Illyria and made war on the Taurisci, allies of Rome who lived in Noricum. In 113, the consul Cneius Papirius Carbo, who had been sent to defend the Taurisci, had sustained a sanguinary defeat near Noreia. Jugurtha, therefore, amused the embassies with discussions while he drew the lines of investment about Cirta ever tighter, as a result of which Adherbal was forced to surrender in 112 and was promptly slain. By what means could the ambassadors have prevented this?

Jugurtha had reasoned well according to the ordinary calculation of expediency, but he failed to reckon with the fact that at Rome the senate, though power-

ful, was not all powerful, and that in addition to the
senate he had to make terms with public opinion.
And public opinion, when the news came of the surrender of Cirta, was violently moved in favour of
Adherbal and against Jugurtha—more especially
because in the taking of the city not a few Italian
merchants had been killed. As Jugurtha had been
the protégé of the oligarchical party, the Gracchan
or democratic party, which had long been waiting
for a good opportunity, exploited this outburst of
public feeling in order to inflict a humiliating rebuff
on their adversaries. The tribune C. Memmius
threatened the senate with scandals and agitations
if they did not avenge Adherbal by declaring war
on Jugurtha. This agitation was so serious that the
oligarchical party had to give way. The senate refused to receive Jugurtha's envoys. War was declared and in the year 111 the command was given
to Lucius Calpurnius Bestia.

Calpurnius, as even Sallust admits, was an honest
man and quite a competent soldier. He chose as
his legates for the expedition men of great influence—
among them M. Scaurus. Now Sallust asks us to
believe that, immediately after this able and honest
commander and his eminent staff landed in Africa,
they allowed Jugurtha to corrupt them, and, instead
of fighting the enemy, accepted his bribes and concluded a disgraceful peace. It is beyond doubt that
Calpurnius opened negotiations immediately after
his arrival and summoned Jugurtha to make peace,
and that Jugurtha agreed to surrender at discretion
to Rome—an arrangement which, after all, does not
appear so very disgraceful to the Romans. The
consul's forbearance may, therefore, be very easily

explained. Jugurtha wanted the kingdom of Massinissa. He did not wish for war with Rome whose
instrument in Africa he desired to be. If he offered
peace, was it not right for a Roman senator to consider whether it was not best to spare Rome a long
and difficult war, which was favoured only by one
party as a move in the party game, even at the cost
of renouncing vengeance for Adherbal? Furthermore,
if Jugurtha were vanquished and deposed, who was
to govern Numidia? Was it prudent to create yet
another province and still further enlarge an empire
which already was too vast?

The negotiations of Calpurnius and Scaurus with
Jugurtha may well have been quite disinterested and
undertaken on good grounds of policy. But the nego-
tiators forgot that the democrats had determined to
use Jugurtha to avenge Caius Gracchus. The peace
highly displeased the public, who were incensed
against Jugurtha, and suspicions of treachery were
rife. Cries of scandal were heard on all sides. The
democrats did their best to inflame the already exasperated minds of the people. C. Memmius not
only made the comitia tributa reject the peace but
persuaded the people to decree that the prætor L.
Cassius should go to Africa and bring Jugurtha to
Rome to be publicly interrogated before the popular
assembly about his misdeeds and his accomplices.

The real meaning of this was that the people were
citing to appear before them for judgment, one might
say, the whole senate, or at any rate the most influential and powerful part of it. And such was the
state of public opinion that the senate did not dare
to gainsay this strange proposal. L. Cassius went
to Africa, and Jugurtha, whose fixed idea was to

reconcile himself with Rome, expressed his willingness to go to Italy. The day came, therefore, when the Romans beheld the king with whom they were at war arriving in the capital, modestly dressed and attended by a small suite. Shortly afterwards he appeared before the Roman people assembled to try him, or rather to make use of his evidence to discredit the senate, the assembly which in the eyes of the world symbolized the power of Rome.

No worse folly had yet been invented by the ingenuity of party spite. But one of the tribunes who must have been a man of sense, rose and vetoed all further proceedings. Threatening cries, invective, and tumult could not move him from his purpose. Jugurtha remained at Rome, holding himself at the disposal of the people, in the position of a man accused on a political charge which could not be discussed. The situation was bizarre and inextricable. The popular party, for whom the ruin of Jugurtha had become an obligation of honour, now tried another method. They discovered at Rome a certain Massiva, a grandson of Massinissa, who for fear of Jugurtha had fled from Africa and taken refuge in the capital, and persuaded him to claim the kingdom of Numidia from the senate. It was a clever move, for Jugurtha hoped that the Romans, in spite of all, would make up their minds to recognize him as king, for the simple reason that it would be impossible to find any one to put in his place. He was not slow to defend himself, and did not hesitate to bring about the assassination of his unexpected competitor. But public indignation was exacerbated by this murder. It was generally felt that Rome had made a mistake in summoning Jugurtha, and the senate used their authority to cut the knot. They expelled Jugurtha from Italy and directed that hostilities should be resumed.

This was accordingly done in 110 by the consul Spurius Postumius Albinus, who, however, carried on the war somewhat feebly. He was unable to compel Jugurtha to accept a decisive battle. The Numidian used all his skill to elude him and tried hard to resume negotiations. Towards the middle of the year Spurius handed over the command to his brother Aulus, and returned to Rome to preside over the elections, which were hotly contested. Aulus, when left at the head of the army, proved so incompetent a commander that at the beginning of 109 he allowed himself to be surrounded and, in order to save his army from annihilation, was compelled to recognize Jugurtha as king and to agree to evacuate Numidia.

This new defeat after so many other shameful reverses roused Rome to a pitch of fury which was all the more vehement because at the same time, at the other end of the empire, aristocratic generals on the Danube and the Rhone had failed to parry the new and more serious blows which were being aimed at the Roman ascendancy in that quarter. It will be remembered that, between 125 and 121, Rome had been at war with the Arverni and had conquered and reduced to a province the part of Gaul which lay between the Alps and the Rhone, and that, after conquering the Arverni, the Romans, in order to weaken the power of their adversaries, had captured or removed to Rome King Bituitus and his son. In Gaul, as in the east, this policy, which aimed at making Rome secure by weakening all her neighbours, soon bore fruit. The first defeat of the Arverni, coupled with the deposition of Bituitus and his dynasty, had overthrown the domination of that people. One by one their vassals had recovered their independence, each under the government of its own aristocracy, and the wars between tribe and tribe had recommenced. Rome had at first profited by this renewal of anarchy to make advantageous treaties with the tribes singly. She had granted to the Ædui the title of brothers and kinsmen and had declared the Sequani and many of the peoples of Aquitania to be her friends. Very soon, however, the weakness of Gaul brought forth the Cimbric peril, which was greater than the Arvernian.

The Cimbri, who in 113 had beaten the consul Carbo in Noricum, had not ventured to invade Italy. Laden with booty they had recrossed the Danube with the intention of crossing the Rhine and invading Gaul. This plan they successfully carried out in 109. If the Arvernian empire had still been in existence, it might have been able to oppose the invasion with the forces of united Gaul. But the empire of the Arverni had fallen, and the Cimbri had no difficulty in forcing their way through the congeries of independent and rival states which had replaced it. Rome had been compelled to come to the rescue of her friends, who were in danger in Gaul, and in 109 had sent thither with an army the consul Marcus Junius Silanus. But at a place now unknown Silanus had been defeated like Aulus in Africa.

To be defeated by the barbarians both in Europe and in Africa was a bitter humiliation for Rome. The Romans were unwilling to admit, what was probably the unpleasant truth, that both these defeats were due to the incompetence of her generals and the decadence of her military institutions. The African disaster, at any rate, they attributed to the now legendary gold of Jugurtha. A tribune proposed that a commission should be appointed to inquire into the African war and this was agreed to. Fortunately, however, in the person of Q. Cæcilius Metellus, a man of real merit had at last been elected consul for 109 by the comitia, and the lot, less blindly than usual, had assigned him Numidia for his province.

After his arrival in Africa, Metellus re-established discipline in the army and began to take the war seriously. In 109 and 108 he repeatedly defeated Jugurtha and compelled him to act on the defensive. Numidia, however, was a country without towns. It was inhabited by nomadic barbarians, rude people who knew every inch of the country and were an extremely mobile enemy, and thus particularly dangerous to a regular army, which was necessarily encumbered by its more complicated requirements. In such a country, therefore, one or more defeats of the enemy in the field did not mean the end of the war. The important point was to deprive the Numidians of their leader, but in this Metellus was not successful. On the contrary, Jugurtha managed to win the friendship of other neighbouring peoples such as the Mauri and the Gætuli, who were not less formidable to the Romans.

74. Caius Marius and the Final Campaign against Jugurtha (107-106 B.C.). While, therefore, the successes won by Metellus partly restored the prestige of the Roman arms and of the aristocracy, the prolongation of the war greatly exasperated the lower classes, who in every delay saw the influence of Jugurtha's money and the corruption of the nobility. The knights were particularly hard hit by this interminable war, which paralysed all their enterprises. The democrats did their best, of course, to foment as much public discontent as possible, and the effect was visible in the result of the consular elections for 108. In this year, which was filled with so much agitation and disquietude, a *novus homo*, a native of the small provincial village of Arpinum, an obscure knight who had failed in business, succeeded in obtaining the consulship and the command of the army in Numidia.

This man was Caius Marius, who, as we have seen, had served with honour under Scipio Æmilianus at Numantia. After this campaign he had continued his political career, which, however, had moved slowly because in all things he had too much at heart the interests of the country and too little those of his party. Thus, as tribune of the people in 119, he had excited the hostility of the oligarchical party by proposing a law requiring that all votes of the people should be taken by secret ballot. When, however, a colleague had come forward with an amplification of the Gracchan corn law, Marius had vetoed it, and thus alienated the democrats. The result was that he failed in his election to the ædileship and had to retire into private life for three years. In 115 he was elected prætor and, in that capacity, had governed Hispania Ulterior with firmness and success. Metellus had taken him to Numidia as his legate, because Marius, in spite of his humble origin, was one of the finest soldiers Rome possessed. He had proved of the utmost service to his general, whose successes were in great part due to him.

At a time when there was such a scarcity of ability

it was entirely legitimate that a man like Marius should aim at the supreme office in the State. He had all the qualities of a statesmanlike consul, being zealous for the public interest and by no means factious. But owing to a mistake made by Metellus, who was himself a statesman, this potent force was suddenly deflected from the true path. It appears that Marius was among those who thought Metellus's method of warfare too slow and prudent. Metellus may have resented this criticism or he may have been blinded by class prejudice; in any case, when Marius applied for leave to proceed to Rome in order to conduct in person his candidature for the consulship for the year 107, Metellus refused his request. Marius was not a man to allow his whole future to be the sport of Metellus's caprice, and insisted so strongly that Metellus was forced to grant the necessary permission. He gave way, however, only at the last moment—twelve days before the election if we may believe Plutarch. Marius flew to Italy, but on his arrival found the whole oligarchical party solidly with Metellus and resolved to resist with all its power, as an affront to the old nobility, the elevation of an obscure knight to the consulship. As we have seen Marius did not belong to the new popular party; but, being opposed in this way by the old aristocracy, what could he do but throw himself into the arms of the democrats?

What was fated came to pass. The scandal of Jugurtha had struck a heavy blow at the prestige of the ancient aristocracy. There was in the air a feeling of disgust and irritation, a universal desire for new things and a new spirit. Marius in his speeches fiercely attacked the oligarchical party in

general and Metellus in particular. He accused them
of purposely prolonging the war and promised that,
if he was elected consul, he would finish it in a very
short time. The democratic party adopted him as
their candidate. The lower classes, peasants and
workmen alike, declared for him. He had the support of the equestrian order. Was he not a knight
like themselves and had he not promised to finish
the war quickly, which was what they desired above
everything? The struggle was hard, and developed
into a conflict between the senatorial aristocracy
and the other classes in the State. But Marius was
elected.

The election of Marius was the first revenge of
the party of the Gracchi. Jugurtha had avenged
Tiberius and Caius. Thanks to the blow struck by
the obscure Numidian prince and his turbid intrigues,
the aristocracy, which had founded the empire and
governed it for so many centuries, was now suspected,
humiliated, and blown upon, though it was probably
to a great extent innocent. The obscure knight of
Arpinum was triumphantly raised to the consulship
and was immediately in a position to inflict a new
humiliation on the senate.

Before the elections, in the hope of frustrating
Marius's designs should he prove victorious, the senate
had already distributed the provinces and had maintained Metellus in Numidia as proconsul. A law
was passed rescinding this decision and satisfying
Marius's ambition to hold the Numidian command.
He had now to fulfil his promise to bring the war to
an end. He immediately set to work and began with
a military reform which was at once simple and very
bold. It instantly rejuvenated the somewhat out-

worn military institutions of Rome, but it upset one
of the principles on which the whole social equilibrium
of the republic had depended for centuries.

Marius's plan was to make a rule of what had
hitherto been an exceptional practice, resorted to
in times of emergency, by accepting for service in
the army all who presented themselves—not merely
citizens with a property qualification but proletarians
as well.[1] It is not difficult to understand the vital
wisdom of this reform and its deadly danger. The
Roman army, as it then was, was composed as a rule
entirely of citizens possessed of a certain capital.
It was the old army of the fourth and third centuries,
and it had ceased to be sufficient for the needs of the
new policy for two reasons. In the first place, the
number of enrolled citizens was now too small for
so many wars and so many provinces, and secondly,
the propertied classes, as we have so often explained.
had become bad military material. All these difficulties disappeared when men of the poorest class,
who had no capital but their physical strength, were
admitted to the army. Not only were the numbers
of his army increased, but for the new recruits military service was not so much a burden as a profession.
It gave them a means of livelihood and of providing
a certain comfort for their old age from their share of
the spoils. It would thus be possible to keep them
with the colours for many years, to submit them to a
course of serious military instruction—in a word to
make them into real soldiers. But, if the advantages
of the reform were manifest, it contained a revolutionary principle, the danger of which was certain to

[1] Sall., *B. J.*, lxxxvi., 2; Plut., *Mar.* ii., 3,1; Gell., *Noct. Att.*,
xvi., 10,14.

make itself felt later on. It was not only that Rome
had gradually converted her national army into a
mercenary force, similar to those led by Alexander,
the Diadochi and the Epigoni, but the middle and
comfortable classes were disarming themselves and
handing over the arms with which they had defended
the empire to the classes of men who had no property.
The effect of the new principle was soon to become
apparent.

For the moment, however, the reform met with
universal approval. The State and the private individual derived equal advantages from it. The poor
found in it a new source of gain, and the rich and
comfortable classes found it easier to obtain exemp-
tions from military service, or to be sent back to their
homes after a short period of service to look after
their property and their business. Marius, therefore, departed for Africa amid the applause of the
people, leaving his quæstor, L. Cornelius Sulla, to
complete the recruiting of men and horses in Italy.
Sulla was a personage who had hitherto figured only
in the *chronique scandaleuse* of the capital. He
was the representative of an illustrious family which
had fallen on evil days. His life had so far been
passed among actors, buffoons, singers, and dancing
women, and (at any rate, according to the ancient
writers) he had recently been able to repair his personal fortunes only because he had inherited the
property of a Greek courtesan!

Metellus did not wait for the arrival of his successor.
He entrusted the command of the legions to his lieutenant and returned to Rome where, in compensation
for his wrongs, the senate had granted him a triumph
and the title of Numidicus. Marius lost no time,

and, in 106, succeeded by skilful manœuvres in making himself master of Numidia. Jugurtha was driven out and took refuge with Bocchus, King of Mauretania, whose ally he was.

But while the war in Africa was proceeding towards the end which was so much desired in Italy, new disasters had occurred in Gaul. There the Cimbri, after defeating Silanus, instead of invading Gaul or threatening Italy, had unexpectedly retired. Rome was able, therefore, for a moment to delude herself with the idea that her great prestige had awed the barbarians in spite of their victory. But it was an illusion. The two defeats which the Cimbri had within a few years inflicted on the Romans, and perhaps also the delays and scandals of the Numidian war, had reawakened the courage of the Gallic peoples subject to Rome, and the appetites of the barbarians that hovered on the frontiers. The Cimbri had gone away only to unite with the Teutones, who had also left their accustomed abode in order to swoop down on Gaul and Italy with their confederates. Shortly after the retirement of the Cimbri in 107, the Tigurini, a brave tribe which formed part of the Helvetii, encouraged by the defeat of Silanus, had invaded Gallia Narbonensis. On the news of the invasion part of the province rose in rebellion, and the Roman garrison of Tolosa had been made prisoners by the rebellious natives. The consul Lucius Cassius Longinus had been forced to march against the Tigurini, who were led by a young and very skilful chief named Divico. On the approach of Longinus, Divico made a pretence of retiring in flight, enticing the Romans in pursuit beyond the frontiers of the province into the country of the Nitiobroges. There he suddenly stopped and took the offensive, encircling the Romans. The consul and the greater part of his army were slain; the survivors escaped by making a disgraceful peace; Tolosa was lost. Half the country was in revolt, and, towards the end of 107, the Roman dominion over Gallia Narbonensis appeared to be on the point of collapse. In 106 it was necessary to send reinforcements to the province under the command of a consul if a catastrophe was to be avoided.

The consul who was sent was Quintus Servilius Cæpio, who was Pontifex Maximus and one of the strongest partisans of the oligarchical party. It is enough to say of him that, amid the grave disorders which then distracted the State, all he sought for was an opportunity to propose a *lex iudiciaria* which would restore to the senate part of the judicial power which had been transferred by Caius Gracchus to the knights. On his arrival in Gaul, Servilius found that the danger which had been so much feared had vanished. Like the Cimbri the Tigurini had retired after their victory, as if all the Gauls feared Rome the more for having defeated her. He turned, therefore, against the Volcæ in order to free Tolosa, and succeeded in retaking that town. He punished the rebellious city by confiscating all the treasures accumulated in the temples by the piety of the faithful[1]—an immense booty, if we may believe the ancients, but destined never to reach Rome. According to the received accounts the escort which accompanied it was waylaid and killed and the treasure stolen.

At Rome, where Cæpio was cordially detested by the knights and by the democrats, it was openly said that he had stolen it himself, a report rather difficult

[1] Strab., iv., 1, 13; Justin., xxxvii., 3,9.

to believe. An inquiry was demanded, a prosecution was launched, and Rome was distracted, in fact, by a new scandal not unlike the affair of Jugurtha. The one man whose reputation with the people increased amid all these sordid and disgraceful episodes was Marius, who by arms and negotiation was rapidly bringing the war in Numidia to a successful conclusion. After Jugurtha's flight to Mauretania, Marius, who did not wish to embark on a long and difficult struggle with Bocchus, had recourse to the arts of diplomacy and used his quæstor, Sulla, as the intermediary for negotiations with the Mauretanian monarch, the object of which was to persuade him to abandon his alliance with Jugurtha and to deliver up the ex-king of Numidia. Sulla handled the affair with much skill. Bocchus hesitated for long, but in the end became convinced that, if he continued to take Jugurtha's part, he ran the risk of losing his own crown and kingdom. After much vacillation he consented, therefore, to betray his ally. In the spring of 105, Jugurtha was made prisoner at a conference which had been ostensibly arranged for quite a different purpose, and was solemnly handed over to the victorious general. The war, after six long years, was finished at last.

75. The Cimbri and the Teutones. The Four Consulships of Marius (105–101 B.C.). Public rejoicing over the victory in Africa did not last long. In 105 the tempest which for some time had been lowering over Gaul burst. The Cimbri and the Tigurini reappeared on the frontiers of Gaul, united and accompanied by two other tribes—the Teutones and the Ambrones. The reason for their mysterious retirements after their victories was now clear. They had retreated merely in order to concentrate and return with new forces. How great the danger appeared is shown by the measures taken by the senate. More than eighty thousand soldiers were sent to Gaul under the command of the consul Cn. Manlius Maximus and of Servilius Cæpio whose command was prolonged with the status of proconsul.

The history of the campaign is little known. It appears that the two generals were of small capacity and that in addition they were not in agreement. Disputes often arose between them and finally insults were exchanged. The senate sent commissioners to bring them into harmony with each other, and again there was much talk and nothing done. The army, like the other armies of that time which had not the good fortune to be commanded by Marius, seems to have been ill trained and undisciplined. The result was one of the greatest disasters which ever befell Rome on the field of battle. On October 6, 105, at Arausium near Orange the barbarian hordes attacked the two Roman armies, each of which seems to have fought a separate battle, and annihilated both of them. There escaped with the two generals a feeble remnant, which was insufficient to defend Gallia Narbonensis against the invader. The dominion of Rome in transalpine Gaul had fallen. A victorious barbarian army was encamped on the main road of communication between Italy and Spain, and had opened for itself the roads in both directions.

It is easy to imagine the terror and the grief at Rome. In this dark hour the one source of hope and comfort for the frightened multitude was Marius, who had remained in Africa to reduce the country he had conquered to order. Of that country, one third, the eastern portion of Numidia, had been annexed to the province of Africa. The western part had been handed over to the King of Mauretania as the price of his treason. The remainder had been bestowed on a cousin of Jugurtha, an obscure prince named Gauda. In the ordinary course Marius could not have been re-elected consul, for the prescribed interval had not elapsed. But the people would take no denial. As in the case of Scipio Æmilianus, a law was passed suspending the ordinary rule. He was elected consul for 104, and, by another law, Gaul was assigned to him. Thus on January 1, 104, Marius was able to make a triumphal entry into Rome and at the same time to commence his second consulship. By his side stood his quæstor, Sulla, who shared in the great honour bestowed on him. Amid the fanfares of the trumpets, the cheers of the troops, and the deafening applause of the crowds, there followed the shadow of what had once been Jugurtha, in chains with his sons, his women, his family, and his court. After the triumph, the conquered monarch, a second Perseus, was thrown into the Tullianum, where he was left to die of hunger.

In her hour of danger Rome depended on Marius to save her from the new Brennus. We do not know how difficult a task the salvation of Rome may have been; but certainly the danger was not so imminent as was then imagined. Now that they had destroyed the Roman army of Gallia Narbonensis, which was threatening their flanks, the barbarians, who were scouring Europe with their raids, wished to plunder Spain and Gaul before they attempted to cross the barrier of the Alps and to invade Italy. Indeed, when Marius arrived in Gallia Narbonensis in the spring of 104, the enemy had retired. The Cimbri had gone to Spain, and the Teutones had turned back to invade Gaul. Gallia Narbonensis, therefore, was quiet, at least in comparison with previous years, and not in danger, in spite of the fact that revolts continued to smoulder here and there as the result of the invasion. Marius, however, being a prudent as well as a clever and astute general, did not immediately set out to follow up the enemy. He not merely allowed the Teutones to invade Gaul but he also permitted the Cimbri to invade and plunder Spain, which was one of the richest provinces of the empire. His chief care was to re-establish the authority of Rome firmly in Gallia Narbonensis, and to exercise and improve the army. According to the information supplied to him the Cimbri would return from Spain in the spring of the following year. It was necessary, therefore, to prepare to give them a suitable reception. Marius had brought with him part of his veteran army from Africa. He also had many new recruits, who had been attracted by the generosity with which he had shared the spoils of Numidia with his troops. There were also contingents summoned from all the subject and allied populations of the empire. His task was to make out of this variegated multitude an army capable of facing the barbarian hordes. According to his custom Marius instructed and exercised his new forces with great care and very strictly.

In addition to this he appears to have introduced into the arrangement and armament of his forces certain reforms which were destined to outlast his day.[1] Hitherto the legion had been divided into thirty

[1] *Cf.* J. Marquardt, *De l'Organisation Militaire chez les Romains* (French translation), Paris, 1891, p. 147 ff.

maniples, which in battle were drawn up in three lines at a fixed distance from each other. A violent and audacious enemy like the Cimbri, strong in the first flush of an attack, might penetrate between the files and separate them, isolating their constituent elements. Marius, therefore, raised the effectives of the legion to 6000 men and divided it into ten bodies of 600 each, which he called cohorts, the name given to the corresponding unit in the allied forces. In this way not only was there a more complete fusion of the contingents of citizens and allies, but the formation of the legion, while not losing mobility, acquired a depth, a power of resistance, and a compactness which were much wanted at a time when the quality of the soldier had on the whole declined. His armament reform abolished the long lance and the huge shield, substituting for them the *pilum* or light javelin (then confined to the first lines) with which it was possible to pierce the shield and armour of the enemy, and the *clipeus*, which was a small light target round in shape.

Those who expected that Marius's arrival in Gaul would be immediately followed by the announcement of great victories must doubtless have been somewhat disappointed. But in the meantime the public were encouraged and were able to await with more confidence the great clash which was expected to take place in the spring of 103. However, while matters in Gaul seemed still to be somewhat in suspense, a dangerous mutiny of slaves broke out in southern Italy and Sicily, and new complications arose in the East. In 104 the rulers of Paphlagonia came to Rome to beg the aid of the republic whose friends and clients they were, against the kingdom of Pontus.

This kingdom had been formed on the shores of the

Black Sea at the beginning of the third century B.C. from the ruins of Alexander's empire. It comprised populations of different languages, manners, and races, and was ruled over by the dynasty of Mithridates,[1] a Hellenized family of the Persian nobility. In this State, hitherto almost unknown at Rome, a young, ambitious, and intelligent sovereign named Mithridates VI., Eupator,[2] had ascended the throne in 111. Helped by Diophantus, a clever Greek from Sinope, Mithridates in the course of a few years managed to rescue the Greek colonies on the Black Sea from the dominion of the Scythians and to conquer Tauris. He had then tried to conquer the whole of the eastern Black Sea basin and to extend the borders of the kingdom of Pontus to the Euphrates. He had sought relations with the barbarous Sarmatians and Bastarni, who led a nomadic existence between the Danube and the Dnieper, with the Gallic tribes that still lived in the valley of the Danube, with the Thracians and the Illyrians. The Scythian kings, who had been expelled from Tauris, had already gone to Rome in the previous year to ask for help; but Rome, alarmed by the disasters which had happened in Gallia Narbonensis, had turned a deaf ear to their complaints.

Encouraged by the inertia of the Romans, Mithridates, apparently in the spring of 104, had invaded and partitioned Paphlagonia in concert with his ally, the King of Bithynia. For the second time Asia came to Rome for help. Rome, having become an Asiatic power by the annexation of the kingdom of Pergamus could not indefinitely refuse this appeal. If

[1] The inscriptions give Μιθραδά της.

[2] On this great historic figure, Th. Reinach has written an excellent work *Mithridate Eupator, roi du Pont*, Paris, 1890.

she was to hold the precious province of Asia securely, she must take care that no neighbour who was too powerful and ambitious should grow up by its side.

The democratic party, then at the height of its power, at once declared itself against Mithridates and in favour of the small principalities which were being threatened. The oligarchs, on the other hand, in a spirit of opposition, took up an attitude which was more impartial if not favourable to Mithridates. Pending the arrival of an embassy from the King of Pontus, no decision was taken.

Gaul almost exclusively occupied the public mind. In the expectancy of the great encounter in the spring of 103, public opinion insisted that the command of the army should remain in the hands of Marius. The popular party had, therefore, no difficulty in securing his re-election as consul for the third time without removing him from Gaul, in spite of the law, and of the nobility, of whose incapacity the successive consulships of Marius were a mute but perpetual reproof. Marius and Marius alone—not the senate and the great families—was the hope, the comfort, the sword, and the shield of Rome! All the elections turned out favourably for the democrats. Among the tribunes for 103 was Lucius Apuleius Saturninus, one of the boldest and most ardent of their party, and during the year was passed the Lex Domitia, which made all the sacerdotal colleges—the pontifices, the augurs, the *XV viri sacris faciundis*, the *VII viri epulonum*— which had hitherto been filled by co-optation, elective offices.[1] Another of the privileges of the great families was thus destroyed.

Not less energetic was the action of the party, when

[1] Cic., *De leg. agr.*, ii., 7, 18 ff. Vell. Pat., 2, 12, 3.

the envoys of Mithridates arrived at Rome. Either they did actually try to convince the senate by bribery, or the democratic party, somewhat corrupted by success, played upon the easily aroused suspicions of the public in order to recreate the scandal of Jugurtha. In any case the ambassadors were assailed by violent accusations and clamorous demonstrations of hostility. Saturninus put himself at the head of the movement, and the senate, being intimidated, had recourse to the expedient of sending an embassy to the East to inquire into the state of matters on the spot.

Meanwhile the spring of 103 had arrived, but without the Cimbri and the Teutones. The Roman legions remained undisturbed in Gaul. This illusory calm led astray the opinions both of the troops and of the Italian public. Many began to murmur against Marius and his method of fighting, and to ask themselves how long the war was likely to last if it was carried on in this way. But, in spite of all this, Marius did not allow himself to be hurried into any movement in pursuit of the enemy. To prevent the soldiers being enervated by idleness, he conceived the idea of using the army to carry out a great public work. The lower course of the Rhone was much silted up with sand and so unfit for navigation, Marius caused a new canal—the *fossa Mariana*—to be excavated, the name and the memory of which are preserved to this day in the village of Foz. By this undertaking he attained three objects: He gave occupation to his soldiers. He assured himself a good avenue for supplies. He greatly gratified the equestrian order, who were his most ardent supporters, as well as the city of Massilia to whose friendship and alliance he attached importance, by assuring the navigation of the Rhone at all seasons and thus opening perpetual access to trade with Gaul.

The business of a general, however, is to fight and not to make canals, and the inertia of Marius complicated the situation. What was to be done in 102? Marius wished to be re-elected consul in order to reap the fruit of his long labours. The popular party wished for this also, because Marius in power was the outward and visible sign of the humiliation of their adversaries. But this time the public hesitated a little, both because Marius's exceptional privileges were becoming excessive, and because many were discontented with the prolongation of the war. Marius had to come and canvas Rome in person. His presence was enough. He was elected consul for the fourth time,—a thing that had never happened before in the whole course of Roman history.

The comitia, after all, had serious reason for what they did. The storm, though delayed, would be all the more violent when it broke. In 102 the Cimbri returned from Spain, the Teutones from Gaul; and on the Rhone the Cimbri, the Teutones, the Tigurini, and the Ambrones concentrated for the invasion of Italy. In Gallia Narbonensis they had destroyed a Roman army. They had sacked Spain and Gaul, and Rome had not dared to come to the assistance of her provinces or of her allies. What could prevent them from believing that they could invade and sack Italy also, and return laden with booty to their own country? They decided, in fact, to cross the Alps in three columns: The Teutones and the Ambrones were to go via Gallia Narbonensis and the western Alps, the Cimbri by the central Alps, the Tigurini by the eastern Alps. Thus, in the second half of 102, a horde consisting of the Teutones and the Ambrones moved across Gallia Narbonensis towards the Roman army, which had been waiting for them and training in silence for more than two years. The encounter took place not far from Aquæ Sextiæ (Aix) and the genius of the Roman general and the discipline of his army vanquished the audacity and the violence of the barbarians. In two successive engagements the Ambrones and the Teutones were skilfully provoked to fight, attacked and destroyed. A hundred thousand dead— if the number is not exaggerated—gave the place in which these proud savages found their graves the sinister name of *campi putridi*.[1]

The great victory of Aix overjoyed Rome. Marius was elected consul for a fifth term, this time without opposition or hesitation. He was directed to repulse the Cimbri who, perhaps in greater force than the Teutones, were invading northern Italy by forced marches. The new danger indeed was not less than that which the genius of Marius had just averted. The consul C. Lutatius Catulus, who had been entrusted with the defence of the central Alpine passes, had not been able to withstand the shock. He had been driven back to the Adige and had been compelled to fall back to the right bank of the Po, abandoning all Gallia Transpadana to the Cimbri. Italy was threatened with an invasion more terrible than that of Hannibal. Marius, and Marius alone, could save her! Fortune once more, and for the last time, smiled on him who had for seven years been her favourite. The Cimbri, instead of pursuing the

[1] On the Battle of Aquæ Sextiæ, *cf.* M. Clerc, *La bataille d'Aix: études critiques sur la campagne de Marius en Provence.* Paris, 1906.

invasion, stopped to plunder the plain of the Po. This gave Marius time to recall his tried legions from Gallia Narbonensis and to effect a junction with Catulus at the time when the barbarians were preparing to cross the Po not far from its confluence with the Sesia. Here, on the plain known as the Campi Raudii, the Cimbri shared the fate of their friends beyond the Alps. Their dead and wounded amounted to more than 120,000; 60,000 were taken prisoners (July 30, 101).[1]

[1] Plut. Mar., 25 ff.

CHAPTER XIV

MITHRIDATES AND THE NEW CRISIS IN ORIENTAL POLICY

76. The Fall of the Popular Party (100 B.C.). The popular party might now call itself master of the State. After Vercellæ the senate itself had proclaimed Marius, with Romulus and Camillus, "The third founder of his country." No one who was present at the triumph celebrated in Rome after that great victory, at which so many prisoners, so many barbarian kings and princes passed in chains before the eyes of the Roman people, could see that immediately behind all this glory lay an abyss as steep as the Tarpeian rock.

And yet so it was to be. Once the danger was over, legalistic scruples, the force of tradition, the principle of equality, resumed the upper hand. Now that the barbarians were finally beaten, Marius could not expect to be again re-elected consul. But success must have blinded both him and his party, for they made a supreme mistake. Under the influence of the Cimbric triumph the democrats proposed the conqueror of Jugurtha and of the Gauls as a candidate for the consulship for the sixth time, along with several other prominent men—L. Apuleius Saturninus and C. Servilius Glaucia among others. This time the aristocracy accepted the challenge. Against Marius they put up his old chief, Q. Cæcilius Metellus. The electoral battle was soon raging all along the line, and not only the consulship but all the other offices were hotly contested. The democratic party was again victorious. Marius was re-elected consul, Saturninus tribune of the people, and Glaucia prætor. This result was obtained, however, with great difficulty. The majorities were small and there was much disorder. The election of Saturninus, in particular, was attended with serious and disastrous violence, for the senatorial candidate lost his life.

This revival of opposition and the circumstances of the situation impelled the democrats to take up a more violent and demagogic attitude. They had got into power and had controlled the State for several years, thanks to the prestige of Marius, the discontent caused by the scandals of the Jugurthine wars, and the Gallic danger. Both wars were now over. The nobility, in spite of all their errors, were firmly entrenched in the senate, and were beginning to raise their heads again. There was only one way to keep in power, and that was to imitate Caius Gracchus and bind the masses by the chains of self-interest to the democratic party and its representatives. Of such a policy Marius was incapable. In spite of his six successive consulships he remained an old Roman in whom were ingrained so many constitutional and puritan scruples that he was no fit leader for a party which had never really been his own. Saturninus was the man who was wanted for this, and in fact he immediately commenced his campaign by presenting an agrarian law, allotting the lands in Gallia Transpadana which had been devastated by the Cimbri and whose owners had disappeared in the course of the invasion. He also proposed a *lex de coloniis deducendis*, which decreed the foundation of numerous colonies in the provinces, in Macedonia, in Achaia, in Sicily, for the distribution of lands to Marius's veterans.[1]

The Gracchan tradition was clearly apparent in these laws, but there was something more in them than the tradition. The new colonies were to consist largely of veterans, and not merely of Roman citizens but also of Italians, to a certain number of whom the honour of citizenship was to be accorded. The popular party had borrowed some of the ideas of Scipio Æmilianus. And in order that this part of the law might be honestly applied and carried out, its administration was placed in the hands of Marius himself. So far as can be judged after the lapse of so many centuries, the two laws were wise and far seeing. But to each was attached an additional clause and a supplementary law. The clause provided that all magistrates and senators should swear obedience to the law within five days on pain of fine and the loss of their dignities. The supplementary law was the *lex de maiestate*. This law still further strengthened, if that were necessary, the political power of the Roman people and its representatives. It declared inviolable the *maiestas* of the Roman people and of the tribunes, and it threatened with serious penalties all who dared encroach on this inviolability. The purpose of the clause and of the *lex de maiestate*, which was destined in course of time to acquire so sinister a celebrity, is clear. Twenty years of practical experience had made it manifest to all that it was much easier for the popular party to pass agrarian laws than to have

[1] For these two laws *cf.* App., *B.C.*, i., 29.

them carried out. The aristocracy, which was firmly established in the senate, in the magistracies, and in the religious colleges, had a thousand methods and contrivances for wrecking a law administratively when they could not secure its defeat in the comitia. It was in order to remedy this fatal weakness of the democratic masses that Saturninus reinforced his two laws with the clause and the *lex de maiestate*.

But this proceeding inevitably gave his legislation a violent and threatening character, which exasperated the nobility and disquieted the knights. The latter had in the preceding years supported the popular party while their hero, Marius, was its leader. Most of them, however, were rich men, who could not approve of many of the laws which aimed at treading down the upper classes for the benefit of the lower. The vote only made the situation worse. There was a violent conflict, in the course of which the aristocrats first tried liturgical obstruction and then the intervention of tribunes. But the veterans of Marius had gathered in large numbers, and retorted by using physical force the result of which was bloodshed.

The laws were passed, but no sooner was an attempt made to put them into operation than it at once appeared how the violence of their provisions reacted against the very party that had proposed them. When, after they were passed, the senate was invited to swear to them, Marius himself, the leader of the democrats, was the first to declare that he could not do it. The clause smacked too much of tyranny! On the entreaties of his party he recanted his refusal and, on the plea that there would otherwise be grave danger of a popular revolt, he swore the oath and induced all the senate to swear with him, except

Q. Cæcilius Metellus, his old rival, who preferred to accept the penalties of the *lex de maiestate* and to go into exile.

The popular party was saved for the moment by Marius's recantation, but the incident estranged them from him. Moreover, it was impossible to propose Marius for a seventh term of office. The democratic party, therefore, fought the elections for 99 without Marius as their candidate and without his active and avowed support. Lacking Marius, who was their hero, the knights also withdrew from the popular party. They came to an understanding with the nobles and agreed to support, not the democratic candidate, Glaucia, but the famous orator, M. Antonius, who was put forward by the aristocracy, provided that the aristocrats backed their candidate, the C. Memmius who had become prominent as tribune in connection with the Jugurthine scandals. On the withdrawal of Marius, many of the veterans also lost interest in the elections. The result was as might have been expected. At the comitia tributa Saturninus was again elected tribune. At the comitia centuriata Glaucia, abandoned by the knights, was defeated. M. Antonius and C. Memmius were elected consuls.

The irritation of the defeated party at their betrayal by the equestrian order was so great that the equestrian candidate, Memmius, was assassinated by the partisans of Saturninus and Glaucia. This time the senators and the knights did not tamely submit to violence. The senate in its anger proclaimed a state of siege and charged the consuls still in office (and therefore Marius himself) to take action against the rebels. He might, on his own personal responsibility, have declined this terrible task. But the conqueror of the Cimbri had not the strength to resist public opinion. Round him gathered the senate, the knights, the tribunes of the people and (wonder of wonders) a great part of the urban population. In the forum there were veritable battles in which he who had triumphed over Jugurtha and the Cimbri had to fight his own veterans of Aquæ Sextiæ and Vercellæ. The party of Saturninus and Glaucia took refuge in the Capitol where they barricaded themselves in and were besieged by Marius. The inevitable result followed. As in the days of Tiberius and Caius Gracchus, Saturninus and Glaucia were killed, and with them a great number of their followers (December, 100). But the Nasica and the Opimius of this new massacre was Caius Marius, who for so many years had been the hero and the glory of the popular party!

77. The Case of Rutilius Rufus and the Rupture between the Senate and the Equestrian Order. The reaction which followed this abortive revolution was violent. The scandals of the war with Jugurtha and the war against the Cimbri and the Teutones were forgotten. The old nobility again became the object of universal admiration. The senate immediately seized the opportunity to recover its old power and its first act was to recall Metellus from exile. The most conspicuous victim of this reversal of fortune was Marius, who had incurred the hatred of the democrats without having regained the favour of the aristocracy. He did not wait for the return to Rome of his old rival, but, voluntarily abandoning political life in which there was no longer any place for him, he set out on a long journey to the East on the pretext of fulfilling a vow made to an obscure divinity at Pessinus.

The aristocratic party was once more governing the empire, and under their rule times became more tranquil if not happier. This was true not only of internal affairs but also of foreign policy. Certainly the ten years between 100 and 91 were not free from troubles or from wars. Spain, which had been upset by the Cimbric invasion, again rose in insurrection, along with the Alpine tribes which had been recently subdued. The new Oriental provinces were devastated (alas too often!) by their barbarous neighbours. Asia Minor was repeatedly disturbed by the intrigues of Nicomedes, King of Bithynia, and Mithridates, King of Pontus. In spite of the commission sent by the senate, these two monarchs had now occupied Galatia. Then, while Nicomedes was intriguing in Paphlagonia, Mithridates had seized the opportunity afforded by the Cimbric war to break off his alliance with the King of Bithynia and seize all Cappadocia for himself. But none of these difficulties induced the senate to transgress the limits of a purely defensive policy, to undertake military or diplomatic interventions, or to make new annexations. The days of Scipio Africanus and Cato seemed to have returned.

In 95, Galatia was given back to the tetrarchs who had previously been its governors. Paphlagonia was declared a free State and Cappadocia placed under the government of a Persian nobleman named Ariobarzanes, who received the title of king. Mithridates himself was treated so handsomely that two years later, in alliance with Tigranes, King of Armenia, he again invaded Cappadocia and drove out Ariobarzanes. Not even this, however, was provocation enough to extort from the senate a declaration of war

against the King of Pontus. The propraetor Lucius
Cornelius Sulla was sent with a small army to replace
Ariobarzanes on the throne, and that was all. About
the same time Ptolemy Apion, King of the Cyrenaica,
died and left to the Roman people the kingdom which
had been his since 116. The Cyrenaica was then a
well-watered, fertile, and prosperous country. But
the senate refused the gift and proclaimed the country
independent.

The aristocratic party did its best, in fact, to
restore order in the empire and to govern prudently.
The severe lessons of the last fifteen years had not
been in vain. But, in spite of the good intentions of
the government, they had the utmost difficulty in
maintaining the equilibrium at which they aimed.
The confused process of decomposition and recomposi-
tion, which the Romans called the corruption of ancient manners, and which we define as the progress
of the ages, was going on. The diffusion of Greek
philosophy, the progress of education, and the increase
of wealth made men feel more vividly the harshness
of many of the strict rigours of the ancient law and the
horrible character of some barbarous superstitions
which still survived. The abolition of the practice of
human sacrifice, of which there were still some traces
in Italy, was on the point of being decreed. The
evolution of law continued, thanks to the praetors
who, in their edicts, were more ready to recognize the
claims of equity. Men were becoming implacable,
however, in their strife for riches, power, culture, and
pleasure, and there was a growing dissolution of the
social order of the State. More numerous than ever
were the nobles and the rich men who built themselves
elegant palaces at Rome, the lords who amused them-

selves by writing books, histories, tractates, and poetry in Greek or in Latin, the orators who, like Antonius and Licinius Crassus, had, by study of Greek models, become masters of every refinement of eloquence. The knowledge and the love of Greek and Asiatic art became widespread. Greek sculptors and painters were now kept busy by the great men of Rome. But this expenditure on Eastern harlots, crowds of slaves, and riotous living ruined many noble families, who were reduced to busying themselves with debts, expedients, and peculation.

Many agriculturists studied the Greek writers on husbandry, borrowed a little capital, planted olives and vines, and did their best to improve methods of cultivation. But inexperience, the want of roads, and excessive usury often ruined those who undertook these enterprises. Every year at Rome and in the cities of the Latins and the allies were opened new schools of rhetoric through which passed numerous scholars, and where was being fashioned a language, a style, and an eloquence of a truly national character. Too many young advocates, however, never found patrons to help them to rise in their profession or even clients to defend. Many of them went into trade, and, if some grew rich at Delos, in Asia, or in Egypt, many failed, Every part of Italy was infested with men who had lost place, or hope, or capital. Small holding was disappearing, the land passing into a small number of hands. Usury flourished. Only the few grew rich, and among them some survivors of the old provincial nobility of Italy, like Caius Cilnius Mæcenas, who, though descended from an Etrurian family of royal blood, did not scorn to come to Rome and take up the business of tax farming, contenting himself with a position among the nobility of the second grade,—the equestrian order.

In such a condition of moral and social disorder a state which, like the Roman Republic, rested on the principle of popular election, could not escape a kind of universal dissolution. The public offices were invaded by adventurers, by persons of ambitious and turbulent characters, by intriguing, meddlesome, and corrupt individuals of all sorts. Honest men were driven out, and had no consolation except to lament bitterly the evils of the times. It was a common opinion, especially among persons of high rank, that the diffusion of culture among the middle class was one of those evils. "The man who studies Greek becomes a blackguard," was almost a proverbial expression. More serious than this was the desire to obtain Roman citizenship, which made rapid progress at this time among the impoverished middle class throughout Italy, who were under the delusion that, if only they could become citizens, they would find a remedy for their miseries; among the young men who had studied rhetoric and were not content to argue petty cases and contest the humble municipal magistracies in their native towns; and, in a word, among all those (and they were many) who longed for the privileges which the citizenship would give them.

In circumstances of this kind the new government must have been weak, even if it could have relied on the concord of its own supporters. The fact was, however, that the reconciliation between the nobility and the equestrian order, which had brought back the aristocratic party to power, was in reality very superficial. The abyss of hatred which had been dug between the two orders first by the *lex iudiciaria* of

Caius Gracchus, then by the successive consulships of Marius, and finally by the course of events, was too wide. The pride of the knights grew greater every day by reason of their riches, their clients, their right to sit in judgment on senators. They now considered themselves at least the equals of the ancient nobility. Many of the latter, on the other hand, were disgusted with the general corruption and disorder, the most obvious cause of which was wealth. They were provoked by their own poverty and by the insolence of the new men; they affected to despise the knights; they lamented the days when the nobility alone had power, and they clamoured for severe laws against the abuses of the publicani. Thus there arose among the old nobility a strong anti-plutocratic party, and among the knights a party antagonistic to the nobility. One single incident, which indeed was serious enough in itself, was enough to shatter the concord of the two orders, on which the maintenance of social order depended, and to unchain a terrible revolution.

Publius Rutilius Rufus was an honest, active, and capable senator, a nobleman of the old stamp, much influenced by tradition. He was a man of culture, but much opposed to the two new forces of plutocracy and demagogy which for a century had been threatening the power of the nobility and the greatness of Rome. He had rendered signal service to the republic. He had been consul in 105 and, in 96, had governed the provinces of Asia as *legatus pro prætore* when Mucius Scævola had returned to Rome to conduct his candidature for the consulship. He had at that time energetically repressed all the abuses of the Italian publicani, doing justice impartially and earning benedictions from the subject populations.

The knights, however, who had so many interests in Asia, decided to make so severe an example of Rutilius that his conduct would not in future be imitated. In spite of his well-known incorruptibility, therefore, they trumped up a charge of extortion against him on his return to Rome in 93, and he was condemned by the *quæstio*, which, under the law of Caius Gracchus, was composed of knights.

78. The Tribunate of Drusus (91 B.C.). Rufus went into exile. But, in spite of the dark colours in which Sallust paints the Roman nobility, they had not yet fallen so low as to tolerate such an affront quietly. A rupture between the two orders was declared. The year 92 seems to have been one of silent fermentation. Its most important incident was the edict of the two censors, Cneius Domitius Ahenobarbus and Lucius Licinius Crassus, which closed the schools of rhetoric at Rome.[1] The latent war between the senate and the equestrian order was openly declared, however, in 91 by Marcus Livius Drusus, a tribune of the people, who was probably the son of the Drusus who had been the most sinister contriver of the ruin of Caius Gracchus. Times had changed, and the son of Gracchus's persecutor now did his best to arrange an alliance between the nobility and the people against the equestrian order, in the very same way as Caius Gracchus had tried to bring about an alliance of the people and the knights against the nobility. He intended to effect this by proposing an omnibus series of bills, one of the sets of *leges per saturam*, which his party had hitherto combated as weapons used only by the democrats.

Drusus's *lex iudiciaria*, indeed, sought to settle the

[1] *Cf.* Suet., *De clar. rhet.*, i.

old struggle for jurisdiction between the senate and the equestrian order on equitable and just lines. It provided that three hundred new members should be admitted to the senate from the equestrian order, and that, from the ranks of the senators, new and old, the *quæstiones* should be recruited by lot. A special *quæstio* was to be set up to try cases of alleged judicial corruption. He also introduced a *lex de coloniis deducendis*, which provided for the foundation of colonies in Italy and Sicily, a suggestion which had been proposed long since but never carried out. There was also an agrarian law, of which we know little, but which seems to have been a renovation of the laws of the Gracchi, and a *lex frumentaria*, which reduced the price at which grain was sold by the State to the people at Rome. The object of these diverse proposals was clearly to obtain by means of the bribes offered in the last three a majority in the comitia for the first. So great was the exasperation of some of the nobility against the knights, and their desire to put an end to their judicial power, that many eminent oligarchs put aside their traditional aversion from land laws and corn laws and supported these proposals.

Drusus's legislation was, however, so disparate and incoherent in character that it could not fail to excite vigorous opposition, not only among the knights but also among the aristocracy. Many senators were displeased at the proposal to increase their body by three hundred new members. The colonial and agrarian laws alarmed vested interests of enormous importance. The *lex frumentaria* burdened the treasury, which was already sufficiently out of gear. An opposition composed both of senators and of knights was, therefore, formed. Then began in the senate, in the comitia, and in the streets an obstinate contest of speeches, legal actions, constitutional and liturgical manœuvring, and even personal violence, which lasted for months and in which the Italians took part. The latter, as in the time of the Gracchi, were much alarmed by the proposed colonial and agrarian laws, which they feared would be carried out at their expense. They had, therefore, flocked to Rome in great numbers to oppose the proposals of the new Gracchus.

It is difficult to make out whether Drusus was a great statesman or a visionary. But it is clear that, instead of allying the people and the nobility against the knights, he succeeded only in splitting the nobility into two parties, in reviving the old animosity between the Romans and the Italians, and in precipitating the most confused conflict of factions and interests that Rome had ever seen. It was a tragic moment. Every one seemed to lose his bearings. Uncompromising oligarchs were ready to vote for an agrarian law if the knights were deprived of their judicial powers. Friends of Rutilius Rufus fought the *lex iudiciaria*, which was intended to vindicate their position, for fear of the agrarian law.

In the midst of these dissensions Drusus could not but be anxious about the growing agitation among the Italians. As C. Gracchus had done, and for the same reasons, he was drawn on to offer them the citizenship as a compensation. He opened negotiations with the Italians and promised that if the laws were passed, he would propose another law making them all Roman citizens. Having by this means obtained the favour of the Italians, he managed, after bitter and violent struggles, to pass all his laws at once. He then endeavoured to fulfil his promise to the Italians by proposing a law dealing with the citizenship. But the senate, on the pretext of a technical irregularity, annulled the laws already passed, and, one dull evening in that melancholy autumn, while he was taking leave of some friends who had come to see him, Livius was struck down by an unknown hand in the atrium of his own house. The assassin was never discovered.[1]

79. The Social War (90–88 B.C.). The death of Livius was followed by the triumph of his political opponents, and of the knights who were at their head. The proposal to grant citizenship to the Italians was so unpopular, even among the lower classes, that Livius's enemies were able to represent this understanding with the Italians as a conspiracy against the State, and to clamour for its exemplary suppression. His body was not cold before the tribune Q. Varius, with the ardent support of the knights, proposed the appointment of an extraordinary commission to investigate the seditious conduct of certain allies and to sit in judgment on their partisans in Rome. As the citizens of Rome always found it rather pleasant every now and then to demonstrate their superiority to the Latins and the Italians, the proposal was passed. This proved, however, to be the last straw. Instead of giving the Italians her citizenship as a compensation for the damage inflicted on them by the agrarian law, Rome was inflicting on them an extraordinary tribunal which was to conduct a partisan

[1] On Livius Drusus may be consulted C. Lanzani, *Ricerche sul tribunato di M. Livio Druso il giovane*, in *Riv. di filologia classica 1912*, pp. 272–292.

persecution! Sooner than endure this, Italy took arms and revolted.

We shall understand the reasons and the spirit of the revolt better if we note the districts in which it was most violent. The Italy which revolted was the poorer and more mountainous Italy of the centre and the south, inhabited by the Marsi, the Peligni, the Piceni, and the Samnites,—the parts, in fact, which had suffered most from the crisis which was changing the face of the peninsula; the regions of the large landed estates and grazing farms, where confiscations of land had been most frequent, where there were fewest roads, and which were farthest distant from the cities and from the great trade routes. On the other hand, the Greek cities of southern Italy, which had continued to prosper by their own strength, and which Rome had freed from the recurring danger of invasion from Bruttii and Lucania; the Latin cities nearest to the sea with their Italian colonies, which exploited the native races on equal terms with the Romans; Umbria, which had known how to change her crops to meet the needs of the time; Etruria, which had been able to profit by the tradition of industry and trade inherited from the days of Etruscan greatness; Celtic Italy, enriched by the business brought by public works and improvements and the construction of military roads—all these either remained quiet or took the side of Rome. To gain the citizenship and with it freedom was, therefore, the last desperate effort of the old Italy, which could not resign itself to extinction.

Rome was in the gravest danger. Half of Italy was in rebellion, and no one knew how far the loyalty of the rest of the peninsula could be trusted. Even

if the latter remained faithful, the rebels had forces
at their disposal which were very nearly equal to those
of Rome. The armament of their troops and their
military system were the same, and the effort they put
forth was very considerable. They had established a
federal government, with a capital at Corfinium in the
country of the Peligni. They had set up a body
representing the insurgent cities, a senate of five
hundred members,[1] which was to have power to
create two consuls, or military leaders, and twelve
prætors. The sole advantages possessed by Rome
were a greater abundance of financial resources, the
command of the sea, and prestige. Would these have
been sufficient? The greatness of the danger is proved
by the preparations which were made for defence.
The republic summoned to its aid its allies outside
Italy.[2] Slaves and freedmen were enrolled. All the
available troops were recalled and the forces were
disposed in two great military zones. One of these
was to the north, between Picenum, the Abruzzi,
and Campania, under the command of the consul P.
Rutilius Lupus; the other to the south, in Campania
and Samnium, to which was sent his colleague, L.
Julius Cæsar. Under the former fought Caius
Marius, the greatest general of his time, who ten
years before had been master of the republic, and who
had himself requested that he might be employed in
any capacity. Against the two consuls were ranged
Pompedius Silo, the friend of Drusus, and Papius
Mutilus, the two best generals of the League.

The first year of the war, 90 B.C., was on the whole

[1] Cf. *C. I. L.* i., 203.

[2] On the Social War, *cf.* App., *B.C.*, i., 39–53; Diod., xxxvii.,
2, 4–14.

none too favourable to the Romans, who had several vicissitudes of success and defeat, and who lost in battle Rutilius Lupus, one of their consuls. The uncertain progress of the war was in itself a triumph for the rebels. In the course of the year 90 the Etruscans and the Umbrians were already beginning to hesitate in their allegiance, and that at the very moment when new dangers threatened from the East Mithridates had for some time been preparing war against the Romans with the object of expelling them from Asia, but was not yet ready to take the field. He seized the opportunity offered by the revolt in Italy to depose the King of Bithynia, substituting for him a younger brother, and to reconquer Cappadocia in concert with Ariobarzanes. Prudence counselled, therefore, that the revolt in Italy should be dealt with not only by arms but also by concessions. Public opinion had been brought to its senses by the danger, and there was a reaction against the equestrian order and its mad policy, which had done so much mischief.

In the tribunician elections for 89 the party of the tribune Varius, the author of the persecution of the Italians, was beaten. Shortly afterwards the consul L. Julius Cæsar proposed and without difficulty secured the passage of a law which granted Roman citizenship to the Italian allies who had remained loyal. Fear had accomplished what justice and reason had been unable to secure! But the Lex Julia merely restricted and did not remove the danger. Central and southern Italy were still in arms. Having taken the first step in the direction of concessions without stumbling, Rome was not long in meeting the remaining rebels half way. Two of the tribunes for 89, M. Plautius Silvanus and C. Papirius Carbo, proposed a new law (the lex Plautia Papiria) which granted Roman citizenship, not only to all the cities which laid down their arms at once, but to all the Italians south of the Po who should ask for it within two months.

This law also was passed without difficulty, and in addition to its enactment the tribune Varius and his followers were driven into exile for what they had done against the Italians, and as being guilty of crimes against the interests and the *maiestas* of the Roman people. Very soon, too, the anger of the people turned against the knights, who were now regarded as responsible for the war. After his law on the subject of the citizenship, Plautius Silvanus induced the comitia tributa to vote a new *lex iudiciaria* depriving the knights of their judicial powers, and providing that the *iudices* should now be elected by the tribes, each tribe choosing fifteen without regard to the social position of the candidates.[1] It was perhaps at this very time that the consul Cn. Pompeius Strabo passed the law which granted Gallia Cisalpina the rights of Latin colonies, in order to make them liable to conscription and so balance the loss to recruiting caused by the revolt of the allies.

80. The Rupture between Roma and Mithridates and the Loss of the Province of Asia. The Italian rebellion had thus been successful, even though the fortune of war remained indecisive. The effect of the concessions was immediate, though all the Italians did not at once lay down their arms. In Picenum, Asculum resisted obstinately, and the consul Cn. Pompeius Strabo was obliged to besiege and take the place by force. Campania, Samnium, and Apulia still fought on. Many Italians, however, now gave

[1] Ascon. in *Corn.*, p. 71 (ed. Orelli).

in. The Umbrians and the Etruscans gave up the idea of joining the League, and, in fact, all the central and southern Italians had returned to their allegiance by the end of 89. It was only in the remote parts of Samnium that resistance still continued.

Italy had hardly begun to recover from these alarms, however, when she was overtaken by a new calamity. We have seen that, in the year 90, on the death of the King of Bithynia, Mithridates dispossessed his legitimate successor, Nicomedes III., in favour of a bastard brother—a certain Socrates Crestus. At the same time, in accord with Tigranes, King of Armenia, he reconquered Cappadocia, whence he had been expelled by the Romans in 92, and placed one of his sons on the throne. The senate, however, did not allow itself to be intimidated, and sent Manius Aquilius at the head of an embassy to restore the two exiled kings to their thrones. Mithridates gave way, either because he did not consider that his preparations were sufficiently far advanced, or because he was daunted by the resolution displayed by Rome.

Asian affairs had been readjusted, therefore, without much difficulty or trouble, which, in these difficult times, was a piece of rare good fortune for Rome. At this point, however, a trifling intrigue among the publicani and the senators suddenly precipitated a catastrophe. Manius Aquilius—so at least the ancient writers assert—had been far from pleased at the complaisance of Mithridates, for he had gone to Asia, hoping to have the conduct of a lucrative war against Pontus. On the other hand, the King of Bithynia while in exile had contracted many debts to the publicani of Ephesus, who now wanted to be repaid. Aquilius gave the king to understand that the sum required could easily be procured by making a raid into Pontus, and in the end Nicomedes, tormented by his creditors, became a silent accomplice of the Roman legate in invading the dominions of his powerful neighbour, thus stirring the smouldering fires into a great conflagration.

At first Mithridates, with great adroitness, merely protested and demanded reparation. Then came the end of the year 89. Italy was in flames, the East was disarmed, Mithridates was ready. Three or four hundred ships of war, fully equipped in the Black Sea ports, were waiting for the summons of the King of Pontus. There was a great concentration of mercenaries, horse and foot, from the more barbarous countries of the near East: Armenians, Cappadocians, Paphlagonians, Scythians, Sarmatians, Thracians, Bastarnians, Celts and, what was worse than all, even Greeks. Great reserves of grain had been collected in Tauris. Treaties and understandings had been concluded with all the more important Oriental potentates and with the barbarians of Thrace and Macedonia. Greece and Hellenistic Asia, groaning under the exploitation of Roman capitalists, only awaited a liberator. There was no need to hesitate longer. In the spring of 88 Mithridates rejoined to the rash and insolent answer which the Roman legate had given to his legitimate protests, by a declaration of war. He reconquered Cappadocia, defeated the Roman troops in Bithynia, drove out Nicomedes III., captured the Roman fleet, and invaded the province of Asia.

A heavier blow could not have been struck at Rome. The social war had impoverished and ruined the landowners of southern Italy, small and great alike. Now the invasion of Asia deprived the treasury

of the revenues of the most profitable of the Roman
provinces, and Rome, and Italy as well, lost their
interest on the vast capital invested in the East.   A
terrible crisis followed at Rome.   The publicani
found it impossible to fulfil their contracts with the
State.   The treasury was empty.   Money was scarce.
Loans were difficult, all but impossible, to obtain; for
the capitalists in their alarm hastened to recall what
they had lent.   Rates of interest which were readily
paid in a period of rapid gain were now regarded as
intolerably usurious.   All the old and obsolete laws
as to debt were appealed to by those who had to pay.
The prætor's court was full of lamentations, protests,
and threats.

In the midst of all this the Italian question again
became acute in the capital.   The senate, on the
specious pretext that the power and number of the new
citizens should not be allowed to swamp too com-
plétely the sacrosanct authority of the original Romans,
proposed that the new citizens should not be enrolled
in all the thirty-five tribes, but should be relegated
to eight of them, or to ten new ones[1] which should
be outside the old constitution.   These proposals
greatly irritated the ambitious Italians who had
flocked to Rome, and the city was soon overflowing
with violent agitation.   While the atmosphere of the
capital was thus highly charged, new and terrible
tidings arrived from the East.   In the province of
Asia, now almost entirely in the power of Mithridates,
on a fixed day about 100,000 Italians[2]—men, women

[1] On the two traditions *cf.* Vell. Pat., ii., 20.   App., *B.C.*,
i., 49.

[2] Appian (*Mithr.*, 22, 23) gives 80,000, Plutarch (*Sulla*, 24)
gives 150,000 victims.   The latter figure need not be regarded as

and children—had been attacked, murdered, drowned, or burned alive by the infuriated populace of the large and small Asiatic towns. Their slaves had been set at liberty and their goods distributed between the royal treasury and the cities from whom tribute was due. Nor was this all. From Pergamus, where Mithridates had established his capital, he now turned to Greece, where all the hot-headed patriots, all the democrats offended by the hauteur of the Roman Government, all the native merchants who had been ruined by the competition of Italian capitalists, all the idle and tumultuous proletariat, began to look to him with hope as the destined liberator. What was more, the plans and hope of Mithridates transcended Greece itself and began to court an understanding with the Italians who were still in revolt. The Samnites and the Lucanians, who were still in arms, sent envoys to him and proposed an alliance, and the King of Pontus replied, promising that he would make a descent on the peninsula exactly as Hannibal had done, and many Italians flocked to his standard.

81. **The Struggle between Marius and Sulla for the Command in the War against Mithridates.** Never, perhaps had the Roman senate had such a terrible task. But there was no hesitation. The province of Asia was so precious a part of the empire that, notwithstanding the revolution which was still distracting Italy, they decided to send one of the consuls thither with a strong army. Of the two consuls the lot designated L. Cornelius Sulla, who had been Marius's legate in 106, who had fought bravely as an

---

exaggerated if it is taken to include women and children, who, however, must have been the minority. On the Italian immigration into Asia *cf.* the description in Cicero *De lege Manilia*, 7, 17 ff.

officer against the Cimbri in 103, and had distinguished himself greatly in the social war. Sulla was not new to Eastern affairs, for as prætor in 102 he had restored Cappadocia to the Roman candidate Ariobarzanes, had for the first time led Roman troops as far as the waters of the Euphrates and, seated in a chair of state, had received the first embassy sent by the King of Parthia to the Romans.

The lot had, therefore, chosen wisely, and the Romans had the more reason for accepting the decision as events were precipitating themselves with ruinous haste in the East. In the spring of 89, Mithridates had despatched an army under the command of his son across Thrace to Macedonia, and a fleet to the Ægean under Archelaus. The news of this was enough to raise in rebellion a great part of Greece, including Athens, which had hitherto been Rome's most faithful friend in Greece. The parts which did not rebel were easily conquered by the army of Mithridates, because the Gauls and the Thracians, instigated from Pontus, had invaded Macedonia, and the governor of that province could send no assistance. Even Delos was taken by Archelaus and the Italian merchants murdered. In short, the whole Roman empire in the East, whether in Greece or Asia, was tottering. Hellenism was making a supreme effort to drive Rome back into Italy, and for this purpose was using the strong arm and well-tempered weapons of a semi-barbarous sovereign from the interior of Asia.

It was at this supreme moment, in the face of Mithridates victorious, when half the empire was invaded and in the hands of the enemy, that a civil war broke out—the last and worst consequence of the struggles of earlier times and of too many rival ambi-

tions. The knights were displeased that Sulla had
been entrusted with the reconquest of Asia. The
fact is certain, though the reason for it can only be
conjectured. It was clear that the consul charged
with the recovery of the lost province must be constituted its supreme and absolute lord and master for
several years, and must be given power to do as he
thought fit there, whether in favour of the interests
of the knights in that country or against them.
Now, for some years since the case of Rufus, there had
been hatred between the senatorial and equestrian
orders, which had been aggravated by the agitations of
Livius Drusus and the social war. Not a few of the
senators detested the knights more than they did the
demagogues, and would willingly have allied themselves with the latter in order to remove the former
from their path. At a critical moment such as this
it was very important for the knights that their pet
province should not fall into the hands of a new
Rutilius Rufus. Hitherto Sulla had not openly
taken part either for or against them. He had kept
himself apart from political struggles, and had occupied
himself chiefly with war and administration. But,
whether his origin made the knights suspect that
he was their enemy, or whether he had actually become so, the fact remains that the equestrian order
were against giving Sulla the Asian command.

On the other hand, Rome had in Marius a great
general in whom the equestrian order to which he
himself belonged, had always had confidence, and who
chafed under the inertia to which he was condemned.
The times were, moreover, troubled and agitated as
never before. The knights madly desired to recover
their judicial powers. Among the Italians new dis-

content was fermenting, owing to the intrigues of the
senate, which was trying by dexterous expedients to
deprive them of part of what had been conceded by the
laws of 89 and 88. The economic crisis filled many
minds with fury and desperation. One of the prætors
had been murdered at his own tribunal by usurers
enraged by his too strict application of the laws against
this trade!

From this dumb ferment of interests, ambitions,
and cupidities was born a vast political intrigue in
which the knights, Marius, the Italians, and part of
the democratic faction all had a hand. Its object
was to restore the ancient powers of the equestrian
order and to take away the Asian command from Sulla,
who was meanwhile collecting an army at Nola. The
man selected to carry out the plan was P. Sulpicius
Rufus whom the conservative tradition as usual de-
picts as corrupt, in debt, and ambitious. In 88 he
was tribune and in that capacity proposed three laws
intended to secure for his party sufficient support to
enable them to pass a law transferring the command
in Asia from Sulla to Marius.

The first law gave the freedmen and the Italians
what they wanted by providing for the enrolment of
the Italians in all the thirty-five tribes and restoring
thereto the freedmen who had ceased to belong to
them since 113, the year in which Æmilius Scaurus
was consul. The second recalled the knights who had
been banished after Marius's political ruin in 89.
The third proposed a reform of the senate which excluded all its members whose debts amounted to 2000
drachmæ.

Sulla hastened back to Rome from Nola to act
in concert with his colleague, Q. Pompeius Rufus, in

opposing these laws, particularly the first, which, in the opinion of many, revolutionized the State from top to bottom. Once again the question of giving the Italians the right to vote threatened to upset everything. Sulla and Rufus, fearing that they could not secure the rejection of the law by the comitia, made the mistake of resorting to liturgical obstruction; that is to say, by declaring *feriæ imperativæ* on every day on which assemblies could be held, they made all meetings of these bodies impossible. This action on the consul's part was no doubt in itself strictly legal, but its obstructive intention was manifest. The interested parties, with Sulpicius at their head, refused to allow themselves to be disarmed by this ingenious manœuvre. Sulpicius in eloquent speeches attacked the *feriæ* as illegal. He collected a bodyguard of six hundred knights, armed squadrons of his supporters among the lower classes, and with these forces he one day invaded the forum, intimidated the consuls, and demanded that the *feriæ* should be cancelled and the comitia held. The consuls tried to resist but their adversaries threatened to resort to arms. Riots followed and Pompeius was so much alarmed that he fled. Sulla himself then abandoned the scene of the struggle and retired to his army at Nola.

By the failure of their opposition the two consuls had lost their authority. One had given way and the other had disappeared. The foundations of the old oligarchical republic were crumbling. Sulpicius and his faction remained masters of the State. Their first step was to pass the Sulpician laws. Next, taking advantage of the moment at which the assembly was full of Italians and the oligarchical party depressed by the defeat which they had just sustained, they

proposed and passed in the comitia tributa the law
regarding the Asian command.   Immediately after
the passage of the law Sulpicius sent two tribunes to
Nola to require Sulla to transfer his legions to Marius.
The coalition which had grouped itself around Sulpicius might congratulate itself on the entire success
of its plan.

That success would, perhaps, have been complete
indeed had the army been the same as of old.   But
Marius had changed its character.   The soldiers
commanded by Sulla were militia recruited, in accordance with the Marian reform of 107, from the poorer
classes of the population.   Most of them, in fact, were
veterans of the Cimbric and social wars, soldiers by
profession, and all of them ready for new experiences
and new adventures.   Sulla knew them all personally,
and had made them promises as great as the discipline
which he exacted on the field of battle in face of the
enemy was terrible in its severity.   They were already
dreaming of the treasures which they would take from
the barbarian King of Pontus and which would be divided among them after the victory. They had a leader
whom they knew to be brave, energetic, eloquent,
and generous, and who had already proved his worth.
What did a law passed at Rome signify to these soldiers
except that the riches on which they had set their
hearts were to go to other hands and other soldiers?
Moreover, it was to be remembered that, though the
two tribunes had come armed with a law passed by the
people to require Sulla to cede the command, Sulla
was still consul and had received that command by
lot according to law.   As is often the case amid
revolutionary disturbances, the legal aspects of the
case were doubtful; and how much more doubtful

must they have appeared to soldiers whose interest it was to doubt? Sulla, who feared the reprisals of his enemies if they were victorious, took it upon himself to speak to his troops and to appeal to them to defend the first legal decision against the second, which it was proposed to substitute for it. The soldiers listened to him, the two tribunes who had been sent to him as envoys were torn to pieces, and Sulla with his legions marched on Rome.

Now for the first time were made manifest the formidable political consequences of the military transformation effected by Marius, the result of which had been that the middle and comfortable classes had consented to disarm and leave the military service to the lower orders. The army had become a mercenary force in the hands of the various factions in the State, to be used in their contests for civil supremacy. This time, thanks to the resolute conduct of Sulla, it was used in the service of the senate and the old conservative aristocracy against the equestrian order, the popular party, and the Italians. But it would not always be so! To enter Rome with his legions was audacity almost sacrilegious, of which no one hitherto could have believed that a consul would be capable. This explains the easy success of the first man who dared to do it amid the general surprise. A short but bloody combat in the streets was enough to clear the capital of the heroes of the legislative triumphs achieved a few weeks before. The whole aristocratic party, except a few who were restrained by constitutional scruples, rallied to Sulla, and, emboldened by the consciousness of success and the presence of the consul and his army, they attempted what we should now call a counter revolution.

The senate, convened by the consuls, annulled the Sulpician laws as illegal because passed on days of festival, and declared twelve of the leaders of the democratic party, including Rufus and Marius, public enemies (*hostes publici*). The consuls then proposed several laws, among them the *lex Cornelia Pompeia unciaria* and the *lex Cornelia Pompeia de sponsu*, the object of which was to give some relief to the debtors. This, besides lessening the pressure of the grave economic crisis which was oppressing them, was, perhaps, also a direct blow at the knights, who were pre-eminently a money-lending class.

The laws were passed. Sulpicius Rufus was assassinated and Marius fled to Africa. The result of the consular elections, however, was a severe check to the Sullan party. Several tribunes and prætors and one of the consuls—Lucius Cornelius Cinna—were ardent democrats. Sulla had succeeded by surprise, but his almost incredible audacity, and his violence, which had awakened the terrors of some and the abhorrence of others, had in most cases aroused that sort of legalistic superstition which was so strong in all Romans. The elections warned the victors not to abuse overmuch the good fortune they owed to their violence, and showed them that already there had begun a reaction against reaction.

This first symptom was soon accompanied by another. The senate, in order to provide also the other consul, Q. Pompeius Rufus, with an army, had prolonged his *imperium* and had assigned to him the legions in Cisalpine Gaul which were commanded by the proconsul Cneius Pompeius Strabo. But the soldiers had assassinated their new general, whether on their own initiative or at someone's instigation could never be discovered. Sulla understood that the defeated party might recover quickly. He made the new consuls swear to respect the existing laws and returned to his army. In the spring of 87, as soon as the weather permitted, he left Italy with no more than five legions, some incomplete auxiliary cohorts, and a few squadrons of cavalry, scarcely thirty thousand men in all. He had little or nothing in the way of a war fleet, and his objective was an enemy whose forces were several times as great as his own.

CHAPTER XV

THE FIRST CIVIL WAR

82. The Mithridatic War and the Revolution in Rome and in Italy (87–86 B.C.). While these grave events were taking place at Rome, Mithridates, owing probably to the necessity of keeping watch throughout all Greece over the party of his opponents, had divided up his army among a large number of garrisons. When Sulla invaded Greece, however, the Pontic generals, Archelaus and Aristion, in order to avoid being defeated in detail in a series of small encounters, concentrated all their scattered contingents at Athens where they shut themselves up to give time for a second Mithridatic army to invade Greece and take the enemy in the rear. They reckoned, indeed, on being able to maintain themselves for an indefinite period in Athens though it was an open place, Sulla having no fleet which could face the Asiatic armada. The besieged were, on the contrary, in a position to use their ships to blockade the besiegers by cutting their communications with Italy.

The plan of the Pontic generals was all the more skilful as they were to find a valuable ally at Rome itself in the party which had been humiliated by Sulla's *coup d'état*. The consul Cinna had re-introduced the Sulpician laws as soon as Sulla's back was

338

turned, including that which enrolled the Italians in the thirty-five tribes. And once again, this terrible question had carried fire and sword into the republic. The other consul, Cn. Octavius, opposed the bill and certain tribunes interposed their veto. Armed bodies had been raised on both sides and had come to blows. Cinna for the moment was beaten and forced to fly before the fulmination of a senatorial decree, deposing him, appointing another consul in his place, and declaring him a public enemy. Outside the walls, however, Cinna found what had hitherto always been lacking to the cause of the democrats—namely, an army. He proceeded to Capua where the forces set to watch the recently subdued Campania were posted. Many of the soldiers were Italians. Cinna presented himself as a consul illegally deposed and despoiled of his office by the senate and the oligarchical party. He succeeded in inducing them to swear fealty to him and began a recruiting campaign among the Italians. Meanwhile, Marius had returned to Italy and with the army of Capua, increased by the new recruits, he and Cinna marched on Rome.

The senate had summoned to defend Rome, Cn. Pompeius Strabo and Q. Cæcilius Metellus with their armies, the former from Gallia Subalpina, the latter from Samnium. There ensued under the walls of Rome what was neither more nor less than a civil war, —a long, obstinate, and confused struggle, interrupted every now and then by attempts to negotiate, and ending with the victory of Marius and Cinna. They succeeded in forcing an entrance into the city at the head of their victorious troops and soon returned with interest the blow struck by the oligarchs through Sulla in 88 at the popular party. The Sulpician laws were passed. A very large number of senators were killed and their property confiscated. Among them was Q. Lutatius Catulus, who in 101 had so gloriously co-operated in the victory of Vercellæ. Sulla was declared a public enemy and dismissed from his command. His patrimony was confiscated and his wife forced to fly for refuge to his camp in Greece. Cinna and Marius were proclaimed consuls for the year 86.

The little army which was to reconquer the Roman Empire in the East was, therefore, abandoned under the walls of Athens to the blows which the army of Mithridates was preparing in Asia. If this army could arrive before Athens capitulated, Sulla and his men were lost. No help or reinforcement could be expected from Rome on whose behalf they were fighting. But Sulla did not lose heart. Whatever opinion may be formed of that enigmatic figure, no historian will be able to deny that he was a man and a leader of men. He gave proof of this in the terrible difficulty in which he found himself. He stuck at nothing which could help to secure the safety of his army. For the construction of machines of war, he felled the groves of the Lyceum and the immemorial plane trees of the Academy, in whose shade Plato and his disciples had philosophized. For the pay and maintenance of the soldiers he subjected Greece to pitiless requisitions. He pillaged the most venerated temples, coined into money all the gold and silver tripods, vases, ornaments, and works of art which had been offered to the gods for many generations. In order that he might contest the command of the sea with the enemy, he sent L. Licinius Lucullus, one of his officers, to run the Mithridatic blockade and collect a fleet among the friendly Mediterranean states. There was not a *ruse de guerre* that might help to end the siege which he did not study. He shared all the labours of his soldiers in order to maintain their spirits, and was always in the thick of the fight or leading a column of attack in person. Above all, he was lavish with the gold he took from the sanctuaries.

Through the whole summer and autumn of 87, Athens obstinately held out in the expectation of relief. Fortunately the army which Mithridates sent to Greece was delayed by difficulties of supply, and, being badly led, made slow progress. Caius Sentius Saturninus, the governor of Macedonia, was, therefore, able to detain it with the small force at his disposal, and to entice it towards the end of the season into Macedonia, where it was compelled to go into winter quarters. Thus Sulla gained the winter months, but in the meantime a more serious danger threatened him in the rear from Italy. Marius had died early in 86, and Lucius Valerius Flaccus, who was appointed consul in his place, had been directed to proceed at the head of 12,000 men to deprive Sulla of his command. This meant that in the spring Sulla would be caught between the Roman army and the army of Mithridates. To take Athens before either Mithridates or Flaccus arrived on the scene was, therefore, a matter of life or death for him. Accordingly he made his preparations during the winter, and on March 7th collected all his forces and launched a desperate attack against the city.

It was successful. First the town and then the Piræus fell into his hands. Archelaus embarked his army and departed. Sulla had now escaped the first and the more serious of the dangers which threatened him, that of being surprised before Athens by two armies and thus being caught in the midst of three enemies. Yet his position, if somewhat improved, was still little less than desperate. He had now to face the forces of Archelaus, which, practically intact, had effected a junction at Thermopylæ by sea with the second army of Mithridates advancing from northern Greece, and, in addition to these, the army of the consul Valerius Flaccus, which was coming from Italy. The approach of the democratic army imposed on Sulla the decision to make a sudden and desperate attack on Mithridates at any cost. With his habitual resolution, he advanced against the Asiatic forces and attacked them near Chæronea in Bœotia where he won a great victory over Archelaus who had taken over the supreme command (86 B.C.).[1]

Chæronea was the first real and considerable defeat inflicted on Mithridates by the Roman arms. It not only produced, therefore, a profound impression on the whole of the East, but greatly altered the situation to the advantage of Sulla and of Rome. For some time back the monied classes of Asia, overborne at the time of the massacre of the Italians, had been regaining confidence, and were now openly intriguing in favour of Rome, skilfully playing on the instability of the poorer class and especially on the discontent caused by the constant levies demanded by Mithridates. At the end of 87 the rich trading city of Ephesus had already risen against Mithridates in favour of Rome. The battle of Chæronea put new courage into the pro-Roman party throughout Asia, and this was in itself a great advantage for Rome. A still greater advantage was that the victory made pos-

[1] On Chæronea *cf.* J. Kromayer, *Antike Schlachtfelder* ii., 353 ff.

sible a sort of tacit accord between Sulla and the democratic party.[1] It appears that Flaccus was a man of sense. When he landed in Epirus, he no doubt saw, what indeed was perfectly clear, that it would be madness to fight Sulla and thus destroy two Roman armies by pitting them against each other, when Mithridates was preparing to send a new force into Greece to avenge Chæronea, and when the two Roman armies united would, perhaps, be only barely sufficient to repel the invader. Sulla in his turn knew well that Mithridates was by himself a sufficiently serious enemy. Further, it may be reasonably supposed that the two Roman armies, instead of fighting each other, preferred to fight Mithridates and to be afterwards led on to plunder Greece and Asia. In view of the proscription which had been declared against Sulla, Flaccus did not venture to unite the two armies; it would seem, therefore, that the two generals came to some sort of secret understanding. As consul, Flaccus had power to requisition the Byzantine fleet, and it was settled that he should attempt an invasion of Asia. Sulla was to wait in Greece for Dorilaus, who was approaching after having embarked in Eubœa ten thousand men saved from the army of Archelaus after his defeat at Chæronea. Thanks to this wise arrangement, the year 86 was fortunate for the Roman arms. Sulla attacked and destroyed the army of Dorilaus at Orchomenus and then retired into winter quarters in Thessaly. Flaccus invaded Macedonia,

[1] That Valerius Flaccus and Sulla had a secret understanding is a conjecture which is very probable, and indeed necessary for the explanation of the whole history of the war. It was first suggested by H. Bernhardt, *Chronologie der Mithridatischer Kriege*, Marburg, 1896.

drove into Asia the last remnants of the Pontic army, and crossed the Bosphorus by means of the Byzantine ships. At the end of the year Mithridates had lost Greece as well as his other European conquests.

83. The Treaty of Dardanus. If the democratic party in Italy had been disposed to follow the wise example which Flaccus had set them in Asia, and had rescinded the proscription of Sulla, Rome would in all probability have soon been gladdened by a victorious peace. This was not to be. The party of the old nobility seemed now to be destroyed: some had been killed; others had fled for refuge to Sulla; the rest had been terrorized into impotence. The democrats were, therefore, more completely masters of the republic than they had ever been before. The offices of State, the military commands, the treasury, the army, and the provinces were all at their disposal. Was it to be expected that they would trouble their heads about the ex-chief of the defeated party, who still remained at the head of a little army in Greece? No one then dreamed that this terrible man might find his way back to Italy with his army behind him. The policy of Flaccus was so little to the taste of his party that not only did his agreement with Sulla remain a secret, but during the winter of 86–85 one of his legates, a certain Fimbria—a violent democrat—succeeded in corrupting the soldiers and in inducing them to murder Flaccus and in making himself general.

Thus the concordat with Flaccus was destroyed and Sulla found himself in the same situation as before, and indeed in a worse position than ever. He could not attack Fimbria owing to the menace of Mithridates on one flank. He could not attack Mithridates owing to the menace of Fimbria on the other. To attack both Fimbria and Mithridates was out of the question. What was to be done? Once more Sulla took an extraordinarily bold course, decisive not only of his own future career but of many grave events in the history of Rome. Not being able to fight both Fimbria and Mithridates at once, and not being able to come to an understanding with Fimbria, he decided to open negotiations with Mithridates. It would appear that Sulla succeeded in corrupting Archelaus, who was induced to dismiss his fleet, and to suggest to Mithridates a peace on the basis of the *status quo ante* 89. By this arrangement Mithridates would retain the ancient kingdom of Pontus, would receive the title of friend and ally of the Roman people, and would pay an indemnity of 2000 talents, in addition to dismantling a certain number of warships. Sulla on his side would grant an amnesty to the revolted cities of Asia.

From the standpoint of the ancient political traditions of the republic, it was little less than high treason, as we should now say, to grant such terms of peace to a monarch who had made war on such a scale against Rome and had slain thousands on thousands of Roman citizens. For much less than the crimes of which Mithridates had been guilty, Antiochus III. had been deprived of half his kingdom, Perseus had been dragged to Rome in chains, and Carthage razed to the ground. But in order to save himself Sulla did not hesitate to treat the *maiestas populi Romani* as cavalierly as in 88 he had treated the principle that Rome could not be violated by an armed force. Moreover, though the conditions were most generous, the negotiations were neither short nor easy. Mithridates, who was

quite aware of the difficulties with which his adversary
was struggling, tried to get even better terms, and
threatened to come to an agreement with Fimbria.
But Mithridates also was in need of peace. The blow
he had suffered in Greece had profoundly shaken
his authority in the East. Asia Minor was gradually
slipping from his grasp. In the spring of 85 Fimbria
invaded Asia, defeated the forces of Mithridates, and
took Pergamus. Lucullus, who had finally succeeded
in collecting a powerful fleet, had appeared off the coast
of Asia and was inciting the cities to revolt. It was,
therefore, best for the King of Pontus to conclude
peace immediately, and the treaty was accordingly
signed at Dardanus in the Troad after a meeting
between Mithridates and the Roman proconsul (85).[1]

84. Sulla in Asia and in Greece (85–83 B.C.).
Fimbria was now finally isolated. Sulla turned on
him suddenly and surrounded him and his army
near Thyatira in Lydia. The soldiers and officers
who had been most attached to Flaccus promptly
deserted to Sulla; the rest, by corruption or by violence, were induced to follow their example. Fimbria,
himself, rather than survive such a disaster, preferred
to commit suicide. Thus Sulla remained master of
reconquered Asia at the head of a powerful army and
fleet and in possession of a treasury bursting with the
indemnity paid by Mithridates.

It was only just that Sulla, the victor of Chæronea
and Orchomenus, and no other, should recover for
Rome her lost Oriental provinces. But the glory of
the achievement was blemished by the treaty of Dardanus. Sulla knew this well, and after making peace
with Mithridates his own idea was to effect a recon-

---

[1] On the Peace of Dardanus, *cf.* App. *Mithr.*, 56–58.

ciliation with the party in power in Italy. His demands were not excessive. Besides the approval of
his Oriental proceedings, he asked only for the re-
patriation of all the proscribed persons who had
taken refuge with him. In order to reach an agreement he remained in Asia and Greece, spending what
remained of 85, the whole of 84, and part of 83 in
negotiations with the Roman government. His
efforts at conciliation, however, were met with immovable intransigence in Italy. The popular party
was now firmly in possession of the government. They
did not wish by granting Sulla's requests, to bring
about the return to Italy of all those members of the
aristocratic party whom they had themselves driven
out, nor did they wish to assume responsibility for the
treaty of Dardanus of which public opinion dis-
approved. It is true that there was a party in the
senate in favour of the return of the exiles. It is also
true that, when the only reply to Sulla's efforts at
conciliation was the preparation of war, the troops
mutinied, and Cinna, who had been re-elected consul,
was killed. These were serious warnings against
taking too lightly the dangers of the civil war which
was threatening. But when was a party which believed itself sure of power, ready to believe in a
danger which was not immediately pressing?

Any remaining chance of an agreement was
extinguished by the intervention of the knights.
Immediately after the recovery of Asia, Sulla had
required the cities of the province to pay the arrears
of five years' annual contributions and a large war
indemnity as well. He had, however, abolished the
old system of farming the Asiatic taxes by public
contract, and had declared his intention of collecting

them directly through his own officials, dividing the province into forty-four districts for the purpose. He did not wish the treasury to share the spoils of conquest with the publicani, and it was because of this that the knights, who were already his enemies, now swore a mortal hatred against him.

Meanwhile Sulla returned from Asia to Greece, where he spent all the year 84 and the first months of 83, continuing his negotiations for an agreement with the democratic party, but at the same time reinforcing his army, which had been reduced by the war, by recruiting soldiers in the Peloponnese, in Macedonia, and in Thessaly. By the spring of 83 he must have come to the conclusion that war was inevitable. The party in power would neither re-admit the exiles nor approve the treaty of Dardanus. To all his proposals they had replied by directions from the senate that all his armies must be dismissed, *i. e.*, that he should surrender unconditionally to the government.

For the new war Sulla prepared with his customary determination. It was not likely to be an easy contest. The party against whom he was fighting represented law and order. Then, as always, that gave them an immense advantage. They had, moreover, the control of the public treasury and of the tribute of all the western provinces. They could recruit troops from all Italy, more especially as, under the threat of a new struggle, they had finally settled the Italian question by distributing the new citizens among all the thirty-five tribes. Finally, they could count on the support of many aristocratic families who recognized their government as legal. Among the most important of these were Caius Norbanus and

Lucius Cornelius Scipio Asiaticus, a descendant of the conqueror of Antiochus, the two consuls of the year, the son of Marius, Cneius Papirius Carbo, who had been consul in 85 and 84, and Cneius Domitius Ahenobarbus. With these were associated some men of humbler birth but eminent by reason of the capacity and resolution which they had displayed in the wars and agitations of the preceding ten years, among whom the most distinguished was Q. Sertorius.

Sulla, on the other hand, had no very precise or clear title to authority, and to the material resources of his adversaries could only oppose the treasures of Asia, about 40,000 soldiers, and those members of the old nobility who had sought refuge with him. It is no doubt true, however, that Italy desired peace and a reasonable accommodation with Sulla, being weary of civil war and not blind to the fact that, if Sulla had made the treaty of Dardanus, he had also inflicted two memorable defeats on Mithridates. This desire was a source of great weakness to the democratic government, for it meant that in Italy they could only arm for their service an undisciplined and ill-trained crowd, as accessible to the ravages of gold as of the sword. Sulla's small army, on the other hand, was a solid block of steel, ready to fight to the death for their leader, who had already enriched them and who had promised them a certain victory and still greater rewards.

85. The First Civil War (83–82 B.C.).[1] The first year of the war showed at once that Sulla was not

[1] On the first civil war the most recent works are E. Pozzi, *Studi sulla guerra civile sillana*, in *Atti della R. Accademia delle scienze di Torino*, voL xlix., 9, 1913–14; C. Lanzani, *Mario e Sulla, storia della democrazia romana negli anni 87–82* B.C., Catania, 1915.

unlikely to win. He landed at Brundusium in the spring of 83, immediately defeated the army of the consul Norbanus near Capua, and then turned on that of the other consul, Scipio, not far from Teanum. Knowing that Scipio was inclined to an agreement and that his soldiers desired peace, Sulla opened negotiations. Scipio agreed to treat. The two generals met and discussed the state of the republic and the remedial measures which were indispensable if peace was to be secured. Finally an armistice was arranged in order that the other consul might be consulted. At the last moment, however, for reasons which are obscure to us and cannot have been clear at the time, Scipio broke off negotiations and returned Sulla his hostages. On this, Scipio's troops, accusing him of deliberately rejecting a just and honourable settlement, mutinied and deserted to Sulla. Scipio was taken prisoner and released by Sulla. He resigned the consulship and retired to Massilia. Sulla remained master of south Italy.

These successes won over to his side many of the nobility who were still wavering, among others M. Licinius Crassus and Cn. Pompeius, son of Cn. Pompeius Strabo, who had been consul in 89. The latter was a young man of very great wealth. He had large possessions in Picenum where he set about recruiting on his own initiative for Sulla, who recognized him as commander of the forces he had raised. These proceedings, however, exasperated the government of the republic. The consul Norbanus sent no reply to the peace overtures made to him by Sulla. The senators who had joined the Sullan party were declared public enemies. The son of Marius was elected consul for 82 with Cn. Papirius Carbo, in order to win over to the government his father's veterans. Arms and armies were prepared by both sides: by the government in northern and central Italy; by Sulla in south Italy.

Hostilities recommenced in the spring of 82. Carbo, who was concentrating in Etruria his contingents, which were coming into northern Italy from all parts, sent his legate, Carrinas, into Picenum to destroy the forces which were being collected there for Sulla, by Metellus Pius and Cn. Pompeius. But Carrinas was beaten by Metellus, and Carbo, who had set out from Etruria to assist him, was stopped and driven back by a startling piece of news. Sulla in person had defeated between Signia (Segni) and Præneste (Palestrina) the young Marius, who had been entrusted with the defence of Rome, and had shut him up in Præneste where he was held besieged. By a bold *coup de main* he had then taken possession of Rome and was already preparing to march against Carbo.

Carbo rapidly retraced his steps in order to come to the rescue of the capital, but found his way barred at Clusium by Sulla's army. There ensued a battle, which was long and sharp, but neither army succeeded in dislodging the other. Rome remained, therefore, in the power of Sulla and the armies of the republic were separated, part remaining in the north and part about Præneste and in central and south Italy. Sulla, however, with his army and his party found himself threatened from two sides—in the north, by Carbo's army, which was still intact and which might be joined by the force which Norbanus was recruiting in Cisalpine Gaul, and, on the other hand, by an insurrection which was brewing on a vast scale in Samnium and Lucania. In these regions the war had rekindled the last sparks of the ancient sentiment of nationality and, with the consent and assistance of the republican government, a large army was being prepared there.

Thus the situation was critical for both parties. The fate of either might have been settled by the slightest error of judgment or failure of fortune. Sulla contented himself with maintaining a strong defensive on the approaches to Rome, and barring them to Carbo, and tried meanwhile to cut the communications between Carbo and Norbanus. Metellus, with considerable forces, appears to have disembarked at Ravenna with a view to marching from there down the Via Æmilia and thus getting in between the two. Carbo on his part, being placed in a difficult position, made a mistake which only a great general would have avoided. Not feeling himself strong enough to annihilate Sulla's army, not wishing to abandon Præneste and Rome to their fate, but realizing the importance of preserving free communication with Norbanus, he divided his forces. To the aid of Præneste he sent eight legions; to Norbanus he sent a reinforcement to help him to confront Metellus, while he kept his main body at Clusium. Norbanus seems to have committed the same error. For, on receiving his reinforcements from Carbo, either because his whole army was not yet ready or for some other reason that we do not know, he marched against Metellus with these reinforcements and with only a part of his own troops.

Scattered in this way these forces all succumbed one after the other, while Carbo's main army was immobilized at Clusium. The reinforcements sent to save Præneste never arrived. Norbanus was defeated by Metellus at Faventia (Faenza) and this gave Sulla several important cities including Ariminum, the key to the communications between Rome and the valley of the Po. On this Norbanus lost his head, abandoned his command, embarked in a small vessel and fled to the east. His flight was at once followed by a catastrophe. The whole of the valley of the Po surrendered to Sulla's generals. On this, Carbo, though he had about 30,000 men, came to the conclusion that all was lost in Italy, and fled to Africa, where he hoped to continue the struggle. Against his leaderless army at Clusium, Sulla launched Pompey, who defeated it without difficulty. Its remnants were dispersed and a certain number of the survivors joined the Samnite and Lucanian armies, which were advancing on Rome from the south.

These armies were not only considerable in numbers but were animated by a fierce spirit of destruction and hatred, and they might have been disastrous to Sulla had they arrived sooner. They did not come, however, until all Italy was already lost to the republic, which retained almost nothing except the ultimate and useless *point d'appui* at Præneste. In the course of this singular campaign, however, Sulla had had to scatter his small forces so much that the great army of the Italians, reinforced by the remains of the democratic legions, succeeded by a skilful night march in eluding Sulla's vigilance and in making an unexpected appearance under the walls of Rome, which were held by insufficient forces. It is difficult to say what they might not have succeeded in achieving had it not·been for the energy of an obscure prætor named Appius Claudius, who saved the city from the ravages of this savage horde exalted by hatred and fanaticism. Instead of yielding to numbers, Claudius, like a new Leonidas, resisted stoutly, losing his own life in the battle. This gave Sulla time to come to the rescue from near Præneste where he was in camp. On November 1, 82,[1] the two armies met at the Porta Collina, not far from the modern Porta Pia. The battle was hotly contested, and, in some of its phases, the Sullans did not have the best of it. The credit for the victory which Sulla won was chiefly due to his legate, Marius Licinius Crassus, who brought up reinforcements at the critical moment. The result was that the Samnites and Lucanians were in the end thoroughly beaten and many of them were taken prisoners.

Shortly afterwards Præneste also capitulated; the younger Marius committed suicide, and Sulla was master of Italy and of the republic. The empire, however, was far from being pacified. The conflagration was still raging in Etruria, Sardinia, Sicily, Africa, and Spain, which were all in the hands of the Marian party. It was then that the man who had astonished the world by his moderation was transformed into an executioner. In the provinces his legates continued to conquer, one by one, the surviving generals of the democracy. At Rome and in Italy, Sulla himself took in hand the task of extirpating by fire and sword what he believed to be the root of all evil. All who had represented or favoured the democratic party were punished with exile, confiscation, or death. Sulla's vengeance fell on their sons, their relatives, their remotest connections. He decreed that the sons and grandsons of proscribed persons were to be for ever incapable of filling any office. Entire cities were mulcted in enormous fines and had their fortifications demolished and part of their public

[1] On the date, *cf.* Vell. Pat., ii., 27.

and private land confiscated. The goods of the condemned and of the exiles, with the lands taken from the Italian cities, were divided among the soldiers and the partisans of the victor. The number of the victims of the proscription could never be ascertained. The Samnites were for the most part destroyed along with their once flourishing cities—Bovianum, Æsernia, Telesia,—which were now reduced to squalid hamlets. About 150,000 soldiers were granted lands in Samnium, in Campania, and in Etruria. Slaves, freedmen, plebeians, impoverished patricians, made or remade great fortunes from the proceeds of murder and rapine. Many of the proscribed fled among the barbarians of Spain or Mauretania or took refuge with Mithridates. Others took to piracy and brigandage.

86. The Sullan Restoration (82–79 B.C.). Confiscation and murder, however, and the surrender to the spoiler of the goods and the lives of the vanquished were not enough. Sulla was too great a statesman not to see this clearly. In 82 he caused himself to be invested with a magistracy, which, though it had an ancient name, had also a new and strange character. He was made *dictator legibus scribundis reipublicæ constituendæ* with power to give the State a new constitution unimpeded by the interference of either the comitia centuriata or the comitia tributa.

His idea was the same as that of Cato. He wished to eradicate from Rome and from Italy the "corruption" which was so much hated and feared, by restoring the institutions of the great days when Italian society, rural, aristocratic, and military in character, was a perfect hierarchy of classes, at the head of which stood a disciplined but unlearned nobility, and at the bottom, a submissive rural population which was patient, comfortable, and not discontented with its lot. By his constitutional reform, therefore, he was careful to annul, one by one, the plebeian and democratic conquests of previous years. He restored the judicial powers of the senate. He restricted the powers of the tribunes, exempting from their intercession the decrees of the senate and bills proposed to the comitia. He enacted that persons who had held the office of tribune should not be permitted to aspire to higher magistracies. He subjected the comitia tributa once more to the preventive tutelage of the senate and possibly went so far as to deprive that assembly of all its legislative power, which was transferred to the comitia centuriata, now perhaps reconstituted on the ancient model of Servius Tullius.[1] He suppressed the distributions of corn, abolished the censorship or reduced it practically to impotence, thus re-establishing the principles of the irremovability and omnipotence of the senatorial order, which was now to be replenished every year only by the addition of the ex-magistrates. The Lex Domitia of 103, making the sacred colleges elective, was rescinded.

Finally Sulla broke the equestrian order. After decimating them by persecution he deprived them of the privilege, acquired with so much difficulty, of seats of honour at the public spectacles. He took away from them the public contracts, the Asiatic

[1] App., *B.C.*, i., 59. It seems improbable that such a great reform can have been carried out by Sulla before the civil war at the time of his first entry into Rome. It is more natural to associate it with the great work of reform carried out during his dictatorship.

taxes, and their judicial duties. When he wished to fill up the gaps made in the senate by war, death, and persecution, he preferred to the knights lesser men of the third estate—even his own old soldiers.[1]

But the Sullan restoration was not limited to this. Sulla also occupied himself with the improvement of the administrative machinery by means of humbler reforms. In this way he solved the difficult problem of increasing the personnel of the government without running the risk, so much feared by the nobility, of increasing the number of the magistracies too much. With this in view, he created the so-called pro-magistracies. It was arranged that consuls and prætors, during their first year of office, should be obliged to reside in Rome, but in their second year, as pro-consuls and proprætors, they should be called upon to govern the provinces. He fixed the legal order and succession of the *cursus honorum* and rigorously re-established the ancient requirement of a two years' interval between tenures of the several magistracies, imposing an additional requirement that ten years should elapse between two tenures of the consulship. In order to put a stop to favouritism, he laid down that provinces should be assigned in advance by lot. He raised the number of the senate to six hundred and, to make the administration of criminal justice more rapid and more efficient, he increased the num-

---

[1] Dion. Halic., v., 77. The contrary account given by Appian (*B.C.* i., 100) to the effect that he introduced three hundred members of the equestrian order, which is in complete contradiction with all the principles underlying the Sullan restoration, may be taken to mean that Sulla put into the senate some of the new knights who were his friends and who had been enriched during the civil war.

ber of courts (*quæstiones perpetuæ*). Similarly, in the interests of civil procedure, he increased the number of the prætors to eight.

The restoration of the ancient constitution was almost perfect. Absolute perfection would have required the repeal of the Lex Plautia Papiria and the abrogation of the citizenship accorded to the Italians. Sulla did not attempt this. No great Roman general, to whatever political faction he might belong, had ever dared to declare himself against the claims of the Italians. It was, indeed, from the generals that the Italians had obtained the advantages, slight as these were, which they now enjoyed. Yet, though he did not abrogate the Lex Plautia Papiria, Sulla deprived of the citizenship many municipia which had declared against him. In 79 he could contemplate with pride and satisfaction the archæological monument which he had raised. The edifice was impressive and apparently indestructible. One thing only was wanting—a breath of the ancient spirit. This he could not supply. His work turned out self-contradictory and, by reason of its insoluble self-contradictions, impermanent. He had wished to restore the patrician estate of the fifth and fourth centuries, but he could not recreate, body and soul, the aristocracy which had been the prop and stay of the old constitution. He had subjected the whole State, the comitia, the senate, the magistracies, the military commands, and the courts of justice, not to a true aristocracy but to a ring composed of his friends, his bullies, his executioners, enriched by the proceeds of confiscations, of deserters from the Marian party, and finally of practically the whole ancient aristocracy, who were now bound to him by ties of gratitude. This ring was feared chiefly because of the prestige of its head, and was held together only by the common interest of its members in the retention of power. It was too heterogeneous, it was too much divided in its tendencies and interests, its ambitions and ideas were too varied to permit of its re-establishing in Rome the ancient order which had prevailed under the genuinely aristocratic régime of the previous centuries. The difficulty of doing this had been enormously increased by the great convulsion produced by the recent revolution. That event, like all other revolutions, had weakened tradition. Sulla's idea may have been to bring back Italy to the rural simplicity of three centuries before and to persuade her to abandon industry and commerce. But as the result of his Oriental campaigns, there had been imported into the country a great number of slaves and freedmen, who were bound to become the teachers of new ideas and new customs. It is, therefore, not surprising that, before he finally laid aside the dictatorship and crowned his great work of restoration by retiring into private life like another Cincinnatus, he should himself have witnessed the beginning of the disintegration of the structure he had raised. The elections of the year 80, the last of his dictatorship, saw the triumph of two men of whom one was a conservative (though a very lukewarm Sullan) and the other, M. Æmilius Lepidus, a declared opponent of the dictator. At the same time a fact of even graver import showed the weakness in foreign affairs of the government founded by Sulla. In the year 80, Alexander II., the last of the Lagidæ, died leaving Egypt in trust to the Roman people. While the senate hesitated, a court camarilla handed over the kingdom to the illegitimate sons of Ptolemy X.

The senate accepted the *fait accompli* and renounced the opportunity of securing without war, by hereditary transmission, what was nothing less than the richest country in the ancient world.   A few months later, when barely sixty years of age, Sulla died at his sunny villa at Puteoli, after having dictated memoirs of his remarkable life, leaving behind him a constitutional achievement of which in a few years nothing was to survive but a few sagacious administrative reforms.

CHAPTER XVI

THE GREAT WARS IN THE EAST

87. The Insurrection of Lepidus and Sertorius (78–75 **B.C.**). When Sulla died, the motley and discordant crew, odious by its associations with murder and rapine, to whom he had entrusted the duties which had formerly been the privilege of the old nobility, no longer possessed the authority necessary to govern the State. All the victims of the restoration immediately began to agitate. One of the consuls, M. Æmilius Lepidus, bluntly proposed the abolition of some of the most important of the Sullan laws. He wished for the re-establishment of the distributions of corn, the recall of the exiles, the restoration of territory, and the vote, to the cities which had been deprived. In Etruria, when these proposals were known, the Sullan colonists were expelled by armed force by the former proprietors. Shortly afterwards, when Lepidus left Rome for Gallia Narbonensis, the province which had been assigned to him, he stopped in Etruria in order to enrol in his army the many destitute persons in this district. In concert with Lepidus another member of the aristocracy, M. Junius Brutus, busied himself with recruiting an army in the Valley of the Po.

Meanwhile revolution was raising its head again in Spain. Q. Sertorius, one of the generals sent by the republic to that country in 83, perhaps for the purpose of recruiting soldiers, had not only held out there after Sulla's victory, but had placed himself at the head of the Lusitani and, by tenacious and unwearied guerilla tactics, had practically detached Spain from the Roman Empire. He had successively defeated four proconsuls. He had gathered about him the exiled and the proscribed, and, in fact, all the malcontents who had suffered by the new restoration. With their help he had finally succeeded in establishing a regular government in opposition to the government at Rome. On the other hand, the Lusitanians and the Celtiberians had recognized him as the upholder of their independence, and, as in the case of Hamilcar and Hannibal, they had given him hostages in the persons of the sons of the principal native families whom he caused to be educated after the Roman fashion. Under his strong and enlightened government Spain was steadily recovering her independence and was in a position, once the defeated party began to bestir itself again in Italy, to offer a strong *point d'appui* for a new revolutionary movement.

It was all the more necessary to repress the revolt of Lepidus without delay. The senate declared him a public enemy and appointed his colleague in the consulship together with the ex-consul, now proconsul, Catulus, and Cn. Pompeius to carry on the war against him. Pompey was the youth who had been Sulla's legate in the civil war. He was not yet thirty and had never held any curule office. He was, therefore, not qualified to hold the command of an army. Pompey had been, however, a favourite of Sulla, who had always had a peculiar weakness for him. So much was this the case that the dictator had entrusted him with the command against the Marian party in Sicily and Africa, and after his success granted him a triumph, contrary to the wish of the senate, and the title of Magnus.   The favour of his all-powerful chief, the reputation which, as a very young man, he had rightly or wrongly acquired of being a good general, the terror felt by the senate at the first signs of a recrudescence of the revolution, the scarcity of competent and loyal officers, and, finally, the ambition and intrigues of Pompey himself overbore all constitutional scruples.   Pompey appeared to be a commander on whom the Sullan confederacy could rely, and an army was entrusted to him.   The attempt at revolution was crushed easily enough in Latium, Etruria, and Cisalpine Gaul.   Lepidus managed to escape to Sardinia where he died suddenly, whether naturally or by violence is not known (77).

When the revolt of Lepidus had been quelled, the senate turned its attention to Spain, and in 77 decided to try conclusions also with Sertorius.   It was a difficult war, which required an able general.   Pompey again came forward as a candidate for the post.   This time a great part of the senate was against him, but Pompey, by clever intrigues, and finally by encamping his armed legions at the gates of Rome, contrived to extort from them the coveted command.

While Pompey went to try his fortune in Spain, Italy began to be exasperated by a new cause of discontent,—the affairs of the East.   While Sulla lived, no one had dared to raise his voice, but now all were exclaiming against the disastrous consequences of the treaty of Dardanus, which had humiliated but not broken Mithridates, and had so gravely compromised Roman prestige in the Orient.   Greece and Macedonia were, in fact, harassed every year by barbarians from the north. The eastern basin of the Mediterranean was infested with pirates, who captured ships, sacked cities, and had set up a kind of state of their own in Cilicia.[1] Mithridates was to all appearance quiet, but it was said at Rome—and perhaps not without justification—that he instigated the Thracians and the Scordisci to invade Greece and Macedonia, that he was secretly helping the pirates, that he was in treaty with Sertorius, and that he was preparing for war on a large scale. In the meantime he had urged the King of Armenia, his kinsman and ally, to conquer Syria as far as the frontiers of Egypt, to invade Great Cappadocia and to assume the pompous title of King of Kings. Was it possible that a new empire was about to arise on the ruins of Syria which would be a greater danger than Pontus?

Here indeed was a fruitful source of reproaches and accusations against Sulla and his party! The Spanish question added fuel to the flames. Sertorius was a very different enemy from Lepidus, and in the year 76 Pompey had succeeded against him no better than had Pompey's predecessor. It was probably in order to explain this failure that he began to accuse the senate of refusing out of spite to send him the necessary reinforcements of men and money. Public discontent increased. Charges against prominent members of the party in power again became frequent. An agitation was begun for the abolition of the restrictions imposed by Sulla on the authority of the tribunes and for the abrogation of the judicial privileges of the senate. By the year 75 the consul Caius Aurelius Cotta had already succeeded in repealing Sulla's

[1] *Cf.* Cic., *Pro leg. Man.* xi., 31 ff.; Plut. *Pomp.*, 24.

law forbidding the election of a tribune of the people to any higher office.

88. The Testament of the King of Bithynia and the New War with Mithridates (75–74 B.C.). The fact was that, once Sulla was gone, the government grew weaker every day, while the bad humour of the public grew more pronounced. In the midst of this confused situation, at the end of 75 or the beginning of 74, while the war in Spain was raging more furiously than ever, the King of Bithynia died, leaving his kingdom to the Romans. To accept the legacy was equivalent to declaring war on Mithridates, for Mithridates could never allow the Romans to establish themselves in Bithynia. Was Rome in a position to undertake a second war against Pontus for Bithynia with revolution smouldering at home, Spain in revolt, and Macedonia threatened? The senate hesitated, and was rather inclined to refuse a succession which involved so much peril. But a violent movement of public opinion constrained them for once to put aside their scruples and their timidity. All who were for any reason discontented with the government, and who knew it to be wavering, clamoured loudly for Bithynia, which, they declared, was as good as another Asia. To those who reminded them of Mithridates, they replied that a second war with Pontus was bound to come in any case, and that it was time to wipe out the shame of the treaty of Dardanus.

The senate could not resist the pressure of public opinion and annexed Bithynia. But those who feared Mithridates proved to be right. For some time the King of Pontus had been getting ready for a new conflict with Rome, and not only had he made all the preparations of which he was suspected, but he

had concluded an alliance with Sertorius. The death
and the will of Nicomedes, however, brought the king
to the point of immediate action. In the spring of
74, while they were placidly discussing at Rome who
should command in the coming war, Mithridates
suddenly set in motion his army, which consisted
of 120,000 men, of whom 16,000 were cavalry. One
part, perhaps commanded by Taxiles and Hermo-
crates, was sent to invade Bithynia. With the rest
he invaded Asia—this time, however, not as before
in his own name, and as a conqueror, but as the ally
of Sertorius whose representative led the way. This
representative was a certain Marcus Marius, who
entered the cities of the province wearing the
insignia of a proconsul, liberated them in Sertorius's name, and proclaimed a partial repudiation
of debt.

Thus, while Pompey was vainly imploring the senate
to send men and money to Spain in order that he might
fight Sertorius, while disorder and discontent were
growing worse in the capital, and while the senate
was falling into impotent hesitations in the presence
of the slightest difficulty, Rome was undertaking a new
war with Pontus. The end might have been disastrous had there not appeared at this critical point in
her history a great man and a great general in the
person of Lucius Licinius Lucullus, who, as we have
seen, had served with distinction in Asia during
the first Mithridatic war under the command of
Sulla.

Lucullus was descended from an ancient and noble
but impoverished family, which during the revolution
had been persecuted by the accusations and the hatred
of the democrats. Like Cato he had lived simply, and,

though an enthusiastic Hellenist, he belonged to the traditionalist party. In 87 he had gone to Asia with Sulla and had rendered signal services to his chief in the several capacities of general, admiral, and ambassador, without seizing the opportunity to enrich himself as he might easily have done. He had returned to Italy with Sulla, and had taken part in the civil war, but he had not stained his hands with the goods of the vanquished. As prætor in Africa he had treated the provincials with gentleness and honesty. He despised the parvenus and the adventurers of his own party, and, in the maturity of middle life, he represented the purest aristocratic tradition of the good old times, but had not attained either great riches or the highest honours in the State.

89. **The First Campaigns of Lucullus in the East: the Conquest of Bithynia and the Invasion of Pontus (74–72 B.C.).** Lucullus was consul in 74. No one was better qualified than he for the command against Mithridates if war should break out. For he had much experience of war in the East. But the question was surrounded by intrigues, struggles, and hesitations, for others were anxious to secure the command for themselves, and at Rome, Lucullus had more enemies than friends. It was only when news arrived that Mithridates had invaded Asia that delays and hesitations disappeared. The direction of the war and the proconsulate of Cilicia were given to Lucullus, but he had to promise that the treasury should as far as possible be relieved of the expenses of the campaign, and that he would content himself with the smallest possible force, which was five legions. The senate did not wish to send to Asia so exigent a commander

as they had sent to Spain. As luck would have it,
Lucullus was really a great general.[1]   He knew how to
do great things with small resources.   When he landed
in Asia, he refused to risk an immediate battle with
the superior forces of Mithridates.   He collected
as much grain as he could and began following the
enemy, step by step, without accepting battle.   Every
night he shut up his forces securely in their camp, and,
by cavalry raids he did his best to make it difficult
for Mithridates to receive the consignments of supplies
which came to him from Tauris.   The army of
Mithridates was very numerous and difficult to revictual, and in the end the embarrassment caused by
Lucullus became unendurable.   As he could not rely
on the ports of Pontus for his supplies, Mithridates
decided to take a great neighbouring seaport and fell
upon Cyzicus, which he invested.   Lucullus followed,
and in his turn besieged the besiegers.   Cyzicus held
out for so long that Mithridates found it necessary
to break loose from the net drawn round him by
Lucullus.   He therefore divided his army into two
parts, the smaller of which he despatched towards
Bithynia hoping to draw off his antagonist on a false
scent, while he himself with the main body sought
safety in another direction.   Lucullus managed to
destroy one division of Mithridates' army on the

[1] The chief authorities for the new and final Mithridatic war,
so far as it is covered by the campaigns of Lucullus, are App.,
Mithr. lxxii. ff.; Plut., *Lucull.*, 6–35.   The most interesting modern
monograph is Th. Reinach's *Mithridate Eupator, roi du Pont*,
Paris, 1890 (pp. 320–372).   On the personality of Lucullus, and
the historical importance and the chronology of his wars *cf.*
G. Ferrero, *The Greatness and Decline of Rome*, New York
and London, 1907, vol. i., Chapters VII. and VIII.; vol. ii.,
Appendix B.

Rhyndacus, the other on the Æsepus. Asia was free and Bithynia conquered by the beginning of 73.

These first successes won by Lucullus caused the greatest delight at Rome. Even in Spain things began to take a turn for the better, not so much owing to Pompey's skill as to the mistake made by Sertorius in allying himself with Mithridates. By this alliance he alienated the sympathy, still lively and far from useless, which the Marian party at Rome had felt for him, and which, perhaps, had had something to do with the senate's failure to send reinforcements to Pompey. The party of Marius, even more than the party of Sulla, whom in this particular they sought to discredit, posed as the defenders of the integrity and the greatness of the empire, which made it impossible for them to approve of Sertorius's alliance with Mithridates.

This was shown by the dignified stand made by a young man who was to be known to history as Julius Cæsar and who had up to this point been willing to risk a great deal for the Marian cause. Cæsar was born in 100 B.C. He came of an impoverished patrician family and was the nephew of Marius, who had married a sister of his father. He was also Cinna's son-in-law, and was, therefore, united to Sertorius's party by a double bond of relationship. To these ties he had remained faithful even in the days of Sulla's omnipotence, for he had refused to obey the dictator's injunction that he should repudiate Cinna's daughter. On Sulla's death he had commenced his political apprenticeship in the ranks of his uncle's party by prosecuting two prominent personages in the Sullan confederacy, Cornelius Dolabella and C. Antonius Hybrida. He had then returned to the

East to continue his studies at Rhodes. Hearing, however, that the neighbouring cities of Caria were revolting against the Roman government in the name of Sertorius and Mithridates, the fervid nephew of Marius turned his back on the anti-Roman policy of the Marians of Spain. He collected a small force and on his own initiative did what he could to stem the rising tide of rebellion. Many other members of the party of Marius followed the example of the young Cæsar and dissociated themselves from Sertorius, and the effect of this was soon felt in Sertorius's own camp. Discord arose, desertions began, and an opposition grew up under the leadership of Perpenna, one of Lepidus's officers, who had collected the remains of his army.

The satisfaction caused by the victories of Lucullus did not last long. Mithridates, defeated on land, had taken to maritime war, making use of his friendship and alliance with the pirates and the tribes and cities of Thrace. There was a panic in Italy. Everyone was convinced that the Pontic fleet meant to threaten Italy from the Ægean, and there was no fleet available for defence! The senate decided that Marcus Lucullus, brother of Lucius and consul in that year, should undertake as proconsul a great expedition to Thrace to destroy Mithridates's allies. They hastily voted 3000 talents to enable Lucius Lucullus to build a fleet. They prolonged his command for a year, and probably also gave him the governorship of Bithynia. Lucullus had taken action, however, in Asia without waiting for the senatorial decision at Rome. He had hurriedly collected a fleet from the maritime resources of the allies and with it he had given chase to the Pontic fleet in the Ægean, destroying its separate squadrons one after another. Meanwhile his lieutenants proceeded to reduce the Bithynian cities which were still in arms, and took much spoil in slaves and other property.

By the middle of 73 Lucullus had reduced all the Bithynian cities but Heraclea, and had forced Mithridates to return by sea to his kingdom, taking with him the remnants of the army which he had led out to conquer Bithynia in the previous year. The mission which the senate had entrusted to him was fulfilled. Many generals thought that he should now rest his troops and await Rome's decision as to what should be done next. Lucullus, however, was of a different opinion. It was now clear that Rome could not securely possess the province of Asia unless the kingdom of Pontus was destroyed. Already Mithridates was retiring into the mountainous interior of his kingdom in order to prepare a new army in the triangle formed by Cabira, Amasia, and Eupatoria, and was summoning to his assistance his son-in-law Tigranes, King of Armenia, Macarus, Viceroy of Tauris, and the Scythians. If, therefore, a final conflict with the King of Pontus was inevitable, it was better to face this at once while he was still weak from the blows he had received in Asia and Bithynia, and before he had time to recuperate his forces. Lucullus, therefore, without waiting for instructions from Rome, crossed Bithynia and Galatia, entered Pontus and rapidly led his legions under the walls of Amisus and Temiscira whose obstinate resistance obliged the Roman army to entrench for the winter of 73–72.

90. **Spartacus and the Slave Rebellion** (73–71 B.C.).[1] Things were thus going well in the East.

[1] On the so-called war of Spartacus, *cf.* especially App., *B.C.* i., 116–20.

This was not the case in Italy, where, in 73, there had broken out a slave revolt, the greatest probably with which Rome had hitherto had to deal. It was led by a certain Thracian named Spartacus who was undoubtedly a man of genius. He had escaped in 73 from the school of gladiators at Capua, and had succeeded in collecting an army composed of slaves and broken men, which was considerable though by no means so immense as it was represented to be by those who found so much difficulty in overcoming it. Spartacus had beaten the local forces of a prætor who made the mistake of supposing that he could easily capture the rebels, and had then thrown himself into southern Italy. There the consuls of 73, when they faced him, were successively defeated.

Discontent with the senate, with the party in power, and with the constitution of Sulla was exacerbated by this scandal. But, as if in compensation, the two Luculli and Pompey were successful in Europe and Asia during the year 72. Lucullus, leaving part of his army to continue the siege of Amisus and Temiscira, attacked and decisively defeated the new army of Mithridates with the rest of his force. At the same time his brother Marcus, proconsul in Macedonia, conquered Thrace, and also the Balkans up to the Danube. In Spain Pompey finally succeeded in bringing the war to a conclusion, not so much owing to his own merits as to the skill of Perpenna, who had slain Sertorius; and was beginning a war of destruction and extermination against the cities which had taken the part of Sertorius or had given shelter to the senators of his party.

In Italy, on the other hand, when the elections for 71 were announced, there was a scarcity of candi-

dates, so terrified was everyone at the idea of having to take the field against the dreaded leader of
the slaves. Such a shameful situation had never
been seen in Rome. In order to put an end to the
scandal the senate entrusted the command to the
prætor of the current year. This was M. Licinius
Crassus, who had distinguished himself in the civil
war by saving Sulla at the battle of the Colline Gate,
and who was, perhaps, the richest man in the senate.
The choice was not a bad one. While Lucullus was
conquering one by one the great Greek cities of
Pontus—Amasia, Amisus, Sinope—Crassus succeeded
in crushing Spartacus, and crucified 6000 of the prisoners he took along the Appian Way between Capua
and Rome. Five thousand of Spartacus's followers
escaped and tried to fly beyond the Alps. But in
upper Italy they were caught by Pompey on his
way back from Spain and exterminated. Shortly
afterwards the two generals, Crassus and Pompey,
arrived together at the gates of Rome.

91. **The End of the Sullan Constitution. The
Consulship of Pompey and Crassus (70 B.C.) and the
New Oriental Policy of Lucullus.** When a man has
enjoyed one privilege, he often thinks it due to himself, or indeed a point of honour, to claim others.
Alone among his countrymen since the beginning
of Roman history, Pompey at the age of 36, without
having held office, and without even being a senator,
had held high commands with the authority of a proconsul and had received the title of *imperator*. Naturally therefore, after conquering Sertorius and restoring
Spain to Rome, Pompey's thoughts turned decisively
towards a candidature for the consulship, the highest
office of all. After having commanded as proconsul

he could not reconcile himself to recommencing the *cursus honorum* as quæstor or ædile. But when Crassus heard that Pompey wanted to be consul, he wanted to be consul too, though the two years' interval prescribed by law had not elapsed since he had been prætor. The senate had to deal, therefore, with two illegal candidatures, for which, moreover, two of Sulla's friends and lieutenants were responsible. It was too much, and the senate indicated that it would offer the firmest opposition. On this, however, Pompey and Crassus came to an understanding, and, what was more important, reached an understanding also with the popular party, which for many years had been waiting for a favourable moment to make a bid for deliverance. If Pompey and Crassus were elected, the promise was made that they would gratify the people by abrogating those parts of Sulla's constitution which had given the greatest dissatisfaction. Both candidates, in the meantime, kept their soldiers in arms under the walls of Rome, thus putting a certain constraint upon the senate. This constraint, the understanding between the two generals, their agreement with the popular party, the discontent of the public, combined with the weariness of the Sullan party, exhausted by ten years of power, overbore all opposition. The senate allowed the candidature of Pompey and Crassus, who were elected consuls for the year 70.

While these events were taking place in Italy, Lucullus had gone to the province of Asia to spend the winter of 71–70, and was endeavouring by various measures to restrain the cupidity of the publicani, without considering what powerful enemies he was making. The mind of the conqueror of Pontus was occupied with much greater matters. Mithridates had fled to Armenia. That country, inhabited by people related by race and language to the populations of Media, Persia, and Asia Minor, had once been part of the Persian empire of which it formed a satrapy. It was afterwards absorbed in the empire of Alexander the Great, but during the wars of the Diadochi it had already recovered its independence, and it was in vain that the Seleucids of Syria had attempted its reconquest. The blow which the Romans had struck at Antiochus III. had indirectly favoured the destinies of the country. During the last fifteen years, by judicious marriages, by conquest, and by negotiation, Tigranes had contrived to extend the borders of his kingdom to the north as far as the Caucasus, where the barbarians of Albania (Schirwan) and Iberia (Georgia) acknowledged him as their sovereign. He had also expanded to the south, east, and west, and had conquered practically all the dominions of the Seleucids, Cilicia, Syria properly so called, and Phœnicia, and he had invaded several provinces of the kingdom of Parthia.

Now Lucullus's idea was nothing less than to invade and conquer Armenia. For this purpose, while he awaited the complete subjection of Pontus, he sent to Tigranes to demand the surrender of Mithridates. Lucullus had already construed the instructions of the senate in a rather wide sense, when, after freeing Bithynia, he had invaded and conquered Pontus. But Pontus was after all the country of Rome's implacable enemy. Lucullus's new proposition was a very different thing. What he meant to do was on his own initiative to conquer a great and friendly country without any excuse or reason whatsoever. His course of conduct, whether he was aware of it or not, implied a real political revolution, which destroyed a vital part of Sulla's restoration. For the authority of the senate in foreign affairs he was substituting the personal initiative of the general. For the senatorial policy which was traditionally prudent and astute, prompt to recede before obstacles, accustomed to protract the discussion of every issue, prone to intrigue and temporize rather than to act, incapable of exploiting a success to the uttermost or of making a decisive effort, he was substituting what we should now call an aggressive imperialism, an audacious policy of expansion which deliberately courted dangers and difficulties.

It was fated that Sulla's work should be destroyed by his friends and favourite pupils. While Lucullus was ruining it in the field of foreign affairs, Pompey and Crassus were making large inroads on it in the sphere of home administration. The two consuls for the year 70 had kept their promises though there was no love lost between them. Laws were proposed by different magistrates, and passed thanks to the support of the consuls, which restored to the tribunes the powers which Sulla had taken away, among the rest the power to propose laws without previously submitting them to the senate. They granted an amnesty to all the survivors of the civil war, not excluding the followers of Lepidus and Sertorius. They reformed the courts of law. The *iudices* for the *quæstiones* were now to be chosen, no longer from the senate alone but promiscuously from the senate, the equestrian order, and the *tribuni ærarii*— a class of persons which we are unable to define with certainty.[1] Further, the censorship, which had been in abeyance for seventeen years, was re-established and the censors, Lucius Gellius and Cn. Lentulus, purified the senate by removing many of Sulla's friends, a measure which gave general satisfaction.

Many of the claims of the popular party had thus been satisfied, and that party would assuredly have secured more if Pompey and Crassus had not quarrelled towards the end of their consulship. It appears that Pompey wished to be sent with a proconsular command to replace Lucullus, whom the senate had been keeping on from year to year, and that Crassus was opposed to this.[2] As things were, both returned at the end of their year of office to private life feeling enmity toward each other, for neither would accept an ordinary province.

92. The Conquest of Armenia and the Intrigues of Pompey against Lucullus (69 B.C.). Meanwhile, in the spring of the year 69, Lucullus found himself in a position to invade Armenia with about two legions and a few thousand natives formed into cohorts—20,000 men in all. He crossed the Euphrates and marched straight on Tigranocerta, repulsing as he went the army of the general Mitrobarzanes, who tried to bar his way. He invested the city, where the king had hidden his treasures and his harem, and when Tigranes approached with a relieving army, he detached 14,000 men from the besieging force and sought a decisive encounter with the new enemy.

[1] On the *tribuni ærarii cf.*, Daremberg et Saglio *Dictionnaire d'antiquités classiques*, articles *Iuduciariæ leges* and *Tribus*.

[2] This is a hypothesis, but a probable one. *Cf.* G. Ferrero, *The Greatness and Decline of Rome*, New York and London, 1907, vol. i., p. 169 ff.

The two armies confronted each other on the banks of the Tigris where one morning Lucullus gave his little army the order to ford the river, in spite of the tumultuous current, launched it against the forces of Tigranes, which outnumbered his by five to one, and gained a complete victory. The king himself was barely saved by headlong flight. Shortly afterwards Tigranocerta capitulated. Lucullus was master of the enemy provinces south of the Tigris, and restored Syria to Antiochus Asiaticus. But Lucullus was not content with this. He led his men back to winter in the gentle climate of Gordiana and dreamed of yet more grandiose operations. He would swoop on Persia and destroy at a blow the empire of the Parthians, whom Rome had never been able to subdue, thus winning for himself and his country glory beyond compare.

By this time, however, the astute Pompey was using his great influence at Rome, and was already beginning the series of intrigues whereby he intended to succeed in the design he had had to abandon in 70, probably owing to the opposition of Crassus, and the object of which was to supplant Lucullus in his command. He had found strong supporters, not only among the democrats but also among the knights who were displeased by the reforms introduced by Lucullus into the administration of the province of Asia. Pressure was brought to bear on public opinion and on the senate by accusing Lucullus of carrying on an illegal war for his own personal profit. The senate with its usual weakness took fright, and, in order to still this outcry, took away the government of Asia for the year 68 from Lucullus and entrusted it to a proprætor. The democrats soon found an unexpected and valuable ally in Lucullus's own army. Though Lucullus was as good a general as Sulla and Marius, he treated his soldiers as if they were still the legionaries of the Punic war. The rigour of his discipline, the parsimony of his largesses seemed truly intolerable to men who had been spoiled by the bad example of previous wars. The most serious grievance against Lucullus was that he gave the legions too small a share of the spoils of victory. Several of his officers who were friends of Pompey (among others Publius Clodius, a youth destined to make some noise in the world) were inciting the soldiers against their general, saying that they had a right to be treated better and recompensed more generously after all the labours they had undergone, and that Pompey was the man for them.

In 68, when Lucullus again attacked the armies of Tigranes and Mithridates on the plains of Lake Van in order to finish the war, he was able to defeat Tigranes once more on the Arsanias, but he failed to take Artaxata, the capital of the kingdom, because his officers and the greater part of his soldiers mutinied. Shortly before this the democratic party at Rome had succeeded in getting him deprived of the government of Cilicia and in having a commission sent to undertake the organization of the new province of Pontus. The mutiny of the legions was a new shock to the authority of Lucullus, which was already tottering, and to which Mithridates soon gave the *coup de grâce*. As soon as he heard that the troops were in revolt, the ex-king of Pontus entered his former kingdom with 8000 men and succeeded in shutting up the legate who had been left behind by Lucullus in Cabira with a handful of men. When Lucullus made as if to go to his assistance, the troops refused to move before the spring of 67. Fortunately Triarius, Lucullus's admiral, was able to disembark reinforcements in Pontus and extricate the legate from Cabira. But he was not strong enough to drive Mithridates out of Pontus. He was, therefore, compelled to spend the winter in the face of the enemy at Gaziura in the heart of Pontus, sending vain requests to Lucullus to send him reinforcements.

93. The Dismissal of Lucullus and the Lex Manilia (68–66 B.C.). The most devoted friends of Lucullus must now have begun to doubt whether he could remain at the head of the legions in the East. However severely they might condemn the intrigues of Pompey and the indiscipline of the troops, it was doubtful whether Lucullus, in the new circumstances, could succeed in reconquering Pontus. A new and unexpected development finally inclined the scales of destiny towards Pompey's side. In the winter of 68–67, Rome and Italy were afflicted by a serious and painful scarcity. This, it was said, was the fault of the pirates, who were intercepting at sea cargoes of grain intended for Italy. But was not the omnipotence of the pirates due to the inertia of the senate and the negligence of Lucullus, who had until very recently been proconsul of Cilicia? A tribune of the people, named Aulus Gabinius, who was a friend of Pompey, was quick to seize the opportunity. He succeeded in passing a law which bore his name (Lex Gabinia) and which embodied a decision unprecedented in the history of the republic. A man of consular rank (unnamed) was to be charged with the conduct of the war against the pirates. He was to have a fleet of 200 ships, a great army, 6000 talents and absolute proconsular authority for three years over the whole Mediterranean and its coasts and for a distance of fifty miles inland. He was to have the power to choose fifteen legates, to recruit soldiers and rowers, and to collect taxes in all the provinces. In a word, there was to be set up a veritable maritime dictatorship, which it was understood, though not explicitly stated, was to be entrusted to Pompey. The senate violently opposed the bill, but the people, being both hungry and angry, threatened to revolt. The law was passed. The powers proposed by Gabinius were even extended and the command was given to Pompey (67).

Pompey got to work at once, and his task turned out to be much simpler than had been imagined at Rome. The power of the corsairs depended on the inertia and negligence of the Roman government. A few operations, a few severe examples, followed opportunely by several acts of clemency, enabled Pompey to relieve the empire of these singular exponents of Mediterranean sea power and to sweep the seas clean, at any rate for a time.

Pompey's dictatorship at sea, however, was intended to be only a stepping stone to something more exalted. In the spring of 67, when his troops permitted it, Lucullus set out with his legions to the assistance of Triarius. But he was too late. Triarius had already given battle to Mithridates and had been defeated. As soon as the news of this reached Rome, the tribunes became active. Gabinius, no doubt with Pompey's concurrence, proposed a new law depriving Lucullus of the command against Mithridates and of the province of Pontus, and transferring the latter, along with Cilicia, to the consul Manius Acilius Glabrio.

This time the senate had to throw over Lucullus and allowed the law to pass. Lucullus made one more effort to impose himself upon his soldiers and to continue to direct the war in spite of the law. The troops, however, refused to obey him. The republic had now in the East a general without an army and an army without a general! The situation was too perilous to last. Towards the end of 67, letters began to reach Rome from Asia that gave an alarming account of the condition of the province. Lucullus had lost his command, Mithridates was master of Pontus once more, Cappadocia was being ravaged by Tigranes. Flying columns had already appeared in Bithynia and were burning the frontier villages.

A new panic arose at Rome, of which another tribune, Caius Manilius, took advantage to propose another exceptional law giving the conqueror of the pirates, in addition to his powers under the Lex Gabinia, the government of Asia, Bithynia, and Cilicia and the command of the war against Mithridates and Tigranes. He was also to have power to declare war and conclude alliances in the name of the Roman people whenever and wherever he saw fit (66 B.C.). The effect of this law was to authorize precisely that personal policy, independent of the will of the senate, for which the popular party had blamed Lucullus and which had been the reason for his recall. But Pompey, unlike Lucullus, was not a solitary and hated survivor of the party of Sulla. He was now the leader of the democratic party, the darling of the knights, and one of the most influential members of the senate. Moreover, the extraordinary provisions of the bill had been supported by the incomparable eloquence of the two greatest orators of the day—

Caius Julius Cæsar and Marcus Tullius Cicero, a young advocate who had suddenly leaped into great renown. It therefore passed into law without difficulty.[1]

94. **Pompey in the East. The Conquest of Pontus, Armenia, Syria, and Judæa (66–63 B.C.).**[2] Pompey moved boldly forward to complete the destruction of a kingdom which six years of incessant war had already brought to the verge of ruin. In 66 he invaded Pontus, and, in the course of a short and successful campaign, succeeded in driving out Mithridates, who had to take refuge in Colchis. He then turned to the conquest of Armenia, intending to attack Mithridates in Colchis in the spring. He was, however, spared the trouble of conquering Armenia by the voluntary submission of Tigranes, who came into the Roman camp on foot and unattended, humbly dressed and submissive in demeanour. Pompey received him civilly, comforted him, restored him all the hereditary dominions of his family, and saluted him as friend and ally of the Roman people, on condition that he paid 6000 talents, fifty drachmæ to every soldier, a thousand to every centurion and ten thousand to every military tribune. He then took his army into winter quarters on the banks of the river Cyrus on the extreme northern frontier of Armenia, where he prepared for his invasion of Colchis in the following year. Meanwhile he entered into negotiations with the Albanians and the Iberians.

---

[1] App., *Mithr.*, i., 97. Cicero supported it eloquently in his historic oration *Pro lege Manilia*.

[2] On the campaigns of Pompey in the East, *cf.* especially App., *Mithr.*, xcvii. ff.; Plut., *Pomp.*, 30–42; Th. Reinach, *op. cit.*, 381–410; Ferrero, *op. cit.*, vol. i., chapters xi., xii. and xiii.

Early in the spring of 65, Pompey invaded the country of the Iberians and reduced them to subjection. Next he passed into the valley of the Phasis and descended upon Colchis, a country full of memories of Medea and Jason and the Argonauts, in order to capture Mithridates. He was too late. The indomitable old man had achieved what all thought was impossible. With his little army he had forced his way into Tauris along the spurs of the Caucasus, thus conquering for himself a new state. The prudent Pompey declined to invade Tauris by sea. He ordered a blockade and himself returned into the valley of the Cyrus (the modern Kur) and led an expedition against the Albanians whom he seems to have surprised by treachery. He then went back into little Armenia and spent the whole year in conquering the last fortresses and appropriating the immense treasures of Mithridates. Early in the spring of the following year (64) he set up a sort of Oriental court at Amisus where he distributed, enlarged, and altered kingdoms. He gave Paphlagonia and Colchis each a new monarch. He increased the dominion of the tetrarchs of Galatia and he appointed Archelaus, son of the defender of Athens, against Sulla, high priest of Comana. He divided the territory of Pontus among eleven cities, in each of which he stored under the supervision of the Roman governor the republican institutions of the Greek πόλις.

Next he turned his attention to the conquest of Syria, a great undertaking which was to give Rome a rich province and to its author eternal glory. The moment was opportune. The country, freed by Lucullus from the Armenian domination, had reverted to a condition of complete anarchy, and pretenders and usurpers were to be counted on its soil by dozens. The chief sufferers by this state of matters were the Greek cities, which clamoured loudly for a liberator. Pompey betook himself, therefore, to Antioch. To Phœnicia and Celesiria he sent his lieutenants, Aulus Gabinius and M. Æmilius Scaurus, and, having methodically occupied the country with his troops he proclaimed it a Roman province. He then turned south. In 63 he was at Damascus for the purpose of settling a great internal dispute which had arisen in the neighbouring country of Judæa.

About a century previously this country had succeeded in regaining its independence of the Syrian empire of the Seleucids, at the time when Rome, in the war with Antiochus III., had weakened the kingdom of Syria and had encouraged every movement, local or national, which tended to disintegrate its unity. At the period which we have now reached, Judæa was again a compact and prosperous state. But it was also distracted by a dynastic conflict behind which there lay a profound cleavage of racial and religious tendencies. A civil war was raging between the pretenders, Hyrcanus and Aristobulus, the one supported by the faction of the Pharisees, the other by that of the Sadducees. The contending parties had already asked for outside assistance, and, when Pompey arrived, both referred their dispute to him for settlement.

One of the many circumstances which so often derange the balance of human judgment led him to decide in favour of Hyrcanus and the Pharisees. Aristobulus and the Sadducees, who were actually in power, did not think fit to bow to the decision of the Roman general, who was accordingly compelled to lay

siege to Jerusalem. The city soon surrendered, but
the Temple, which was surrounded by powerful
fortifications, made a protracted resistance, and its
reduction gave a great deal of trouble to the besiegers.
Finally, however, the besiegers prevailed, the defenders capitulated, and the royal seat of Saul and
Salome became a Roman conquest and was annexed
to the province of Syria. While Pompey was lingering
in Syria and Palestine, he received the most welcome
news of the death of Mithridates. The old king
in his new and little kingdom of Tauris had conceived
a most audacious plan. His intention was to put
himself at the head of the barbarians of South Russia
and the valley of the Danube and with them to swoop
down on Italy from the central or eastern Alps like
Hannibal or the Cimbri. To carry this out, however,
required very different forces from those of the dispossessed sovereign of Pontus. The blockade was
ruining the commerce of the country. His subjects,
groaning under the taxes made indispensable by his
extraordinary armaments, murmured threateningly.
In the end Pharnaces, one of his sons, raised the
standard of revolt, and the aged monarch was constrained to put an end to his life by poison.

Thus fortune relieved Asia and the Roman general
of this tenacious enemy. Pompey was able to rest
in the East for the remainder of the year 63, and the
whole of 62, visiting all parts and reorganizing in
various ways the vast territories that had been
conquered. Pontus and Bithynia were fused into a
single province, but still kept the name of the old
kingdom of Mithridates. To Mithridates' son Pompey gave Tauris, where were buried his father's
unavenged ashes. Ariobarzanes, King of Cappadocia,

obtained some increase of territory. Paphlagonia was reconstituted, Galatia divided into three principalities, Armenia was left independent, but was deprived of most of her ancient conquests. After all this had been completed Pompey returned by easy stages to Italy and was received everywhere with more than divine honours. Nor was this undeserved. In ten years the consequences of the momentous step taken by Rome in accepting the legacy of the King of Pergamus had matured. By accepting that legacy Rome became an Asiatic Power. She was now the greatest Power in the East and she had become so thanks to two men, Lucullus and Pompey, seconded at Rome by small but active groups of politicians. The senate, on the other hand, as a body, had remained a passive spectator of this great revolution which had so rapidly changed the face of the Mediterranean world and which was destined to have so much influence on the history of Rome and of mankind.

CHAPTER XVII

THE DEATH STRUGGLE OF THE ARISTOCRATIC GOVERNMENT

95. Cæsar, Crassus, and the Egyptian Question (66–64 B.C.). While Pompey was carrying out with so much good fortune the enterprise with which he had been entrusted, there were many people at Rome who had good reason to envy him for being so far away, and who would have been glad to exchange his easily acquired glory for the trouble of dealing with the thorny questions agitating the capital. Of these the two most important were the question of Egypt and the question of debt. The glory which Pompey had won in the East had inspired Crassus with the desire for a similar celebrity, and his thoughts turned to the conquest of Egypt,—the richest, the most civilized, and the most fertile country then known.[1] The testament of Alexander II., who had left Egypt to the republic, afforded a pretext, and if Egypt were conquered, Rome would never again want for bread. In the senate, however, there was considerable opposition to this project of Crassus. This may have been due to the fact that the recent practice

[1] On this ambition of Crassus *cf*. Plut., *Crass.*, xiii., 2; and G. Ferrero, *The Greatness and Decline of Rome*, vol. i., chapter xiii., and vol. ii., Appendix C.

of authorizing extraordinary commands offended the sense of constitutional propriety of many of the the senators, or to the strength of the party which was against any extension of the empire. It may also have been that the influence of Egypt, the richest, and consequently—according to the ideas of that time—the most corrupt country in the Mediterranean basin, was particularly dreaded.

Crassus in any case decided to make use of the people to secure what he wanted, and with this in view he came to an understanding with Caius Julius Cæsar, the nephew of Marius, to whom we have already referred. Cæsar was an elegant and intelligent youth, active, popular, and of an ancient family. But he was still a minor personage (in 66 he was a candidate for the ædileship of the following year), because his connection with Marius had retarded his career, and also because his family was poor and he was in need of help to pay the necessary expenses of a political apprenticeship, which in those days were very heavy. The bargain was struck. Crassus was to help Cæsar to be elected ædile; Crassus and Cæsar were to make a joint effort to secure the election of two friendly consuls who were favourable to their plans, and then they were to try to arouse a great popular agitation for the conquest of Egypt.

Cæsar was elected, but he and Crassus failed to secure the election of friendly consuls, though they spared no pains to achieve this result, and, it was whispered, even went so far as to form a conspiracy to gain their ends. But, though the consuls were against them, they did not give up their plan of an Egyptian expedition, and commenced a series of complicated intrigues to influence the public to that end. Crassus, who was the censor of the year, proposed to enter all the inhabitants of Gallia Transpadana in the lists of the tribes or, in other words, to make them Roman citizens, thus increasing the number of the electorate. As ædile Cæsar gave magnificent public shows, and it was thanks to him that one morning the trophies of Marius, which had been removed by Sulla, were found re-erected on the Capitol. For several days, crowds flocked to the Capitol to view with reverent curiosity the effigy of the old hero who had been the deliverer of Italy. Many old soldiers were openly moved to tears by the sight and by the memories it evoked. But when Cæsar, thinking that the minds of the people had been sufficiently prepared, commenced his agitation for the conquest of Egypt, the Sullan group, which was the party of the old nobility, opposed him resolutely, affirming that Rome should not desire to annex all the countries in the world and to pick a quarrel with the universe. Public opinion favoured this view and the agitation was a failure.

At this moment, indeed, Italy was thinking not of Egypt but of her debts—the eternal torment which every now and then became acute. The growth of luxury and the efforts to improve agriculture by planting vines and olives everywhere seem to have been the chief causes of the aggravation of a burden which was becoming intolerable to many. Crassus was, nevertheless, not discouraged, and in 64 returned to his scheme of the previous year, which was to secure the election of two consuls and many tribunes who would favour his aims. The candidates in that year were seven, and of these Cæsar and Crassus suppported Lucius Sergius Catilina, an old officer of

Sulla, who had already been a candidate in 66 and had been excluded from the senate on a technical disability, and C. Antonius Hybrida, who had also served with Sulla. Among their adversaries was M. Tullius Cicero, the great orator, who, though he came of a modest and not very wealthy equestrian family of Arpinum, had hitherto been elected to the usual magistracies with the consent of all parties. His genius, culture, modesty, and honesty, and the decorum of his private life had raised him above the ordinary kind of competition. This time, however, Cæsar and Crassus wanted for their own purposes the place to which he aspired, and they opposed him strongly, and with him the popular party. The conservatives, on the other hand, feeling themselves unable to beat Cæsar and Crassus with men of their own side, resolved to adopt Cicero's candidature because he had attracted to himself the most moderate elements in the democracy. Thus it came about that Cicero entered on the electoral campaign as the nominee of the aristocratic party.

The fight was lively but the result indecisive. Cicero was elected, and with him C. Antonius, one of the candidates of Cæsar and Crassus. Catiline was beaten. But, though the consular elections had not gone well, several tribunes devoted to Crassus had been elected, and they were not long in making themselves felt. One of them, P. Servilius Rullus, proposed an agrarian law providing for the appointment of five commissioners. These commissioners were to be elected by the people for five years. They were to be irremovable, irresponsible, and not subject to the tribunician veto. It was proposed to empower them to sell all the property in or out of Italy which had come into the possession of the State in 88 and thereafter, and all property whose sale had been decided upon by the senate since 81. They were also empowered to investigate the shares of war booty taken by all the generals except Pompey, and to compel these generals to return any share that they were shewn to have retained illegally. With the money thus acquired, the commissioners were to buy land in Italy for distribution to the poor.

It appears that this law was proposed as a means of solving the Egyptian question indirectly, as the commissioners were to have power to declare that Egypt by the testament of Alexander had become Roman property, and consequently to order its conquest. This at any rate was suspected by the opponents of Crassus, who opposed the law as being calculated to subvert the fundamental institutions of the State.

96. The Consulship of Cicero and the Conspiracy of Catiline (63 B.C.). This was the first struggle which Cicero had to face as consul, and he was brilliantly successful. He succeeded in securing the rejection of the law by two speeches, in which he exerted himself to prove that the law was of no advantage to the people. It was certainly too complicated and obscure and upset too many vested interests. The people themselves were afraid of it, and Crassus and Cæsar sustained a new defeat, the odium of which fell chiefly on Cæsar. Crassus was so rich and powerful that no one dared to manifest displeasure too openly against him. Cæsar, however, could be made to suffer for Crassus, and from that moment there arose against him, in senatorial circles and among the great

families attached to the party and the tradition of
Sulla, an animosity which pursued him for ever afterwards. His manners and morals were implacably
criticised, his debts were exaggerated, his acts and
intentions distorted. Thus attacked, Cæsar defended
himself by all the means in his power, and did not fail
to take advantage of an opportunity which presented
itself for a counterstroke. At the beginning of 63,
Metellus Pius, who had been Pontifex Maximus, died
and, with the help of Crassus, Cæsar managed to
revive the ancient form of popular elections to this
office, which had been abolished by Sulla, and also to
secure his own election in the teeth of the strongest
opposition which the oligarchical party could bring
against him. This was a striking success and a great
encouragement to Cæsar in his intended candidature
for the prætorship. These personal successes were,
however, but small compensations for the failure of
the grand design on Egypt. But Crassus did not
give up his plan, and prepared to support at the
elections for 62 the candidates who were willing to
favour it. For the consulship he had selected Lucius
Licinius Murena and Decimus Junius Silanus,
abandoning Catiline, who was discredited by his two
failures, and seemed quite out of the running. An
unexpected move, however, on the part of the candidate whom they considered impotent and exhausted
upset all their plans. Though deserted by Crassus
and Cæsar, Catiline resolved to stand a third time,
and, as without their assistance he could not depend
for success on the command of money or supporters,
he formed the idea of arming himself with a programme which by its clearness and simplicity was
certain to be popular. Without hesitation he chose as

his electoral watchword the abolition of debt.[1] The
programme was revolutionary, but it does not follow
that Catiline was already preparing an armed insurrection. His whole object was to move the masses by
making a proposal which no doubt seemed criminal
to the creditors, but for which the minds of the majority were not unprepared, and which was to be carried
out by due process of law. Moreover, reduction,
condonation, and even abolition of debt were frequent in Greek history, then so much studied, and had
also been so in Roman history from the earliest times
down to the year 86, the last occasion on which resort
had been had to such a measure.

This time Catiline had not miscalculated. His
name instantly became most popular, not only in
Rome, but in all Italy, among those who were groaning under the burden of debt, and they were many.
When it was seen that the agitation conducted by
Catiline was so successful, the upper classes of Rome
were panic-stricken. No one would lend any more
money. Bankruptcies were multiplied; from all sides
came the cry that the election of Catiline would be the
signal for a new civil war. The equestrian order
emerged in great agitation from the reserve which it
had maintained since the dictatorship of Sulla, and
spontaneously offered to unite with the senate for the
defence of public order. The alarm was so great
that all the feuds and discords among the great seemed
for an instant to vanish. Even Crassus and Cæsar
suspended their intrigues. Catiline, for his part

[1] The programme of the Catilinarians is clearly indicated by a
letter from them to the senate. This document is preserved by
the most important—and most hostile—historian of the conspiracy (Sall., *Cat.*, 33).

seeing the coalition of the rich and powerful closing its ranks against him, carried on the fight with any means that came to hand, and collected a band of partisans, who were of course all armed, from Etruria, a region where there were many landowners deeply in debt and hopelessly ruined, especially among the ex-soldiers of Sulla.

The struggle was very violent. On Cicero devolved the duty of directing all the forces opposed to Catiline and the revolution which, according to his enemies, Catiline personified. The result was that the united forces of the knights and the senatorial order triumphed over the party of the debtors. Cæsar was elected prætor, but Catiline was not elected consul. It was at this point that, driven to desperation, Catiline decided to attempt a revolution. The means at his disposal were inadequate, and indeed trifling. All he could do was to direct his friends in Etruria to recruit an army among the Sullan veterans, who had been reduced to poverty. But who could seriously hope to conquer Rome and destroy the legal government—to repeat, in fact, the achievement for which Sulla had required so many years and so many legions—by assembling the *canaille* of one out of the many districts of Italy?

News of the plot, moreover, soon began to leak out. In the month of November, Catiline was compelled to fly from Rome, and his friends who remained there precipitated the catastrophe by a supreme imprudence. There were then at Rome certain ambassadors from the Allobroges, who had come on a special mission in the interests of that people. Catiline's party formed the plan of winning them over, with the vain idea that by their means a conflagration might be raised in Transalpine Gaul similar to that kindled by Sertorius many years before in Spain. The Allobroges, however, denounced the clumsy intriguers, who were thrown into prison by Cicero's orders, brought before the senate and tried on December 5th.

Catiline had friends and adherents in all classes, and among the accused there were senators and magistrates, men belonging to the highest families. Public opinion in all ranks, however, exasperated by the intrigue with the barbarians, demanded so furiously that a severe example should be made that the first speeches in the debates were all for inflicting the extreme penalty of death on the conspirators. Crassus did not dare to speak, but Cæsar, who stood alone, in a speech which seems to have been really fine, sought to show that condemnation by the senate without appeal to the people was an unconstitutional and unconscionable proceeding. It was not right, he claimed, to decide while they were angry, and in any case it would be more politic to inflict on the guilty, not the penalty of death, but that of detention for life, together with confiscation of their goods.[1] Cicero finally spoke ambiguously, allowing it to be understood that he inclined to Cæsar's view.[2] Though Cæsar's speech and his subsequent replies profoundly moved the more moderate party in the senate, the extreme opinion prevailed, chiefly owing to the speech of Marcus Porcius Cato, a descendant of the famous censor, who had for some time been acquiring considerable ascendancy in the senate. The death penalty was accordingly voted, and the conspira-

[1] The debate in the senate and the speech of Cæsar are fully reported in Sall., *Cat.*, 50–54.

[2] This was the so-called fourth Catilinarian oration.

tors were conducted to the Mamertine prison and strangled.

The people, the majority of the senate and the knights paraded Rome with exuberant manifestations of delight that the republic should have escaped so grave a peril. The consul was acclaimed as the saviour of his country. There were hostile demonstrations against the friends of the Catilinarians. Cæsar himself, as he left the senate house, was threatened by an armed band of knights. A few months later Catiline was defeated near Fæsulæ (Fiesole) in Etruria and the ill-armed crowd of his followers was dispersed.

Thus the anxiety of the moment was dissipated, and public interest turned anxiously to Pompey, who had been absent a good five years and was now returning from beyond the sea.

97. Parties at Rome and the Return of Pompey (62–60 B.C.). The Catilinarian conspiracy had profoundly disturbed the already unstable equilibrium of party politics at Rome. The extreme and intransigent section of the oligarchical party, with Cato at its head, prevailed. Cato was an honest but obstinate and narrow-minded man who from this time forward became one of the important figures of his time. The democratic opposition, reacting against this state of matters, necessarily became more bitter. As had always happened at critical moments in the internal struggles of Rome, the knights had deserted the popular party. The reconciliation between the equestrian order and the senate was the political masterpiece of which Cicero never tired of boasting.[1]

---

[1] Cic., *Ad. Att.*, i., 18–3, *Exagitatus senatus, alienati equites romani. Sic ille annus duo firmamenta rei publicæ, per me unum constituta, evertit.*

The popular party now turned, therefore, to the *humiles*, the small men, who, owing to the commercial and industrial expansion of Rome, had of late grown very numerous, and had organized themselves in various organizations (*collegia* and *sodalicia*). They were a rough crew, by turns apathetic and violent, moved by nothing but their immediate interests or by some gust of vehement passion. The State was, in fact, at the mercy of two extreme parties, exasperated by furious hatred, and fighting with poisoned weapons.

The whole of the year 62, while the people were waiting for Pompey, and Cæsar was prætor, was distracted by continual skirmishes, disputes, scandals, and exchanges of insults between the parties. The conservatives accused the whole of the popular party of being Catiline's accomplices. The democrats began to accuse the senate of having, not executed, but illegally assassinated, the conspirators. This was the condition in which Pompey found the republic when he disembarked at Brundusium towards the end of the year. On his arrival, there was a moment not devoid of anxiety, for many predicted that he would not disband his army and would use it to impose no one knew what on the senate. This turned out to be a false prophecy. Pompey quietly disbanded his army and went his way to Rome to make arrangements for his triumph.

Just before he arrived, in the early days of December, a singular scandal came to light in the capital. The mysteries of the Bona Dea, at which only women could be present, were being celebrated at the house of the prætor when Publius Clodius—the same who as a friend of Pompey had incited the legions of Lucullus to revolt, and as a member of the youthful aristocracy had given abundant occasion for scandal—was found on the premises disguised as a female slave. It was said, truly or falsely, that he was the lover of Cæsar's wife. But Cato and his party took the matter seriously, demanding that a new example should be made, since the fate of Catiline had not sufficed, in order to repress the insolence of the rising generation, which was growing even more cynically riotous and dissolute than its predecessors.

The act committed by Clodius was sacrilege, and he should, therefore, have been tried by the college of pontiffs. But Cato and his friends did not trust the priests, and demanded that a special tribunal should be constituted. This proposal let loose a conflict which agitated the republic for several months. The popular party, out of spite, took Clodius under its protection. The oligarchs out of revenge stood fast. There were intrigues on every side. All the prominent personages in the State had to declare either for or against Clodius. Even Cæsar postponed his departure for Spain, which had been allotted to him as propraetor. Even Cicero declared definitely against Clodius. In the end the trial took place and Clodius was acquitted, to the great annoyance of the oligarchs and the great joy of the democratic party, which was inclined to regard Clodius's acquittal almost as a revenge for the condemnation of the accomplices of Catiline. The trail of hatred which this absurd scandal left behind it was not long, however, in showing itself—and with disastrous consequences.

98. The Triumph of Pompey and his Difficulties with the Senate (61–60 B.C.). When the trial of Clodius was over, Cæsar was able to leave for Spain and

Pompey to celebrate his triumph, which took place on September 29 and 30 in the year 61. It was the most magnificent triumph that had ever been seen; but after the festivities were over and Pompey, once more a private citizen, asked for confirmation of his acts, and for recompense for his veterans, he found himself confronted by an obstinate, complex, and determined opposition which, with all his power, influence, and reputation, he was quite unable to vanquish. It was in vain that, during the last six months of 61 and the first of 60, Pompey sought to arrive at an agreement. In vain, finally, was his request to Cato for the hand, some say of the latter's two daughters, some of his two nieces, for himself and his son.

Behind this opposition, there no doubt lurked old feelings of ill-will. Lucullus had never forgiven Pompey for deposing him. Crassus had never forgiven him for being more fortunate than himself. The senate as a body had not been able to forget the Lex Manilia whereby Pompey had dispossessed them of their prerogatives and reduced them to the rôle of spectators of his enterprises. The opposition was strengthened by the knights and all who were interested (and they were many!) in the company which had undertaken the contract for farming the taxes of Asia. They claimed that, as the revenues of the republic had been increased by Pompey's victories, the terms of their contract should be made more favourable by the grant of a rebate. Pompey, on the other hand, proposed that the greater part of the increased revenue should be spent for the benefit of his soldiers. Yet it is certain that all this opposition would not have been able to stand against Pompey's influence and the logic of events had it not been reinforced by one very important consideration. By approving the annexation of Pontus and of Syria, Rome became an Asiatic Power on an immense scale, indeed almost entirely an Asiatic Power, for her European dominions had become a mere trifle by comparison with her possessions in the East. This could not fail to disquiet all those who, for reasons based on tradition or deduced from the existing state of things, feared that excessive increases might ruin the empire or, at any rate, that the East would acquire too much influence over its destinies. The senate hesitated to recognize the tremendous revolution in Eastern affairs, whereby Rome had now been made mistress of Asia Minor.

99. The Consulship of Cæsar (59 B.C.). However that might be, the conqueror of Mithridates and of Syria, on the day after his brilliant triumph, was placed by this obstinacy in a position as embarrassing as it was ridiculous. At the same time the senate increased still further its own discredit, for there were many who considered it intolerable that this body was, out of spite, as it would seem, refusing territories the conquest of which had added so much to the power, the glory, and the revenues of the republic! At this point, towards the middle of the year 60, Cæsar arrived at Rome from Spain in order to stand for the consulship, and soon discovered that Cato's party was no more inclined to conciliate him than it had been to conciliate Pompey. That party opposed his candidature by every means in its power, but failed to prevent his election. Then it took advantage of the public discontent with the senatorial policy regarding the new provinces, to decree, as if in deference to the feeling of the comitia, that the pro-consuls of 59 were merely to carry out an administrative task of quite secondary importance—the supervision of forests and roads. This was a clear intimation of the intentions of Cato's party. Dominated by that individual and his friends, the senate had given warning that, as it had tried to nullify the work of Pompey, so it was preparing to hamper Cæsar. In other words, as the senators did not wish to be mere spectators, and were unable themselves to be the motive power of the new policy, they would hinder it as much as possible.

It was necessary, therefore, to face the prospect of a bitter struggle and to seek for any form of support, old or new, that could be found. Cæsar, who was a man of large views, conceived the idea of opposing these tendencies in the senate by nothing less than a coalition consisting of Pompey, Crassus, Cicero, and himself, all reconciled and all in agreement for the purpose of governing the republic with more energy than the senate was capable of shewing. This was a bold scheme, but the moment was propitious; for the oligarchical party, led by Cato, went on quarrelling with everybody. Pompey was, of course, ready to make any sort of concession if he could only escape from the impasse created by the non-approval of his administration in the East. Crassus's old ambitions were still unsatisfied, and Cicero had still to make the people forget how he had crushed the Catilinarian conspiracy. Cæsar worked hard, and in strict secrecy to secure this understanding during the months he spent at Rome between his election as consul and his entry into office. His overtures to Cicero were in vain. Crassus and Pompey, on the other hand, accepted Cæsar's proposals and entered into a secret agreement with him towards the end of the year 60.[1]

Cicero's refusal deprived Cæsar's government of a force which would have tended to moderation and balance; but, in spite of this, he began his consulship with conciliatory speeches and actions. His aim was to acquire sufficient popularity and influence to obtain approval for Pompey's acts in the East and a good province for himself. His method was the same as that used by the Gracchi and all their imitators, and consisted in legislating so as to favour the interests of certain social classes outside the aristocracy, beginning as usual with an agrarian law.

Accordingly, he brought forward a bill providing for the appointment of twenty commissioners to distribute to the veterans and to the poor all that remained of the public domains in Italy (excepting Campania as in the time of the Gracchi), in addition to the new land to be acquired with the proceeds of the spoil won by Pompey. Cæsar hoped to be able to propose and pass the law with the concurrence of the majority of the senate, and therefore, before presenting it to the comitia, he asked for the senate's approval. But he was mistaken. The majority of the senate rebelled furiously. It was scandalous that a consul should propose an agrarian law, thus robbing the tribunes of their dismal trade! No consul had

[1] That the negotiations and agreements for the first triumvirate were concluded after Cæsar's election as consul is not only affirmed by Suetonius (*Cæs.* 19) against Dion Cass. xxxvii., 54; Plut. *Cæs.*, 13; *Pomp.*, 47, *Crass.*, 14; App., *B.C.*, ii., 9; but is confirmed by the explicit testimony of Cicero, *Ad. Att.*, ii., 3, 3. *Cf.* also Ferrero, *The Greatness and Decline of Rome*, vol. i., pp. 284–285.

ventured on such an infamy for four hundred years, since the days of Spurius Cassius! At first the senate contrived to adjourn consideration of the measure by skilful obstruction, but finally the senators declared that they did not consider the times opportune for any innovation. Cæsar then retorted that he would present the law to the comitia forthwith. Cæsar's colleague, Bibulus, who belonged to Cato's party, thereupon began a course of obstinate liturgical opposition. Cæsar agitated among the people, and having tried every conceivable method of moving Bibulus, he had recourse in the end to a final expedient. He openly called Crassus and Pompey to his aid. They came into the forum and declared that, if persuasion failed, Bibulus's opposition must be overcome by force.

It was then—and then only—that the Roman public became suddenly aware that Cæsar, Crassus, and Pompey had come to the agreement about which there had been so many whispers, and had formed the coalition which a man of letters of the day afterwards referred to as the "three-headed monster," and which modern historians improperly call "the first triumvirate." The amazement and the terror caused by this revelation were immense. If Cæsar, Pompey, and Crassus had come to an agreement, who would be able to resist them? Pompey had on his side his veterans and part of the aristocracy, Crassus part of the aristocracy and the knights, Cæsar the middle classes and the urban proletariat. The whole State, in a word, was in their hands. It would henceforth be difficult for anyone to obtain a magistracy, a military command, or a *legatio libera* without the consent of this triarchy, which, so long as it held together, would dominate the republic.

The opposition to Cæsar's bill melted away rapidly. Many senators, if they did not forthwith pass over to the party of the triumvirs, much modified their attitude. The credit of Cato and his followers vanished in the twinkling of an eye, and the law passed by the people in the comitia tributa was sworn to by the senate, including Cato and his friends.

100. The Complications in Gaul and the Lex Vatinia (59 B.C.). This was the coalition's first great victory. Once more fortune had favoured audacity. But towards the end of February, 59, while all these agitations were at their height in Rome, Q. Metellus Celer, the governor of Cisalpine Gaul, died—an event which was destined to have momentous consequences. Cæsar thought the moment had come to rescind the decree of the senate assigning him for his proconsulate the duty of supervising the State forests. Transalpine Gaul had been for some time disturbed by wars, which from time to time offered pretexts for foreign intervention. In 61, the Allobroges, who had saved Rome from the Catilinarian conspiracy, had revolted. More to the north, east, and west of the Saone (the ancient Arar), the Ædui and the Sequani had been contending for the supremacy of central Gaul and the possession of the valuable traffic dues from the river. But the Sequani had been beaten, and, since their adversaries had for long been allies of the Romans, they turned for help to the Suevi, a Germanic tribe living beyond the Rhine, and to their king, who was named Ariovistus. With the help of the Suevi the Sequani in the end conquered the Ædui and their allies. Ariovistus, however, having effected an entry into new territory, had commenced a policy of slowly but constantly immigrating his

Suevi, thereby establishing a genuine German hegemony in Gaul. He had already subjected the
Ædui to a regular tribute, and had deprived the
Sequani of most of their dominions.[1] To free themselves from this domination had now become a national problem, but the means by which this was to
be accomplished had become the subject of renewed
controversy and discord. One party pinned its faith
to assistance from Rome. Another looked to the
Helvetii, the ancient allies of the Cimbri, who, after
the disastrous failure of the great Germanic invasion,
had shifted their quarters to the western regions of
Switzerland, between the two lakes of Constance and
Geneva, the Jura, and the Alps. Some time before
this, the Ædui, among whom the party favourable to
the Romans predominated, had sent envoys to Rome
to point out, while exaggerating, the danger. The
Helvetii, they said, had increased in numbers and were
in need of land. They were on the point of invading
Gaul and, if Rome once allowed them to get a footing
there, they would soon again be threatening Italy and
even the capital as in the time of the Cimbri and the
Teutones. Metellus had died when on the very
point of setting out to open a campaign against the
Helvetii.

Gaul, then, was a field in which glory and honour
could be gained. Cæsar wished to secure it for
himself; but it was impossible to ask the senate to

---

[1] *Cf.* Cæs., *B. G.*, i., 31-4, ff. The whole account of the first
part of the Gallic campaign of Julius Cæsar here given differs
widely from the traditional one. The reasons for this divergence
are set forth at length in Appendix D. to vol. ii. of *The Greatness
and Decline of Rome* under the title *The War against the Helvetii
and the Suevi.*

reverse its own decree. Since the struggle for the agrarian law the rupture between him and the majority of the senate was complete. He could no longer hope to govern in agreement with the great council. There was no other alternative, therefore, but to govern without the senate with the help of the comitia, and to complete the deposition of the senate which Pompey and Lucullus had begun.

Cæsar did not hesitate. Disquieting rumours were spread of threats of invasion from the new Cimbri, and, to meet the danger, the tribune Vatinius proposed a law making Cæsar governor of Cisalpine Gaul and Illyricum for five years from the day on which the law should be promulgated. The provision was drawn in this form so that, if war should break out before the end of the year, he might, like Lucullus, leave without delay to take over the command. The law was promulgated on March 1st.

Seeing that he was master of the comitia, Cæsar next proceeded without delay to bring forward laws to deal with all the questions which had been so long outstanding. The Egyptian question was settled by a law declaring Ptolemy Auletes a friend and ally of the Roman people, thus removing a long-standing source of discord between Pompey and Crassus. By another law the people granted a rebate on the contract for collecting the Asian taxes. A third gave final approval to all Pompey's acts in Asia. Finally he presented a second agrarian law which attacked Campania, the last remaining fragment of public land in Italy, which had been respected by even the Gracchi and subsequent legislators, and ordered it to be distributed among poor citizens who were fathers of several sons. In order to tighten the bonds which united him to Pompey, he gave the latter his daughter in marriage.

101. Cæsar and Clodius. The senate had never been so completely stripped of power. Never had the principle of the collective responsibility of the consuls been reduced to such a shadow as in this year. Bibulus had at first attempted obstruction based on the auspices, but in the end he had to abandon the attempt to intervene at the comitia. The jest of the day was that the two consuls in office were not Cæsar and Bibulus but Julius and Cæsar.

It was even more ominous for Cato and his friends that Cæsar obviously meant to prolong his tenure of power beyond the year of his consulship during the years in which he was to be proconsul in Gaul. He was trying above everything to bring it about that the magistrates of the forthcoming year should all be his friends. In this he was almost wholly successful. His opponents had some success in the elections to the prætorship, but both the consuls for 58 were firm adherents of Cæsar, Pompey, and Crassus. Among those who were designated tribunes of the people was P. Clodius Pulcher, notorious as the hero of the scandal of the Bona Dea, who was not merely a partisan but a tool. Clodius was a patrician and belonged to the Claudii, one of the most ancient and celebrated of Roman families. Before the scandal of 62 he had been, as was to be expected, more inclined to the oligarchical party than to the democrats. He had followed much the same courses as Pompey, who was a friend of his. But after the scandal he had been rejected by his order and by his party, and his only alternatives were to retire into obscurity for ever or to throw himself into the arms of the democratic party. Cæsar saw that he could make advantageous use of the great name and considerable political aptitudes of this sprig of nobility. He caused a law to be passed, therefore, authorizing the transfer of Clodius from the patricians to the plebeians, helped to secure his election as tribune for 58, and arranged that he should organize the lower orders in the city in such a way that Cæsar might effectively control the comitia, the legislative organ which had been used to strip the senate of its power, and on which Cæsar, Pompey, and Crassus relied as their instrument for crushing further resistance on the part of the senate, should any such be attempted.

For some time before the Sullan restoration the *collegia* or workmen's unions, which were numerous at Rome, had assumed a political character and had as a rule favoured the popular party. When left to themselves, however, they had always been at the mercy of the impression of the moment and, owing to ignorance or apathy, were often absent from the assembly, or weakly represented there. Cæsar's idea was to give these people, who were very numerous, and who, being resident in Rome, might easily form a permanent majority in the comitia, a solid electoral organization. This task was entrusted to Clodius, who was to drill the crowded cohorts of electors and win their favour by laws favourable to their interests, and by public benefactions.

The senate, meanwhile, every day more completely lost confidence in its own strength and the will to oppose Cæsar, Pompey, and Crassus. Such was the terror inspired in the majority of the senate after the humiliation inflicted on the senators by the triumvirs by means of the comitia, that Cato and his party were now reduced to a small group, isolated and without influence. Cæsar by himself could not have lorded it in this way. But who could presume to oppose the united forces of Cæsar, Pompey, and Crassus? The result of the elections for 58, which had been so favourable to the all powerful three, put the finishing touch to the senate's discouragement. So much was this the case that, immediately after the elections, on the proposition of Pompey and Crassus, they amplified Cæsar's proconsular powers perhaps rather more than was prudent, and conferred on him, in addition to the province he already had, that part of Transalpine Gaul which was a Roman province, with the command of a legion.

On December 10th, immediately after he took up office, Clodius set to work to carry out Cæsar's behests, and launched the programme whereby the triumvirate intended to control the assembly, which was to be their instrument of government. There was first a *lex frumentaria*, giving poor Roman citizens the right to receive corn, not, as hitherto, at special prices, but gratuitously. There was a *lex de iure et tempore legum rogandarum*, which freed the comitia tributa from all liturgical restrictions and enabled political assemblies to be held, not only on all *dies fasti* but also on public holidays. The effect of this was to make it easier for people living in the country to take part in the proceedings of the popular assembly. There was a *lex de collegiis*, which removed certain restrictions imposed by the senate on the workmen's unions, and finally a *lex censoria*, which limited the power of the censors to exclude from the senate persons who had occupied the magistracies necessary to qualify them for admission to that body. These laws were passed almost without opposition a few days after the close of Cæsar's consulship and were in a sense a posthumous victory for him.

102. The Political Character and Historical Importance of Cæsar's Consulship. Cæsar had produced—or at least attempted—a change in the Roman polity which was all the more profound because his contemporaries perhaps hardly realized it. So far as the laws proposed by himself or by Clodius are concerned, Cæsar is merely the continuator of Caius Gracchus and his successors. We find the same provisions as to the land and the supply of corn, the same legislation in the interest of the knights, the same proposals to restrict the authority of the senate. But among these laws there was none which, like Gracchus's agrarian laws, or his law relating to the citizenship, was the end, to secure which the others were simply a means. For Cæsar these laws were all means for bringing about a political revolution, which was, in fact, the real work of his life. In what did this political revolution consist? Not in monarchical aims and ambitions, as too many modern historians have somewhat naïvely supposed, but in the substitution, in fact if not in law, of a government on the model of the Greek τυραννίς for the old aristocratic rule to which Rome had been accustomed.

The new government might be described as a "triarchy," the personal rule of three citizens more powerful than the rest, each of whom was at the head, not of a political party but of a group of interests. The coalition of the three dominated the comitia and the senate, distributed the magistracies as they thought fit, and had the whole policy of the empire in their power. They did not, ostensibly, alter the constitution, but merely worked it for their own advantage. As masters of the comitia, the triumvirs had the public offices at their disposal, and this being so, they controlled the majority in the senate and the whole State. It is obvious that in this way the Roman government, which had hitherto been in the hands of an aristocracy divided into large family groups, was profoundly altered. There is no ground for thinking that Cæsar's motive in effecting this change was an immoderate personal ambition. The needs of the time and the exigencies of the situation were stronger than any ambition of his. He did his best to substitute this government by interests for the aristocratic rule of the senate because Sulla's reforms had distinctly failed, and the aristocracy were no longer capable of working the Roman constitution or of governing the empire through the senate.

Moreover, it was no longer an aristocracy in the strict sense of the term—compact, homogeneous, active, energetic, and sufficiently harmonious. It was a congeries of ancient and recent families, of soldiers, diplomatists, men of business, lawyers, men of letters, persons of fashion, all differing in origin, traditions, tastes, and ideas, jealous and envious of each other, distracted by all the influences of the complex and discordant forces of the life of the day. The growth of power and wealth, Greek culture, civil war, and political strife—all these had combined to bring about this dissolution of the Roman authority, the most manifest sign of which was the weakness and inconsequence of the government of the empire since the death of Sulla. In these twenty years no one, in truth, had governed Rome—neither the senate, nor the comitia, nor the old nobility, nor the knights, nor the democratic party. The mood of the moment, traditional routine, and the fleeting violence of party spirit had been all powerful. The finances were in disorder. The elections were every year the sport of some caprice of public opinion or of some surprise attack prepared by interested parties. Piracy and brigandage were rampant on sea and land. The army was disorganized. The effectives of the legions were reduced to half their proper number. There was no training, or next to none, for the recruits who volunteered for service. The generals and the other superior officers were improvised from among the ranks of the politicians. Only the centurions— obscure professional soldiers—knew anything by experience of the profession of arms, and it was only they who held together what was now a disintegrating army. The foreign policy of the republic was equally wanting in vigour and intelligence. When there was no Pompey or Lucullus who would take it on himself to decide at his own risks and perils, the action of the senate was confined to dragging out protracted negotiations and discussing questions interminably without solving them. What long hesitation there was, for instance, before accepting the extremely productive countries of Pontus and Syria, which Pompey offered ready subdued!

When a powerful organization grows weak with old age, it always happens sooner or later that another and more vigorous organization grows up and seeks to take its place. This was exactly what Cæsar did. He took advantage of the weakness, the errors, the discord, the conflict of interests which divided the class traditionally entrusted with the government of the empire. He succeeded in effecting an agreement between Pompey, Crassus, and Clodius and in collecting about himself and these others a group of interests sufficient to constitute a party capable of supremacy in the senate and the comitia, and therefore in the republic.

His attempt, which was carried out unexpectedly and with great energy, succeeded for the time. But the new government was hastily founded and its vitality depended on whether it could maintain itself and continue to do great and useful things. For in so ancient a republic aristocratic traditions were deeply ingrained, and an enterprise of this kind, once the first surprise was over, was certain to meet with serious and obstinate opposition. From this moment, indeed, the Roman senate was no longer divided into oligarchical and popular parties. There was but one, which we may call the senatorial party, whose aim was to defend the traditional powers of the senate against the invasion of the personal power of the triarchy. The question of the senate's rights and privileges was behind all the agitations which were henceforth destined to vex the State; and the nucleus of the "senatorial party" was, of course, formed from the small group of which Cato was the head and which alone had not bowed the knee to the triumphant power of Cæsar, Crassus, and Pompey.

CHAPTER XVIII

THE ANNEXATION OF GAUL

103. The Exile of Cicero (58 B. C.). In the early months of 58, Clodius brought to a conclusion the task which had been set him, and indeed went rather farther than the triumvirs desired. Not only did he secure the passage of the laws he had proposed but he succeeded in eliminating Cato and Cicero, the two most important persons who were in a position to interfere with the schemes of Crassus, Pompey, and Cæsar. By a law which Clodius proposed, the former was directed to carry out the occupation of Cyprus though the island then enjoyed self-government, and Cato, much against his will, was forced to obey the commands of the people. A worse fate awaited Cicero. Clodius wished to be revenged on him for the hostile evidence he had given at the famous trial. Early in 58, therefore, he proposed a law threatening *interdictio aqua et igni*—that is exile—against any one who had condemned a Roman citizen to death and deprived him of his right of appeal to the people. This was precisely the case of Cicero and the Catilinarian conspirators.

The great orator and his friends, at first tried to resist, to rouse the people in Cicero's favour, to solicit the intervention of Cæsar, Pompey, and Crassus. But the moment was not propitious. The people were apathetic; Clodius was at the height of his popularity. The three heads of the government found him so useful that they could not well take strong action. Thus it was that he to whom the senate, and Pompey himself, had given the title of *Pater patriæ* had to go into exile early in March without waiting for the passage of the law. Cicero went in the direction of Macedonia, and immediately after he was gone Clodius hurried his bill through all its stages and confirmed the exile of his enemy by another law, which banished him four hundred miles from Rome, confiscated his property, and ordered the destruction of his houses and villas.

104. **The Campaign of Cæsar against the Helvetii (58 B. C.).** Meanwhile Cæsar stayed on at Rome instead of leaving for his province, where some months earlier there had been rumours that a terrible outbreak of war was imminent. He did not move until about the end of March, when the Helvetii definitely began their migratory movement.[1] If Cæsar really believed that the Helvetii were the Cimbri and the Teutones over again, it must be said that his conduct was singularly imprudent. For he allowed himself to be surprised by the Helvetic movement with only one legion in Provence, while three others remained in their quarters at Aquileia. Fortunately, when he arrived at Geneva after a hasty journey, he found only an embassy, which humbly requested permission for the Helvetii to cross the province in order to establish themselves in Gaul. The horde were so modest that they made no diffi-

[1] On the numbers of the Helvetii *cf*. Ferrero, *The Greatness and Decline of Rome*, vol. ii., pp. 3, 4.

culty about acceding to Cæsar's request that they should wait a few days for his answer. Meanwhile he sent for his other three legions and fortified the points at which the Rhone was easy to cross between the lake and the Jura. In this considerable interval the barbarians did not attempt to force a passage, which they might have done without serious difficulty. On April 13, Cæsar, who was now sure of being able to repulse an attack, refused their request. The new Cimbri and Teutones did not press the matter farther, but went instead to the Sequani to get permission to cross their territory!

Rome did not wish the Helvetii to establish themselves in Gaul, fearing a new Cimbric peril, and the senate had ordered the governor of Gallia Narbonensis to defend the Ædui, who had asked Rome for assistance against the new invasion. Cæsar was entitled, therefore, to consider it his duty to pursue the Helvetii into the interior of Gaul. He returned to the Cisalpine province and there raised two new legions. Then he crossed the Monginevra Pass to Grenoble and, turning northward, marched towards the frontiers of Provence. The slow rate of march of the supposed enemy, who had with them their women and children, their household goods and provisions for three months, had given the Roman general ample time to carry out these complicated operations. For a moment indeed Cæsar, who, with about 25,000 men, crossed the frontier of Provence about the beginning of June, hoped to come up with the Helvetii while they were in the act of crossing the Saone in order, after traversing the territory of the Sequani, to enter that of the Ædui. With all his haste, however, he succeeded in cutting off only a small rear-guard which had been left on his side of the river. He then crossed himself with his army and set out in pursuit of the enemy.

At this point another embassy from the Helvetii unexpectedly presented itself. At its head was no less a person than Divico, an old acquaintance of the Romans, who many years before had taken part in the invasion of the Cimbri and the Teutones. This embassy declared that the Helvetii had no intention of making war on Rome, and that they merely wished to establish themselves in Gaul with the consent of the Romans. Their claims could not have been more moderate; but he who made them was a former leader of the Cimbric hordes, and Cæsar did not trust him. He therefore refused their proposals and continued at a respectful distance to pursue the Helvetii, who had resumed their march. He did not immediately attack them, partly because he was waiting for a favourable opportunity, and partly because his own movements were continually hampered by lack of supplies. The Ædui had been charged with the task of keeping him well provided, but too often they failed in their duty on various pretexts. Cæsar made up his mind to discover exactly how things stood. He held an enquiry, and then for the first time discovered that in pursuing the Helvetii he had plunged into the tremendous wasps' nest of Gallic factions. True, the Æduan government had asked him to defend them against the Helvetii, but there was a party—and a very powerful one—which regarded the Helvetii as friends and wished to favour them in every possible way. Among the Ædui,—and the same applied to almost all the Gallic peoples,—the old nobility, which up till that time had held the reins of power, had begun to be impoverished and had fallen into debt, very much as the ancient aristocracy of Rome had done in the second century B. C. On the other hand a small plutocracy was growing in power and wealth. They had contrived to amass capital and to get possession of much land. They monopolized the collection of the taxes and made great profits by money lending. This plutocracy with the support of the lower orders, whom they did their best to favour at the expense of the dominant aristocracy, were struggling to deprive the nobles of their political power and to establish, instead of the old oligarchical republic, a system of personal government not unlike that which Cæsar, Pompey, and Crassus had set up in Rome. This party had invited the Helvetii to come to Gaul, for it hoped to be able to use them as soldiers for the purpose either of driving out Ariovistus or of consolidating its own power. This was why that party sought to favour the Helvetii by impeding the supplies of the Romans.

Cæsar had entered Gaul as a liberator and a rescuer. He was now confronted with the situation that some of those whom he wished to save were on the side of the enemy, with whom they were secretly plotting to destroy their saviour. The situation caused him so much anxiety that he decided to retrace his steps in order to make more definite provision for revictualling his troops. At this point, however, the Helvetii made a sudden attack on the Romans. The encounter was long and difficult. Cæsar was unable to extricate his main body without grave losses. Therefore, while the much pursued enemy was able to continue his journey undisturbed towards the north, Cæsar was obliged to remain for three days on the battlefield to bury his dead and remedy the disorganization caused by the surprise attack. It is difficult to say what

would have been the result if Divico had repeated
the assault on the following day. The Helvetii,
did not wish, however, for war *à outrance* with Rome.
They were wearied by their long march, impressed by
the difficulties attending their emigration and by the
hostility of the countries through which they were
passing. Perhaps, too, they were frightened by
their own successes, and by the vengeance which they
foresaw might be exacted by Rome. They therefore
made new offers of peace, and they obtained peace on
terms which clearly showed how little Cæsar regarded
himself as their conqueror. Those who wished were to
return to their former territory, but they received from
Cæsar the title of "allies of the Roman people."
Those who wished to remain in Gaul were to receive
grants of land from the Ædui (58).

105. **The War against Ariovistus (58 B. C.).** Cæsar's
first undertaking in Gaul was finished. He had won
no great victory, and, what was more, he had alienated
from Rome the sympathies of the national party and
of the mass of the Gallic people. Ariovistus alone
had profited by the operation of Rome against the
Helvetii. This was soon made clear to Cæsar at the
general assembly of the Gauls, which met spontaneously after peace had been made with the Helvetii
and at which the Gallic cities demanded that Cæsar
should rid Gaul of Ariovistus. Cæsar had come in
the guise of a liberator—well it was not the Helvetii,
but Ariovistus who was the enemy of Gaul.[1] Cæsar

[1] On the interpretation of the complicated question of Gaul
at this time *cf.* G. Ferrero, *The Greatness and Decline of Rome*,
vol. ii, Appendix D.; also *Le premier livre des Commentaires et les
critiques de M. T. Rice Holmes*, by the same author, in *The Classi-
cal Quarterly*, 1910, p. 28 ff.

knew that his own prestige and that of Rome would be a thing of the past if he did not immediately make war on Ariovistus and free Gaul from the Germanic danger.

The difficulty was not only that the King of the Suevi was a powerful enemy, but that in the previous year the senate had declared him "a friend and ally of the Roman people." There was, therefore, no legal pretext for war, and this increased the risk run by Cæsar if he were to commence hostilities and afterwards be defeated. The situation left no room for hesitation, however, and so he at once began to look for a *casus belli*. He required Ariovistus to bring no more Germans into Gaul, to restore to the Ædui the hostages he had taken from them and still held, and to cease molesting or making war upon this people and their allies. But Ariovistus replied that the senate, in declaring him a friend and ally, had recognised his conquests in Gaul, which were anterior to that declaration. On this Cæsar, taking as the centre of his operations Vesontium (Besançon), the capital of the Sequani, marched in the direction of the Rhine. The battle between his legions and the host of Ariovistus took place in upper Alsace, probably not far from Muhlhouse. This time the military superiority of the Roman army prevailed over an enemy, who was reputed cruel and ferocious. The Germans were thrown back beyond the Rhine and Ariovistus himself had great difficulty in escaping death by flight.

106. The Question of the Recall of Cicero and the First Breach in the Triarchy. The Germanic domination of Gaul was at an end for centuries. Gaul was restored to herself. Cæsar had this time won a real and a great victory, the effects of which were to endure for hundreds of years. But contemporary judgments of events are often fallacious, and this victory, which opened to the Latin language and the Latin spirit one of the privileged lands of Europe, made no impression at Rome. Rome was intent on quite another question, the question of Cicero. When he sent Cicero into exile for condemning the conspirators, Clodius had struck too rashly. After the first shock there had been a reaction in public opinion.

All those who, especially in the senate, had been discontented with the government of the triarchy had at once seen that this question might be used as a means of injuring Cæsar, Pompey, and Crassus. They had, therefore, spared no pains to arouse public feeling in favour of Cicero. The public by whom Cicero was beloved and admired had gradually become passionately excited on the question, and even some of the *collegia* of artisans and many towns of Italy had demanded his recall. In short, while Cæsar was fighting Ariovistus, Rome, forgetting all else, thought only of the manner and method of getting Cicero to come back. In deference to public opinion Pompey himself, who, like Cæsar, had tolerated rather than desired the vindictive measure of the tribune, promptly declared himself in favour of the great man's return. Clodius, however, made Cicero's exile a personal question, and did not hesitate to rebel against Pompey. He attacked his Oriental policy; at the head of armed bands he set himself to disturb the public assemblies. He agitated the capital with constant demonstrations and tumults, and did his utmost to overawe the feebleness of the authorities by a reign of threats and terror. This exasperated his opponents, who were all the more determined to secure Cicero's return at any cost. The elections, which turned on the question of Cicero, were favourable to the distinguished exile, more especially as Pompey had drawn nearer to the senatorial party. Cicero's cause, therefore, made triumphant progress, and already the consuls and the tribunes were preparing a law providing for his recall. Clodius, however, was not a man to give in so easily and, though he had lost his office as tribune, he began to obstruct the passage of the law by force.

107. The War against the Belgæ (57 B. C.). On the whole things were going rather badly for Cæsar at Rome. There they were taking no notice of what he was doing in Gaul, and the personal government of the three great men threatened to make shipwreck owing to the discord which had arisen between Pompey and Clodius over the question of Cicero. The electoral coalition by means of which he had planned to dominate the republic threatened to split. For Cæsar, therefore, it was doubly necessary to achieve something in Gaul during the following year that might overtop what he had accomplished before. In the winter of 58–57 he had heard that northern Gaul, the powerful country of the Belgæ, and north-western Gaul, which was called Armorica, or in other words all the Gallo-Germanic tribes bounded by the Rhine, the Scheldt, the Atlantic, and the Seine, were in a state of unrest. The cause of this was the proximity of the Roman legions wintering in Gaul. Cæsar decided to confront the danger boldly in the following spring, and to interpret the instructions of the senate in as broad a sense as Lucullus had done in the last Mithridatic war.

The enterprise was no easy one. Fifty years

previously the Belgæ had been able to oppose a strenu-
ous resistance to the Cimbri and the Teutones, who
had beaten the Roman armies. Their warriors were
said to number as many as 350,000. Their country
was unknown. The recent friendship of the central
Gauls could be regarded by Cæsar only as a weak and
perhaps a treacherous support. Cæsar enrolled two
new legions and many archers and slingers in Asia,
Crete, and the Balearic Islands. He persuaded the
Ædui to invade the country of the Bellovaci, the
strongest of the Belgic tribes, and he himself awaited
the possible advance of a Belgic horde in an entrenched
position on the Aisne.

The Belgæ came on and entrenched also. The
two armies confronted each other for four days, each
expecting the other to attack, but neither wishing to
play the enemy's game. Finally, one day, after a few
skirmishes, the Belgic army retired. Cæsar was
greatly surprised, and at first suspected an ambuscade.
It was not until later that he discovered that the
Bellovaci, anxious about the invasion of the Ædui,
had insisted on withdrawing to defend their own
country. This defection, imperfect transport arrangements, and an exaggerated idea of the Roman power
had sufficed to bring about the dissolution of the league.
Fortune had wondrously served Cæsar, who realized
that the time was come to pursue the scattered enemy
and to subdue one by one these valorous but fickle
tribes. One after the other the Suessiones, the Bellovaci, the Ambiani, the Aduatuci, and finally the
terrible Nervii, the most warlike of the Belgæ, were
brought to subjection either by peaceful or by violent
means (57 B. C.).

108. The Annexation of Gaul (56 B. C.). While

Cæsar was fighting so successfully in Gaul, matters had come to a head at Rome. Cicero had in the end returned, and had been received with enthusiastic demonstrations of welcome all over Italy. But to make this possible, Pompey had to find a tribune of the people, Titus Annius Milo, who, by means of a band of gladiators and cut-throats he had collected, was able to enforce the passage of the law of recall amid scenes of tumult, rioting, and bloodshed. But Clodius declined to admit defeat. He announced his candidature for the ædileship for the following year. He tried to raise the people against Pompey by spreading the rumour that Pompey had purposely created a scarcity in order to be proclaimed King of Rome. He did his best through tribunes who were friends of his to prevent Cicero from being compensated for the destruction of his house. Finally, during the elections for 56, he brought to the assistance of the senatorial party which was opposed to the triarchy the unexpected support of his faction, and in consequence secured the victory of that party's candidates for all the prætorships and both the consulships.

As if all these troubles were not enough, the Egyptian question had been unexpectedly reopened. Ptolemy Auletes, whom Cæsar had caused to be officially recognized as King of Egypt, had been driven out by a revolution and had claimed the protection of the republic. There were, however, too many candidates for the honour of restoring him to his throne, and among these Pompey came first. The senate, as usual, would not hear of his undertaking the duty, and their opposition was openly or secretly supported by Clodius, and, it would appear, also by Crassus. The personal government, founded on groups of clients,

which was to take the place of the impotent and
decadent senate, threatened to collapse before it had
done anything.

Towards the middle of 57, Cæsar could no longer
disguise from himself that, unless some powerful and
extraordinary remedy could be applied, his government was threatened with a catastrophe. Clodius, in
order to revenge himself, had now completely gone
over to the senatorial party. So complete was his
conversion that he had already launched an attempt
to secure the repeal of his own laws of 59. It was at
this difficult moment that Cæsar's great and courageous mind conceived a grandiose idea which was
destined to have tremendous historical consequences
and to produce effects which to this day are vital and
profound. His victories over the Belgæ had made a
deep impression at Rome. Cicero said shortly after
this that the generals of the republic, even including
Marius, had hitherto been content to repulse the
Gauls, but Cæsar had carried the war into their country. What would be thought if Cæsar were suddenly
to announce to Rome that Gallia Transalpina might
now be considered subject to the Roman empire like
Spain, Macedonia, and Syria?

This was the idea which Cæsar had been meditating
since his victories over the Belgæ. In order to carry
it out, he sent his lieutenant, P. Crassus, with one
legion, into western Gaul to receive the formal submission of the tribes scattered between the mouths
of the Loire and the Seine. Another lieutenant,
Sulpicius Galba, was despatched with another legion
to the upper Valais, near the great St. Bernard. After
this he returned rapidly into the Cisalpine province,
and announced to the senate that it might decide on

the annexation of Transalpine Gaul, and send the usual ten commissioners to organize the new province in concert with the proconsul.

Never was a more audacious blow struck by any Roman general. His claim was that two compaigns had been sufficient for the conquest of a vast country the majority of whose cantons had never seen the helmet of a Roman legionary or the toga of a Roman magistrate. His sudden decision was destined to bring about a series of wars in Gaul much more terrible than any which he had hitherto had to wage. But the solemn pledge by which he bound the republic in the presence of the peoples and the provinces, gave the Romans the strength to complete a conquest which distracted them from facile successes in the east and definitely inclined the axis of civilization towards the west.

109. The Conference of Lucca and the Consulship of Crassus and Pompey (56-55 B. C.). Cæsar's announcement threw Italy into a delirium of enthusiasm. The Roman people decided to send Cæsar a deputation of senators to congratulate him on his success. The senate, carried away by the wave of public sentiment, ordained a *supplicatio* of a fortnight, the longest period hitherto known. Many of the adverse critics of the year before now suddenly became Cæsar's most ardent admirers. In a moment he had become the idol of the populace, and he made use of this favourable opportunity to reconstitute the government of 59. This was all the more urgently required as, soon after Cicero's return, Cato also had come back from Cyprus. Cæsar therefore invited Crassus and Pompey to meet him at Lucca, where they arrived attended by a regular court of senators; and there he expounded to them a vast design whereby their common authority, now endangered by the revival of the opposition, might be preserved.

Crassus was to reconcile Clodius and Pompey. Crassus and Pompey were to be candidates for the consulship for the year 55. During their year of office they were to secure for Cæsar the prolongation for another five years of his command in Gaul, and the provision of funds to pay the legions he had recruited in addition to those assigned to him by the senate since the beginning of the war. In these five years he would conquer Britain and push his legions beyond the Rhine. After his consulship Crassus was to receive the province of Syria and was to complete the conquest of Persia. As for Egypt, both Pompey and Crassus were to surrender their ambitions in that quarter, and Gabinius would be directed to restore Ptolemy without waiting for the senate's authorization, on condition that Ptolemy paid a considerable sum to each of the triumvirs. In compensation for this, Pompey, after his year of office as consul, was to be made governor of the two Spanish provinces.

We do not know what was the course of the discussions which took place between Cæsar, Pompey, and Crassus, but it is certain that they came to an agreement, and that the effect of this agreement was the final confirmation of the species of political revolution adumbrated by Cæsar in the year of his consulship. Three groups of clients, each ruled by a powerful chief were to govern the senate and the republic. The new aggressive imperialism was to prevail over the ancient temporizing policy of the senate; the conquest of Gaul was to be followed by that of Britain and Persia. For a moment, in fact, the republic really appeared to have returned to law and order under an energetic government. All idea of abrogating Cæsar's agrarian law was abandoned. In the senate Cicero, in his historic oration, *De Provinciis Consularibus*, replied triumphantly to those who, now that Gaul was conquered, would have wished to reduce the duration and the extent of Cæsar's proconsular powers. The proposal to organize the whole of Gallia Transalpina as a province and to send in that behalf the ten senatorial commissioners, was agreed to.[1] The Gallic tribes, like the Ædui and the Sequani, with whom Rome had treaties of alliance, that is to say the richest and most civilized tribes of the centre, were to retain their independence with the title of allies. The barbarous populations of the north and west were subjected to the Roman dominion. Finally, in order to prevent the consuls in office from using their powers to obstruct the election of Pompey and Crassus, means were found to put off the elections until the beginning of 55, so that they might be held under the presidency of a friendly interrex.

Crassus and Pompey were elected, and immediately took steps to secure that the remaining offices should be filled by their friends. Thus Cato's candidature for the prætorship went down before that of P. Vatinius, the author of the law which in 59 had conferred on Cæsar the governorship of Gaul. In accordance with the law still in force, the senate had already provided

---

[1] Gallia Transalpina was actually constituted a province in 56 B.C. *Cf.* Cic., *De Prov. Cons.*, xii., 29; xiii., 32–33; xiv., 34; Cic., *Ad Fam.*, i., 7–10; Dion Cass., xxxix., 25, 1; G. Ferrero in *Revue archéologique*, 1910 (15), pp. 93 ff., and for a more extended account C. Barbagallo, *L'Opera storica di G. Ferrero e i suoi critici*, Milan, Treves, 1911, 197–209.

that the consuls of the year should, in 54, receive Syria and Further Spain respectively. But Crassus and Pompey immediately corrected this. C. Trebonius, one of the tribunes, proposed that each proconsulship should be for five years, and that not only Further Spain but Hither Spain as well should be given to Pompey. When this law was passed, the consuls proposed and passed another law prolonging Cæsar's command in Gaul and Illyria for a further five years. The Egyptian difficulty still remained; but, before anything could be done, it was announced at Rome that Ptolemy had been restored to his throne, that his daughter Berenice, who had usurped the kingdom in his absence, had been killed, and that the Egyptian problem had been solved. All this had been done by the governor of Syria, A. Gabinius, who had acted under Pompey's orders without waiting for the directions of the senate.

CHAPTER XIX

THE CRISIS IN CÆSAR'S POLICY

110. The Invasion of Britain: Crassus Meets with Disaster in the East (55–53 B. C.). The difficulties, which had for a moment been settled, soon reappeared. While Pompey and Crassus were carrying out at Rome the decisions arrived at during the conference of Lucca, Cæsar was beginning to feel the effects of the hasty annexation of Gaul. In 56 he had already had to undertake a campaign lasting several months in order to repress an insurrection of the Armorici and the Veneti, which threatened to spread. He had succeeded in crushing this rebellion and had taken much spoil, having commenced the systematic pillage of Gaul which was to furnish him with the means for his expensive policy in Italy. He had even prepared for his invasion of Britain, which he intended should take place in 55.

When, however, he was on the very point of setting out for this new conquest, he was delayed by a Germanic invasion which had burst upon Gaul and which this time was received by the inhabitants, not with terror, but as the advance guard of an army of liberators. The invaders were the hordes of the Usipetes and the Tencteri. With his usual rapidity Cæsar turned to meet them. By means of a rather dishonest stratagem he captured their leaders, who had come to him as envoys and then led his army against the main body of the Germanic forces, which were left without generals. The defeat which Cæsar inflicted on them was crushing, and was followed up by a brief incursion made beyond the Rhine. This war had, however, consumed so much time that it was no longer possible for Cæsar to attempt his projected invasion of Britain in that year. He contented himself, therefore, with a sudden raid on the island, disembarking two legions, and postponed the main expedition until the following year, 54 B. C.

In the year 54, therefore, Rome was attempting nothing less than the conquest of the Parthian empire in Asia, and in Europe the subjection of the great island separated from the coasts of Gaul by a narrow arm of the sea. Like Pontus and Armenia, the kingdom of Parthia had arisen, about the middle of the third century B. C., in the heart of the great monarchy of the Seleucids, and had progressed as that great hellenistic empire had disintegrated. Hitherto, perhaps owing to the remoteness of Parthia, the relations of that country with Rome had never entered on a decisive phase. The Parthians had been indifferent spectators of the first Mithridatic war. In the second they had gone so far as to ally themselves with Pontus and Armenia against Rome. Later, however, they abandoned this line of policy and, when Pompey replaced Lucullus, they took the Roman side and assisted in the conquest of Armenia. Then again they revolted and attacked Armenia, which had become a vassal and a client of Rome. Once more, however, they drew back and gave up this attack.

Rome on her side oscillated between two policies,

without resolutely following either the one or the other. Lucullus had intended to conquer the kingdom of Parthia, but had had to give up the idea because his soldiers had refused to follow him. Pompey had at first come to an understanding with the Parthians, but, after a time, had inclined to the idea of fighting them. In the end he had decided to remain on friendly terms with them. After Pompey's return to Italy this uncertainty had continued. One party —which was very strong in the senate[1]—wished to live at peace with the Parthians. Another party wished to make war on them and conquer the ancient kingdom of Persia, repeating the achievement of Alexander. The most ardent supporters of this view were to be found among the officers who had been with Lucullus and Pompey in the East, and among the friends of Crassus, Pompey, and Cæsar. The conference of Lucca had decided to satisfy the aspirations of the war party, and Crassus had been entrusted with this difficult enterprise.

It is possible that he had an even more vast design than the mere conquest of Parthia, that he meant to penetrate Iran, following in Alexander's footsteps, and to carry the Roman eagles as far as the banks of the holy Indus. In any case he left Rome about the end of the year 55, embarking at Brundusium 9 legions of 3500 men each, 5000 cavalry, and 4000 auxiliaries, 40,000 men in all. He landed at Dyrrhachium, and, following the Via Egnatia, he crossed Epirus, Macedonia, and Thrace, and passed the Bosphorus during

[1] This party had won a great victory in 55 B. C. When A. Gabinius, Governor of Syria, meditated war against Parthia, the senate resolutely forbade him to carry out his plan. *Cf.* Strabo, xii., 3, 34.

the winter.   In the spring of 54 he entered northern
Syria and relieved Gabinius of his command.   Then,
having completed his preparations, he invaded Mesopotamia during the summer of 54.   The country was
not defended; Crassus occupied the different cities
and then stopped.   His plan, which was no doubt
clever enough, was to attract the enemy into Mesopotamia, in order that he might be attacked as far as
possible from his base of operations.

Meanwhile in the summer of 54, Cæsar had invaded
Britain with five legions and a great fleet.   He had
been able to penetrate into the interior of the country
beyond the Thames and to defeat the forces opposed
to him.   Nevertheless, he soon returned to the continent, contenting himself with a vain promise of an
annual tribute.   The situation in Gaul had become
too dangerous to allow him to involve his forces in a
serious attempt to conquer the island.   The Carnuti,
the Senones, the Aduatuci, and the Treviri were all
either in open revolt or in a state of acute unrest.   Not
only, therefore, was he compelled to give up in 54–53
his usual plan of wintering in Cisalpine Gaul, but he
had to spend that unpleasant season fighting, holding
his own as well as he could with a view to a more
vigorous resumption of hostilities in the spring of 53,
the same time when the Romans and the Parthians resumed the struggle in the East.

Here Crassus's manœuvre seemed at first to be
successful.   In the spring of 53 the garrisons left
by Crassus in Mesopotamia were besieged by the
Parthians, who appeared to be falling into the trap he
had set for them.   In reality, however, the King of
Parthia had sent practically all his cavalry, heavy and
light, under the command of their Surena or general-

issimo, into Mesopotamia with the object, on his part also, of enticing the Romans as far as possible from their base. Both adversaries, therefore, were making use of the same stratagem; but the Parthians were operating on ground which they knew better than their opponents, and with an army which had had more practice in this method of fighting. To make matters worse for Crassus, he was too easily convinced that he had succeeded in deceiving the enemy, and immediately crossed the Euphrates in order to go to the rescue of the besieged cities. On this the enemy at once raised the siege and, as if struck with panic, retreated precipitately into the interior.

This sudden retirement aroused the suspicions of many of Crassus's staff, who urged him to stop and collect more information. Crassus, however, fell into the snare. He thought he saw his chance of finishing the war quickly, and he launched his army in pursuit. Day after day, he followed the Parthians across the desert without overtaking them. Every step forward quickened his desire to catch his flying adversary at any cost. Every day increased the weariness and the anxiety of the army, which was driven on by the hope of fighting on the morrow a battle which was always delayed. At last, when the Romans, having just passed the city of Carrhæ, were on the point of reaching the banks of the Belik, the Parthians suddenly stopped and turned to give battle. The longed-for engagement had come, but at a moment which was singularly inopportune for the exhausted army of Crassus. The officers wished to postpone action and await a more favourable opportunity, but Crassus, obsessed with the fear that the enemy might escape him, ordered an attack.

It was a strange combat, of a kind to which the Roman army was not accustomed. The heavy Parthian cavalry delivered strong attacks on the Roman cohorts and eluded by skilful evolutions all counter attack, while mounted archers and slingers showered on their adversaries a perpetual hail of missiles. These repeated attacks failed to break the legions, but inflicted such very serious losses that towards evening Crassus had to give the order to retreat. His retreat, however, was continuously molested by the extremely mobile enemy. His army was discouraged and full of strange terrors. It was not long, therefore, before discipline gave way and the retreat became a disorderly rout. The formations began to fall to pieces, and finally there came a day when the soldiers, instigated by emissaries of the Surena, who promised that they should be allowed to return to their own country in safety if Crassus would agree to treat for peace, compelled their general to accept the Surena's invitation to a conference. Crassus preferred being killed by the enemy to being murdered by his own soldiers and went to the fatal interview. He was slain on June 9, 53. His head was sent to the court of the King of Parthia, his body remained unburied, and his soldiers were dispersed or made prisoners.

111. **Anarchy at Rome (54–53 B. C.).** This was a reverse equal in its gravity to the greatest disasters Rome had suffered for centuries. The news arrived at Rome in the month of July, at the very moment when public opinion had been exasperated by a very serious internal scandal. The scandal was that not until July, 53, after seven months of interregnum, had it been possible to elect the magistrates for that year, whereas the elections should have been held about the

middle of the previous year. How was such a long delay possible? The personal government of Cæsar, Pompey and Crassus had again led to anarchy as in 58, but in a different way. Owing to the eclipse of the senate, whose traditional authority was still able to impose some limits on the desperate ambitions of contending politicians, the elections had become a veritable pandemonium. The number of candidates was so great, their intrigues on such a scale, violence, corruption, intimidation, and obstruction on the part of the rival factions were so serious, that no magistrates whatever could be elected. Pompey, who, instead of going to Spain, had remained in the neighbourhood of the city, had shown his usual weakness and irresolution, and had done nothing.

This disgraceful state of affairs had damaged the government and its chiefs not a little in the public estimation, and Cæsar above all, as he was the most discussed and criticized. The tragic end of Crassus's enterprise could not but increase the displeasure of the people. Cato and his friends, therefore, who had always opposed the fatal expedition and the whole of the rash policy of the three masters of the republic, were justified by events.

It was worse still when the elections for 52 gave the signal for a new outburst of anarchy. The candidates for the consulship were Milo, Publius Plautius Hypsæus, and Quintus Cæcilius Metellus Scipio, the adopted son of Metellus Pius. For the prætorship was standing the ubiquitous Clodius, and for the quæstorship Marcus Antonius, one of Cæsar's officers who had come from Gaul for the purpose. The fury of contending ambitions flared up more strongly than ever. Pompey abandoned Milo. Clodius, in order to spite the latter, supported the other two candidates, and bands of partisans of one side or the other began to fight pitched battles in the streets. The consuls made several vain attempts to hold the comitia. Finally the senate in despair decided to propose to the people a law providing that in future no magistrate should receive a province until five years after he had been in office. It was hoped that this might somewhat check the mad competition; but meanwhile the end of the year had come, no magistrates had been appointed, and it was not even possible to nominate an interrex, as a tribune interposed his veto.

The State had thus fallen into complete anarchy. At this point, in the beginning of 52 and, to be exact, on January 18, Clodius, returning with his followers from Bovillæ, met Milo going to Lanuvium attended by his band on the Appian Way. The two parties came to blows and Clodius was killed. This deed of violence was enough to precipitate a sort of revolution. The lower orders of Rome, excited by the clients of Clodius, after celebrating his funeral with savage splendour, used the flames of the pyre on which the body of their idol had been consumed to set fire to the senate house itself. The conflagration spread to the basilica Porcia, and from thence to the greatest and most venerable monuments of Rome. For many days the city was full of tumult, fire, rioting, and clamorous demonstrations.

112. **The Great Revolt in Gaul (53–52 B. C.).** After so many centuries of aristocratic government, Rome was not the city best fitted for the imposition of a personal rule. The political system conceived by Cæsar was once more falling to pieces. For these reasons Cæsar had left Transalpine Gaul about the

end of 53 and had approached the borders of Italy, feeling that it was necessary to help Pompey and his faction to restore some semblance of order to the disturbed republic. Hardly, however, had he turned his back on the still disturbed Transalpine province when he was overtaken by couriers from Gaul who brought very grave news.

The flames of rebellion had blazed up once more. The Carnuti had massacred the Italian merchants in their midst and were again in rebellion. The Arverni had upset their government, which was favourable to Rome, and under the leadership of a young prince named Vercingetorix, who had once been a friend of Cæsar, had raised the standard of revolt. The Senones, the Parisii, the Cardurci, the Turones, the Aulerci, the Lemovices, the Andes, and all the tribes on the Atlantic coast, had risen and had recognized Vercingetorix as their chief. The Sequani were hesitating. The Ædui, who had remained loyal, and with them the Roman legions, appeared to be enclosed in a ring of iron. One enemy was already marching on Gallia Narbonensis, while another invaded the territory of the Bituriges, who were tributaries of the Ædui.

Cæsar did not hesitate for an instant. He left Italy, Rome, and Pompey to their fate and hurried to Gallia Narbonensis. He reinforced the defending forces there as well as he could, and with a few cohorts, it being then the depth of winter, he crossed the snow-covered Cevennes and threw himself on Arvernia, wishing to give the enemy the impression that he was invading the whole country with large forces. Vercingetorix was, in fact, deceived by this attack, and rushed his army to the defence of his fatherland.

Then Cæsar, having recrossed the Cevennes and
returned into Provence, collected a small body of
cavalry he had left there and went back to Gaul. By
riding night and day, while the insurgents thought he
was in the country of the Arverni, he managed to
arrive unexpectedly in the country of the Lingones,
to put himself at the head of the two legions stationed
there, and to direct the concentration at Agedicum
(Sens) of the rest of his forces which were scattered
throughout Gaul.

Thus, within a few days, the general found himself
again at the head of his army, which consisted of
35,000 infantry, over and above the Gallic auxiliaries
and some contingents of cavalry. This was the whole
force at his disposal, and it was not much. But there
was no time for hesitation. Audacity alone could
save him. And, exiguous as his army was, Cæsar
with the country in flames all round him, resolutely
took the offensive. In the course of a few days, he
attacked and took Vellaunodunum (Beaune), burned
Genabum (Orleans), crossed the Loire, and entered the
country of the Bituriges, laying siege to Noviodunum.

Vercingetorix, finding that he could not stop Cæsar,
resolved on a new plan of campaign. This plan was
undoubtedly very able and, had it been ruthlessly applied, might have proved the ruin of the Romans. It
consisted in burning and destroying everything, so as to
make a void before and around Cæsar's army, which
meanwhile would be harassed and starved by sudden
cavalry attacks, cutting off the revictualling convoys.
But when Vercingetorix began to put his plan into execution, the Bituriges implored the implacable champion
of Gallic liberty to spare their capital Avaricum, the
future Bourges, which they promised to defend to

the last. Vercingetorix was weak enough to comply. Cæsar, instead of wandering in a wilderness, therefore, and pursuing an elusive enemy across a desert, had a solid objective at which to strike, and laid siege to Avaricum. Vercingetorix did not dare to come to the rescue of the city. The Bituriges had overrated their strength. After a vigorous siege lasting a few weeks, Cæsar took the place, killed all the inhabitants, and captured all the provisions which had been stored there.

This success was important because it not only enabled Cæsar to rest and refit his army in a rich and well provisioned city, but revived the prestige of the Roman arms as much as it discouraged the insurgents. Had not Cæsar destroyed Avaricum under the very eyes of Vercingetorix, who did not dare to come to the rescue? Was not this a decisive proof that Cæsar was the stronger? Cæsar must have really believed that his victory was decisive, for it seems to have induced him to divide his forces. Four of his ten legions were sent under the orders of Labienus against the Sequani and the Parisii, who had lately joined the insurgents, while he himself with six legions was to strike a blow at the heart of the rebellion by attacking the territory of the Arverni and obliging Vercingetorix to accept the battle which would end the war. This plan he carried out. Vercingetorix tried in vain to prevent him from crossing the Allier. By means of a stratagem Cæsar eluded his vigilance, invaded Arvernia, and laid siege to Gergovia, which it was his intention should share the fate of Avaricum. But he now had only six legions, and Gergovia resisted obstinately. The siege was protracted, and its prolongation began to revive the courage of the Gauls. Cæsar, wishing to make an end of it, attacked the town, and was repulsed with such heavy loss that he had to make up his mind to raise the siege and return to the north to effect a junction with Labienus.

The division of his forces had been a mistake the consequences of which were sufficiently serious. The failure at Gergovia, which was announced and exaggerated everywhere, shook the tribes which had remained loyal. In the end the Ædui went over to the enemy, depriving the Romans of their best base of supplies and cutting Cæsar's communications with Labienus. Cæsar understood that he must join Labienus immediately, and at any cost. In order not to lose time in building bridges, he plunged into the Loire with his army and crossed it on foot. Then, turning north, he managed by forced marches to reach Labienus, probably at Agedicum.

Labienus had been successful in his campaign against the Senones and the Parisii, but of what use were his victories? The whole of Gaul was now in revolt and full of enthusiasm for the cause. A national convention had been summoned to meet at Bibracte to organize the resistance of all the Gallic peoples. What could be done with a force of little more than 30,000 men in a country which was in rebellion from end to end? Cæsar considered the question of temporarily abandoning Gaul and retreating into Provence. But to retreat with his little army through the Gallic conflagration seemed to him an enterprise so perilous that before he moved in that direction he determined to go to the western frontier of Germany in order to raise a large force of cavalry. Thus it came about that the general who seven years before had entered Gaul in order to put an end to the German danger now meant to use the Germans against the Gauls and to pay the former with the gold he had extorted from the latter.

But Cæsar's extreme danger was destined to be transformed into a great triumph, more through the errors and discords of the enemy than owing to the help of the German cavalry. At Bibracte there had already been much discussion as to who was to command and what plan was to be followed, whether guerrilla tactics were to be continued or warfare on the grand scale was to be attempted. Partly in order to please those who wanted war on a large scale and partly because guerrilla warfare required few troops of high quality whereas the Gallic army was large, heterogeneous, and mediocre. Vercingetorix was compelled to change the methods which had hitherto been so successful. When Cæsar, probably in the early part of August, began his retreat towards Provence, Vercingetorix, leaving his headquarters, which he had established at Alesia (Alise St. Reine in the Department of the Côte d'Or), and, giving up the system of small attacks which he had hitherto followed, came out into the open and tried to bar Cæsar's way. When the contest was reduced to a pitched battle, the Roman legions, the genius of their leader, and the dash of the German cavalry in the end prevailed over the enemy offensive and defensive.[1] This battle was enough to change the issue of the war. Vercingetorix was beaten and retired upon Alesia. Cæsar gave up the idea of retreating to Provence and suddenly decided to invest Alesia. Vercingetorix, seeing him-

[1] The scene of the battle is uncertain. Some think it took place on the banks of the Vingeanne, others between Brevon and the Ource, others again near Montigny or not far from Allofroy.

self shut up, with immense labour summoned all Gaul
to his assistance.

In this way he collected an immense army, more
than 250,000 men according to Cæsar,[1] which should
have swooped down on the Romans while the latter
had to meet the shock of a desperate sortie by the
besieged. Had this plan succeeded, the Roman army
would have been crushed between two enemies. Not
feeling himself strong enough to resist the double
assault in the open, Cæsar did not hesitate to construct
round the first line of trenches a second set of fortifications on a great scale, behind which his army,
besieging and besieged at the same time, was to have
resisted the new and formidable attack which was
expected. The expedient was new, ingenious, but
daring. Its success would have been very difficult to
secure if the relieving army had methodically belea-
guered the Roman forces even at the risk of starving
the army of Vercingetorix along with that of Cæsar.
But the new army had more than one leader. There
were disagreements in the camp. They were too eager
to save Vercingetorix, the raw tribes of the Gauls
were impatient and ill-provided with materials of warfare and food. Instead of methodically investing the
besiegers, they tried to storm Cæsar's camp and
exhausted themselves in furious attacks, which lasted
only a week and were all repulsed. This desperate
struggle was followed by a progressive decline of
energy. In the meantime, Vercingetorix, vanquished
by famine, which had made terrible ravages among the
soldiers and among the inhabitants of Alesia, came

[1] *Cf.* Caes., *B. G.*, vii., 75–76. Though the long series of figures
composing this total may have reached us in a corrupt form the
final result is on no interpretation less than 250,000.

and delivered himself up as a prisoner into the hands of the conqueror (September, 52).

The great Gallic insurrection was quelled. Cæsar's little army, operating in the depths of a country ablaze with rebellion, had been able to do what Crassus's forces had failed to achieve on the treacherous plains of Mesopotamia. The new province of Gaul after eight years of insurrections and perpetual fighting was safe. The West, as had been the case in the Cisalpine province and the two Spains, cost Rome decidedly more than her easy conquests in the East. But the prize of victory was shown' in the course of history to be much more glorious and precious. By shedding her blood on the mountains and plains of Transalpine Gaul, Rome was laying the foundations of peace for her empire and for the world, and of the history of the European civilization of the future.[1]

[1] On this period of Roman history *cf.*, the very detailed account given by G. Ferrero, *The Greatness and Decline of Rome*, vol. ii., chapters iv.–vii.; also C. Jullien, *Vercingetorix*, Paris, 1907; *Histoire de la Gaule*, iii., chapters xi.–xiv.

113. Pompey Sole Consul (52 B. C.). At Rome in the meantime, while Cæsar was fighting in Gaul, Pompey and the senatorial party had come closer together. Both were alarmed by the unceasing disturbances, the decay of the republic, the disaster which had overtaken Crassus, and the revolt in Gaul, and they had agreed to forget their old feuds and animosities. The situation was so serious that even the most obstinate opponents of the triarchy were inclined to be conciliatory. As for Pompey he was too rich and powerful, too much spoiled by good fortune, not to prefer supremacy with the senate's consent to supremacy against their wishes. Thus, when the persistent tumults made a reconstruction of the whole system of government absolutely necessary, the proposal that Pompey should be sole consul—it was desired to avoid the name of dictator—was approved of even by the most intransigent of the senators, even by Cato himself.

Pompey made haste to satisfy the conservative section of the senate by carrying out in a few weeks what they had been demanding in vain for years. By two laws, *de ambitu* and *de vi*, he shortened the proceedings in trials and increased the statutory penalties for acts of political corruption committed since the year 70. He made the procedure in cases of electoral violence more rigorous and more rapid and gave a powerful impulse to the prosecutions which were pending. In a few weeks a large number of *populares*, partisans of Clodius and Cæsar, were condemned, along with some of the more turbulent members of the conservative party. Not even Pompey's old friend Milo was spared. He next revived a proposal unsuccessfully made in the previous year by the senate, and brought forward a *lex de provinciis* by which it was laid down that no consul or prætor should become governor of a province until five years should have elapsed from the end of his year of office. He also introduced a *lex de iure magistratuum* which confirmed the ancient provision forbidding persons to become candidates for the consulship while absent from Rome, excepting only such as had received, or might receive, permission from the people. This exception applied to Cæsar, who, shortly before this, had been authorized by a law promoted by his friends to become a candidate for the consulship in 48 without being personally present in the capital.

Order had been re-established in the city. The senate breathed again. Pompey's credit revived and his government of Spain was prolonged by five years without discussion. Cæsar's position, on the other hand, was not improving. The government he had founded was now practically overturned. First the death of Crassus and then the slow conversion of Pompey, and the discredit which the disaster in Parthia, the revolt of Gaul, and the anarchy at Rome had thrown on the policy of the Lucca conference, had destroyed the triarchy. Cæsar could not but fear that, if he returned to Rome as a private citizen at the end of his proconsulship, his enemies would find a way of cutting short his political career by means of a prosecution, and of revenging themselves on him for the blows they had suffered at his hands and at those of Pompey and Crassus as well.[1] There was only one way of escaping this danger. That was to secure his re-election as consul and the grant of a long new proconsulship, for every magistrate was inviolable during his term of office. His proconsular powers expired, however, on March 1, 49, which was the tenth anniversary of the day on which the Lex Vatinia had given him Gaul as his province. He could stand, therefore, as a candidate only at the elections which would take place during the year 49 and thus be elected consul for 48. In the ten months between March 1, 49, and January 1, 48, Cæsar would have had to remain at Rome as a private citizen, exposed to the prosecutions which would be brought against him by his enemies. True, a law had been passed permitting him to stand for the consulship *in absentia*, but of what use would that be to him when his powers expired on March 1st.

[1] There were several reasons or pretexts of which Cæsar's adversaries could have made use in launching a prosecution against him—his "unconstitutional" war against Ariovistus, the "friend and ally" of the republic, the deception involved in his premature annexation of Gaul, his war against the Usipetes and the Tencteri, which his enemies described as treacherous and for which Cato's party in the senate had demanded that he should be handed over alive to the enemy (Suet., *Cæs.*, 24); his use of the enormous spoil of his wars to corrupt senators, tribunes, and other magistrates at Rome. Owing to this vigilant animosity against Cæsar at Rome, the news of his defeats was more rapidly spread than that of his victories. *Cf.* Cic., *Ad Fam.*, viii., 1-4; Plut., *Pomp.*, 57; *Cæs.*, 29.

114. The Conflict between Cæsar and the Senate (51–49 B. C.). In order to escape the danger which threatened him, Cæsar made up his mind to ask the senate at the beginning of the year 51 to prolong his proconsular powers from March 1, 49, to January 1, 48, affirming that this prolongation was implied by the law giving him permission to stand for the consulship during his absence from Rome. Cæsar's destiny now depended on this request, the answer to which was almost entirely in the power of Pompey. The senate would no doubt grant or refuse it according as Pompey supported or opposed it. From this moment, therefore, Pompey, as arbiter of the situation, was as much courted by the friends as by the enemies of Cæsar. But, though now opposed to Cæsar and favourable to the senate,[1] he took refuge in a reserve which became more impenetrable as his power increased. In April, when Cæsar's request was discussed in the senate, he gave no opinion one way or the other, and a tribune, by interposing his veto, extricated him from the difficulty of having to declare his views.

The consul Marcellus, however, who was a fanatical enemy of Cæsar, raised the question again on June 1st, by formally proposing that Cæsar should be recalled from Gaul. This time Pompey could not remain silent, but he evaded the difficulty by saying that the question of appointing a successor to Cæsar could not be discussed before March 1, 50. The senate agreed. Marcellus did not press the point, but returned to the charge on September 30th, proposing that, on March 1st of the following year, the senate should discuss the question of Cæsar's successor, and that any veto which might be interposed by a tribune

[1] *Cf.* Cic., *Ad Fam.*, ii., 8, 2; *Ad Att.*, v., 7.

should in advance be declared null and void. These proposals gave rise to a lively discussion. The first was approved, the second suspended by the veto of the tribunes. The most important result of the sitting, however, was that Pompey had to express his opinion. His opinion was that, if on March 1st, Cæsar's friends among the tribunes made use of their right of intercession to obstruct the proceedings, Cæsar should in his opinion be considered as a rebel and "punished" accordingly. The breach between Pompey and Cæsar thus continually widened.

The position of Cæsar, who was engaged in overcoming the final resistance of Gaul, now became continually more critical. Pompey was deserting him and had practically broken the weapon of the veto in his hands. After what Pompey had said, to use the services of his friends among the tribunes was equivalent to breaking with him openly. Cæsar did not wish to do this, and, in order to avoid it, he hit upon a very curious expedient. There had been elected tribune for the year 50 B. C. a certain Scribonius Curio, a young man full of talent and burdened with debt, a great orator and writer, and, in addition to all this, a keen opponent of Cæsar. By promising to pay his debts Cæsar managed to win him over to his side and to persuade him to accept a very difficult mission. This was to obstruct the discussion about his province on March 1st, while ostensibly acting as his enemy and as the supporter of all that was just and constitutional. If the senate was prevented from coming to a decision owing to the intervention of one of his enemies, Pompey could not blame him.

Curio discharged his task with remarkable skill. With affected impartiality he affirmed that it was time to have done with all extraordinary powers, whether they were Cæsar's or whether they were Pompey's. By proposing laws, some conservative and others democratic in tendency, by posing as the impartial defender of legality and of public peace, and by attacking Cæsar while at the same time striking at Pompey, Curio succeeded in becoming so popular with the great public which wanted peace that he was able, by means of his veto and by other expedients, to postpone from month to month until the end of the year 50 all debate on the subject of Cæsar's successor. Pompey, who was paralyzed by illness during several months of the year, pretended to have forgotten the threats he had uttered during the sitting of September 30th, and the majority of the senate was glad enough to postpone the solution of this terrible problem. These skilful manœuvres, in which the hand of Cæsar was soon detected, exasperated Pompey and the other enemies of the proconsul, who were anxious to revenge themselves at any cost. On the other hand, the end of Cæsar's term of proconsular power was approaching and it was necessary that the matter should be settled.

It was in these circumstances that the historic sitting of the senate on December 1, 50, was held. The consul Marcellus began by proposing that Cæsar should be recalled from Gaul on the expiration of his proconsulship, that is on March 1, 49. The proposal was passed by a large majority without opposition from Curio. Then Marcellus, warming to his work, proposed that Pompey also should resign his command in Spain, which, as we have seen, had been prolonged until 45. This new proposal was rejected by a large majority. It was not until this point in the proceedings that Curio rose to make a third proposal, which he introduced in an extremely clever speech, and which, from a strictly logical point of view, was in contradiction with the decisions already arrived at. He suggested that both Cæsar and Pompey should simultaneously surrender their proconsular powers. This motion corresponded so closely with the desire of all parties, senate and people alike, that the house, contradicting itself, passed it by 370 votes to 22.

It was a wise decision, but the enemies of Cæsar could not make up their minds to accept such a defeat. Pompey, moreover, was not willing to surrender before the appointed time the powers which the senate had prolonged. Marcellus and the more violent opponents of Cæsar in furious haste conceived a plan and submitted it to Pompey, who was still at Naples. Marcellus was to move in the senate that Cæsar should be declared *hostis publicus*. If the senate did not agree, or if the proposal was vetoed by the tribunes, he would on his own authority declare a state of siege, and Pompey would be entrusted with the duty of preserving the public safety. The senate would then be intimidated into doing anything they were told. Pompey signified his approval from Naples probably on December 9th, and immediately afterwards Marcellus carried out his *coup d'état*. He proposed that Cæsar should be declared a public enemy and that Pompey should be directed to take command of the two legions which were waiting at Luceria for orders to leave for Syria. When Curio vetoed this, Marcellus left Rome and betook himself to Pompey at Naples in order to invite him to undertake the defence of the republic as Nasica and Opimius had done in their day.

115. From the Rubicon to Brundusium (Jan. 7, March 17, 49 B. C.). There was still one remaining hope. Cæsar wished for peace. He wished it because he knew how dangerous and how wicked it would be to unloose upon the empire the horrors of a second civil war, not because of great political issues such as had brought about the first, but to satisfy the offended dignity of two quarrelsome politicians. He determined, therefore, to make a supreme effort for reconciliation. Curio, who had left office immediately after the vote had been taken in the senate, had gone to Cæsar's camp. He was sent back to Rome with a letter which was to be delivered to Marcus Antonius, an ex-officer of Cæsar who was now a tribune, and which the latter was to read publicly at a meeting of the senate. In the letter Cæsar declared himself ready to lay down the command in Gaul at once and to return to Rome as a private citizen, provided Pompey would take similar action. In the contrary case, he added, he would have to defend himself against the violation of his rights. The letter was conceived in terms which were at once firm and respectful, and Cæsar counted a great deal on the effect it was likely to produce. Had not the senate clearly shown at the sitting of December 1st that it was anxious by a just settlement to put an end to the dispute between the two great men and their followers?

In the meantime, however, Pompey had accepted the mission of saving the republic, which had been entrusted to him by Marcellus, and had taken command of the legions at Luceria. Moreover, Cæsar's enemies had not been idle. The result was that, on January 1, 49, the feeling in the senate was very different from what it had been a month earlier. Cæsar's letter was taken as a threat, and was received with interruptions and protests. Cæsar himself was declared a public enemy if he did not lay down his command in the course of the following July. Some days later the senate proclaimed a state of siege. Cæsar's attempt to keep the peace had failed. As he would not give way, Cæsar was now compelled to resort to extreme measures. Only one weapon remained to him, and it was double-edged. If it failed, war would be inevitable. This was to make it clear that he was prepared for anything, and by threats to bring to their senses the senators who had rejected proposals of conciliation. Accordingly he left Ravenna one night about January 10th with 1500 men and violated the frontier which separated his province from the republic by crossing the Rubicon. He surprised and seized Ariminum (Rimini) and in the course of the next few days also occupied Pisaurum (Pesaro), Fanum Fortunæ (Fano), Ancona, and the principal coast towns, besides thrusting out several cohorts in the direction of Arretium (Arezzo).

The second civil war had begun, though neither side had seriously desired it, and though all Italy with one accord longed for peace.[1] No misfortune could have been more disastrous at that moment than a civil war. Three years previously, in 52, Italian merchants had for the first time been able to export to the provinces oil made in Italy. This fact by itself is enough to show how much hard work had been done in the peninsula and how much progress had

[1] Cic., *Ad Att.*, vii., 6, 2. *De republica valde timeo nec adhuc fere inveni qui non concedendum putaret Cæsari quod postularet potius quam depugnandum.* *Cf.* also Cic., *Ad Fam.*, xv., 15, 1 ff.; Plut., *Cæs.*, xxxvii., 1; App., *B. C.*, ii., 36, 48.

been made in the sphere of agriculture. It also proves that, beside the ruined landowners and the idle and otiose holders of *latifundia*, there had grown up an agricultural middle class, men who, by means of capital and labour and with the assistance of clever slaves imported from Greece and the Orient, had successfully attempted the most scientific cultivation known to the ancient world.

At the same time the tastes and habits of all classes had become more refined, and this fostered industrial progress, which again owed much to Oriental slaves and freedmen. In Cisalpine Gaul from Vercellæ to Mediolanum, from Mediolanum to Mutina, in Etruria at Arretium, there were now numerous manufactories of pottery, lamps, and amphoræ, which in later years became famous. At Patavium (Padua) and Verona, artisans and merchants were beginning to produce the carpets and rugs which shortly after this period were universally used in Italy. At Parma and Mutina were woven splendid woollen stuffs from the fleeces produced by the flocks reared in the neighbouring country. At Faventia (Fænza) they had begun to spin and weave linen from the flax produced in the district. Genua (Genoa) at the foot of the wild Ligurian mountains had become a crowded mart for the timber, the hides, the honey, and the cattle which the Ligurians produced from their lonely valleys. The iron mines of Elba were now being worked on a large scale, and Puteoli smelted the ore which Elba produced and manufactured all sorts of iron ware. Naples had become the city of perfumes and perfumers, and Ancona possessed a flourishing manufacture of purple dyes.

The cities of Italy were becoming larger, richer,

and finer. In them a new middle class was growing, in numbers, in comfort, and in influence. With the rising standard of living and the participation of the lower classes in public life, old social feuds and conflicts had been appeased. The ferocity of the old struggles between plebeians and patricians, between rich and poor, between Romans and Italians, was a thing of the past. The one question which interested everyone was the question of debt. But this universal desire for peace failed to preserve Italy from the scourge of civil war, which was let loose upon the country owing to the rancorous rivalries of party politicians whose endeavours to intimidate each other by threats finally made a conflict inevitable.

The step taken by Cæsar, who was still in hopes of persuading his enemies to come to some agreement, failed of its effect, not because it did not terrify them enough but because it terrified them too much. When it was known at Rome that Cæsar had successively occupied Ariminum, Ancona, and Arretium, it was generally believed that he intended to march with his legions on the capital. A great panic broke out, and Pompey directed the consuls and the senate to leave Rome and retire to Capua. Cæsar, who wished to come to an understanding with the senate, understood at once that this flight made peace more difficult, and tried, by means of letters and by every other expedient in his power, to persuade as many senators as possible to remain in Rome. Meanwhile, however, Pompey's generals were recruiting soldiers in Picenum and Samnium, and Cæsar could not allow such a menace as this to grow up on his flank unchecked. He therefore recalled his legions from Gaul and advanced. He took Auximum (Osimo) and Cingulum (Cingolo) and compelled the generals whom Pompey had sent to collect recruits to fall back upon Corfinium in the ancient country of the Peligni, where was concentrated a sound nucleus of an army under the orders of one of the most influential members of the Pompeian party, L. Domitius Ahenobarbus, who had been consul in 54. Cæsar felt he could not leave Corfinium to become a formidable *point d'appui* for Pompey. With his usual rapidity he took the legions which had arrived from Gaul, and to which he had made large promises, and marched against Corfinium. He laid siege to the place and after a week forced Domitius to surrender. Cæsar wished to come to terms with his enemy, and therefore was generous. He set free Domitius and the Pompeian noblemen who were with him.

By his rapid advance and by the victory of Corfinium Cæsar in less than two months had succeeded in disorganizing what we should now call the mobilization of the other side; that is to say, all the measures they were taking to raise soldiers in Italy. After two months of war Pompey had in Italy little more than the two legions concentrated at Luceria for the campaign in Syria. He had lost most of Italy and was in great danger of having his communications with Spain, where he had his best legions, cut by Cæsar. All the more ready should he have been to listen to the offers of peace which Cæsar, shocked by the precipitate course of events, made to him through different channels. Now, however, Pompey's pride was touched. He did not wish it to appear that he had accepted peace from Cæsar as though he had been conquered. As he had lost half Italy, and as he could not hope with the forces at his disposal to reconquer the country and so reopen communications with Spain, Pompey at once decided to leave Italy, taking with him the senate, the magistrates, and the army. He would leave Brundusium for the East, where the provinces and the allied princes would at once assist him with all their resources to rebuild his army.

When Cæsar learned of his adversary's intention, he was much disturbed. He knew well that it meant the devastation of the empire by a terrible civil war if he could not contrive to make peace with Pompey in Italy. By forced marches he hastened to Brundusium in order to blockade the enemy there and finish the war by a single stroke. But he was too late; Pompey, the senate, and the army had embarked and abandoned Italy to Cæsar.

116. The War in Spain (March–November 49 B.C.). The lot was cast. Cæsar had to fight a civil war on a great scale—the second in the history of Rome. But his own situation was full of anxiety. He had been abandoned—alone at the head of his army—in Italy, which was without magistrates and separated from the most important provinces. Cæsar did not lose courage, and above all did not lose time, but immediately sent what force was available to occupy Sardinia, Sicily, and Africa. He himself went to Rome without delay to reorganize the government as best he could, and to replenish his supply of money. He arrived towards the end of March, collected the few senators who had remained, and regarded them as constituting the senate. In concert with them he found substitutes for the absent holders of the chief offices of State, made various provisions in favour of the people, repealed the law made by Sulla excluding the descendants of proscribed persons from office, and finally took possession of the treasury, threatening with violence the tribune L. Cæcilius Metellus, who made as if to prevent him from forcing its doors. Then, after a stay of a few days, he left for Spain.

Cæsar's plan of campaign was simple and daring. He intended to fly to Spain and there destroy the best and most important nucleus of Pompey's forces. This being accomplished he would return to Greece to fight the new army which Pompey was collecting there. Success, however, depended on rapidity of action. And on his way to Spain, Cæsar immediately found himself confronted with an obstacle in the shape of Massilia, a free city which was devoted to Pompey and had determined not to allow its neutrality to be violated in any circumstances. Cæsar recalled three legions from Gaul and besieged Massilia. But, as the delay caused by the step seemed to him dangerous, he resolved to withdraw all the remaining troops in Gaul and to send them to Spain with those he had in Gallia Narbonensis—five legions in all—under the command of his lieutenants, while he himself brought the siege of Massilia to a conclusion.

His generals had no success in Spain, so he left Caius Trebonius and Decimus Brutus to carry on the siege of Massilia, and went in person to take command of the Spanish operations. He pitched his camp north of the Ebro near Ilerda (Lerida) but failed to induce the enemy to give battle as was necessary to his plan. He then tried to cut the enemy's communications with the town but suffered a serious and sanguinary reverse, while the hostility of the natives, increased by his failure, and an unexpected rise of the river, which carried away the neighbouring bridges, nearly led to a catastrophe. Towards the middle of July, however, the position of the inhabitants of Massilia, who had been defeated and blockaded by sea by Decimus Brutus, began to appear desperate. The Spaniards feared that the legions besieging the city would soon be set free to fall on the Pompeians and their native partisans. They changed their minds, therefore, and went over to Cæsar, supplying him with victuals as they had previously supplied the Pompeians. The result was that the scarcity passed from one camp to the other, and Pompey's lieutenants, L. Afranius and M. Petreius, were forced to retreat beyond the Ebro. Cæsar pursued them, and by a series of marvellous manœuvres, succeeded—as they had not done with him when they had the chance—in following them up, encircling them, and finally starving them into unconditional surrender (August 2, 48). Once more Cæsar offered magnanimous conditions to the vanquished. They were to be free to act as they thought fit—either to betake themselves to Pompey, or to join Cæsar's party or to retire into private life. Shortly afterwards the two legions in Further Spain under the command of M. Terentius Varro, one of the greatest scholars of his time, followed the example of their comrades and capitulated. All Spain was then in Cæsar's power.

After this Cæsar returned to Italy where he had already been made dictator by a law proposed by the prætor M. Æmilius Lepidus. The new and democratic Sulla, however, had no intention of carrying out reprisals, and, for the time, he did not propose to make any profound changes in the constitution. He contented himself with presiding over the elections by which he was made consul for 48, and with proposing a practically universal amnesty for all political offenders since the year 52, and a law of debt, prudent and considerate in its provisions, which attempted to minimize the economic effects of the war. This law provided that interest already paid should be set off against the capital indebtedness. Debtors were to be allowed to pay what they owed by handing over their real estate, and the value of the latter was to be calculated, not at the actual much depreciated rate, but at the rate obtaining before the war. In cases of dispute the matter was to be settled by arbitration. On the other hand, in order to promote the circulation of money which the war had affected adversely, he revived an old enactment, which had become obsolete, forbidding citizens to hoard more than 60,000 sesterces in gold or silver. All this was done in a period of eleven days of dictatorship after which Cæsar resigned his extraordinary powers and set about his final enterprise against Pompey.

117. Pharsalia (48–47 B. C.). Cæsar's victories in Spain had been counterbalanced by serious reverses in Africa and Illyria. Curio, who had been sent to Sicily and Africa by Cæsar, had occupied Sicily and had driven out Cato. He had then proceeded to Africa with a force of only two legions, and had defeated the Pompeian general, P. Attius Varro. But he had afterwards been enticed into an ambuscade by Juba, King of Numidia, a friend of Pompey, and had been surrounded and slain. Again P. Cornelius Dolabella, another of his lieutenants, who had ventured on an attempt to conquer Illyria, had been defeated and had lost a portion of the fleet, while part of the forces sent to him from Italy by M. Antonius had been made prisoners.

Pompey, on the other hand, had collected 50,000 men and a powerful fleet in the East. To these forces, Cæsar could oppose only twelve war-worn legions whose effectives were reduced to 25,000 men, and a much weaker fleet, which was capable of carrying little more than half his army.

The enterprise in which Cæsar was embarking was, therefore, very perilous. But to attempt it was the only way to peace. Cæsar counted much on surprise. On January 4, 48, therefore, after assuming consular authority, he left Brundusium with as much of his army as the fleet could embark—that is to say, about 15,000 men, and, having without difficulty eluded Calpurnius Bibulus, Pompey's admiral, who did not expect him till the spring, he landed at Oricum in an unfrequented bay on the coast of Epirus. He occupied Oricum and then Apollonia, and tried to seize Dyrrhachium. In this he failed, for Pompey anticipated him by occupying Dyrrhachium with all his army. Cæsar then encamped on the Apsus to the south of Dyrrhachium, and there awaited the part of his army which had remained in Italy. It did not come, for Bibulus was now on his guard, and provisions also failed to come. Very soon Cæsar found himself isolated in a hostile country with only 15,000 men and short of provisions, while on the other side of the river he was faced by Pompey with an army at least three times as great.

Why did not Pompey attack there and then? In order to explain this extraordinary inertia and indecision we must suppose either that Pompey was wanting in the energy necessary for the conduct of war or that, wishing to spare the effusion of Roman blood, he intended to end the war without fighting. Why should he risk a sanguinary battle between Romans when Cæsar himself had put his neck in the noose?

His communications with Italy being cut, his little army must sooner or later disintegrate and surrender owing to hunger and exhaustion. Thus the two armies confronted each other for several months of uncertainty, Cæsar being in a much worse position than Pompey.

Time, however, if it wearies armies, also brings opportunities and strokes of luck by which bold spirits may profit, and so it happened on this occasion. Bibulus died, and under his successor the blockade of the Pompeian fleet was relaxed. One fine day, therefore, the Cæsarian generals in Italy managed to cross the Adriatic and effect a junction with Cæsar. On this Cæsar, who required a speedy end to the war, offered battle, but in vain. Pompey, who had declined to attack before when the enemy had fewer men, did not think fit to change his plan because Cæsar had been reinforced. It was in vain that Cæsar tried all manner of provocations and finally tried to cut his adversary's communications with Dyrrhachium. Pompey, who was able to communicate with the city by sea, would not move. At last Cæsar in his exasperation conceived the plan of blockading Pompey in his own camp, hoping to repeat the miracle he had performed four years before at Alesia.

Pompey's camp, however, rested on the sea, which he controlled, while Cæsar's lines were tormented by scarcity. The siege was labour lost and ended in a disaster. One day a skirmish, which took place near the trenches, flared up into a great battle, the result of which was a defeat for Cæsar. A thousand of his soldiers were left dead on the field, and thirty-two standards fell into the hands of the enemy. Cæsar raised the siege and withdrew his army towards Thessaly to seek supplies and to join two of his lieutenants, Domitius Calvinius and Lucius Cassius, whom he had sent to Macedonia shortly before this time to meet Pompey's forces.

Victory was in Pompey's hands. He had only to choose one of two equally effective plans. He might immediately pursue and destroy the retreating enemy, or he might return to Italy, and, having refitted his forces there, he might set out to reconquer the East where Cæsar might easily be isolated and surrounded now that he was reduced to the position of a leader of a few legions in revolt against the lawful government of the State. Pompey followed neither the one course nor the other, but merely pursued his enemy at a distance, being, as it were, dragged on by him. Perhaps he hoped that Cæsar's forces would disintegrate owing to famine and capitulate as his own lieutenants had done in Spain. Having adopted this plan, which might, if perseveringly followed, have given him the victory, he should have carried it out consistently. But he did nothing of the kind. When the two armies reached the plain of Pharsalia, Pompey accepted the battle which he had hitherto refused under conditions more favourable for himself.

How are we to explain this sudden resolution? The war of attrition by which Pompey had intended to wear out Cæsar, though it avoided serious risks, made great demands on the patience, not only of the general and the soldiers but also the senators who, whether as officers or as friends, accompanied Pompey. Among these there were many who were now utterly weary of the life they had been leading for so many months. All of them were confident of victory. And the impatient and the ambitious and the amateur strategists talked over Pompey into fighting the battle of which—quite rightly—he had hitherto fought so shy. The fight took place on August 9th on the plain of Pharsalia. In such a battle in the open field Cæsar's tactical genius and the valour of his legions prevailed over the greatly superior numbers of the enemy. In the confusion Pompey lost his head and could think of nothing better than to mount his horse and seek safety with a handful of troopers in shameful flight.[1]

118. Cleopatra and the Alexandrian War (48–47 B. C.). Pompey had fled without any clear or precise idea where he was going. He first went to Amphipolis and thence to Mytilene. Then he coasted along Asia Minor, not touching anywhere, and reached Cyprus. At Cyprus he finally decided to betake himself to Egypt, to the court of the children of Ptolemy Auletes, who had owed him both his throne and his life. At that moment, however, Egypt was in great confusion. The two sovereigns, Ptolemy XIII and Cleopatra, were in conflict with each other, and the latter, a beautiful, intelligent, and ambitious woman, who was the elder of the two, had been deposed and driven out. The Egyptian diplomatists no doubt saw clearly that the uncertain position of Ptolemy was not likely to be consolidated by an ally who had been defeated, perhaps decisively, and that any help that he might give would undoubtedly induce the fugitive Cleopatra to invoke the vengeance of his rival. Thus it was that on September 29th, shortly.after Pompey's arrival at Pelusium, as the great general was landing

[1] On the battle *cf.* J. Kromayer, *Antike Schlachtfelder*, ii., p. 401 ff.

from a barge sent by the King of Egypt to receive him, an assassin's dagger put an end to his life and delivered Cæsar from the greatest of his rivals. Thus perished the man who had triumphed over Mithridates, who had given Rome a new empire in the East, and had annexed to the Roman dominions the country which was one day to be the birthplace of Jesus and the cradle of Christianity.

Meanwhile Cæsar, having sent his lieutenants to receive the submission of the vanquished and the submission of the whole of Greece, hastened by long stages with a small escort after the flying Pompey. When he arrived at Alexandria, he received the news of his rival's death. But, instead of turning back to conquer the remains of the Pompeian army and finally impose his authority on Italy, he came within an ace of ruin in one of the most dangerous intrigues ever known in Egyptian politics. His first intention had been to stay in Egypt in order to replenish his finances, more especially as the father of the sovereign had not entirely paid off the old debt which he had contracted in 59 towards the triumvirs as payment for the recovery of his throne. Cæsar, however, could not ask the Egyptian government to pay Ptolemy's debts before they had decided whether he was, in fact, their rightful king, and he therefore directed Ptolemy and Cleopatra to submit themselves to his judgment. Both obeyed, and Cleopatra came in person to defend her case. Ptolemy and his ministers, however, when they heard that Cæsar had made the acquaintance of the fatally fascinating Cleopatra, were quite sure that he would decide in her favour. They therefore stirred up the people, who were already annoyed by the exactions, the intrusions,

and the manners of the Roman soldiers, to revolt, and
finally declared war on Cæsar.

The Alexandrian war, which had broken out so
suddenly, could not but be long and difficult. Cæsar
was almost entirely without troops. The King of
Egypt, on the other hand, in addition to an army
which, though small, was not to be despised, had the
co-operation of the Alexandrine population. Cæsar
had to entrench himself in the royal palace and sustain
a regular siege for five months while he awaited
the assistance which he had summoned from all sides.
In the spring his reinforcements at last arrived.
The Alexandrines were beaten, Ptolemy fled, and
perished by drowning in the Nile (March 27, 47), and
the thrones of Egypt and Cyprus were bestowed on
Cleopatra.

But Cæsar's enforced inactivity at Alexandria
had produced grave disturbances in Italy and, what
was more serious, had given time to the Pompeian
party to recover. After the battle of Pharsalia,
Cæsar had been appointed dictator by the Roman
people for the whole of the year 47, and before he had
been blockaded by war and winter in Alexandria
he had had time to appoint M. Antonius his *magister
equitum*. In sole possession of the dictatorial power
in Italy, Antony had not known how to prevent
the occurrence of a kind of social revolution. The
civil war had aggravated the economic crisis. Many
were no longer able to pay the rent of their houses
or the interest on the money they had borrowed.
The burden of debt had become intolerable.

As a remedy for these evils the tribune Dolabella
forthwith proposed that debts should be annulled
and that the payment of rent to the owners of house

property should be suspended. The result had been a very serious panic among the monied classes. It was already manifest that the extreme party among the Cæsarians—the adventurers, the malcontents, the cranks—and with them the Catilinarian tradition, were gaining the upper hand! The richer, wiser, and more moderate section of Cæsar's party, led by the tribunes Asinius Pollio and Trebellius, opposed Dolabella's measure. Disturbances had broken out. The senate had proclaimed a state of siege and Antony had been compelled to resort to sanguinary acts of repression.

At Rome the Cæsarians were divided into a moderate party on the side of law and order, and an extreme and revolutionary party, and were fighting among themselves. Meanwhile the Pompeians were profiting by Cæsar's absence to reorganize themselves. In Africa, Pompey's sons, with Cato and Labienus, had collected the remnants of Pompey's army and had formed an alliance with Juba, King of Numidia. They were recruiting archers, slingers, and Gallic horsemen. They were preparing an army and a fleet and were trying to raise a rebellion in Spain. In the East, Pharnaces, son of Mithridates, had reappeared with an army in Pontus, in Little Armenia, Cappadocia, and Armenia, and had defeated Domitius Calvinus, governor of the province of Asia. Cicero was not far from the truth when he affirmed that the chief cause of all the ills which afflicted the empire after Pharsalia, was Cæsar's long absence.

Yet Cæsar was in no hurry to return, even after he had reconquered Alexandria and given the throne to Cleopatra. With the queen he made a journey on the upper Nile and then spent a further period at her court, indulging in feasts and banquets, games and all kinds of pleasures. It was not until the early part of June that he left for Syria, after losing nine precious months. Even then he did not at once return to Italy where he was so impatiently awaited. Before going back he wished to set the affairs of the East in order. On August 2, 47, he fought and conquered Pharnaces at Zela in Pontus. Thereafter he convoked a great diet at Nicea, where kingdoms were made and unmade, friends rewarded and enemies punished, and a stock of treasure amassed. Then at last he went back to Italy, disembarking at Tarentum on September 24, 47.

It was too late. Immediately after Pharsalia, there had been in Rome and Italy among all classes, even among the aristocracy, a general movement in favour of Cæsar. Since fortune had been on his side, all were inclined to hope that he would restore peace and order. A year later there was almost no trace of this movement. The new army which the Pompeians had organized in Africa, Cæsar's long delay in Egypt, the rumours, true or false, of his amours with Cleopatra, the discord which lacerated the Cæsarian party, the proposals of Dolabella—all this had perplexed and checked, or even antagonized, the upper and richer classes. This was dangerous for Cæsar, who was soon to leave for Africa to carry on a long and difficult war. But time pressed, it was no easy task to harmonize all the conflicting interests involved, and, as the rich and powerful chose to turn their backs on him, he decided to adopt the somewhat perilous policy of leaning on the discontented masses. He reproved Antony for his repressive policy. He did nothing to check Dolabella; on the contrary, he adopted several of his proposals. He decreed the remission for a year of house rents in Rome under 2000 sesterces, and in the remainder of Italy of those under 500 sesterces. He imposed a forced loan on rich private persons and on municipalities. He confiscated and sold the patrimonies of several citizens who had perished in the civil war—among others that of Pompey. In the Cæsarian party, therefore, the left wing was prevailing over the moderate and reasonable elements. Cæsar presided over the elections as dictator, and for all the offices he secured the election of his own partisans. He himself was elected consul for 46, and in December left for Sicily on his way to the new seat of war.

CHAPTER XXI

THE DICTATORSHIP AND DEATH OF CÆSAR

119. Cæsar's Position and Plans after the Battle of Thapsus. The new campaign in Africa lasted about five months, from December, 47, until June, 46. It had various vicissitudes and was decided on April 6th by the battle of Thapsus, in which the Pompeian army was defeated. In the months that followed Cæsar was occupied in dealing with the last remnants of the enemy still holding out. Among these was Cato, who had shut himself up in Utica. This campaign differed from its predecessors in the ferocity with which it was carried on. This time Cæsar showed no mercy. The leaders who fell into his hands alive were put to death. Many, like Cato, who knew what was in store for them, committed suicide. We cannot blame Cæsar for this. It is an eternal law that a struggle, as it is protracted, becomes more ferocious. By prolonging their resistance the Pompeians were not merely endangering the position and the life of Cæsar; they were exposing the empire and the whole social fabric to the danger of universal disaster. What was happening in Italy showed this clearly. Cæsar might well feel in perfect good faith that his severity was justified, not only in his own interest but in the interest of the State.

But these executions made final and irreconcilable the antagonism between the upper and cultivated classes and Cæsar, which had arisen during the fatal nine months of his absence after Pharsalia. The killing had begun! Cæsar was merely another Sulla, and the executions would be followed by confiscations! However bitter the feuds of parties and factions had been, there was no Roman and no Italian who was not grieved at the disappearance in a civil war of so many illustrious members of the great Roman families, and who did not feel a sort of rancour and hatred against the man who appeared to be responsible for their fate. But this growing aversion on the part of the classes who were most influential by reason of their wealth and their culture inevitably drove Cæsar to rely more and more on the poor and ignorant masses. This was in itself a danger, and another and a greater danger soon arose. In Cæsar's party there were, as we have seen, two groups. One of these was the more moderate, the more attached to traditional and legal forms, whose desire was that Cæsar, however powerful and eminent, should be merely a citizen of Rome. The other contained the more extreme and turbulent men whose one object was to increase Cæsar's power every possible way in order that they might exploit his omnipotence for their own advantage. As the educated upper classes who were faithful to tradition were gradually alienated from Cæsar, this extreme wing prevailed over the moderate elements and drove Cæsar further and further in the direction of formally setting up a real tyranny.

This had become clearer since Thapsus. While the better part of Italy wrapped itself in melancholy silence, depressed by the death of so many illus-

trious men, Cæsar's more violent partisans busied
themselves with voting him more extraordinary
honours than ever. He was to have the dictatorship for ten years, the authority of censor under
the title of *præfectura morum*, the unheard of right
to propose the candidates for the tribunate and the
plebeian ædileship. The impression produced by all
this was terrible. What was a dictatorship for ten
years but a monstrous tyranny before which even the
dictatorship of Sulla paled? So adverse, indeed, was
public opinion that, when Cæsar returned to Rome,
he refused the ten years' dictatorship[1] and immediately did his best to make Rome forget the bloodshed
of Thapsus by the generosity of his government and by
administrative reforms of advantage to the public.
He expended a great part of the spoil taken in Africa
in paying the citizens and the soldiery the sums he had
promised during the civil war. Each citizen received
300 sesterces, each soldier 24,000, each centurion
48,000, each military tribune 96,000. There was also
a gratuitous distribution of grain and oil to the people,
and he took measures to secure that his old agrarian
law of 59, which had become practically a dead letter
owing to the malevolence of the government, should
be properly carried out. He set about founding colonies in Campania and he began to work out the Lex
Julia municipalis, the future foundation of the relations between Rome and the Italian communities,
which for forty years had enjoyed the rights of Roman
citizenship. He even carried out certain other reforms
which the conservative party had been demanding for

---

[1] Cæsar was not to assume his third dictatorship until the end
of 46, *cf.* Ferrero, *The Greatness and Decline of Rome*, vol. iii.,
p. 270.

a long time. Thus he reduced the number of poor citizens entitled under the Lex Clodia to participate in gratuitous distributions of grain at the public expense, and he broke up the *collegia* of workmen which Clodius had reorganized, and of which Cæsar himself had made use so extensively both before and after 59.

All these were wise reforms, but they were not enough to soothe the unrest among the educated upper class, which was, indeed, increased by a new political anxiety. How long did Cæsar intend to retain his extraordinary powers? That he should have assumed them during the civil war was natural enough. But the civil war was now over, and, when Cæsar had restored order, would he restore the republican government, as even Sulla had done? Every form of personal government was still so much detested in Rome and Italy that many grew more acutely anxious about this question every day, as they saw the numerous indications which appeared of a contrary intention on the part of Cæsar.[1] In the presence of this fear all the benefits which Cæsar showered on the country counted for nothing. No contemporary, viewing these events from close at hand, realized that it was impossible for Cæsar to lay down his plenary powers even if he had wished to do so, and that, in a sense, he had been made prisoner by his own victory. He had made too many promises, raised too many hopes, assumed too many obligations, excited too many animosities; he had too much disturbed the equilibrium of Italy and the empire to be able to abdicate before he had resettled a perturbed world. But, in order that this might be done quickly, there was need

[1] Cic., Brutus, xcvi., 330, xcvii., 332, and passim. "*In hanc reipublicæ noctem—hæc importuna clades civitatis.*"

of an energetic centre of authority, a concentrated and resolute use of power such as could never have been obtained under the antiquated forms of the republic. Facts were soon to demonstrate that the only result of his disappearance would be a catastrophe which would shake the whole empire.

As a matter of fact, Cæsar was not thinking of restoring the ancient institutions of the State but of resuming one of the plans he had made many years before at the conference of Lucca. His intention was to avenge Crassus and conquer Persia. The conquest of Persia would give him glory, influence, and the treasure necessary for the reconstruction of the State and the salvation from ruin of Italy, where many of the middle and lower class had been reduced to desperation owing to the state of never-ending crisis in which they lived.

120. The New Pompeian Insurrection in Spain (46–45 B.C.). But this vast design was hindered by a new difficulty which arose in Spain, the province which had been so easily reduced to obedience in 49. Cæsar's lieutenants had been guilty of misgovernment. Pompeian agents had been active. Pompey's sons, Cneius and Sextus, went about demanding vengeance for their father and excited much sympathy in a country where Pompey had left many friends. Spanish aspirations to national independence were latent but not exhausted. All these circumstances tended to produce a new conflagration and a new danger. Towards the end of 46 Cn. Pompeius apparently had forces enough at his disposal to disquiet Cæsar's lieutenants so seriously that they felt his personal presence to be necessary. Cæsar could not set out for Persia leaving Spain in danger, so he decided to postpone his expedition against the Parthians. Before his departure for Spain, however, he assumed the dictatorship which he had refused on his return from Africa, and required that he should be elected sole consul for the year 45. This being done he left the city without convoking the comitia, having appointed eight *præfecti urbi* to whom he entrusted all the duties of the prætors and some of the duties of the quæstors during his absence. It was an inevitable necessity from which neither Rome nor Cæsar could escape, but the irritation and the grief caused by this open increase in Cæsar's personal power was great at Rome.

The Spanish war was no easy one. Cæsar himself was obliged to fight in the ranks, and was in danger of being taken prisoner (March, 45). However, in the end he won again, and, though Sextus Pompeius managed to effect his escape into the northern part of Spain, Labienus and Cn. Pompeius were killed. The discontent felt at Rome by all who feared that Cæsar meant to turn the republic into a tyranny was increased by this new massacre of noble Romans, by the length of the war and the difficulty with which a bare victory had been secured. On the other hand, the more zealous of his partisans had seized the opportunity offered by the victory of Munda to secure new honours for their leader—the right to use as a hereditary *prænomen* the title of *Imperator*, the consulship for ten years, the right to name the candidates for the offices of tribune and ædile. There was no longer any room for doubt. Cæsar meant to reign alone over the ruins of the republic.

The effect of these new honours was not merely to widen the abyss between the Cæsarians and the Pom-

peians, but to exacerbate the differences within the
Cæsarian party between the moderates and the rest.
So apparent was this that immediately after his return
Cæsar tried to conciliate the malcontents. He reconciled himself with M. Antonius, who had been in
disgrace since the repressive measures of 47, and abolished the *præfecti urbi*. The optimists were comforted by a flicker of hope. Cæsar really meant, they
thought, to restore the institutions of the free republic.
But, as Cicero warned them, this was an illusion.
Cæsar was not thinking of restoring the republic but
of conquering Persia, of enlarging and embellishing
Rome, of diverting the course of the Tiber, of draining
the Pomptine marshes, of founding libraries, of cutting a canal through the Isthmus of Corinth, of opening a new road across the Apennines, of building a
great harbour at Ostia, of codifying the Roman law,
of revising the land survey and assessment throughout the empire. The disagreement between Cæsar
and the educated upper class was growing more and
more serious. He wished to give Italy a magnificent,
active, and beneficent government. They wanted a
government in conformity with the political traditions
of the republic in which the senate and the magistrates
would again have their ancient authority.

Discontent grew, even among the moderate Cæsarians, who did not wish to be the instruments of a
personal rule, and the situation became ever more
uncertain and unstable. While Cæsar was eagerly
preparing his Parthian expedition, the senators, and
among them many who were of his own party, were
anxiously asking themselves what was to be the
political future of Rome. Cæsar's every act was
scrutinized, dissected, and bitterly commented on as

a new sign of his treasonable ambition. Finally, in the first fortnight of February 44, a proposal was made to the senate and to the people that Cæsar should be dictator for life!

121. The Conspiracy of the Ides of March (March 15, 44 B. C.). The proposal was, of course, approved. Perhaps it was a real necessity, as Cæsar intended to leave Rome in the following month for the war against the Parthians. In the circumstances, it would not have been prudent for him to leave Rome on an undertaking which might last several years without having as much as possible consolidated his authority. For the Romans, however, a dictatorship for life was the same thing as a tyranny. It had for centuries been an unquestioned principle of public law that a dictatorship could not last for more than six months. Sulla himself, though he had taken possession of the State and had been master of its armies, had hastened to lay down this office immediately after order was restored. If Cæsar had decided that his dictatorship was to be perpetual, it was clear that he meant to be tyrant of Rome, to annihilate the authority of the senate, and to transform the Roman magistrates into his own servants.

It was at this point that a senator who belonged to the Cæsarian party persuaded himself that in order to save the republic, the senate, the Roman tradition—and therefore Rome and Italy—it was necessary that Cæsar should be killed. That senator was C. Cassius, who had been quæstor to Crassus during the ill-fated Parthian expedition. In the civil war, he had fought for Pompey, but, after Pharsalia, he had been reconciled to Cæsar, who had admitted him to his friendship and entrusted him with important offices. In murdering Cæsar, Cassius had certainly no personal advantage to gain, and what he did was, therefore, done in good faith, on the theories held by the educated and upper classes of the day, theories which he merely carried farther than others, as was to be expected from a man of his rough and intolerant character.

Cassius opened his mind to a few confidential friends, who all agreed that it was necessary to win over to the cause of the conspirators his relative, M. Brutus. Brutus was another of the Pompeians who had gone over to Cæsar after Pharsalia. He was a student, an idealist, a puritan, who had much influence owing to his ancient lineage, his distinguished connexions, and his fanatical admiration for the heroic civic spirit of the old republic. He gloried in his descent from the first Brutus, the founder of the republic, to whose salvation he had sacrificed his own son. Cæsar, who had been a great friend of the mother of Brutus, was very fond of him and had loaded him with favours. Yet, by working on his republican sentiments and his attachment to tradition, Cassius had no difficulty in persuading him that he should place the good of the State before any consideration of personal gratitude. Having won over Brutus, the conspiracy extended rapidly, and, amid the general discontent, found many adherents among the Pompeian party in the senate, as well as among the more moderate Cæsarians. That the conspiracy had profound political motives is demonstrated by the fact that early in March, 44, there were no less than sixty or eighty senators among its members, and that these may be said to have included all that was best in the Cæsarian party itself. Personal government and a life dictatorship were still too repugnant to Roman ideas.

The conspirators had to act at once, because it was most difficult to keep for long a secret which was known to so many people. Moreover, Cæsar was on the point of setting out for his great Parthian expedition. His veterans had been recalled to the colours and were flowing in from all sides. No less than sixteen legions and 10,000 cavalry were concentrating in Macedonia and Greece. On Cæsar's suggestion the senate had already decided that before his departure the magistrates should be elected for three years, the supposed duration of his absence. Moreover, it was rumoured that Lucius Aurelius Cotta, the quindecemvir, would propose in the senate that, in accordance with an ancient Sibylline oracle, the leader of the Parthian expedition should be proclaimed king over all the Roman provinces outside Italy. It was then decided that Cæsar should be killed on the Ides of March, the date of the next meeting of the senate.

For this meeting the senate had been summoned to the Curia of Pompey in the Campus Martius, not far from the modern Campo dei Fiori. There was a large attendance of senators, but Cæsar did not come. He was kept at home in his official residence (*domus publica*) as pontifex maximus by a slight indisposition and not by any suspicion, and he had decided not to attend the sitting. The conspirators decided to send Decimus Brutus to discover the reason for his absence and to persuade him to come. And this gallant officer, who had been Cæsar's lieutenant in Gaul, who had covered himself with glory in the struggle with the Veneti in 57 and at the siege of Massilia in 49–48, did not hesitate to lead to the slaughter a man from whom he had received so many benefits and who trusted him absolutely!

Cæsar allowed himself to be persuaded by Decimus and went to the senate. Immediately after he had come in and taken his seat, he was approached by Tullius Cimber, one of the conspirators, who made as if to plead the cause of his brother, who was in exile. Meanwhile Trebonius had undertaken to detain outside the chamber Marcus Antonius, who, having been reconciled to Cæsar and made his colleague in the consulship, had been kept in ignorance of the plot. While Tullius was speaking to Cæsar, the other conspirators crowded round, and suddenly the suppliant gave a slight pull to the dictator's toga, uncovering his bosom. This was the signal. The conspirators drew their daggers and threw themselves upon Cæsar, raining on him a storm of blows. In a few moments he was lying in a pool of blood at the foot of Pompey's statue (March 15, 44).

122. Cæsar and His Work. The dictator was gone, and, with his life, his life's work was destroyed for ever. What remained behind? What can be reconstructed or inferred from the scattered surviving fragments of his ideas and his achievements throughout his by no means long but momentous career? The ancient historians saw in him only the destroyer of republican liberty, himself condemned to inevitable destruction. Modern writers have been inclined to see in his life something much greater than this— something like a plan, organically complete, faithfully followed from his earliest youth, whereby he intended to restore—and partly did, in fact, restore,— the crumbling fabric of the Roman State. That this was not so and that his work will not bear this interpretation has, we think, been clearly shown in the narrative contained in the preceding pages. But if we must deny that his work had any organic, still more any miraculously prophetic, significance, this does not affect our estimate of its greatness. Cæsar was in very truth a great man, a scholar and an artist, and at the same time a soldier and a man of action. He knew how to bring all his faculties to bear on any kind of work in which he happened to be engaged, and on all with the most remarkable effect. His grandiose imagination, the prodigious lucidity of his intellect, his indefatigable activity, his mental agility, his inexhaustible fund of nervous energy, would have made him a great figure at any period in history. But no politician can lay down in his childhood a plan by which all his conduct shall be preordained. All must be the servants of the great historic forces which dominate their epoch.

Cæsar lived at a time when Italy and the empire were encumbered with the ruins of a history which had come to an end, and which had to be destroyed in order that a new era might be initiated. His work, therefore, was one not of creation but of destruction, for the time for reorganization had not yet come. The Gallic war and the civil war, two great works of destruction, were, in fact, the two greatest achievements of his life. The Gallic war destroyed the ancient Celtic Gaul and threw open the continent of Europe to Græco-Latin civilization. It was only because Gaul had been Romanized that it was possible for Great Britain and Germany to be gradually made civilized and ultimately Christian, and for Europe to enter on the great historical career of which we are, perhaps, about to witness, or perhaps have already witnessed, the culmination. By the civil war, on the other hand, Cæsar hastened the final crisis in the history of the immemorial institutions of the republic, which were already impotent and worn out with age. All that he did in the way of creating new organs of government on the ruins of these institutions was provisional, transitory, and insecure, for the decomposition which he had hastened had not reached its fullest development at the time of his death. This was proved by the tremendous convulsion by which his death was followed and which will be related in the next volume. After it was over, it required the slow patience of several generations to create a new order, which this time was destined to be really solid and to endure.

END OF VOL. I

INDEX

T